CITIES IN SPACE: CITY AS PLACE

Third Edition

David T. Herbert

Professor of Geography
University of Wales Swansea

and

Colin J. Thomas

Senior Lecturer in Geography
University of Wales Swansea

John Wiley & Sons, Inc.

New York   Toronto

David Fulton Publishers Ltd
Ormond House, 26–27 Boswell Street, London WC1N 3JD

First published in Great Britain by John Wiley & Sons Ltd 1982, titled *Urban Geography: A First Approach* (reprinted 1986 and 1988)

Second edition published in Great Britain by David Fulton Publishers 1990
(Reprinted 1991, 1992, 1994, 1995)

Third edition published in Great Britain by David Fulton Publishers 1997

British Library Cataloguing in Publication Data
A catalogue record for this book is available from the British Library

Distributed in North America by
John Wiley & Sons Inc.
605 Third Avenue
New York, NY 10158-0012
USA

Library of Congress Cataloging-in-Publication Data available upon request

ISBN 0470-24405-4

Typeset by Textype Typesetters, Cambridge
Printed in Great Britain by the Cromwell Press Limited, Melksham

Contents

Preface

The study of urban geography remains an important part of the geographical curriculum both in schools and in higher education. We live in an urban society and in a world which is being transformed by the processes of urbanization: to study urban geography is to study environments and phenomena significant to our everyday lives. There is a wider field of urban studies that encompasses all concerns with cities and their impact on society. A geography of the city, with its interests in place, space and spatiality, adds a dimension to that wider field without 'ring-fencing' any of its own particular concerns. There are particularities about an urban geography which give it distinctiveness but in their contributions to the general and problem-oriented field of urban studies, geographers are less concerned with disciplinary labels than with advancing the research frontier and helping to forge the kinds of policies that can improve the urban condition. As urban geographers have become more immersed in the philosophies and methodologies of the social sciences and the humanities, they are more obviously less constrained by the 'fetishism of space'. The heritage of locational analysis and its focus on the geometry of space is, properly, still there, but it offers techniques and approaches to be used where appropriate rather than ubiquitously. Urban geography continues to hold a range of perspectives and stances and it is important to see these as a source of strength rather than mere eclecticism. If locational theory injected a strong scientific competence to human geography, new cultural and historical approaches have added scholarship of a different kind.

The title of this book captures the two main scales at which urban geographers have studied the city. *Cities in Space* draws upon the locational analysis tradition. Cities are points or locations with complex patterns of interaction, growth and decline. The ideas of systems and networks and the wider processes of urbanization fall within this orbit. *City as Place* introduces the second major concern, that of the territory occupied by an urban place, its components, resident populations, movements and change. The city as place has a variegated built environment, ranging from its monuments to its derelict and vacant lots. It has a range of economic activities and a diverse population forming the social mosaic of the urban area. The two parts are of course not discrete, above all the city is part of society and processes of globalization and change affect urban systems and specific cities alike. Again, cities have become closely associated with problems from economic decline, to urban riots and a rising wave of homelessness, poverty and disadvantage. Cities have no monopoly over these phenomena but they do tend to be the stages upon which they are enacted. There are urban qualities, if only density, concentration and accessibility, which lend themselves to these roles.

This is an introductory text which aims to present both more traditional and newer approaches to urban geography in an accessible and educational way. There is a strong record of achievement and a discipline needs to state its heritage and track record as well as to evaluate what is new at the research frontier. This is the third major revision of a text first published in 1982 with the title *Urban Geography: A First Approach* and in 1990 as *Cities in Space: City as Place*. Both titles have been reprinted several times. It is our belief that urban geography is academically challenging, has a proven record of relevance to the problems facing urban societies, and has considerable intrinsic interest. These are the qualities we aim to represent in this text. We are grateful to our colleagues at University of Wales Swansea for their encouragement, help and active assistance. Nicola Jones and Anna Radcliffe provided the cartography and graphics; Lynn Muir and Leighan Evans helped with the production of the type script. Our families of course lent their support and forbearance and to all we are grateful

David Herbert
Colin Thomas

Department of Geography
University of Wales Swansea

February 1997

CHAPTER 1
The concerns of urban geography

Griffith Taylor could still state in the 1940s, at a time when many classic urban studies had already been written, that urban geography was in its infancy. This statement reflected the restricted visions of geography as a discipline at this time, centrally interested in the relationship between people and environment and the natural science paradigm of environmentalism. Most geographies studied rural and regional landscapes with the few urban studies reflecting their disciplinary context. There were

- site and situation studies, concerned with the physical qualities of the land over which urban settlements had developed and with locational qualities
- urban settlement studies that examined the spatial distributions of towns and cities, networks of urban places and their connectivities, and notions of hinterlands or market areas
- urban morphologies that studied the internal structure of the city, its morphology or physical fabric, the types of buildings, layout of streets and general town plan, and the relation of these to the historical phases of urban growth
- studies of the historical evolution of the cities and their regional settings that demonstrated the diversity of urban forms, changes over time and cultural variations at a regional scale.

These themes reflected the concerns of geography as a discipline and made for a distinctive urban geography with a particular contribution to the literature. Taylor (1949) used the terms 'infantile, juvenile, mature, and senile' to characterize stages of urban growth, classified towns by site and situation – 'cities at hills, cities at mountain passes' – and developed examples from different parts of the world. Dickinson (1948) saw the determination of site and situation as being the first task of the urban geographer. This mode of analysis provoked a response from Crowe (1938) who criticized its focus on inanimate objects of landscape rather than upon people and movement. Perhaps the last of the early urban geographies was Smailes's *Geography of Towns* (1953) with its themes of the origins and bases of towns, settings, towns and cultures, towns and regions, and morphology. Several of these topical areas from early urban geographies survive in modern forms. Urban morphology, for example, has continued to develop as a research theme, while urban change and its regional variations are too clearly facts of the real world to be ignored, and studies of urban systems have inherited the city and region themes.

The second half of the twentieth century witnessed significant changes in the place of urban studies in geography. At the beginning of the 1950s, it remained at the margins of the discipline: 'It is rather surprising that there is so little regular study of the characteristics of urban geography' (Taylor 1949: 6). For Mayer (1954) urban studies had been one of the most rapidly developing fields of study in geography in the post World War II period. The rate of change gathered pace and in 1982 we suggested that:

> Whereas in the early 1950s a separate course on urban geography . . . was quite exceptional, today the absence of such a course would be equally remarkable.
>
> (Herbert and Thomas 1982: 11)

These statements are evidence of growth but by the later 1990s the ways in which urban geography was researched and taught had changed. First, there was a process of 'fragmentation' with the emergence of many specialisms within urban studies. A broad urban geography is typically followed or replaced by more specialized courses such as urban-social geography, the urban economy, urban services or race relations within cities and the literature reflects this focusing of interest around specific themes. Second, geographers along with other social scientists have found that there are many issues for which it is not necessary to regard the city as a discrete phenomenon or even an appropriate frame of reference. Unemployment and social deprivation, for example, are strongly associated with cities but they are essentially societal problems which find expression in urban places. The whole question of 'urban' as discrete space is contested. Third, with the analysis of a specific issue, like deprivation, disciplinary boundaries need not be a central concern. The shift away from 'spatial chauvinism', or the tendency to emphasize space to the exclusion of other key dimensions, reflects the integration of a 'geography' into wider social science perspective. Evidence for the widening horizons of urban geographers is accompanied by the increased awareness of non-geographers of the significance of space and place. Sociologists such as Urry (1995), with his study *Consuming Places,* and economic analyses of regional economic variations in the growth and decline of cities have exemplified this trend by the attention they give to place, space and spatiality.

A further feature of the development of urban geography has been the change in subject matter. Central topics of the 1960s are little regarded in the 1990s, 'births' and 'deaths' of research topics, reflecting broader trends, have been numerous. The plethora of central business district (CBD) delimitation studies of the 1960s, for example, reflected a preoccupation with land-use and the notion of definable 'segments' of urban space, but a 1990s survey of urban financial services would be much more concerned with process and interaction within a global economy and with social networks that were not constrained by geographical space. Central place theory in the earlier period epitomized a positivist geography with its focus on model-building and the generation of spatial laws, whereas later analyses of consumer behaviour signalled a shift to decision-making, behaviouralism and the interplay between structure and agency.

Figure 1.1 summarises this pattern of change as traditional urban geographies emphasizing form and function gave way to studies concerned with the roles of people in the urban system. Initially, with spatial analysis, human activities were summarized in mechanistic ways but stronger interests in activities, feelings, and the richness of human diversity prevailed. Earlier concerns with topics such as rank-size rules, economic base

	Cities in Space	City as Place
TRADITIONAL	urban origins and growth city and region	site and situation urban morphology
SPATIAL ANALYSIS	urbanization processes rank-size rules economic base studies classifications central place theory	social ecology natural areas social areas segregation
BEHAVIOURAL	urban systems urban services labour markets financial services	residential change consumer behaviour housing markets images of the city
RELEVANCE	impacts of urban economies planning urban systems control of flow, investments	urban problems area policies
STRUCTURALISM	hidden strutures social formations	hidden structures problems as manifestations
HUMANISM	quality of life life-worlds	meaning of place people in the city
NEW CULTURAL	post-modern cities	social construction semiotics of the city

Figure 1.1 Changing themes in urban geography

studies, urban hierarchies and social areas reflected the thrust towards modelling, quantification and generalization of largely static structures. Later, behaviouralism had its focus on processes, movement and decision-making and, contemporaneously, there was a growing awareness of structuralism and the imperatives of political economy, and the fact that any spatial manifestations of patterns and processes had to be related to the deeper societal forces which underpinned them. The call for relevance also produced a reaction against descriptive studies with their reliance on mechanistic and abstract models, and a renewed interest in humanism prompted the need to understand more fully the affective values people held for place. With the 'new' cultural geography of the later 1980s and 1990s, the roles of human agency and the whole meaning of city as place became ever more central to geographies of the city. The road from studies of site and situation to those of the social construction of urban space has been travelled in a relatively short space of time but has been accompanied by a complete transformation in the ways geographers research the city.

Definitions

Issues of definitions, though seemingly tedious, are always necessary. Besides clarifying basic terms, definitions illuminate the subject matter with which they are concerned. One basic definition is that of urban geography *per se*. Definitions of geography consistently involve the three benchmarks of space, place and environment. These tend to be constants though a particular perspective or paradigm may emphasize one at the expense of the others. Space,

	Topic:					
	Historical	Economic activities	Social institutions	Cultural dimension	Political institutions	Area study
Subdiscipline						
Historical geography	•					
Economic geography		•				
Social geography			•			
Cultural geography				•		
Political geography					•	
Urban geography	•	•	•		•	•
Rural geography	•	•	•		•	•

Figure 1.2 Subdisciplines of human geography

for example, was central to the positive science of spatial analysis, place is the key concept for a humanistic and cultural approach, and environment was both a focus of earlier approaches and a new concern of studies of the sustainable city. A definition of urban geography, developed with reference to the discipline as a whole and recent experience of actual research, is

> Urban geography studies the patterns and processes which occur between and within urban places; the objective form which these take, the subjective manner in which they are interpreted, and their mode of origin at both local and societal scales.

Among the subdivisions of human geography, urban geography sits somewhat uneasily as Figure 1.2 shows. Whereas economic geography and social geography are distinguished by thematic concerns, urban geography studies an area. Frey (1973) commented on this type of issue with the suggestion that geography considered both single elements or *topics* which could be studied systematically, or assemblages of *areas* which could be studied regionally. As an area-based study, an urban geography can cover a catholicity of interest. More commonly, however, studies of individual cities focus upon historical, economic, social and political aspects and have some specialist interest. Urban geography consists of a range of studies of different aspects of the city as a human place and is centrally concerned with those economic, social and political forces that find expression in urban areas. In modern terms these characteristics serve the subdiscipline well. The analysis of 'the city' gives it a holistic approach, as much concerned with interactions as with the separate strands of urban life. Another significant definitional issue is that raised by the question: what is urban?

Problems arise because words such as urban, city and town tend to be time and culture-specific evoking different meanings at different historical periods and in different parts of the world. Use of the term 'city' in the UK, for example, is historical and legal, whereas in the USA it has far more ubiquity. Historically, there were city-states in European countries

urban	•	population size, densities
	•	economic base functions
	•	administrative functions, art, culture
	•	central place funtions, city as exchange
	•	urbanism, lifestyle characteristics
urban place	•	extent of built-up area
	•	links with contiguous areas
	•	labour-market area
	•	population-size thresholds
	•	the perceived city, sense of place

Figure 1.3 Definitions of urban and urban place

such as Greece and Italy and diversity in terminology is embedded in the literature. Practical attempts to define urban have used criteria related to population size, urban functions, and the concept of urbanism (Figure 1.3), and the qualities of these can be summarized.

Population size

Undeniably, urban places are larger than rural places, so the point at which the village becomes a town should be identifiable at some point along the population-size continuum of settlements, though this point varies over time and space. For several Scandinavian countries, including Denmark and Sweden, any settlement which has more than 200 inhabitants is classed as urban in the national census; at least 1,000 inhabitants forms the required threshold in Canada, but 2,500 is the minimum for the USA. Many countries impose much higher thresholds, such as Greece, with 10,000 inhabitants and Japan with 30,000. This diversity is initially confusing, but has some logic if considered within its societal context. Given the physical geography of Scandinavia, for example, and the ways in which its settlement patterns have evolved over time, a settlement with over 200 permanent inhabitants may well be regarded as urban. In a country like Japan, on the other hand, with a relatively limited land area and considerable population pressure, virtually all settlements exceed such a low threshold and 30,000 provides a more realistic line of demarcation. By no means all of the inconsistencies can be explained in these ways, but there are grounds for recognizing order in the apparent diversity. In addition to size, population density is sometimes used on the assumption that urban places have typically higher densities, they are intensive ways of occupying space.

Urban functions

Most official censuses adopt a population-size definition of urban, largely in response to the fact that it is simple and easily measured. There are more telling criteria and Plato provided clues in the *Republic* when he stated that

> The origin of a city is, in my opinion, due to the fact that no one of us is sufficient for himself, but each is in need of many things. . . . Then the workers of our city must not only make enough for home consumption; they must also produce goods of the number and kinds required by other people. . . . We shall need merchants . . . a market place,

and money as a token for the sake of exchange . . . We give the name of shopkeepers, do we not, to those who serve as buyers and sellers in their stations at the market place, but the name of merchants to those who travel from city to city.

Plato developed his argument in terms of other urban needs such as doctors, education, laws and justice and his definition centred on the functions and activities of the city. Urban places have at least two kinds of activities that distinguish them from rural settlements First, they are non-agricultural, and second, they are primarily concerned with the exchange rather than with the production of goods. On the first of these qualities, arguments revolve around the **economic base** of a settlement or its dominant economic activities. Activities in rural settlements are exclusively concerned with land as a resource and with agricultural production. A simple definition of urban, based upon activities, is one which reflects the dominance of non-agricultural functions. Such a criterion, combined with population-size, is employed in Israel, where a settlement must have in excess of two-thirds of its labour force engaged in non-agricultural work to be classed as urban, and in India, where a threshold of 75 per cent of the adult male population is used.

Other definitions of urban are allied to the economic-base approach. Many settlements have specialized functions which are not rural and can fairly be described as urban. Cities established to control or administer regions of a country were allocated administrative and political functions. Greek and Roman cities are early examples and the tradition has been carried through to modern capital cities such as Canberra, Ottawa and Brasilia. Early urban places were often multifunctional with religion, defence and culture contributing to their primary roles. Religion has provided a key specialist function for many urban places from the religious centres of the Middle East and southern Asia to the cathedral cities of medieval Europe. Although there were craft and mining-dominated urban settlements in the ancient and medieval worlds, the manufacturing centre only really dominated settlement evolution with the progress of industrialization in Europe in the later eighteenth and nineteenth centuries. Industrialization has undoubtedly created settlements which are urban. Distinguished by size, density and the dominance of industrial employment, they were, in Britain at least, the new towns of the nineteenth century. Single-function settlements, whether religious or cultural centres or manufacturing towns, often persist in their original roles over long periods of time. As cities develop, however, they are likely to add to these original roles or even to replace them and this may have the effect of consolidating their urban status.

Another approach to definition has focused upon the functions of distribution and exchange and the marketing role of urban places. Pirenne (1925), in his study of the emergence of urban settlements in medieval Europe, placed great emphasis upon the **town as a market place** and, for him, the city was a 'community of merchants'. This emphasis on marketing and exchange became explicit in studies of central places and the urban hierarchy emphasizing the roles of urban places as institutional centres for a surrounding territory or hinterland. It is the demand for services that calls the urban settlement into being and once established it develops a network of functional relationships over the region. Work stimulated by Christaller's (1933) **central place theory** made this centrality or nodality status of urban places its central focus. Most of the empirical work focused on economic services, particularly retail and wholesale trade, but retained an awareness of the significance of non-economic institutions and services. As Mumford (1938) suggested, the city should not be over-regarded as an aggregate of economic functions, it is above all a seat of institutions in the service of the region, it is art, culture and political purposes. This latter description applies to many early cities.

Urbanism

A further strand in the definitional debate came from sociology and Louis Wirth's (1938) statement on urbanism as a way of life. Wirth argued that urban places could be distinguished by the lifestyles of their inhabitants which were different from those of rural people. The qualities of population size, density and heterogeneity in their environments combined to make 'urbanites' different from 'ruralites'. Relative anonymity and a paucity of face-to-face relationships were seen as the hallmarks of an urban lifestyle and this hypothesis was supported in the **theories of contrast**. Tönnies, Weber and Redfield (see Reissman 1964) were among those who postulated rural–urban contrasts such as sacred–secular, traditional–rational and personal–impersonal. Such contrasts, although conceptually attractive, could not be sustained in empirical studies and have limited credibility. Lewis (1966) made a detailed re-examination of Redfield's work in Tepoztlan and found that factors other than place were of central relevance in understanding these differences. There is, he suggested, a 'culture of poverty' which unites poor urbanites and rural peasants throughout the Third World. Studies of particular districts of Cairo, populated by migrants from specific rural areas, revealed rural values and lifestyles, derived from those areas and perpetuated in an urban setting (Abu-Lughod 1961). Differences were less between urban and rural than between rich and poor.

The outcome of this kind of research is that there are no consistent, measurable, abrupt changes of attitudes and values between 'urban' and 'rural' populations. In many ways, poor urban dwellers have more in common with their rural counterparts than with the professional and business elites who occupy the same cities. The more telling question, however, is whether poor urbanites in, for example, one Latin American city, have more in common with poor urbanites in another, than they have with the rural peasants of the same region. There is some sense in believing that this may be so. The whole rhythm and content of life in urban places is different from that in rural areas and this difference deepens with length of urban residence. Key factors include the nature of urban–rural relationships, the efficacy of transport and communication networks, and the form of spatial diffusion processes; in many Third World situations the effect may be that urban places are places apart and their populations, over time, become more distinctive. With modern trends such as counter-urbanization in advanced societies, the distinctiveness of urban living is again drawn into question. Professional and business people can relocate to rural settings and conduct their affairs with electronic mail and information 'super-highways'. They have lifestyles and values that are urban and geographical location becomes a secondary consideration.

Critiques of Wirth's urbanism and of the theories of contrast have followed rather different paths in European and North American studies. Numerous studies (Young and Willmott 1957; Gans 1962) have demonstrated that social cohesiveness and face-to-face relationships exist within urban localities and that neighbourhoods or communities serve as the territories for such interaction, countering the argument that anonymity and impersonality distinguish urban places. It is now also evident that the progress of western urbanization has reduced urban–rural differences to a point at which they become almost meaningless as transport and communication networks are so efficient that residential location loses some of its significance. Certainly, some traditional differences remain and there are residual rural enclaves, but urbanization is a pervasive societal process. It can be argued that as all settlements are outcomes of the same societal forces, the form of the outcome is less important than the nature of the forces.

Evidence of lifestyle differences between urban and rural places is therefore ambiguous and contrasts may be more real at some stages of societal development than at others. Urban–rural differences are blurred in many advanced western societies, as they are, for different reasons, in Third World societies which have experienced recent and large-scale rural-to-urban migration. There are many situations, however, in which urban places exhibit distinctive lifestyle characteristics. These are not necessarily urban–rural differences but are as likely to be inner city–suburban or small town–large city contrasts. These contrasts are products of social dimensions, such as class or race, rather than of place.

Urban places

Cities are physical concentrations of people and buildings and have economic, social and political qualities which are often culture-specific. Another approach is less concerned with defining urban as a quality, than with defining urban place as an entity. Two central objectives of this approach are, first, to recognize the reality of urban regions, comprising city and hinterland, and second, to provide a framework of standardized urban units which will make the tasks of comparative analysis easier. By the mid-1970s, most countries had adopted some criterion of an 'extended city' to measure urbanization. This **city-region**, defined normally by population size, density and journey-to-work area, was labelled a standard metropolitan statistical area (SMSA) in the USA; a census metropolitan area (CMA) in Canada; and a labour-market area in Sweden.

The concept of the extended urban area was pioneered by the USA Bureau of Census in 1910 and the definition of an **SMSA** summarized its key features:

1. Either one central city with a total population of 50,000 or more, or two contiguous cities constituting a single community with a combined population of 50,000 and a minimum population of 15,000 for the smaller of the two.
2. The remainder of the county to which the central city belongs.
3. Adjacent counties, if
   (a) 75 per cent or more of the labour force is non-agricultural;
   (b) at least 15 per cent of workers in the outlying county work in the central county, or 25 per cent of workers in that county live in the central county, i.e. there are significant journey-to-work links between areas;
   (c) at least 50 per cent of residents in a county meet density requirements or non-agricultural employment thresholds.

This definition included measures of population size, centrality and economic functions.

It was standardized across the USA to allow comparative analyses and formed a study-base which approximated the services and labour catchment area of the central city. The term **metropolitan statistical area** (MSA) has been used since 1983 and **consolidated metropolitan statistical areas** (CMSA) are formed by two or more contiguous MSAs.

British attempts to define urban places followed similar lines. The Standard Metropolitan Labour Area (SMLA) consisted of a core together with a metropolitan ring and had a population of more than 70,000. Among criteria for a 'core' are job densities over 5 per acre (13.75 per hectare) and more than 20,000 jobs in total. An SMLA 'ring' consisted of contiguous administrative areas sending at least 15 per cent of their labour force to work in the 'core'. A development of this system was produced by the Centre for Urban and Regional Development Studies (CURDS), at the University of Newcastle. They gave the term 'core' to a continuous built-up area containing a concentration of employment and retailing activities. To each core is attached its primary commuting field or 'ring', from which at least 15 per cent of those employed travel to work in the core, and more travel to that core than to any other. Core plus Ring formed the Daily Urban System and to this is allocated the Outer Areas which are districts more closely linked to them in commuting terms. Local labour market area (or LLMA) is the given term for the whole 'urban place'. In 1981, 61.6 per cent of the British population lived in Cores, 16.6 per cent in Rings and 6.6 per cent in Outer Areas. Using international data, Cheshire and Hay (1989) developed the conceptually similar **functional urban regions** (FURs) to compare changing patterns of urbanization throughout western Europe. Using the CURDS criteria, Prestwich and Taylor (1990) calculated that there were 228 FURs in Britain which could be aggregated into 20 **metropolitan regions**, each with a dominant urban centre. Additionally, there were 115 relatively self-contained 'freestanding' **urban regions**.

This research has attempted to answer the question, ' What is an urban place?' rather than 'What is urban?' though its focus on larger urban places excludes many small towns and cities. Development of the methodology has involved cooperation between academic researchers and those departments of government which have an interest in monitoring urban change and in providing standardized data-recording units. Whereas the question of defining urban can remain a topic for academic debate, the question of defining urban places has practical implications and of necessity some answer must be found. Progress has been made but there are methodological difficulties and any definitions need to be capable of adjusting to the pace of urban change.

Urban geography and urban studies

Urban geography is largely a division of convenience. The city, however defined, has no monopoly of social problems, economic disadvantage, or more general population attributes. Most subject matter has a societal rather than an urban frame of reference. There is a distinction to be made, for example, between problems in and of the city. Problems in the city are general problems that affect society as a whole, they simply find expression in urban places and their causes lie in economic or socio-political structures rather than in spatial structures. But there are also problems of the city that are brought about, or exaggerated, by the specifically urban conditions in which they occur. These categories are not necessarily exclusive but they do point up the dangers of assuming that differences emerge solely from places. This distinction between problems in and of the city is similar to that between people policies and place policies. The former target people wherever they live, the latter focus on places and their inhabitants. A people policy is individualized, a place policy is aggregate and may create errors of inclusion and exclusion.

Although an urban geography has central concerns with space, place and the urban environment, geographers have moved considerably from a preoccupation with spatial patterns and distributions for their own sake. Modern urban geography has an awareness of broad and deep-rooted social processes and with current policy needs. The focus on urban place allows a particular perspective to emerge but the essential task is to understand the phenomenon rather than to show its immediate association with geographical space. Urban geographers have moved closer to the multidisciplinary field of urban studies and Short (1984) expressed the position well when he suggested that urban geography identifies the city as a useful object of analysis but not one which is independent from the nature of the wider society. The task is not only to identify and explain those features which distinguish cities but also to see them as integral parts of the societies in which they are placed.

Human geography contains a variety of perspectives and **paradigms** which demonstrate that there are many ways of looking at the city. Paradigms change over time but the trilogy of positivism, structuralism and humanism is a useful starting point.

Modern perspectives

Modern perspectives can be initially summarized under the broad headings of positivism, structuralism and humanism which, while not wholly exclusive, are equally not entirely complementary. Some texts in urban geography have been written more specifically towards one or other of these positions. Walmsley's (1988) *Urban Living* belonged to the behaviouralist and humanist perspectives, whereas Badcock's (1984) *Unfairly Structured Cities* has a structuralist and political economy stance. This text undoubtedly has its biases but seeks to use good research from different theoretical stances to illustrate particular aspects of the city. There is much to be gained from what have been termed 'openings' or a willingness to see complementarity between approaches and the structure–agency debate may be seen as less concerned with a dichotomy than with an accommodation. It is important that students should be aware of different approaches and sources of explanation and hence be able to form their own judgements in what remains an open and continuing debate.

Positivism

Positivism was proposed by Comte to distinguish science from religion and received its fullest expression in the school of logical positivism known as the Vienna Circle in the 1920s. The positivist method seeks to explain events in the natural world by showing that understanding of a single event can be deduced from certain general statements or theories which contain one or more universal laws. Positivism was expressed in geography as **spatial analysis**, the study of human activities which result from the operation of universal processes of decision-making whose characteristics could be identified by a combination of modelling, observation and statistical analysis of the outcomes of those decisions. (Johnston 1980).

Spatial analysis had several distinctive features:

- It focused on general laws rather than exceptional cases.
- It used numerical methods and was quantitative in its approach.
- It had predictive power and could be used in public policy.

Two statements can be made about the conditions under which these characteristics affected urban geography. First, many of the ideas were derived from other disciplines and reflected the more general impact of normative, scientific approaches on the social sciences. Second, although one can find examples of generalizations in human geography from much earlier periods, the discipline in practice was centrally concerned with exceptionalism and stood in sharp contrast, for example, with the search for general laws in several branches of physical geography. From the isolated examples, such as Weber (1899), Christaller (1933) and Lösch (1954), a much more general shift towards a nomothetic discipline, in which the search for laws and models was a central concern, was one highly significant change which struck traditional geography at its very core. Associated with this shift was a much greater emphasis on quantitative analysis and statistics, an emphasis which not only added a 'degree of difficulty' to the new paradigm but also better equipped geographers for the development of a new scientific methodology.

Schaefer's (1953) plea for a move away from exceptionalism was a significant single event, more important in the longer term was the systematic development of spatial analysis by other US-based geographers, notably Garrison and Berry. Based initially at Seattle, the interests of this group were very much with spatial laws of two main kinds. The first were concerned with the patterns of points on the earth's surface, of which the main examples were clearly urban places; the second were of flows of goods and people, based upon a view of humans as exceptionally rational beings who reacted to the various costs of moving from one place to another by keeping them at a minimum. Their main stimuli were clearly from economics, both those provided by Christaller's central place theory and those from regional scientist-economists such as Isard and Lösch. Their work was strongly mathematical, focusing, for example, upon operational models developed in linear programming, though they also adopted statistical procedures to present their morphological and associational laws and to test their notions about the economic rationality of men. Urban geography proved especially amenable to the impact of this move towards increased quantification and the role of Brian Berry, who promoted the analysis of settlement patterns and sought spatial order in size and location of towns and cities, villages and hamlets, neighbourhood and regional centres, was considerable. Urban geography had some additional advantage in that the rediscovery of central place theory, a process helped by the English language version of Christaller (1966), provided a comprehensive spatial model, which, both as a whole and in its many individual facets, provided a rich testing ground for many elements of an emerging quantitative methodology with all the assumptions of normative behaviour and a positivist-scientific approach.

The new methods of spatial analysis were by no means confined to central place studies. They were applied to classifications of settlements, to examination of urban population sizes, and to the analysis of population densities within cities. On internal urban structure, a considerable amount of research was aimed at the comprehension of land-use and associated land-value gradients. Of the various texts, that by Haggett (1965) was among the most influential, and the application of models as a general panacea reached its height in Chorley and Haggett's work (1967).

During the early 1960s, interest in urban geography had shifted significantly towards social aspects of city life. This shift became associated with the increasing influence of spatial analysis and gave quantification and model-building a new and vigorous platform. Research focused upon the classification of residential areas within cities and the issue of residential segregation. As multivariate statistical techniques and the use of high-speed computers were developed, factorial ecology became the most widely adopted methodology. Much of this thrust towards quantification which, though synonymous with positivist ideas, was data-based and coincided with the availability of census small area statistics.

As the methodology of spatial analysis was extended and made more precise, it became more scientific with greater use of symbolic language and the formulation of mathematical models. Doubts began to grow as analyses became more sophisticated but yet remained descriptive, while optimizing solutions served the needs of suppliers rather than consumers. With its emphasis on the geometry of space, spatial analysis produced theories based on mechanistic assumptions of human decision-making. These involved the concept of 'economic man', a perfectly rational being whose location decisions were based on perfect knowledge, optimization of opportunities and minimization of costs. The later behavioural approaches still adhered to positive theory, but centred on processes rather than on patterns. More general reactions to the shortcomings of a positive science approach led to the introduction of other perspectives. It is important to stress, however, that despite these shortcomings, positivism and spatial analysis gave urban geography an important methodology and perspective which it retains. Many valuable skills presently included in the training of geographers are those derived from the practice of spatial analysis. As new methods, such as geographical information systems (GIS) and multilevel modelling, are introduced, they again arise from the same source.

Structuralism

As it entered geography, structuralism was in some ways a reaction against positive science and spatial analysis, although its standing as a social theory, especially as Marxist theory, was well established outside geography. Structuralism is first and foremost a theory of society, but its initial adoption by urban geographers had a more pragmatic catalyst with the civil disorder and public unease that shook western urban societies in the late 1960s. At that time, it was initially a critique of the lack of **relevance** in spatial analysis and Harvey (1973) argued that there was a clear disparity between the sophisticated, theoretical and methodological frameworks geographers were using and their ability to say anything meaningful about events unfolding around them.

Structuralism is a generic term but two meanings in particular have assumed significance:

- Relationships among component parts are more significant than the individual parts themselves; the correct terms of reference are societies and established orders rather than individual agencies.
- All human actions are underlain by hidden structures which influence and condition these actions. Explanations, therefore, cannot be found in observed phenomena or spatial outcomes but must be sought in the general structures to which these relate.

These general themes and, in particular, the notion of hidden structures and the impacts of dynamics of change in capitalist societies, have dominated Marxist approaches to the city. Whereas there is more than one type of hidden structure, structural symbolists working in the cultural/symbolic tradition, for example, talked of the 'rules of the mind' which govern actions and are embedded in the mores of a society, the key source for urban geography was derived from political economy and Marxist theory. According to Marx, every society is built upon an economic base which contains the modes of production and exchange. From this economic base or structure develops a superstructure of social and political institutions (legal systems, religions, customs). Economic bases may vary over time and space but in the modern world it is the capitalist system which dominates and provides the structural imperatives. Marxism explained recurrent crises in urban land markets as the results of conflict between opportunities available and the volume of profit seeking reinvestment. Massey (1984) argued that the 'rounds' of investment meant that geographical inequality was actually inherent in spatial structure itself and Harvey (1989) spoke of the 'annihilation of space through time'. The tone of the structuralist (political economy) position through much of the 1970s and 1980s was summarized by Bartelt *et al.* (1987) as the general assertion that large cities are what the larger economic order makes them. Bartelt *et al.* (1987) suggested three positions:

- Urban structure is a mirror of class, economic and social interests in which the urban landscape is a mosaic of financial interests and an outcome of investment patterns.
- Segregations of classes and ethnic groups are products of the inequality of wages and economic order. The city is an arena where conflicts over consumption of land are played out.
- Traditional approaches must be modified by an understanding of the ways in which economy is organized across space.

Modern Marxism is far from being a single perspective and there are divergent views on issues such as the relative significance and autonomy of base and superstructure and on the role of human agency. Harvey (1982), for example, recognized the duality of the worker as an object for capital, on the one hand, and as a living, creative subject on the other, a duality unresolved in Marxist theory. Marxism's basic divisions of labour and capital, workers and bourgeoisie, the concept of class as a collectivity, and class struggle have all been subjected to revisionist writing. Massey (1984: 117) pleaded for a stronger recognition of the significance of geographical differentiation: 'No two places are alike . . . most people still live their lives locally, their consciousness is formed in a distinct geographical place.'

During the 1980s in the UK, there was a major empirical research project, founded on the political economy perspective, which stimulated the 'localities debate'. The research projects, based on geographical localities, were criticized for empirical fact-finding at the expense of economic rigour (N. Smith 1987). Some argued that what occurred in localities was determined elsewhere, others wished to ascribe greater discretion to local agencies who had the power to influence trends and outcomes. This latter argument moved the debate towards an alignment with other, non-Marxist interpretations. Weberian class theory, for example, rested on voluntarist principles, with class positions which were negotiable and the appearance of conflict as these negotiations occurred (Jackson and Smith 1984). On the one hand, localities could be regarded as segments of the political economy in which the main forces came from structures and international markets, on the other, as 'arenas' in which local agencies such as local authorities or alliances of business people played important roles with the aim of 'urban boosterism'. The idea of local agencies with some autonomy and discretion, sits much more comfortably outside Marxist theory. These are issues in the structuralism debate, but for the moment it serves as a generic term for a highly influential set of approaches within modern urban geography.

Humanism

Humanism was also in many ways a reaction against positivism and its tendency to ignore human agency. Humanistic geographers looked to different philosophies, such as phenomenology, which evoked subjective descriptions of the life-worlds of human experience. There was no one founding philosophy for humanism and this made it more difficult to find its focus than Marxism which rests on a single source. Humanism rejected the absolutism of scientific thought and accorded idealism and mental activity a primary explanatory role independent of the material order (Jackson and Smith 1984). Human awareness, human agency, human consciousness and creativity were hallmarks of humanism with the aim of placing people back at centre-stage and studying human experiences as key sources of understanding. For humanistic geographers, an essential question concerned an understanding of the ways in which groups developed shared meanings and the intersubjectivity which imbued places with special values. Seamon (1979), for example, stated that people came together in time and space recognizing each other from daily, taken-for-granted impersonal dynamics: these spaces of activities evolved a sense of place that each person helped to create and sustain.

An understanding of the **meanings of place** had far more significance than that of the **geometry of space**, people were to be regarded as central figures in the city rather than anonymous components of models or laws. The priorities and methods of humanism were vastly different from those of positivism as qualitative methods replaced quantitative, place superseded space, and the inner meanings of people's life-worlds were explored rather than their outward spatial forms.

The triad of positivism, structuralism and humanism sets the broad parameters for the debate which underpins the practice of urban geography. Since their statement in these terms, however, both the theory and practice of urban geography have continued to evolve. Scientific method remains a powerful set of tools in urban analysis though its former dominance as a paradigm has long since been lost. Structuralism has diversified and changed and is accommodated in a variety of interpretations. The basic messages of hidden structures and imperatives remain valid and no analysis of an urban problem or issue can ignore the lessons of structural theorists. Most recent debate has two dimensions which can be elaborated in more detail. The first contains attempts to reconcile structure and agency and the second to develop the cultural approach to the city.

Structuration theory is the most notable attempt to find touching points or openings between the structuralists and humanists. Giddens (1984), as the founder of structuration theory, has played a major role in this debate. Giddens criticized the structuralists for their ability to see social, political and economic constraints but yet to ignore the purposefulness of individuals. He also criticized the humanists for their vision of the ideals and cultures of individuals and groups that omitted social, political and economic constraints. For Giddens, any social theory must not only recognize people as knowledgeable and capable subjects but also acknowledge the realities of societal constraints (Cloke *et al.* 1991). Structuration theory was a means of transcending the two perspectives and finding common ground. The theory has many strands but useful concepts to illustrate its essence are **signification**, **legitimation** and **domination**, each of which marks this complementarity of the agency, individual or group as one position, and the wider context within which they are placed as the other.

- **Signification** describes ways in which people interact by means of communication in a set of individual exchanges, but still work to a set of semantic rules established within society.
- **Legitimation** describes ways in which individuals or families may apply sanctions to some forms of behaviour as individual decisions but, in doing so, they draw upon a wider set of moral rules.
- **Domination** is concerned with the use of power to control or achieve results. Such power has a local expression but may also derive from wider authority to distribute resources. The personal, transient encounters of daily life are invariably bound up with more permanent guidelines of social institutions.

The **new cultural geography** has developed some of the earlier humanist ideas in ways that add to our ability to understand patterns and processes in the city. From this perspective, culture is a process in which people are actively engaged. A key process is that of **social construction** whereby people attach meanings to places and interpret them in a variety of ways:

> In constructing cultures, . . . people construct geographies. They arrange spaces in distinctive ways; they fashion certain types of landscape, townscape and streetscape; they erect monuments and destroy others; they evaluate spaces and places and adapt them accordingly; they organize the relations between territories at a range of scales from the local to the international.
>
> (Anderson and Gale 1992: 4)

The new cultural geography emphasizes people's values and ideas but remains attentive to the material bases of social life, it has a focus on human agency but shares structuration theory's concern to reconcile the two forms of analysis. This kind of cultural geography has much stronger concerns with the urban than did earlier, more traditional forms of cultural geography; it is concerned with the city as a centre for consumption, with the significance of gendered space and the relevance of the semiotics of the city to its research objectives.

Emergence of the 'post-city'

As a reflection of both empirical change and new theoretical positions, a series of new adjectival urban forms are now part of the lexicon. All have in common the prefix **post-** and the most widely used are post-industrial, post-structural and post-modern. Some words of explanation are warranted in this introductory chapter and more detailed examples will follow.

- The idea of the **post-industrial city** is based upon the empirical fact that manufacturing and industrial activities have fallen in significance during the second half of the twentieth century. Most urban employees are now in a wide range of service industries and cities have become products of an 'Information Age' in which producer services such as banking, finance and insurance and leisure and consumption services dominate the urban economy. Post-industrial is a statement that cities in advanced societies have moved from pre-industrial, through industrial to a new economic base and its set of associated characteristics.

- The descriptor **post-structural** is more an observation on shifts in ways of theorising urban forms and processes. It has alignments with the 'cultural turn' that became a dominant research trend in the 1990s with its focus on meanings, values and cultural processes. Bovaird (1993) argued that this post-structural approach 'ate at the heart' of Marxist perspectives by placing a debate about meanings, rather than about the social relations of material production, at the centre of human interaction. The shift in research interest from patterns of production to those of consumption (Jackson and Thrift 1995) has similar implications.

- The term **post-modern** again has theoretical bases but it has become commonplace to refer to the **post-modern city**. As a perspective, post-modernism advocates a return to the idiographic, the exceptional and the qualities of uniqueness. It celebrates differences and uniqueness and distrusts grand theory (Cloke *et al.* 1991). These tenets distance post-modernism from both positive science, with its quest for models, and structuralism, with its base of grand theory. Post-modernism finds expression in many ways but it is its impact on architecture that gives the clearest urban expression. The grand plans of modernist architecture are rejected by a return to a much more variegated urban landscape in which many styles can find expression. Le Nouveau Paris (Jahn 1991) proclaimed the new iconography of the city as demonstrated by a range of constructions such as the Grand Arch at La Défense, La Pyramide du Louvre, Les Halles and the Centre Pompidou. For urban geography, the implication is that cities are not explicable with simple logic nor can they be described with simple models; the very complexity of cities is such that the description, post-modern, is appropriate.

This chapter has traced the evolution of urban geography and has identified its main concerns. It has also discussed the theoretical positions which have underpinned ways in which urban geographers have studied the city. In the chapters which follow, there will be opportunities for the relevance of these theoretical positions to the practice of urban geography to be examined in greater detail.

CHAPTER 2
Urban origins and change over time

As there are problems in defining urban, so there are related difficulties in establishing the origins of urban settlements. Much of the available evidence for early forms of settlement is archaeological and goes back several millennia in time, but, at site investigations, the scale and sophistication of the built environment, with its accumulation of artefacts, leaves little doubt of the existence of an urban centre. Archaeological evidence, however, is often characterized by its unevenness and in some parts of the world there is little or no evidence of early cities. Lack of evidence may indicate either that cities did not exist or that insufficient proof has survived in recognizable form. Archaeological investigation is expensive and time-consuming and many of the major investigations were completed before the advent of major technological advances such as remote sensing and dating techniques. Without such studies, few statements are possible on those parts of the world thought to have experienced early urbanization. McGee (1967), for example, could suggest only that the origins of south-east Asian cities are obscure and may be related to the diffusion of Chinese and Indian forms of political organizations in the first century AD. Where detailed evidence is available, as for Catal Huyuk in Anatolia (Jacobs 1969), it is typically for one site and cannot easily be generalized to encompass regional systems of settlements. Many writers have examined the question of urban origins and, perhaps inevitably, the answers vary.

The traditional theory of urban origins

There is a **traditional theory** of the origins of cities, sometimes termed ecological or environmental, and linked with Childe (1950), which many would support. A basic tenet of this theory is that the emergence of cities followed agricultural change and that the Neolithic revolution, which advanced society from a stage of primitive hunting and gathering to one of food producing, was the necessary precondition for the emergence of towns. Domestication and cultivation led first to more permanent villages. An increase in carrying capacity of the land and a rise in population not only gave more villages, but also freed some members of the community from the rhythm of agriculture and the new seasonality allowed for periods of lower activity. There is evidence, for example, that the standard Mayan plot could produce twice as much corn as was necessary to support an average family unit. This freedom from the routines of agriculture gave conditions under which specializations could develop, producing initially priests, leaders and craft-workers and, eventually, a class of merchants. It was this scope for specialization and non-agricultural concerns that produced the conditions for urban settlements.

This traditional theory required a favourable natural environment. Urban evolution was most likely to occur in those parts of the world favoured with the topography, soils, water supply and climate which made agricultural change possible. These favourable, natural conditions had also to be matched by an advanced level of human endeavour through which critical changes in agriculture might be achieved and the key steps to urban specialization taken.

Childe had argued that agricultural surplus was the catalyst for change and Mumford (1961) extended this notion of surplus back to the cave painters of the upper Palaeolithic period. These painters were specialists, perhaps with religious roles, released from the primary functions of hunting and gathering by an abundance of game, and exhibiting some of the first signs of an urban tradition. A key question has been not the fact of surplus but its roles in emerging city civilizations. It is useful to note, however, that the traditional theory is contested. Jacobs (1969) argued that the concept of transition from rural to urban did not bear close investigation either from the archaeological evidence, or from modern interpretations of the relative roles of cities and countryside. Catal Huyuk, she argued, was the first form of settlement in that region and change in rural areas followed rather than led the process of urbanization. Catal Huyuk was a mining centre in a previously unsettled area and it was in response to demand generated by the city that significant changes in the surrounding rural area occurred. Jacobs argued that rural areas have rarely been sources of invention, innovation and change, rather these are the roles of cities. This argument has force but not generality. There are modern examples of mining centres in uninhabited areas which have provided stimuli for local agricultural change, but they tend to be exceptions rather than rules. Administrative and political cities also had this effect and have often been parasitic upon the rural hinterland. Again, cities are centres of innovation, but rural areas have not been devoid of such roles. It is reasonable to assume that changes that affect only rural areas, and are outcomes of a long process of evolution, will originate within those areas. The case of Catal Huyuk is valid but exceptional.

There are more general criticisms of the traditional theory of urban origins. Friedmann and Wulff (1976) discounted the term urban 'revolution' and argued for an evolution occupying many centuries, and taking a variety of forms in different parts of the world. A considerable debate, with two main parts, surrounds the issue of *where* cities first evolved. First, there is the basic question of where the earliest urban civilizations were located; second, there is the related question of whether some areas were primary and others were derived, independent development or diffusion. Attempts to list early urban civilizations vary but share a common core. Sjoberg (1973) included Egypt, Mesopotamia and the Indus valley, with later nuclear areas in North China and Middle America. Braidwood and Willey (1962) concluded that south-west Asia, Meso-America, Peru, India and China had urban civilizations by the beginning of the Christian period. Wheatley (1971) suggested seven areas of independent or primary urbanization: Mesopotamia, the Indus valley, the Nile valley, the North China plain, Meso-America, the central Andes and south-west Nigeria (Figure 2.1). Both Braidwood and Willey, and also Wheatley, would argue that these were independent developments, though this argument is at odds with earlier theories of

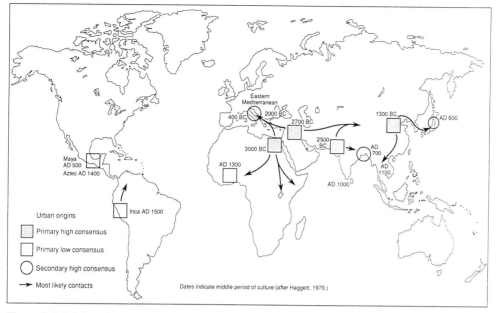

Figure 2.1 Origins of urban places

diffusion from a single centre or from a small number of centres. The concept of a single centre of diffusion in the Near East is difficult to maintain, especially with the urban developments in central and South America. Most writers accept that there were 'secondary' or 'derived' urban civilizations, as in Crete, south-east Asia and Etruria and there were cities 'transplanted' as imperial or colonial extensions of political control. Several independent centres of early urbanization existed in both the Old and the New World which did not coincide in time and had different features. Meso-American cities, for example, did not have animal husbandry, the wheel, nor an extensive alluvial setting. Diffusion may have become more important in later periods when towns were used as instruments of control and administration. Both Childe (1950) and Sjoberg (1965) stated that urbanization spread much more rapidly during the first five centuries of the Iron Age, with growth of empires, such as those of Persia, China, India, Greece and Rome, than during the preceding fifteen centuries of the Bronze Age.

The concept of surplus

Harvey (1973) produced a succinct statement on the origins of cities and the concept of surplus:

> there is general agreement that an agricultural surplus product was necessary for the emergence of city forms. Much controversy, however, surrounds the manner in which we should conceive of surplus and the way in which surpluses arise, are acquired and are put to use.

(Harvey 1973: 216)

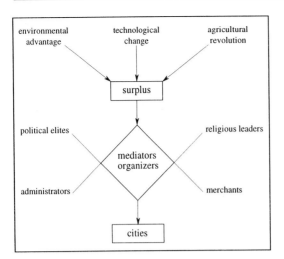

Figure 2.2 Derivation of surplus and its effects

Surplus can be viewed only in relative terms as the threshold of need, beyond which a surplus exists, may vary from one society to another and ultimately among individuals. As Wheatley suggested:

> No primitive people have ever spent all their waking hours in eating, breeding and cultivating: even the most debilitated, by squandering some of their resources in non-utilitarian ways, have demonstrated the existence of a surplus.
>
> (Wheatley 1971: 268)

Whereas there are always potential surpluses, they must be measured not merely against biological needs, but also in relation to the social conditions in which they occur. Harvey (1973) warned against a 'formless relativism' in the context of surplus and outlined the merits of Marxism as a general theoretical context which allowed surplus to be measured against 'the universal human requirements of man's existence as a species'.

The key is the way in which surplus is translated into the chain of events which leads to the emergence of cities (Figure 2.2). Here the focus is on those key individuals, institutions or groups whose role is to initiate and perpetuate the processes of change once the right conditions exist. Any causation process is likely to be multi- rather than single-stranded:

> It is doubtful if a single, autonomous, causative factor will ever be identified in the nexus of social, economic, and political transformation which resulted in the emergence of urban forms.
>
> (Wheatley 1971: 318)

For Carter (1977: 26), 'The catalyst was probably the intricately related role of temple, fortress and market place' and Clark and Slack (1976) drew these considerations together into the two general conditions for the emergence of urban settlements, a complex social structure and a sophisticated political order. Urban places, they argued, needed organization, order, stability and control and the circumstances to achieve these had to be present.

Many assume that there are important economic bases to urbanism. Pirenne (1925) regarded trade, commerce and the market function as the 'creators' of medieval towns, but Carter (1977) was sceptical of this view and showed that many markets and fairs were itinerant and never led to permanent urban settlements. Defensive functions are relevant as most early cities were fortified, but these are manifestations of social and political order, or disorder, rather than reasons for cities in their own right. For Marxist theorists, social institutions were secondary in comparison with fundamental changes in the economic bases of society. As economic change led to a transition from reciprocal exchanges to market economies, the expropriated surplus was invested into permanent form as the city. These 'forms', palaces, temples, market-places, guild-halls and city plans, all were the monuments of urban culture, standing as symbols of an economic and urban order.

Cities in traditional societies

Although urban geography has focused its attention squarely upon modern cities, there is a significant literature upon the nature of cities prior to this period. If the later eighteenth century, with the Industrial Revolution and its enormous influence on people and settlements, is taken as a divide, there is a preceding period of the order of 5,000 years when cities existed in one or more parts of the world. Over this period, urban civilizations grew and declined, periods of urban dominance were followed by times during which cities were abandoned or destroyed and rural forms of society gained ascendancy. These phases have been well documented (Mumford 1961; Chandler and Fox 1974) and resemble a cycle of urban change. A time-period of these dimensions is clearly capable of detailed classification, but a convenient two-fold division is into 'traditional' and 'modern' societies. Cities of the pre-industrial period are those which emerged as parts of 'traditional' societies.

Compared with cities of the modern world, the **pre-industrial cities** were generally small in population size and relatively few in numbers. In 1300 BC, for example, Thebes was the largest city with a population of about 100,000 and there were only twenty cities with populations in excess of 20,000. By the fifth century BC, Babylon may have approached 250,000 in size and in AD 100 Rome's population was put at 650,000. At this latter time, it is estimated that there were about 60 cities with populations of more than 40,000. These were mainly **primate cities**, disproportionately larger than any others within their urban system. Langton (1978) noted that, in 1730, when the vast majority of English towns had fewer than 5,000 inhabitants, with some larger regional centres and ports of up to 25,000 population, London had already exceeded 500,000.

The concept of the pre-industrial city

Sjoberg's (1960) concept of the **pre-industrial city** was in many ways a pace-setter in this field. It has proved controversial and has been subjected to detailed criticism, but the debate has helped understanding the process of urban change. Sjoberg saw cities as products of their societies. He also, perhaps less correctly, saw technology as the central force for differentiation and change, and his main distinction, between pre-industrial and industrial cities, rested upon the time-divide of the Industrial Revolution, giving the ability to use inanimate sources of energy to power tools. In the long time-period prior to this 'divide', Sjoberg hypothesized that a single broad type of city existed that he labelled **pre-industrial** and it is this generalization that has been contested. Society at this time was feudal with a social stratification system which could be separated into a small, wealthy elite and a much larger lower class of the poor. Radford (1979) argued that a vital component of Sjoberg's concept was control of the city by an elite whose dominance was derived from non-economic, extra-urban sources. In Charleston, South Carolina, for example, wealthy, low-country planters built town-houses in which they spent only part of the year but they still constituted the urban elite. For Sjoberg, this two-part stratification of pre-industrial society had generality and could accommodate even multi-stratified societies such as India with its caste system.

These pre-industrial cities were multifunctional and were not principally centres of economic activity. Religious, administrative, political and cultural functions were dominant and were reflected in the power structure of the pre-industrial city, in its institutions, its built fabric and land-use. There were economic activities, trades and crafts, but these were of limited importance. Sjoberg's model extended to the morphology of the pre-industrial city and its patterns of land-use. The city walls, which served as defences, as means of segmenting within the urban area, and as mechanisms for controlling the inflow of migrants and traders, were key features. The internal morphology was typified by narrow streets, congested routeways, and an absence of order, by 'houses, jumbled together, forming an irregular mass broken at intervals by open spaces in front of a temple or governmental building' (Sjoberg 1960: 35).

Sjoberg's model generalized upon the internal arrangement of land-uses and socio-spatial differentiation of the pre-industrial city. There were three broad generalizations. First, the elite population groups of pre-industrial cities were typically located close to the central area, near to prestigious buildings and sources of power. This residential location may have had the additional advantage of placing the rich well within the defensive walls and away from the more noxious elements of urban life. Their choice of a place to live was also affected, however, by the non-material factors which helped produce an exclusive, high-status core. As Langton (1975) suggested:

> Tight segregation was further encouraged by primitive transport technology, bad road surfaces, a street system designed more for house access than intra-city travel, the physical repulsiveness of the garbage-strewn, poorly built and crowded non-central area, and the tightly-knit structure of elite society, which was often reinforced by bonds of kinship and inter-marriage.
>
> (Langton 1975: 2)

The first feature of the social geography of the pre-industrial city was, therefore, a prestigious central area occupied by the elite: from centre to periphery there was a set of zones of progressively less prestigious areas occupied by less prosperous people (Figure 2.3).

Second, Sjoberg recognized that outside the central core there were differences in residential patterns of a more detailed kind. These ethnic, occupational and kinship divisions were at finer levels of segregation and took the form of quarters or precincts. Third,

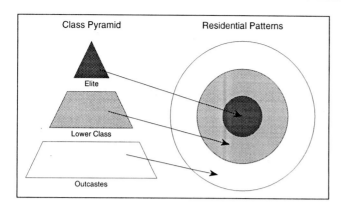

Figure 2.3 Sjoberg's model of the pre-industrial city

Sjoberg argued that over much of the pre-industrial city there was a lack of functional differentiation of land-use. Plots were put to multiple uses, the separation of workplace and residence was uncommon, and nothing which resembled well-defined land-use zones or sectors could be seen to exist in any detail or uniformity.

Sjoberg presented an attractively simple and graphic account of the nature and form of the pre-industrial city but there were questions on the accuracy of his interpretation. How acceptable, for example, is the idea that one basic type of city existed in different parts of the world, for varying phases of time, over a timespan of about 5,000 years? As Sjoberg himself argued, cities are parts of the societies within which they occur and reflect contrasts between those societies. As Egyptian society in the Ancient World differed from medieval society in western Europe, so the cities of those societies should mirror those differences. Similar overgeneralization, and some misuse of nomenclature, is revealed by Sjoberg's use of the term 'feudal' to describe **all** societies before the Industrial Revolution, when, in the proper sense of the word, some were feudal and others were not. It is in his general use of historical data that Sjoberg has been most severely criticized. For Wheatley (1963: 183), he had treated the evidence of the past in a 'cavalier' fashion and had grossly understated the significance of cultural and religious factors. Burke (1975) was of the view that Sjoberg had based his concept upon secondary sources of information, of questionable quality, from limited parts of the world.

A further example of overgeneralization is provided by Sjoberg's two-fold division of pre-industrial society into an **elite** and a **lower class**. Feudal stratification in medieval Europe had intermediate classes, such as clergy and bourgeoisie, and some societies were further complicated by intricate castes of priests, warriors, commoners and slaves; there were also migrant and ethnic groups who played a large part in shaping the residential mosaic. Langton (1975), in his study of seventeenth-century Newcastle upon Tyne, recognized a sharp stratification within the merchant community and, similarly, the craft guilds were differentiated by wealth and power. Social stratification, then, was far more variegated than Sjoberg implied.

Several authors have taken issue with Sjoberg over his depiction of the pre-industrial city as an essentially unplanned and disorganized collection of streets and dwellings. Wheatley (1963) showed that early Chinese cities had straight broad roads radiating from a nexus, with the wealthier people living on these roads and the poor in the interstitial areas behind. There was a remarkable uniformity of plan in Chinese cities, with a square or rectangular

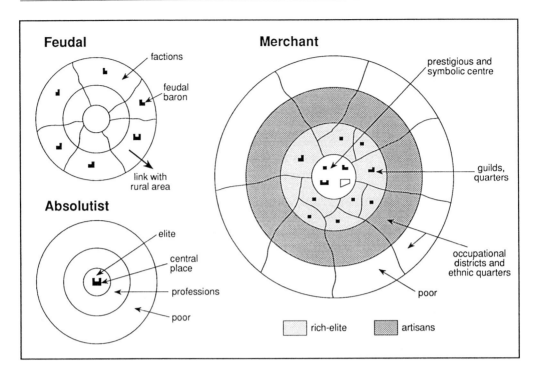

Figure 2.4 Feudal, absolutist and merchant cities

form and walls surrounding a great cross and gates at the end of each of four arms. There are many other examples of planning in pre-industrial cities such as Roman towns, and the Renaissance or Baroque cities, which had walls, processional ways and a grid-iron plan. Mabogunje (1974), writing on the pre-colonial development of Yoruba towns, described the palace and market as forming a 'hub' from which processional ways radiated.

Sjoberg's spatial model of the pre-industrial city had a zonal form and there is ample evidence that cities in traditional societies possessed this spatial arrangement, with prestigious central areas and low-status urban peripheries separated by zones of decreasing status. De Planhof (1959) recorded Marco Polo's description of Lut, an Iranian city, as comprising a series of seven concentric walled circles, protecting various quarters, each of which was occupied by members of a single social class. The status of these classes increased towards the central citadel, progressing from peasants, through artisans, to tradesmen, warriors, and doctors of law. At a different place and time, Zweig (1942) described pre-industrial Vienna as a clearly ordered city. Nobility and their palaces occupied the heart of the city, diplomats the next districts followed successively by industry and merchants, petty bourgeoisie and workers. Langton (1975) examined studies of British cities in the seventeenth century and concluded that three of the five largest English cities, together with Dublin, exhibited spatial patterns similar to those postulated by Sjoberg with evidence of wealth declining towards the urban periphery. Radford (1979), in Charleston, South Carolina, discovered a prestigious centre, a gradient towards the periphery of the city, and segmented slave quarters. The key to the validity of the Sjoberg model is its level of generalization and, at more detailed levels of empirical investigation, divergences and distortions become evident. White (1984), for example, showed that in Italian feudal cities a centrally located elite was not the norm. This group did not cluster at the centre until a later stage when cities were dominated by a single ruler (Figure 2.4). There are two further considerations. First, there is the nature and **symbolism** of the functional centre of the pre-industrial city; second, there is the extent to which segmentation into districts and quarters distorted the broader zonal pattern.

Institutions and symbolism

While the pre-eminence of the central areas of pre-industrial cities was clear, its constituent institutions varied. For the medieval Muslim, the key landmarks of the city were the mosque, market and public baths; for the early dynastic Mesopotamian it was the temple; for the Carolingian, the keep, church and market; in Mauryan India, the palace and market, and so on. These institutions reflected the power bases and cultural values of their societies and gave strong symbolism to the central area. This symbolism came through most strongly in societies where religious institutions were paramount. McGee (1967) has described the south-east Asian city of Angkor Thom, built between AD 1181 and 1219. At the centre of the city was the Bayon, the largest temple, a huge mountain of stone designed to symbolize the magical mountain which is the axis of the universe and abode of the gods. 'Surrounding the Bayon there was an enclosure in which the palace of the king was located and surrounding this were the walls and a wide moat, some eight miles in circumference, which represented the mountain, walls, and the sea of the cosmological universe' (McGee 1967: 37).

Wheatley stressed the **cosmological** significance of the whole plan and ethos of the pre-industrial city: 'No account of the spatial relations of pre-industrial cities in East and South Asia can afford to ignore the cosmogonic significance of the ritual orientation of urban space' (Wheatley 1963: 182).

Besides the prestige and wealth of the central areas, there was a religious symbolism and the ceremonial cores of the Mayan cities, with their grouped pyramids, courts and plazas, had similar attributes.

Districts and sectors

Outside the central areas of pre-industrial cities, the evidence for zoning was not always clear. Tuan (1968) described the ninth-century city of Ch'ang-an as being divided into two parts by a long and very broad street. On one side of this street was the imperial court and its associated entourage, on the other were the merchants and other citizens. This simpler pattern is reminiscent of London. Regent Street was the boundary between the West End, with its complex government buildings around Westminster and St James and homes occupied by nobility and gentry, and the East End, with its narrow streets and mean houses, occupied by mechanics and traders.

Segmented or compartmentalized pre-industrial urban forms were found in many parts of the world. In Yoruba towns, each street formed a quarter consisting of a number of family compounds. These compounds were enclosed spaces with single entrances and many internal subdivisions; individual families occupied each subdivision but the compound was united on a kinship basis. Square or rectangular compounds were the most common, but they varied in size and form in ways which reflected the status of their occupants. Whereas compounds of poor families would cover no more than one-fifth of a hectare, those of chiefs would have an area in excess of one hectare. In the pre-industrial, colonial cities of South America, a fortified, 'monumental' centre, dominated the urban area, but around it were native compounds housing the Indian population.

The merchant cities, which emerged in the long period between the Dark Ages and the beginning of the Industrial Revolution in Europe, marked an important phase of urban development. This was a time of transformation from a feudal to a capitalist society, producing a merchant class, the 'third estate', after the aristocracy and the church. The merchants, as traders and exchange-dealers, needed urban settings and their activities became part of cities. Medieval guilds, with the roles of regulating entry to professions and controlling the supply of goods, accompanied the growth of crafts and industries. The need for a money economy and for financing as a profession became imperative; the word 'bank' comes from the Italian *banco* or the table on which money-changers conducted their affairs. The merchant cities of Europe brought new forms of society, architectural expressions and economic organizations.

These merchant cities took the typical form of the segmented or compartmentalized city in medieval Europe during the 'pre-capitalist' period (Vance 1971). The critical stage in transformation to the capitalist city was that at which people began to own rather than merely to hold land. In the medieval city, land-ownership was mainly functional, affording workers a place to practise a trade and to shelter family, apprentices and journeymen. The burgage plots, or land-holdings, were intended to provide suitable urban locations rather than personal wealth. The guilds had key roles and guild membership was the means of entry to established urban life. Individual guild-halls were foci of activity and their members, living within the precincts, created distinctive, occupational districts. The guild as an organization offered security, entertainment, social contact, surveillance of business and religious orthodoxy – all effective bonds which cemented the territorial districts into cohesive communities. This 'factionalizing' role of the guild had a strong impact upon the social geography of the medieval west European city and was paralleled by other social divides. There were ethnic divides with early ghettos dating from the twelfth century when Jews were excluded from Christian quarters. Political rivalry within cities led to physically identifiable and separate quarters such as the *societa della torri* in Florence. For Vance, the medieval city in western Europe was segregated and multicentred and it was the guild system that underlay most of this compartmentalization.

> The supervision of the quality of products, the conditions of manufacture, the ways the goods were sold, became important offices of the gild, and roles that encouraged the clustering together, in gild districts within the city, of the individual practitioners of the various 'mysterious arts'.
>
> (Vance 1971: 105)

Vance also recognized a more general zonal form in the medieval European city, with patrician, high-status guilds occupying more central districts and some gradation outwards. There was a distinctive vertical arrangement of land-uses and social classes, with ground floors of buildings used to transact business, the first floor serving as the family home and upper floors reserved for employees and others. Separation of workplace and home was not the general rule.

Langton (1975), in his detailed study of seventeenth-century Newcastle upon Tyne, stressed the complexity of the city in traditional societies and the danger of overgeneralization. From an analysis based upon the taxed population of 1665, he showed that occupational groups were, to a significant degree, segregated into distinctive concentrations. Four groups of activities – mercantile, victualling, shipping and manufacturing – corresponded with clusters around strategic facilities, and some crafts were also found in spatial clusters. In Newcastle, any emerging 'class' zones also contained occupational groups united by comparable levels of wealth.

> Newcastle was not a feudal pre-industrial city, nor was it a pre-capitalist or capitalist city. A merchant clique was pre-eminent in wealth and municipal power. Its social dominance was expressed geographically in the existence of a mercantile quarter in that part of the city where its economic purposes were best served and where the institutions through which it dominated the city were located. In addition, the city possessed other regularly patterned occupational districts which were in some areas reinforced by 'class-zoning' and in others countervailed by it.
>
> (Langton 1975: 21)

There is ample evidence to show that while spatial models of the type proposed by Sjoberg, with their proposals of zones, quarters and gradations, have some generality, detailed, empirical studies of the city in traditional societies reveal divergences, contrasts and exceptional features. Whereas technology has some value in monitoring differentiation and change over the pre-industrial period, culture, tradition and social values may be more telling explanations of diversity. These values underpinned early cities, as Vance (1977) argued, and helped us to understand the strong contrasts within medieval Europe between merchant towns and Renaissance cities:

> No more revealing picture of the distinction between the city as the workshop of man and as the monument to enshrined and narrowly-held power could be furnished than by comparing Bristol in the West Country of England with the several dozen princely towns in Germany and Italy possessed of similar status.
>
> (Vance 1977: 223)

Any generalizations must also allow for diversity and change. Cities have rarely been static and the concept of urban change is as important as those of form, composition or ethos.

The city in transition: nineteenth-century change in Europe and North America

For much of the nineteenth century the city in western societies was, at varying speeds and impacts, in a process of transition. This transition had implications for the social geography of the city, but it was underlain by far-reaching changes transforming the overall nature of society. Economic change allied with industrialization was a dominant trend, another was the change from a traditional 'feudal' to a capitalist society. Sometimes the needs of the new economies brought immediate and specific changes, more usually – and especially in terms of residential structure – there was a slower and more varied response. Whereas the wealthy could initiate change and provide the means to achieve it, the large mass of urban population was governed by constraints and their opportunities came far more slowly.

The period of transition, mainly centred in the nineteenth century, was from the city in traditional to that in modern societies. At a basic level, a set of stages by which urban transition was achieved can be identified, and **pre-industrial** and **industrial cities** can be seen as such stages. These ideas about stages and models retain some general value but cannot adequately cope with the complex processes of change or their expressions in urban forms and organizations. An organizing framework of stages and models is helpful, but the details of process and pattern are at least as significant. As a post-modern perspective suggests, the search for order and compartmentalization should not distract geographers from acknowledgement of the complexities of an urban life where disorder and variation may be more common than their antitheses.

For Vance (1971) the terms, pre-industrial and industrial, are less appropriate than pre-capitalist and capitalist. The latter, in his view, more adequately described the changing relationship between employer and worker and social transformation of land and housing in the new capitalist order. Industrialization and the emergence of capitalism had many expressions and the segregation of residential areas, for example, mirrored increased specialization in work, differential rewards and social stratifications. Class became a basis for separation and difference in geographical space. Allied to these changes was the revolution involving the relationship between workplace and home. During the long age of the city in traditional societies, separation of workplace and home had been extremely limited. When the **workshop economy** was the norm, social stratification was reflected at different floors of individual buildings rather than in separated residential space, with variants of the 'upstairs-downstairs' syndrome.

With increasing social differentiation, a more general separation of workplace and home became common. This separation occurred during the nineteenth century and was the central process in understanding the changing social geography of the city. Essential adjuncts of this process were the development of a housing market to supply accommodation, and the evolution of a transport system which allowed home and workplace to be linked in a daily rhythm. Access to housing and transport was limited initially to those sections of society who controlled wealth and power but these facilities gradually became available to other sections of the population.

Many of the geographies of the nineteenth-century city provide snapshots of residential structure at different points in time. These identify patterns, demonstrate change over time, and reveal the local processes of residential mobility which underpin that change. The additional task is to relate these patterns and processes to more general forces of social transformation and to reveal the roles of the agencies which provide the conditions under which change can occur.

Marxist geographers interpret these forces as integral parts of the process of capital development which began, in the early nineteenth century, to force rapid urbanization, new patterns of production and new divisions of social life (Walker 1978); urban outcomes are sharply defined by the structural imperatives of the capitalist mode of production. Ideally, from this standpoint, the spatial organization of the city should be designed to facilitate the circulation of capital, commodities and information. The 'fractions' of capital, such as industrial, commercial, financial and property, are closely interdependent in the grand scheme of capitalism, with urban space as the arena in which capital, rent and state interact (Badcock 1984). Marxist geographers acknowledge that this optimal organization for the circulation of capital is difficult to achieve as there are obstacles of inertia, time lags and conflicting class interests, but the imperatives of investment flows, movements of capital, and the interests of the dominant classes will prevail. These imperatives ensure uneven development, inequalities, exploitation and injustice. Capital then is the linchpin that explains both the organization of the city and the relations between city and society. This line of argument is persuasive during the period of the rise of the industrial city and its close correspondence with the developing capitalist ethic. As a grand theory it is most appropriate to particular phase in urban history, but has continuing relevance.

The capitalist ethic transformed the nature of social relationships and established both land and housing as **commodities** to be owned rather than held. Whereas the offer of employment had often carried the obligation to house the employee, this became far less common and it was ability to pay rent that determined the availability and quality of housing. This is not to say that the industrialists had no role in the housing of their workers. Provision of such housing became an investment in which both owners and speculators were involved. Lack of transport meant close juxtapositions between workers' housing and factories. All of this involved different and more impersonal relationships and new attitudes towards rent, property and profit.

Urban form adjusted to these changing circumstances. Buildings were extended upwards, creating the tall house in northern Europe, or backwards to infill the burgage plot. With these changes, containment of the extended family under one roof remained typical under the workshop principle, with master, workers and apprentices all accommodated (Figure 2.5A). Vance (1966) noted the mill villages in both Rhode Island (Figure 2.5B) and Nottinghamshire as early examples of the separation of workplace and residence. With the factory system, the **separate** place of work became normal and short daily journeys by workers bound the small groups of residences to the factory. In these examples, the industrialist was still the provider of housing, as an adjunct of production, but an initial stage of separation had been achieved. For the labour force of these early factories, the employment link was short, direct and highly specific.

As the change to the factory system gathered pace, a demand for new labour was generated. These workers had to be accommodated in cottages and tenements which were constructed in the alleys and courts behind the main street façades. Infill now became a more direct source of profit and congestion began to appear in the inner city (Figure 2.5D). The merchants who occupied main-street housing were faced with choices. Depending on

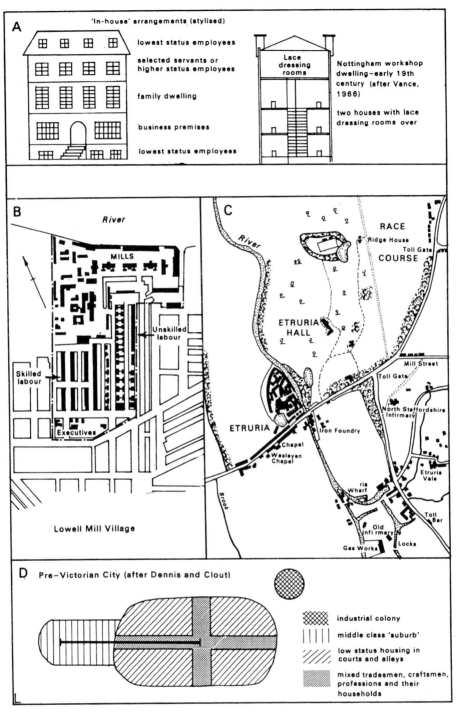

Figure 2.5 Changing work–residence relationship

    A Social stratification by floors within a building

    B Lowell mill village with designated residences

    C Wedgwood's Etruria with potbank and cottages

    D Early transport and emerging suburbs

the profitability of infill and the availability of new peripheral land and transport, ground and first-floor space could be released for business expansion; managers rather than owners remained the inner-city dwellers. As the attractiveness of the central city waned with increasing congestion, higher-income groups began to accept short journeys to work to displace themselves from both the workplace and the 'classes' they aspired to leave behind. Daunton (1990) noted that for middle-class families, home became part of a retreat from urban stress, central city to suburbs, and Georgian terrace to villas set in gardens. Preferences for suburbs could become a general trend only when investment capital realized a profit by building houses on the urban fringe. This began in London at places such as St John's Wood and Regent's Park and soon spread elsewhere.

It would be wrong to locate the origins of these trends in the nineteenth-century city as, even in twelfth-century London, there were high-status residences, the isolated mansions and country houses of the rich and powerful, around the edges of the city. Similarly, in the eighteenth century, early industrialists had left the towns in which they had established their production processes; Wedgwood, for example, left the Potteries town of Burslem to find a more rural setting for his Etruria Hall (Figure 2.5C) and, nearby, he built both a new factory, alongside the canal, and housing for his workers. It was during the nineteenth century, however, that the trickle became a stream as professionals and businesspeople sought to emulate the new residential examples of the elite. The change in housing contract between employer and employee had deleterious effects: 'housing generalization led to the creation of slums . . . it grew out of the abandonment of the self-correcting mechanism of enlightened self-interest that had existed in factory-tied housing' (Vance 1966: 324).

As employers lost a sense of proprietal care, social distances widened and the **urban proletariat** was created. That there were new attitudes to housing provision is clear, whether prior attitudes were necessarily good, and subsequent bad, is less obvious. For example, the use of the term 'slum', as a generalization upon Victorian low-cost housing, has been questioned (Ward 1975).

For the new professionals and businesspeople, the distancing of housing from the industrial areas brought new attitudes. High-income residential **areas** gave exclusion and the opportunity to create symbols of affluence and power. The emerging high-income groups acted concertively to develop particular kinds of residential districts and imbue them with lifestyles and social flavours which set them apart (Cowland 1979). There may have been accompanying changes in family lifestyles. As employers loosened bonds with the workplace, they generally chose to live as nuclear families, but in low-income areas the extended family remained the norm. As the higher-income and later the white-collar groups acted on a preference for 'rural' settings, an aversion to place of production and crowded living areas, and a desire to avoid the rising taxes of the central city, the advantages became clear to others. For the working classes, the mid-nineteenth century was a time when it would have been desirable to secure less crowded and unhealthy quarters but their exodus had to await the development of trolley-buses in the late 1880s (see Hall 1988). The railroads had brought transport possibilities to the white-collar groups in the 1830s but, as Ward (1964) suggested, innovation and expansion of the street-car system was achieved more rapidly in the USA than in Britain. In US cities, production and circulation concentrated in the central city, where economic enterprises were interwoven with workers' homes; there was an outward residential thrust of the bourgeoisie towards suburbs and a dramatic increase in the economic and social differentiation of urban space. The essential mechanisms of these changes were a transport system, a building and construction industry, and a set of new agencies to administer the urban housing market.

> The character of the place and its different neighbourhoods, was determined by the builders themselves, or more strictly by the developers – those large builders . . . who took large leases of building land and organized its disposition, saw to the laying out of the lesser residential roads, the making of sewers and the provision of water supply, and who generally arranged sub-leases with smaller builders for individual houses or small groups of houses.
>
> (Thomson 1977: 108–9; quoted in Shaw 1979: 195)

Residential patterns in the nineteenth century

Most empirical studies of nineteenth-century cities sought to identify the 'dimensions' or 'bases' of residential differentiation and the extent to which they found spatial expression. Shaw (1977; 1979) studied Wolverhampton in 1851, when it had a population of 49,985 and 1871 when it had reached 68,291. At the earlier date it was well into the process of transition from pre-industrial to industrial city and even in 1851, social status was the clearest basis of residential separation, linked with household composition and domestically organized trading. An Irish ethnic dimension was evident and the social geographical divide was between areas of relatively high social status, where servants were common and the head of household was involved in business, and the industrial districts where social class was low, servants were rare and there were many children in employment. By 1871, family status or household composition was more significant and, in the central district, business households, containing single adults but no children, were run by a manager as the proprietor and his family had moved to the suburbs. Higher-income suburbs had developed in the western part of the urban area.

A study of Liverpool (Lawton and Pooley 1975) found the transition towards the modern industrial city to be well advanced at mid-century: 'the rapidly growing city of the mid-Victorian period exhibited a high degree of residential differentiation: the main social dimensions of city structure had clear spatial expression and were reflected in distinctive social areas' (Pooley 1977: 364).

The bases of separation were demographic, economic and social, the central area had long since ceased to be residential, and trends towards suburbanization were evident. Goheen (1970), in a detailed study of Toronto, analysed evolving residential patterns in Toronto between 1850 and 1900. At the beginning of this period, the wealthy were segregated but remained in the city centre where they could both take advantage of urban amenities and exercise influence on urban affairs. By contrast, the unskilled workers, segregated at the urban periphery, had most disadvantaged environments and locations. Between these extremes, and accounting for a large part of the urban population was considerable heterogeneity of functions, classes, and residences. By 1879, economic, family and ethnic (Roman Catholic) segregation were distinctive and independent dimensions, even though they had limited territorial expression. By the turn of the century, both the scale and texture of urban life had become transformed to resemble those of the modern city. Radford's

(1976) study of Charleston, South Carolina, a 'slave city', between 1869 and 1880, found detailed patterns of segregation but a displacement of the free blacks to the urban periphery. More generally it has been argued that there was little residential segregation in the nineteenth-century American city; the destitute were clustered but elsewhere there were admixtures of lesser professionals, craftsmen and labourers. These were still, however, cities in transition displaying processes of economic and social change.

The industrial city

The growth of industrial capitalism affected the nature of economic activity, the social and political organization, and the spatial configuration of urban places. The pace of change was unprecedented and was paralleled by major advances in areas such as medical science and technology which magnified its effect. Industrial capitalism was accompanied by demographic transition, a population explosion which was to find its main expression in the urban areas of the industrial era: this became truly the **age of great cities**.

The factory system brought specialization of labour, workers undertook single tasks involving the continuous use of equipment, and the 'conveyor-belt' syndrome of Fordism became the norm. With its greater scale of production, economies of scale, increased productivity and higher levels of output, the factory system transformed industry and manufacturing. The factory system needed a large pool of available workers, and factories tended to cluster together in order to make optimum use of labour pools, markets, ancillary suppliers and services. This clustering led to the form of **industrial city**. Some were new cities, such as mining towns on coalfields, shipbuilding settlements on tidal rivers, and transport towns at strategic points of conflux but others were grafted on to pre-existing urban settlements such as market towns, rural service centres and merchant cities, transforming them with this new urbanizing force. The 'great cities' were those in which the urban-industrial process was most successful and acquired its own momentum. Successful industries attracted other activities, the demand for services was multiplied, the availability of work drew in workers, the generated wealth began to find civic expression in the new 'monuments' of civic buildings, cultural institutions and infrastructures of roads, rails and services. The urban hierarchy, once established in nineteenth-century Britain, became affected by the spread of innovations in an uneven way, with innovations filtering downwards from larger cities to smaller towns in the urban hierarchy.

Industrial capitalism also led to realignments of social structures, by creating two main classes, the owners of capital who invested in labour to produce a profit or surplus, and the labour force that sold its skills to the owners of capital in order to earn wages. This division between capital and labour, the keystone of Marxist theory, had profound implications for relationships within city and society. All power was now concentrated into the hands of the holders of capital, cities were formed to suit their needs and the industrial city was the physical manifestation of the imperatives of the capitalist system. These imperatives had expressions which subsumed the pre-industrial legacies of the merchant cities. In Europe, industrial capitalism spread from Britain to Belgium, hence to Germany, France, the Netherlands, Scandinavia and the Alpine countries and later to southern Europe.

The scale of this urbanization was spectacular. Lawton (1972) estimated that almost all of

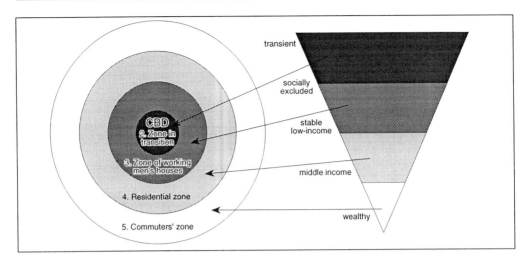

Figure 2.6 Burgess's model of the industrial city

the 27 million increase in British population from 1801 to 1911 was absorbed by urban areas. White (1984) commented on the growth of German cities and showed that the Ruhr had a population of 237,000 in 1843 but 1.5 million in 1895. The industrial city had its own social stratification, the 'bourgeoisie' of successful industrialists, business people and professionals, but more spectacularly the new working classes, the urban proletariat. Initially, it was in the interests of capitalists to provide houses to rent for their workers, a labour force close to the factory gates was a priority. As the industrial city grew in scale, this was less typical and existing properties were subdivided for rent or added to by an emerging, speculative building industry. Much of this housing was of low quality and the pressure of population growth meant overcrowding and congestion. Again, White (1984) recorded that poverty and squalor generally characterized the living conditions of the new proletariat and at Bochum, Germany in the 1870s, three-quarters of the population was at subsistence levels.

The industrial city was of a radically different form from that of its predecessors, and infrastructures were stretched to impossible limits by the pressures of growth. Public sanitation and water supply services were overwhelmed, the lack of control meant high levels of pollution and low quality housing and services. Engels (1872) wrote of conditions in London where houses were occupied at high levels of overcrowding and had fallen into severe states of disrepair with narrow courts and alleys filled with filth and rubbish. Such conditions led inevitably to contagious disease and ill-health and to a breakdown in social order with high rates of crime and vice. Hall (1988) characterized these places as 'cities of the dreadful night'. Eventually society was to respond to these malaises with alternative communities such as garden cities and social reforms in attempts to control standards of living. For many years, however, these piecemeal measures did little to ameliorate the worst urban conditions.

With the industrial city there were new economic and social organizations of geographical space. The vestiges of the pre-industrial city, where they existed, were swept away. The city centre was the commercial heart of the new society, and the wealthy, with their power to exercise choice, opted for space and more open surroundings on the edges of the industrial city. The poor were left at the heart of the city in their crowded tenements and high density terraces using space which others had discarded (Figure 2.6). Perhaps the best known British description was that provided for Manchester:

> Manchester contains, at its heart, a rather extended commercial district, perhaps half a mile long and about as broad, and consisting almost wholly of offices and warehouses. . . . unmixed working people's quarters, stretching like a girdle (around this commercial district), averaging a mile and a half in breadth . . . Outside, beyond this girdle, lives the upper and middle bourgeoisie, the middle bourgeoisie in regularly laid out streets in the vicinity of working quarters . . . the upper bourgeoisie in remoter villas with gardens . . . in free wholesome country air, in fine comfortable houses.
>
> (Engels 1844: 80)

In terms of a spatial model, Engels recognized a broad concentric zonal form which became ever more apparent as an improving transport system, moving from horse-drawn carriages, to trams, street-cars and railways, gave means of mobility to those sections able to move outwards towards the city periphery. As the term **pre-industrial city** described one general urban form, and the **industrial city** described another, so this stage of change is a category in its own right. The '**city in transition**' is a term appropriate for older cities which became modified to the industrial city form. The rich gradually moved out from central locations, the city centres became commercialized, the inner city gradually assumed its 'locus of poverty' character and the new suburbs grew. But those changes happened over decades and during this time they were cities in transition containing vestiges of the old, portends of the new, always modified by local conditions and the impact of change (Ward 1975).

Transition to the industrial city developed first in Europe as an effect of the industrial revolution itself and its early impact in that part of the world. In the late nineteenth and early part of the twentieth century, these processes were still unfolding in North American cities and there were further complexities. Hiebert (1995) showed that the late-nineteenth-century North American city was typified by the persistence of tightly knit ethnic neighbourhoods with mixtures of social classes. It was only in the 1920s that these enclaves began to separate along class rather than ethnic lines. One precipitating factor was the mass in-migration of urban poor, creating an underclass and forcing class divisions. Other evidence pointed towards a growing gap between work and residence in the mid-nineteenth century and this established an elite, though the working-class areas still divided ethnically. There was a conflict between the politics of race and of community. Hiebert (1995), with evidence from Toronto, supported the persistent significance of ethnicity but also agreed that ethnic areas did tend to be sorted along class lines. As the city reorganized in space, the places where people lived became more homogeneous but the actual attainment of homogeneity should not be exaggerated. Class and ethnicity were commonly interwoven and only groups seen as 'different' tended to occupy sharply distinguished and separate social worlds.

Suburbanization

The growth of suburbs was the clearest expression of the expanding city. Enabled by improving transport systems and infrastructures, lower density residential areas on the edges of cities were the main response to the long process of migration from the central city. This peripheral growth added significantly to the land area of the built urban environment which doubled and trebled in size from the 1920s onwards. The scale of suburbanization was the key to urban expansion. In the USA public policy fuelled suburban growth. Between 1944 and 1961, the entire US transport budget of $156 million was diverted to road construction and, at its peak in the 1960s, this amounted to over one-third of all Federal grants (Badcock 1984). Modern suburbanization was wedded to private transport so this input of public funds had powerful implications for peripheral growth. At the same time, the funding of housing construction and purchase began to make home-ownership a highly desirable state and the suburbs offered this opportunity. Mid-twentieth-century suburban development dwarfed nineteenth-century urban growth, though public support for suburban road programmes and funding for suburban homes was regressive. It meant less money for public transit systems, no compensation for inner city families displaced by road programmes and a starvation of housing finance for the inner city. In the UK the much stronger public sector intervention in housing gave more balance with new local authority estates as well as private suburbs on the urban periphery.

There are different views on the forces behind suburban development.

- One view is that suburbs arose from preferences within the private housing sector and the role of agency was paramount. Individual households of nuclear families with access to transport chose spacious, modern dwellings in relatively rural settings. There were push factors from the congested inner city. Status was also a factor on two counts – an escape from the poor image of the inner city and a place to live in a higher status suburban community.
- Another view is that suburbs attracted investment to stimulate consumption and create fresh demand for industrial goods in housing, domestic appliances and motor cars. This was a means of switching investment into the 'secondary circuit' – the finance-capital market as part of a capitalist strategy for reproduction. In other words, suburbs grew as capital was diverted into new investment opportunities. Harvey (1977) argued that the promotion of home ownership, principally through suburbanization, was a method of achieving social stability by giving a sense of property to a much wider range of people. Suburbs avoided a situation of 'under consumption' whereby industrial surpluses could not be absorbed.
- There were also socio-economic-political processes which created suburban municipalities that were independent from the central city. The idea of an 'outer city' with high levels of autonomy and different lifestyles. Exclusionary political processes, such as zoning policies, were used to maintain the suburban landscape and the character of its community.
- Even during their period of building, there was evidence for the social construction of suburbs. Names such as Crestwood Heights and The Glades gave new suburbs a particular kind of image as they were marketed and sold as commodities. The persistence of old suburbs such as Shaughnessy Heights, Vancouver was in large part

due to the concerted efforts of residents trying to preserve a symbolic place. Such suburban communities are sustained not merely by political and legal processes but also by the localistic and humanistic concerns in which a suburban sense of place is grounded.

In the post-industrial city, the suburb has a major role. There is a hierarchy of suburbs from inner rings to outer rings, reflecting stages of urban growth with status differences including the public sector/private sector divide. Beyond the physical limits of the city, suburbanization continues and the growing small town and villages of outer metropolitan rings and in 'rural' areas to which the term counter-urbanization applies may well, at least in part, be suburbanization writ large.

Whereas in the UK, North America and Australia the suburb played a major part in urban growth, it was less significant in west European societies. As White (1984) showed, this arises from different cultural contexts where access to urban facilities is rated more highly than access to rural settings. Because land prices are high at the centre, it is the poor who are commonly relegated to the urban peripheries. There are suburbs in European cities but they defy simple classification. Industrial suburbs cluster around local industries which act as nuclei for a mixture of residential developments; many working-class suburbs in Europe are high rise and large scale, such as the Bijlmermeer complex housing over 100,000 people in Amsterdam, and the many 'grand ensembles' of Paris each with up to 80,000. Middle-class suburbs in European cities are limited in scale of development for several reasons:

- Continued preference for city centre residence
- New city centre apartment schemes
- Inadequate financing arrangements
- Significant numbers of second homes which allow an escape to rural areas.

The notion of sharp, easily visible and meaningful segregation, drawn along class lines, may be too seductive. The post-modern message of differences over time and space, difficulties of generalization, and the inappropriateness of grand theory, may again be worth heeding.

The post-industrial city

The **post-industrial city** is a generic category to summarize the significant changes of the second half of the twentieth century. Like industrialization, 'post-industrialization' is a societal process that has impacts upon the city. Bell (1974) identified five primary characteristics of the post-industrial society:

- Changes in the economy which lead to a focus on services rather than manufacturing.
- Changes in social structure which give greater eminence to professional and technological classes.
- Changes from the practical to the theoretical as a source of ideas; and increased emphasis on research and development and its relation to policy.
- Change in the control of technology, greater concern for the impacts of technological change.
- A form of intellectual technology allied to advanced information systems.

Johnston (1982b) suggested five distinguishing features of late capitalism:

- **Concentration** or the process whereby a number of large and dominant companies emerged from the competitive market and many small firms either close or are subsumed in the process.
- **Centralization** which leads to strong central control of finance and policies within these large and often multi-site enterprises.
- **Service sector expansion** as manufacturing processes became automated and computerized, requiring fewer workers but more being required for personalized services in tertiary (buying and selling) and quaternary (control functions of finance) sectors.
- **High status material goods** assume much greater significance and fuel the demand for production in late capitalism.
- **Government** has to assume significant roles as the regulator of the system, balancing out wilder fluctuations and protecting the main institutions.

These trends had a considerable impact on the spatial organization of the city. The central city was no longer an appropriate location for manufacturing and industrial activities and as they declined, there was a movement towards green-field sites on the urban periphery. Other forms of economic activity, such as some forms of wholesaling and retailing as well as offices, were similarly affected. Again, the process was uneven. Harris (1993) noted that the decentralization of manufacturing in New York City was much slower than elsewhere as industries such as garments and printing retained their central locations. Yet in the period 1900 to 1940, there was a gathering pace of industrial decentralization and a loosening constraint on journey to work.

There is ample evidence for these trends in post-industrial societies. For Hartshorn (1992), the period 1920 to 1970 was one of manufacturing and industrial dominance in the economy of the USA. Its features were the Fordist industrial system of mass production processes, and the Taylorist principles of scientific management. The subsequent decline of manufacturing is well documented and, by the early 1980s, some 2,000 US firms disappeared each year. Greater automation led to considerable shedding of workers from manufacturing (though this was not the only factor); the shift was to employment in the service sector and to high-technology industries. In the UK, steel tube manufacturers lost 28 per cent of their workforce between 1976 and 1980, iron and steel 26 per cent and motor manufacture 16 per cent. This 'deindustrialization' affected most western countries. Although the shifts to other forms of employment occurred, the 'new' industries with automated, computerized and robotic processes required much less labour. Although the growth of services predates deindustrialization and economic restructuring, it has assumed major significance in the last third of the twentieth century. When Daniel Bell (1974) proposed the **post-industrial society**, a key indicator was the point at which the non-manual, white collar workforce exceeded 50 per cent. By the 1980s in the USA, the UK and Australia this workforce was around 60 per cent.

These changes had considerable implications for the form of the post-industrial city and there were several discernible trends.

- The larger urban centres acquired greater significance as they assume roles as **World Cities** interacting on a global scale. The idea of **globalization** effects emphasizing the links between producers and consumers and of major organizations operating at that scale revolves around the world cities. Financial markets in particular operate in this kind of way, status addresses are important, and face-to-face contacts in close social networks underpin urban decision-making. Late capitalism enhanced the dominance of the largest urban centres as they accrued multiplier effects and control, smaller urban places have been allocated relatively subservient roles.

- A second trend, **counter-urbanization**, describes a situation in which smaller towns and semi-rural areas beyond the traditional metropolitan rings begin to act as magnets for people and activities. Gordon (1988) identified two processes at work in Britain: an extension of the suburbanization process and a form of product system dispersal in which small towns became new centres of activity. The activities are often high-technology industries, freed from the constraints of location, and able to follow qualitative preferences in their choice of location.

- Some of the changes in economic activity, following the decline of traditional manufacturing, had significant regional effects. In the USA, the Sun Belt industries of south and west with high-technology industries, research and development and resource-led activities led to redistributions. In Britain, Hall (1985) identified three Outer Metropolitan Area corridors outside London, based around the motorway system, where there had been substantial increases in employment.

- A final comment on the form of the post-industrial city relates to the information base upon which it rests and the potential of intercommunicative systems. With the revolution in information transfers, the friction of space becomes less imperative and the ties which many activities have to specific locations are likely to diminish. The post-industrial city belongs now to the information age yet the momentum for urban growth, albeit in a more dispersed form, remains undiminished. Major institutions, including multinational headquarters, financial centres and government, remain in the larger cities. Access, face-to-face contact, social networks and interactions – the qualitative dimension to business – remain of central importance and sustain the city. A feature, none the less, of post-industrial society, is that 'urban' is more difficult to encapsulate in 'place'. Rural-urban differences are increasingly blurred as both urban people and urban activities continue to disperse to non-urban environments

The progression from the pre-industrial to the post-industrial city spans many centuries. It has had variable effects on different parts of the world and is one basis for global differences. As always the urban form reflects the changing nature of its society but the massive redistribution, principally outwards of people and activities, can be related to specifics which include transport technology, communications, preferences, space and environmental quality. Increasingly, the post-industrial city is a place of **consumption** rather than of production with the commodification of heritage, conservation, tourism, entertainment and the sale of 'goods' as general trends

Urbanization as a process

Fundamental to the emergence of the urban system was the nature of the **process of urbanization**. This process has varied and is closely reflected in the types of cities that have developed. Cheshire (1995: 1,047) expressed this relationship well: 'Before the historic

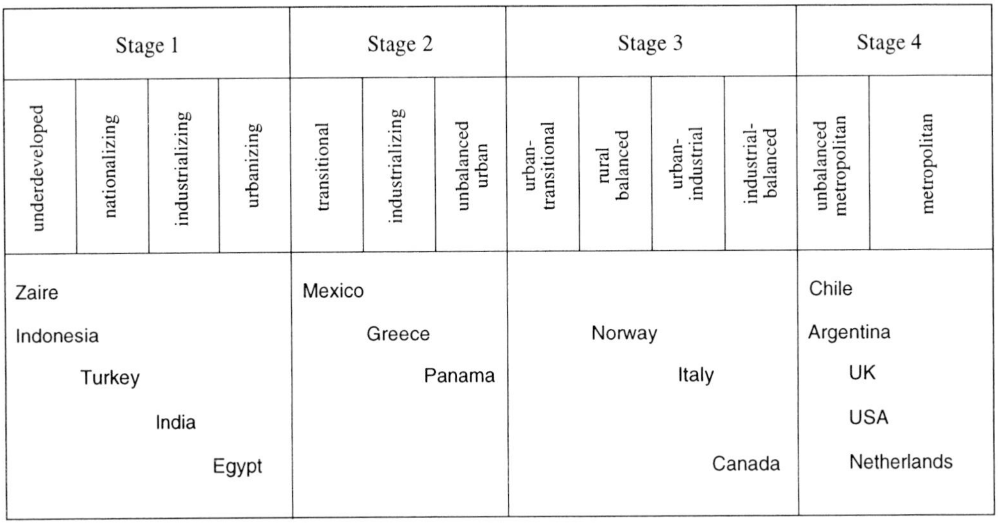

Stage 1				Stage 2			Stage 3				Stage 4	
underdeveloped	nationalizing	industrializing	urbanizing	transitional	industrializing	unbalanced urban	urban-transitional	rural balanced	urban-industrial	industrial-balanced	unbalanced metropolitan	metropolitan
Zaire				Mexico							Chile	
Indonesia					Greece			Norway			Argentina	
		Turkey				Panama			Italy			UK
			India									USA
				Egypt						Canada		Netherlands

Continuum monitored by measures of urban status, industrial status, prevalence of middle class and prevalence of nationalism

Figure 2.7 A staged model of modern urbanization

phase of industrialization, the functions of cities were administrative, commercial, cultural and, of course, defensive. The process of industrialization transformed cities into centres of goods production and distribution.'

Industrialization was the clearest driving force of large-scale urbanization and there was a close correlation between industrial growth and the rise of cities. As the concentration of employment opportunities in cities emerged, large numbers of migrants were drawn into urban areas from rural districts, new forms of local government and organization appeared, and rapid urbanization typified the 'advanced' economies of western Europe and North America.

Reissman (1964) recognized urban status, industrial status, the prevalence of a middle class, and the prevalence of nationalism, as key components of urbanization. Urban status was measured by the percentage of people living in cities over 100,000; industrial status by percentage of net domestic product contributed by manufacturing; prevalence of middle classes by *per capita* income; and prevalence of nationalism by rate of literacy. Whereas there is a considerable gap between these concepts and their empirical measures, they add up to an index of economic development closely related to industrialization. Reissman's typology of stages gave some indication of the positions of individual countries along this scale of urbanization in the middle part of the twentieth century (Figure 2.7). Zaire with a small percentage of urban dwellers, little industrial development, low per capita income and low rates of literacy was placed in stage 1 of the model, whereas the UK, with opposite characteristics, was in stage 4.

Jakobson and Prakash (1971) used a three-sector theory of urban-economic development, in which the sectors are labelled as primary or agriculturally based, secondary or industrially based, and tertiary or services based, linking the process of urbanization with stages. The secondary, transition stage is divided into three parts labelled take-off, expansion and achievement. The 'tertiary curve' in their model (Figure 2.8) was the S-curve of

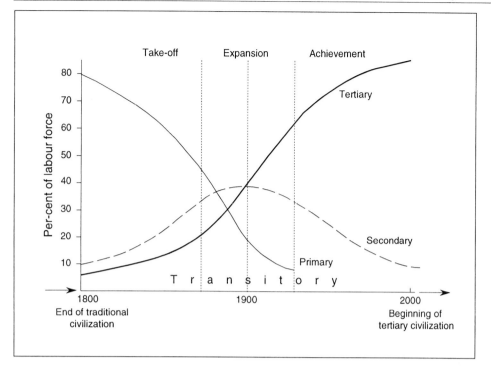

Figure 2.8 Urbanization and the progression from traditional to modern

urbanization, progressing from 10 to 80 per cent levels of urbanization in a society. Whereas the primary period is dominated by resource locations and the tertiary period by market factors, the transitory or secondary period had elements of both. During the take-off phase, urban growth occurred in discrete nodes whereas during the expansion phase metropolitan areas form and these become megalopolis during the achievement phase. The theory is closely tied to economic and technological development but identified attributes associated with pre-industrial, industrial and post-industrial cities.

During the key **transition** stage, industrialization, modernization and urbanization were the integral features. The rate of transformation was affected by four sets of factors: physiographic (natural resource base), ecological (area and population size), geopolitical (insularity and relation to world markets) and socio-cultural (ethnic homogeneity, norms and values). At this point, the framework begins to resemble that of Reissman and the problems of fitting empirical measures to concepts appear.

The strongest and most consistent line of argument in explanation of the urbanization process in modern western experience proposes close links with industrialization and economic development. Starting with Weber's (1899) analysis of urban growth in the nineteenth century, a large number of studies have demonstrated the close correlation between industrialization in general and between specific indices, such as per capita income or percentage of the labour force in manufacturing employment, and the level of urbanization. 'Increased division of labour and increased specialization, the necessary concomitant of increased productivity, inevitably became forces promoting population concentration in cities. Associated with this population shift . . . was a shift in the occupational structure of economies' (Berry 1973a: 4).

As western societies industrialized and became technologically more advanced, so they became urbanized and emerged as nations of large cities.

Other views of urbanization focused on the contrasts that emerged between city and countryside. The **theories of contrast** are linked with social scientists such as Wirth (1938). Essentially, these are sociological or anthropological perspectives that emphasize life style and rural-urban differences. Theories of contrast and Wirth's concept of urbanism were provocative but probably had little relevance for the twentieth-century city: 'He offered a theory upon which to build future research. In actuality, his theory was a peroration on a city that had passed' (Berry 1973a: 36).

Another view of urbanization recognized its links with **demographic processes** and the increasing concentrations of population in space (Lampard 1965).

The general theories of urbanization are well known but others seek to introduce a more explicit spatial dimension to the urbanization process. Friedmann and Wulff (1976: 11) specified a **core** and **periphery** model which was designed to accommodate the interactive relationship of city and region: 'Urbanization is thus perceived as a complex of spatial processes and their associated patterns, although the spatial relations of power (decision-making and control) are identified as the critical process to which all others are ultimately related'.

Decision-making and control, or the distribution of effective political and economic power, was viewed as a major determinant of the evolution and spatial organization of an urban system and was the first of four major spatial processes which Friedmann and Wulff (1976) considered to be part of the urbanization process. A second spatial process was identified as capital flows, or ways in which capital is mobilized and invested; a third was spatial diffusion, the process by which innovations, entrepreneurship and modernization reached both down the urban hierarchy and outwards from core to periphery. For their fourth major spatial process, Friedmann and Wulff specified the migration process. Their emphasis on migration and on the **spatial** quality of urbanization depicted a process of changes in the distribution of population which, in turn, reflected a changing society. People are arranged in space both as a consequence of initial urbanization and as a necessity for its continuance; as the industrial city grew it had need for a large pool of available labour irrespective of the socio-political system from which it emerged.

Global experience of the urbanization process over the last third of the twentieth century has led to reassessments of its nature and directions; these reassessments have focused on trends observed in Europe and the USA. In these societies there has been a considerable slowing-down of the rate of urbanization and a redistribution of people down the settlement hierarchy. Champion (1995) cited World Bank figures to show that the proportions of population living in cities of a million or more inhabitants fell between 1965 and 1990. There are fluctuations in the urbanization process which may resemble a **cyclical** set of stages or even a **life-cycle** form. An **urbanization** phase, characterized by rapid growth in the core of an urban region, is followed by a **suburbanization** phase of slower growth in the core but rapid growth at the urban peripheries. **Disurbanization** is a stage at which there is decline in the core and some losses or slow growth in the suburban areas; **reurbanization** experiences some selective return to core areas. Cheshire (1995: 1,058) saw this last phase in more general terms for larger cities in the European Union: 'The regular march of decentralization appears to have faltered and, in northern Europe, it has halted, even reversed.'

There was a similar situation in the USA, as Frey (1994: 161) suggested: 'The new urban revival in the United States represents a return to urbanization after the counter-urbanization phenomenon of the 1970s'.

The idea of a cycle is based on careful empirical observation and needs to be explained. With reference to reurbanization, for example, Cheshire (1995) noted the attractions of larger cities able to offer opportunities and good living conditions to skilled professionals; the roles of **local** policy-makers in enhancing the urban environment; and the natural advantages to many **services** of central locations. Cheshire concentrated on one stage of the process, but any general explanation of urbanization in advanced societies has to accommodate a range of factors. Demographic and economic factors retain their central significance but have to be reconciled with others such as business cycles, housing market fluctuations, economic restructuring, globalization processes and locational preferences. Some of the outcomes of this volatile mixture of interrelated factors may be what Frey (1994) termed **period effects**, time-specific instances where several factors combine to introduce a short-term phase. Counter-urbanization may have this character and Champion (1995) also placed some industrial disinvestment, following turmoil in world oil markets, in that category. Proponents of a longer-term view support the idea that much longer cycles underlay urbanization. Berry (1991) used the notion of the 50–60 year 'long waves' of **Kondratieff cycles** to account for changing urban growth in the USA. The **fifth** of these cycles may now be in place (Hall 1985) oriented around advanced technologies and new industries, which, through their imperatives, may reorder the urban system. Hall linked his thesis of long-wave cycles with the idea of innovation concentration in specific geographical locations. This view has been contested and Massey (1988), for example, doubted the value of a deterministic interpretation of 'places which innovate'.

Yet many have argued that cities are not merely passive outcomes of the urbanization process; they can themselves be foci of change. Friedmann (1973) argued that cities are organizers of economic, cultural and political space; centres of innovation; environments of opportunity and seedbeds of democratic change: industrialization led inevitably to large cities which became autonomous 'power engines' in their own right; their dependency links with hinterland and growth of large cities from capital accumulation stimulated the growth of the nation. This view of the city as a **catalyst** of change is by no means universally accepted and it has acquired new significance with the **localities** debate and its interest in the roles of local agencies.

These observations can be put into perspective. First, cities are manifestations of wide-reaching forces of societal change rather than separate phenomena. Although there is force in the view that cities may act as catalysts of change, the driving forces are derived from the societies of which they are part. Second, there are variations within advanced societies and any comparison with non-western cities raises, in much sharper focus, the facts of differential urban experiences. Berry (1973a: xii) was a powerful advocate of the need to disavow any view that urbanization is a universal process: 'Not only that we are dealing with several fundamentally different processes that have arisen out of differences in culture or time, but also that these processes are producing different results in different world regions, transcending only superficial similarities'.

Third World cities: some general characteristics

Although this text has a focus on the western city, this chapter will consider cities in other parts of the world which are products of the global process of urbanization. It is still possible to classify cities as 'Third World', 'socialist' and 'colonial', but these are categories of convenience. First, no one category is independent of the others; the key processes of urbanization and globalization are shared. Second, the categories are broad and contain considerable internal diversity. The term 'Third World' is adopted, though modern usage favours 'North' and 'South'.

Urbanization as a global process

The industrial city was the product of the first major phase of modern urbanization which began in the late eighteenth century. The 'logistic curve' (Figure 3.1) demonstrates this process of change as western societies moved to a point at which around 80 per cent of their population could be classed as living in urban settlements. By 1990 the level of urbanization had reached 73.4 per cent in the whole of Europe and 78.9 per cent in the European Union (Champion 1995); in the USA in 1980, 74.8 per cent lived in metropolitan areas (Fox 1985). The UK led a process that involved significant social change with the underpinning forces of economic development and rural-to-urban migration. As western societies industrialized, so new cities emerged and rural areas began to export migrants and eventually to depopulate. This massive transfer of people was the major source of urban population growth. Western urbanization coincided with the expansionary phase of the demographic transition process but it was some time before natural population growth became the dominant contributory factor.

In Third World societies, the 'modern' process of urbanization is still unfolding. It has some of the characteristics experienced by western societies but is substantially modified by its own cultural contexts and by the fact that it is occurring in a radically different global and temporal framework. Figure 3.2 shows that many Third World countries remain relatively un-urbanized with great differences among those countries. Yet progress towards urbanization is constant and Gilbert (1994) saw virtually every country in the Third World following a path to an urban future. The urban population in low and middle-income countries rose from 557 million in 1965 to 1820 million in 1990, an increase of 226.8 per cent.

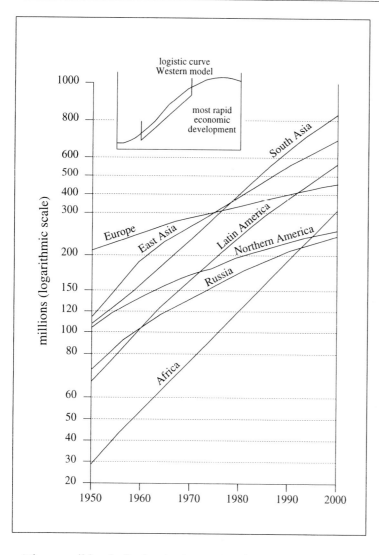

Figure 3.1 Logistic curve of urbanization and trends between 1950 and 2000

The overall level of urbanization in South-east Asia in 1981 (Ginsburg 1986) was 24 per cent, with a range from Singapore (100 per cent) and Brunei (64 per cent) to 14 per cent in Thailand. An average for Sub-Saharan Africa was 23 per cent, with a range from 50 per cent in South Africa and 38 per cent in Zambia to less than 10 per cent in Malawi and Mozambique. By contrast, Latin America was generally urbanized with an average of 62 per cent. Argentina, Chile and Venezuela (all over 80 per cent) were fully urbanized, Bolivia (33 per cent) and Guatemala (39 per cent) were the only countries less than 40 per cent urbanized. Although African countries lag behind in levels of urbanization, they are now experiencing some of the highest rates of urban growth.

Whereas all countries are moving towards increased levels of urbanization, western experience may well not be replicated. A highly urbanized future world is one credible scenario, but many Third World countries will never approach levels of urbanization as high as 70 or 80 per cent and may remain predominantly rural societies. Whatever the longer term outcomes, it is clear that major changes, expressed more dramatically in absolute urban

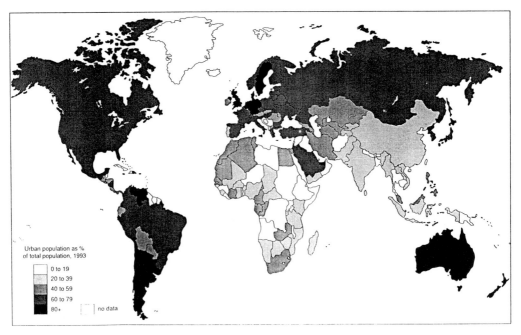

Figure 3.2 World urbanization by state, 1993

growth rather than percentage change are affecting Third World countries in modern times (Table 3.1A) and projections suggest that this will continue. The 'great cities' of the Third World are likely to overshadow those of the western world in their dimensions and absolute population size. Singh and Singh (1986) showed that in India the numbers of urban places have increased only modestly between 1951 and 1981 (from 2,867 to 3,301) and the country remains less than 25 per cent urbanized but, in that time, the number of urban dwellers has grown by over 150 per cent from 62.1 million to 157.4 million.

Table 3.1 Selected indicators for Third World cities

A Absolute population change in selected Third World cities

City	1960 City	1960 Urbanized area	1977 City	1990 Urbanized area (000s)	2000* (000s)
Bombay	4,941,000	-	5,970,575	12,272	18,121
Buenos Aires	2,966,816	7,000,000	2,982,000	10,623	11,378
Cairo	2,852,000	2,933,000	5,084,463	8,633	10,731
Calcutta	3,040,000	5,919,000	3,148,746	10,741	12,660
Karachi	1,912,598	2,060,000	3,498,634	7,965	12,079
Mexico City	2,832,133	4,666,000	8,988,230	15,085	16,354
Beijing	4,010,000	-	7,570,000	10,872	14,206
Shanghai	6,900,000	-	10,820,000	13,452	17,213
São Paulo	3,164,804	-	7,198,608	14,847	17,803

Sources: UN Democratic Yearbooks;
* Habitat (1996) An Urbanizing World, Oxford University Press.

B Migrants as a percentage of population growth

City	Period	Inc. (000)s	Migrants as % of total	One-room housing units (1990)
Bombay	1951–61	1,207	52	70
Caracas	1960–66	501	50	22
Djakarta	1961–68	1,528	59	-
Istanbul	1960–65	428	65	3
Lagos	1952–62	393	75	-
São Paulo	1960–67	2,543	68	-

Source: Extracted from Berry (1973).
Note: Evidence suggests that since the 1970s, higher proportions of total population growth in cities are accounted for by natural increase.

C Squatter settlement in some Third World cities

City	Total population	Squatter	% 1990
São Paulo (1980)	c 8,000,000	c 3,000,000	-
Hong Kong (1979)	5,010,000	500,000	3
Delhi (1983)	5,000,000	c 1,500,000	17
Rio de Janeiro (1979)	c 5,100,000	1,200,000	16
Manila (1973)	4,510,000	1,356,000	6
Mexico City (1977)	8,988,230	c 4,000,000	-
Lusaka (1981)	540,000	250,000	-
Madras (1985)	3,700,000	1,100,000	-
Dar es Salaam (1995)	1,734,000	-	51
Kingston, Jamaica (1995)	c 1,000,000	-	33
Karachi (1995)	9,863,000	-	44

Modernization theory

Many attempts have been made to understand the nature of the urbanization process in Third World societies. **Modernization theory** argues that the change from traditional agricultural to modern 'industrializing' societies occurs through the spread of western technology, capital, institutions and sets of values. Modernization focuses upon urban centres which diffuse its impacts to surrounding rural areas. Observers look for something resembling the western city as an indicator of the progress of urbanization. Writers in this vogue often identify a state of over-urbanization or pseudo-urbanization in Third World societies as urban growth occurs but is not being matched by sufficient economic development, industrialization and technological change to make it viable. The cities are structurally weak with inadequate economic bases and are 'formal' rather than 'functional' cities, parasitic to the rural societies within which they are placed. Whereas the evidence for high unemployment and low economic growth of indices supports this contention, there is no general acceptance of the over-urbanization thesis. Bose (1971) argued that Third World countries in the later twentieth century were comparable to western societies at similar stages of development. For him, urbanization was an essential element in the process of economic growth and social change in South and South-east Asia, a change involving the transformation of traditional, rural, agricultural into modern, urban, industrial economies. The universality and indeed desirability of this scenario is contested and Gwynne (1996a) argued that the connection between industrialization and urbanization has been less close in Latin American countries than in nineteenth-century Europe or twentieth-century East Asia. Latin American industrialization relates to cyclical patterns in the world economy and has been typified by inward-looking industries serving internal markets and relying on foreign technology: the outcome has been highly concentrated urbanization and the dominance of **primary cities**. Gwynne stated that demographic change, including urban fertility and rural-urban migration far outweighs any manufacturing growth in accounting for urbanization and Stren (1992) noted similar evidence for Africa where the mass of low-income migrants resolve their employment problems informally.

Demographic change

Demographic change is an integral component of urbanization in the Third World and again there are important points of difference with western experience. First, it can be said that as urbanization occurs, many of these countries are experiencing unprecedented rates of general population expansion. Death rates have fallen, birth rates have remained high and, with a very few exceptions, have declined only slowly giving very fast rises in population. This 'explosion' has affected all kinds of areas, both urban and rural, and the continuing increase of rural populations has masked the relative impact of urban growth. Second, there are no sharp contrasts between natural rates of increase in urban and rural areas. In the UK case, for example, urban populations, because of demographic imbalance and bad living conditions, were not self-propagating for part of the nineteenth century and only the inflow of migrants caused growth. In Third World countries, this situation does not exist and there is some evidence that cities, as places from which medical and other innovations are diffused, are healthier than rural areas. Third, the role of rural-to-urban migration is different. In all Third World countries there are migrations from rural areas to cities (Table 3.1B) and these have significant impacts upon those cities in demographic and social terms. Many societies have used controls to limit the impact of migrations and where these are relaxed major changes occur. China's economic growth in the late twentieth century was fuelled by millions of rural workers moving to take advantage of new job opportunities (World Bank 1995). There have been inequalities of wages aggravated by policies that favour cities and prompting movements of rural workers into urban areas. Attempts to reverse these policies favour only the richer farmers and land-owners. These migrant streams, however, are by no means the sole source of urban population growth, neither have they always led to large-scale rural depopulation. Urbanization in the Third World needs to be viewed in the whole demographic context within which it occurs: the scale and nature of rural-to-urban migration, for example, means that the distinction between city and countryside is not as clear as modernization theory assumes. There are return flows to rural areas, partly for cultural and social reasons, and partly as a reaction against the declining opportunities in urban areas.

Dependency theory

Dependency theory offers another approach. It implies, broadly, that less developed countries are 'used' by advanced countries over long periods of time from colonial to modern. Gilbert (1982: 16) argued that in Latin America, 'The social and economic structures that have emerged in the region represent the outcome of a historical process of interaction with Iberian, then British, and late North American expansion'.

Dependency theory related the economic development of Third World countries to the demands of the world economic system into which they were inexorably drawn. International capitalism dictated the role of less developed countries and in so doing influenced the urban response. As external considerations were dominant, indigenous urban populations were marginalized and their consumption needs had low priorities. Again, Gilbert offered a useful summary:

> Today the essential decisions about technology, employment, and economic growth are made in the metropolitan centres of Europe and the United States, and Third World urban functions and form have come to reflect their provincial status. The Third World city forms part of the world economy but its population does not share equal access to the world's resources.
>
> (Gilbert 1982: 25)

Preston (1996) stressed the need to account for both **dependence** and **independence**. Local economies are subordinate to, and dependent on, larger organizations whose decisions are taken elsewhere, but there are local effects and prerogatives. 'Dependency is a useful concept but has its limitations. It implies the superiority of North over South and of global economic might over local or regional power, which is not always true and demeans those in the South' (Preston 1996: 6).

Globalization and world systems

Dependency theory remains valid but has been stated as a subset of the wider concept of **globalization** of the world economy. The wider concept is not particular to the Third World but does have universal application there. Its principle is that outcomes in any locality are the products of decisions made at higher orders of the economic system. Economic growth in any Third World country needs to be analysed in terms of its relations with a wider world economy that is dominated by the USA, Japan and the European Union. As Preston (1996) argued, the functioning of the capitalist world economy affects Latin America at every scale from continent to household. A relevant historical model was provided by Wallerstein (1989) with his **world systems** model. Wallerstein proposed three aspects of his world systems perspective: 'the world system as the unit of analysis in the study of social behaviour, the significance of specific historical periods of human development, a view of the world capitalist economy'.

These ideas add up to the 'small world' view of economic (and indeed cultural) interdependence. What happens in one place affects others but the significant flows of influence are downwards from higher order to lower order places. It is the higher order places and organizations that are empowered to control events and their imperatives prevail. The debate on globalization questions the overriding significance of the macro forces, local effects may yet have formative inputs.

Colonial cities

Dependency theory lends itself to an understanding of the colonial period and the class of colonial cities which was implanted in the Third World as means of control and of exploitation. McGee (1971) argued for the significance of the colonial city in any system of urban classifications:

> Perhaps the greatest failure of Sjoberg's twofold division of cities is that he failed to take account of cities that have grown as links in the interaction of two civilizations. Such towns were flourishing even in the pre-industrial society.
>
> (McGee 1971: 50)

Horvath (1969) saw the colonial city as discrete with characteristics that distinguished it both from the industrial and the pre-industrial models. Others have recognized that technology, used to distinguish pre-industrial and industrial, was not apposite to the colonial city case. On the basis of a detailed study of Oaxaca, Mexico, in the seventeenth and eighteenth centuries and a belief that its emergence could best be understood within the framework of a colonial variety of commercial capitalism, Chance (1975) argued:

> It is his failure to acknowledge commercial capitalism as a socio-economic system prior to the industrial revolution of the nineteenth century which constitutes a major flaw in Sjoberg's argument and the chief reason why his model does not apply to the Latin American case.
>
> (Chance 1975: 225)

Horvath viewed the colonial city as one expression of a colonial period dominated by external powers. Some colonial cities were new towns, others were grafted on to pre-existing nuclei, most were major ports which acted as receiving and exporting centres for the colonial empires. These often became 'primate' cities in which colonial power and interest were concentrated. In its fullest expression, the colonial city was the microcosm of colonial society and served as a political, military economic, religious, social and intellectual entrepôt between colonizers and colonized. Not all European countries founded urban settlements in their colonies; whereas, for example, the founding and maintenance of towns was a deliberate part of Spanish colonial policy, this was not true of the Portuguese.

Colonial cities were set apart from the rural societies in which they were placed, and the gulf has tended to diminish only slowly over time. In Latin America, hundreds of new cities adopted planned designs imported from Spain and Portugal with precise layouts and areas designated for different groups. Bromley (1979), writing on small colonial towns in the Central Highlands of Ecuador, suggested that their colonial characteristics have persisted into the modern era, allowing them to remain ethnically and culturally distinct. Colonial cities had predominantly white populations, administrative functions and a thriving commercial tradition. Studies have suggested more plural features of population com-position within larger colonial cities; they could accommodate separate communities, each with different lifestyles. Horvath (1969) recognized a stratified system with three major components in Latin American colonial cities. Top of the hierarchy was the Spanish-speaking elite, followed by a mixed-blood group and supported by the indigenous population. K. Davis (1974) identified the *peninsulares* or Spanish colonists with little knowledge of industry; the *creoles,* who imitated the elite and were parasitic; and the native Indians and negro slaves who formed the labouring classes. Radcliffe (1996) spoke of *gente blanca* (white or European); *mestizo* (mixed race); *negro* (black) and *indígena* (native Indian). Where demand for urban labour necessitated the transfer of Indians into towns, they were kept in segregated compounds. This kind of social stratification, with its subservient groups, reflected that nature of dependent capitalism.

Several generalizations emerge from this summary of the main features of colonial cities. As a type, they were distinctive as extensions of political power, cultural transference and commercial capitalism. They were parasitic and separate from the societies in which they were placed. This **dualism** signified the failure of western urbanization to integrate with Third World societies in historical periods and its continuity reflects inertia and contemporary divisions in society. Roberts (1978) viewed backwardness and uneven development in Third World countries as products of an expanding dependent capitalism. There is variation with smaller towns retaining distinctive forms and traditional roles, and larger colonial cities integrating into international urban systems and developing stronger relationships with their regional hinterlands.

Characteristics of Third World cities

Colonial cities provide a useful bridge with western civilization but by no means all Third World cities originated in this way. Urban places form a rich diversity, inherited from different traditions and cultures and mediated by contemporary forces for change. Friedmann and Wulff (1976) usefully classified the features of Third World cities under the headings of morphology, social ecology, social organization and economy.

Morphology

In their **morphology** and land-use patterns, Third World cities often reflect dualism with the two forms, colonial and traditional, coexisting in a weakly integrated way. The traditional, pre-colonial city had a mixture of land-uses and few clear functional areas. Open spaces occurred only around institutions such as the mosque or temple and many transactions were conducted in the streets. Walls and narrow streets made for congestion and difficulty of movement; older, prestigious residences faced interior courts, seeking a level of privacy denied by their densely built-up environs. The modern city, in contrast, has a more spacious layout and geometry and features reminiscent of advanced societies. In cities where an urban nucleus did not predate colonialism, as in Lagos, dualism is less evident, but elsewhere, such as in Delhi/New Delhi, it is a clear and dominant feature.

Social ecology

Social ecology in Third World cities does not contain the spatial segregation typical of western cities. Ethnicity, caste, religion, language and other cultural variables 'overlie' economic and demographic conditions, giving complex patterns of residential differentiation. Yet, once again, there is empirical variation. Gilbert (1996) noted that in all

Latin American cities there were clearly segregated areas of land-use, such as modern industrial zones, commercial and retail centres, high-income residential areas, office developments and large swathes of low-income housing. For the urban poor, choices were limited and the spaces they occupied were those, often flood-liable or polluted, which others did not want. With continuing flows of rural-to-urban migration and the accompanying struggle for an urban foothold, 'migrant status' is an important variable. Districts in the city into which rural values have been imported, persist and Mabogunje (1986) talked of the 'peasantization' of African cities as peasant values and productive practices were imported on a massive scale; the urban economy lacked the capacity to allow them to make the transition to urban dwellers.

There are signs for both convergence with, and divergence from, western experience. Whereas the elites aspire to western modes of urbanism and move in those directions, the differences inspired by socio-cultural values and inertia remain. Until recently in Latin America, the rich lived centrally, close to the *plaza major*, cathedral and public buildings in a pattern reminiscent of the pre-industrial city. Now improving transport has allowed a movement outwards towards suburban housing. The aspirations of the elite

> may simply come to nothing under the impact of accelerating migration and the growing inability of the urban economy to absorb the incoming workers in productive occupations. The Third World city under dependent capitalism is predominantly a poor city, and the poor are growing in both absolute and relative numbers. The resultant ecology of poverty may be a very different one from the essentially middle-class cities of North America and Western Europe.
>
> (Friedmann and Wulff 1976: 45)

Social organization

In their **social organization**, urbanites in the Third World can be located both in a horizontal social dimension of kinship and social networks and in a vertical class structure. The persistent strength of kinship alliances is evident in many cities and is particularly critical among recent rural migrants who have strong locality-bases resting on communal ties, shared services and mutual support. Whereas these 'havens' allow migrants to find a place in the city and are essential parts of a supportive, survival strategy, they inhibit assimilation into fuller forms of urban living.

> Throughout the Third World, the proto-proletariat is encapsulated in a kind of ghetto, blocked from participation in wider social realms, only marginally absorbed by the urban economy, exploited by the elites, ignored by the middle strata and viewed with deep suspicion, if not hostility, by the blue-collar workers.
>
> (Friedmann and Wulff 1976: 47)

Class structures are inflexible with enormous gulfs between elite and poor. Voluntary associations may sometimes link classes and cross social barriers but their impact is limited. Poverty increased in most parts of Africa and Latin America during the 1980s, though it declined in much of Asia. Most spectacular was the rise in urban poverty recorded in Africa, Asia and Latin America as real wages fell in value and costs of living rose. As Gilbert

(1993) argued, the debt crisis and recession had greater impact upon cities than upon rural areas.

In addition to kinship and class, there are other dimensions of social organization in Third World societies. The **internal colonialism** model is strongly related to race. It proposes that there are dominant and subordinate groups which are ethnically different and that the spatially segregated, subordinate ethnic group is subject to separate administration and laws. Generally, in Latin America, whites were more segregated from blacks than they were from mulatto or mixed races. Intermixing was common and large numbers of mulatto children led to a large, free, mixed population. Radcliffe (1996) has examined the significance of **gender differences** in Latin American societies and the progression from traditional images of *marianismo* or female submissiveness and *machismo* or male aggressive virility. Class differences interact with gender roles. Elite households maintained women at home but for the urban poor they were essential workers and women now form around 25 per cent of the total labour force. About one-fifth of households are female-headed and mostly single parent as traditional nuclear families become less universal. Female migrants are drawn to cities for domestic service and a class of *empleadas* has arisen. In most prosperous parts of South Asia, the phenomenon of the Filippina maid has led to large numbers of international migrants.

Changing family structures and the diminution of the strength of family networks bring new problems to Third World cities. Children are parts of the informal economy and have important roles in family-income generation. The street-children of Latin American cities have become a feature of the last part of the twentieth century. As children are abandoned to their fates, so are the old. The ability of states to care for elderly people varies and dependence on a vulnerable extended family tradition is high. In Brazil, workers over the age of 40 are considered too old for some kinds of work and loss of income can lead to social marginalization.

Economy

The **urban economies** of the Third World are still imprecisely understood. Economic models are either descriptive or 'structuralist' and offer only grand historical speculations about dependency, immiseration and revolutionary potential. It is in relation to the impact of industrialization and economic development that variations within the Third World become most striking. Parts of South-east Asia have moved dramatically into more advanced economies; in Singapore, manufacturing now forms 28 per cent of the gross domestic product compared with 12 per cent in 1960. It is the third largest oil-refining centre in the world with a gross national product growth which has outpaced that of Japan and is on par with that of oil-rich Middle Eastern countries. Singapore, Taiwan, South Korea and Hong Kong are the 'tiger' economies of East Asia and in that region as a whole, Gross Domestic Product (GDP) per worker more than tripled between 1965 and 1993. McGee (1986) argued that there has been a substantial growth in the fluidity and availability of capital in the market economies of Asia aided by the growth of financial institutions. If these are indicators of successful economic growth, there are those of failure. Mabogunje (1986) stated that urbanization in many African countries is more a measure of despair than of hope; rather than economic development, it is the symbol of the failure to achieve that goal. Recent pressures on a global scale have had significant impact on the urban economies of developing countries and Gilbert (1996) noted that recession and the debt crisis had badly affected cities in Latin America.

Most societies have some industrialization and a formal sector of the economy which varies in size and form from city to city. Such sectors are diverse and have achieved some success in stimulating economic growth. Whereas reliable statistics are scarce, unemployment remains very high and only bureaucracy appears to proliferate. The western experience of a link between urbanization and industrialization has not been replicated and the informal sector occupies 60 to 80 per cent of urban populations. McGee (1971) suggested that the cities of south Asia could be divided into two economic sectors. A modern sector which is capital-intensive and a bazaar sector which is labour intensive: 'The persistence of this dualistic structure, basically a symptom of economic under-development, is the most important variable affecting the function of contemporary Asian cities'. (McGee 1971: 165)

A central feature of the traditional bazaar economy is its capacity, drawn from both its intensive use of labour and its self-inflationary qualities, to absorb labour. As more participants enter the bazaar economy, additional activities and transactions are generated. Kinship allegiances underpin a system that has strong links with the peasant economy. Roberts (1978) identified, in Latin America, a large-scale sector on which modern economic growth was concentrated and a small-scale sector operating on low wages and low profits, providing cheap services, and absorbing workers into a large reserve of unskilled and casual labour. Unlike the bazaar economy, however, the small-scale sector did not cater for a special segment of the population and had no neighbourhood base. Gilbert (1996) argued that in Latin America the informal sector did not consist wholly of petty services but also contained small artisans, repair services and crafts sometimes complementing the formal sector. This interrelatedness of the two sectors has been a consistent finding and the poor in the informal sector are part of the overall urban economy. As Latin American countries are integrated into world markets and develop patterns of consumption similar to those of advanced capitalist societies, the state has enabled the persistence of the small-scale sector at the expense of investment in social infrastructure. In Africa, Mabogunje (1986) saw the informal sector as the continuation of a 'preferred peasant reactive strategy' to the development of cities in which they have no part. The informal sector grows by 'involution' whereby tasks and returns are continually subdivided to absorb more people. Migrants come to Nigerian cities to buy and sell in the bazaar tradition with no illusions of job opportunities in the formal sector.

Housing and squatter settlements

As in most western societies, the rich exercise considerable choice in terms of housing and have traditional locations near prestigious institutions in the central city. While these locations often persist, there is evidence that the elite has abandoned the older core areas for more peripheral locations. These trends vary regionally but are marked in large urban areas. There are also significant cross-cultural variations in the type of new prestige housing; while preference for low-rise and space remains, much new construction is typically of high-rise, luxury apartments. Below the elite, Johnston (1972) isolated two middle-class groups in Latin America which he labelled as 'upper-class mimickers' and 'satisfied suburbanites'.

Whereas the former are upwardly mobile and seek housing, which has filtered downwards, near to upper-class areas, the latter are less status-conscious and their priority in housing is the security of tenure they normally find on the urban periphery.

The poor live in situations of extreme hardship. Abrams (1964) suggested that in terms of housing there were three classes of poor urbanites. First, the homeless or street sleepers often numbered hundreds of thousands and included the recent migrants, refugees, disabled or elderly people and abandoned children, all living in abject poverty. Second, the slum or tenement dwellers, especially in south Asia, occupy densely built-up areas of the old cities. Their problems are of overcrowding in multi-occupied buildings with severe shortages of basic facilities; 'home' could be a small, windowless cubicle, shared by between six and ten people, in the centre of a tenement block. Third, the squatters, or occupants of the shanty towns, are, by definition, illegal occupants of urban space though many, through length of tenure, have achieved a kind of *de facto* legality. Turner (1967) first advanced the idea that squatter settlements should be viewed as acceptable facets of urban growth and policy should aim to improve their quality. Generally, city governments oppose squatter settlements and this leads to conflict over space. Gilbert (1996) saw signs of change and argued that although some cities do not permit 'land invasions', these often occur with the covert help of politicians or administrators. Self-help housing can improve only where residents can afford better building materials and governments provide services. Some land, such as the *ejidos* on the edge of Mexico City, is sold illegally. Rakodi (1995) showed that there were a variety of forms of tenure other than owner-occupation and rental, involving different contractual arrangements between providers and occupants.

As Third World cities have grown in population, so the formal housing market has proved unable to cope and squatter settlements or spontaneous housing have provided the only form of shelter. There was an estimated deficiency of 5 million dwelling units in Mexico City in 1980 as rates of house construction failed to meet the demand for shelter. Spontaneous housing is found throughout the Third World and may form between 10 per cent and 30 per cent of total housing stock in individual cities. The African situation may be worse and Mabogunje (1986) described the environmental conditions of many African cities as the most visible expression of what he termed 'backwash urbanization' or the flood of rural peasants into urban areas. One half of Lusaka's population lived in squatter housing with vast sprawls of *bidonvilles* or urban slums.

As with other things, diversity is the key. Squatter areas were almost unknown in China before the 1990s and those most desperately in need of housing occupied overcrowded tenements in the inner city, often in courtyards and lacking basic facilities. Chinese rehousing centred on major, high-rise schemes of 12 to 15 storeys on the urban periphery, such as Beijing's Tuanjielu quarter which houses 30,000 people, 70 per cent of the families/households in two-roomed apartments. In Singapore, all slums and squatter districts have been demolished in an urban renewal programme, home-ownership is encouraged in state-built housing and 90 per cent of the larger apartments are owner-occupied. Hong Kong retains its boat dwellers but over 1 million squatters have been rehoused in multi-storey resettlement schemes and the 'walled city' in Kowloon, one of the last and worst tenement areas, was cleared in 1989–90.

The quality of shanty dwellings is normally rudimentary and initial squatter settlements used thatch, cardboard, wood, zinc sheets or any constructional material which happened to be locally available. In areas of general poverty or with a refugee problem, shanties persist in these forms but in others, where some foothold in employment or security of tenure is possible, space may be added, materials replaced and *in situ* improvement occurs. Severe absence of public services is often a problem. Unpaved roads, crude systems of sanitation, inadequate water supplies, educational and medical services, all are common features. Such deficiencies have often led, particularly in Latin America, to land invasions and the 'overnight shanties'. These are often clustered around high-status residential projects to which they are attracted by the possibilities of tapping supply lines for water or electricity.

Who occupies the shanties may seem an unnecessary question and for the most part it is the urban poor and especially recent migrants. Several Latin American studies, however, have made it clear that it is not only the poor who occupy shanties. They attract families from inner city tenements who have outgrown their cramped conditions, they suit specific groups – such as single women with children – and are not infrequently occupied by small businesspeople or professional people who are trying to accumulate capital. Squatter settlements often have real attractions – a strong sense of community, a spirit of self-help and protection, and often some organized cooperative endeavours. Settlements of these qualities have the capacity to improve and Gilbert (1996) showed that more affluent tenants would wait for better housing opportunities in this sector.

The potential for shanty improvement is widely recognized but less widely acted upon. There is still a paucity of consistent policies to tackle housing problems, and most official policies have the character of 'benign neglect' but can still be intrusive. In Manila, 3,000 shanties were destroyed in a three week period and Venezuela has had a selective policy of destruction of *ranchos* since the 1950s. Turner (1967) was critical of some of the state housing projects in comparison with self-help shanties. The latter offer much more space, scope for initiative and the possibility of making an investment – the great need is for better services and security of tenure. Turner argued for the provision of materials, the legalization, wherever possible, of squatter settlements, and more investment in services. Not all would agree. At one extreme are those who view squatter settlements as undesirable 'infestations', whereas at another are those who see shanty improvement as a diversionary exercise. As Roberts (1978) argued, squatter settlements show what can be achieved by people with few resources, who are neither a social problem nor a solution. If token improvement schemes are introduced, squatter settlements may be used by governments as a means of patronizing low-income population at little cost. Between these two extreme viewpoints are involved the politics of the Third World.

> The activism of the poor, however, is a factor in urban politics since their behaviour constitutes an unknown element which is alternatively feared and sought after depending on the strength and political complexion of the government of the day.
>
> (Roberts 1978: 157–8).

The socialist city

Many societies, including the former USSR, eastern Europe and China, developed state-planned or command economies during much of the twentieth century and this form of central control is reflected in their cities. They arose from an organization, based upon Marxist principles, in which the state had the power to determine the pace and form of urban development. Cities within such societies were not uniform, there was no monolithic response to socialist principles and variations occurred for historical, social and even political reasons. There were, however, distinctive features which gave an 'urban type' in socialist countries. Urbanization proceeded at differing rates. At the time of Russia's October Revolution of 1917, only 18 per cent of the population was urban despite the fact that the rural population of European Russia migrated in huge numbers to industrial towns in the later nineteenth century. In 1917, less than 20 per cent of the population of Albania, 44 per cent of Czechoslovakia and 67 per cent of East Germany were urban. China had about 15 per cent of its population living in towns or cities in 1917 and 29 per cent in 1993. By 1993, the urban population of Russia had increased to 75 per cent, Poland to 64 per cent, Czechoslovakia to 65 per cent and Albania to 37 per cent (World Bank 1995)

Socialist countries have also experienced the growth of large cities. In 1959 Russia had 3 cities with a population of 1 million or more, by 1976 it had14. Moscow's population grew from 6.0 million in 1959 to 7.5 million in 1975, Warsaw's from 804,000 to 1,431,000 and Budapest from 1,590,000 to 2,083,000.

In socialist societies many new towns of 1,100 inhabitants or more were constructed in the former USSR. Many cities, though, predated socialism and retained their historical imprint, often with medieval street plans and historic monuments; St Petersburg (formerly Leningrad) and Kraków, for example, are 'socialized' cities rather than socialist cities. St Petersburg was the largest Russian city in 1914 with a population of just over 2 million; it was an orderly city with broad thoroughfares, common building lines and materials, and its historic buildings remain within the framework of the modern city. Kraków in Poland offers the clearest example of the old, historic city juxtaposed with Nowa Huta, the new planned industrial town. The socialist city has also evolved over time, at first with piecemeal planning and economic imperatives given priority over housing. Thomas (1988) traced key features of the transformation of Moscow. In 1917, only about 5 per cent of working-class people lived in the low density core bounded by Garden City Boulevard. This core was made up of many public buildings, commercial premises and large mansions set in spacious grounds and rural peasants were absorbed into northern, eastern and southern outskirts. After 1917, the state expropriated the mansions and subdivided them into flats, and constructed wooden buildings in their grounds with high levels of overcrowding. In the 1930s public transport began to appear and five-storey buildings provided housing. By the 1960s, 82,000 to 120,000 apartments were being built each year to house 390,000 to 530,000 people and high-rise blocks of 12 to 22 storeys became the norm. Overcrowding had always been a problem and the new high-rise blocks provided families with no more than two or three rooms. Clapham (1995) suggested an east European housing model, one phase of which was a centralized system of housing construction using industrial assembly methods. Since the rapid political change in eastern Europe and the former USSR, major changes have occurred. These include restitution, or the return of homes to private owners; transfer of types of housing, e.g. cooperatives to condominiums; and the sale of state housing. Recent research makes the basic assumption that housing systems will converge with western models but this process will take some time and the legacy of the socialist system will remain (Clapham 1995).

Dwyer's (1986) study of Chengdu in China traced the modern urban growth of this city of 1.4 million people. A new physical plan removed the ancient city wall and replaced it by a ring road and developed manufacturing employment. Before 1949, there were many single-storey wood and plaster houses in a poor condition but much of this was demolished and replaced by six- or seven-storey blocks on the urban periphery. New housing had a space allocation of 6 or 7 square metres per person compared with the average of 2.5 square metres, but there was still overcrowding in inner areas where some courtyards had 15 rooms shared by 9 families.

Although China has not experienced political upheaval of the kind witnessed in east Europe, there is clear evidence of major change. China has entered a peak phase of industrial urbanization and a massive influx of rural migrants into cities has occurred in the early 1990s. A level of about 35 to 38 per cent urban is estimated for the year 2000 (Zhao and Zhang 1995) and the growth of large metropolitan regions in five areas: Shanghai/Yangsi, Shenyang/Dalian, Beijing/Tianjing/Tangshan, Guangzhou/PearlRiver/HongKong, and Chinqing/Chengdou. Although policies to restrain urban growth remain, the conditions under which they can be implemented are changing.

Socialist cities have been developed with strategic plans that are only about 20 per cent realized. For an individual city, hierarchical arrangements were common. In Moscow, the neighbourhoods (*micro-rayon*) had an ideal 10,000–12,000 population; the residential districts (*zhiloy-rayon* or groups of neighbourhoods) had 30,000–50,000; the groups of residential districts (*gorodskoy rayon*) had 100,000–300,000; and urban zones (*gorodiskaya zona*) 800,000–1,000,000. These cities had other common features:

- An adherence to the idea of optimum size and therefore to policies designed to control growth.
- Equitable opportunities for access to housing and services.
- Minimal journeys to work and by public transport. This is an ideal as homes are often too far from workplace and public transport may be far from efficient.
- A rational, planned spatial ordering of functions with industry or residence separated by green belts.
- A rational distribution of services with local provision of basic retail, health-care, education, recreation and welfare. Again this ideal is by no means achieved.
- A central area which may preserve some historic forms but is often dominated by heavy, grandiose 'Stalinesque' architecture such as Warsaw's Palace of Culture, with broad roads and central squares.
- Blocks of flats, often prefabricated, formed the standard housing response and estates housing up to 120,000 people have very little variety of style or quality.

All of this combines to give uniformity of time and place to the Socialist city that extended to street furniture, statues and slogans. As French and Hamilton (1979) stated:

Indeed, if one were transported into any residential area built since the Second World War in the Socialist countries, it would be easier at first glance to say when it was constructed rather than to determine in which country it was.

(French and Hamilton 1979: 15)

The contrast between the socialist city and the western city emanates from the elimination of land speculation, central control of rent and massive public sector intervention in housing provision and all aspects of infrastructure. Soviet cities were only weakly differentiated by function and the core of the city was densely occupied with no true central business district. Spatial segregation of social groups was limited but not entirely absent as there were the rudiments of a private, housing sector, and, in Bulgaria, 90 per cent of housing was owner-occupied by the late 1980s (Clapham 1995). Services were poor and employment was dispersed. Commuting from hinterlands was increasing and Thomas (1988) estimated by 1984 there were inward flows of 600,000 and outward flows of 140,000.

Socialist cities still form a distinctive group based upon the fundamental differences in the forms of society – Marxist/Leninist as opposed to capitalist – planned as opposed to free market, from which these cities have emerged. The socialist cities had variations as well as similarities. Convergence theory suggests that as socialist cities relax their rigid precepts and as western cities accept the need for some control, the gap will narrow. Events of 1989–90 in eastern Europe have produced far-reaching political change, the repercussions of which will affect cities and rural areas alike. However, as urban forms, socialist cities are likely to remain apart for some time as lack of private ownership of land and of inheritance, general austerity and control by central planning priorities, will ensure that change is a relatively slow process.

CHAPTER 4
Understanding the urban system

Chapters 2 and 3 considered the question of urban origins and traced the patterns and processes involved in the development of early cities. This perspective focused upon urban settlements as discrete elements in geographical and societal space. However, as individual cities became less localized in their impact and acquired functions of trade, commerce, industry and communications, urban interdependence increased and networks of towns forming an urban system became functional realities. Throughout the nineteenth century, the urban system of western societies became functionally and formally more complex; population in general, and urban population in particular, was increasing dramatically. Individual cities became functionally more integrated into the wider urban system and through increased physical extension created an integrated and larger economic and social system at the intraurban scale; both 'systems of cities' and the 'city as a system' became accurate descriptions of urban development.

This process was evolutionary and Bourne (1975: 12) proposed a schematic representation (Figure 4.1) which is still applicable to western industrial countries:

1. A national system dominated by metropolitan centres and characterized by a step-like 'size' hierarchy, with the number of centres in each level increasing with decreasing population size in a regular fashion.
2. Nested within the national system are regional subsystems of cities displaying a similar, but less clearly differentiated hierarchical arrangement, usually organized about a single metropolitan centre, and in which city sizes are smaller overall and drop off more quickly than in level 1 above with movement down the hierarchy.
3. Contained within these are local subsystems or daily urban systems representing the life space of urban residents which develop as the influence of each centre reaches out, absorbs and reorganizes the adjacent territory. In small countries levels 2 and 3 may be difficult to differentiate, whereas in larger countries both of these levels may show further subdivision.

Many aspects of the urban development process and of everyday urban life continue to occur within a national framework. Consequently, the notion of interrelated national, regional and local urban systems offers a broad introductory framework for the analysis of the physical and functional articulation of urban systems. This forms the focus of this chapter. However, since the early 1970s the system has also accumulated an important global dimension associated with the progressive globalization of the world economy. This

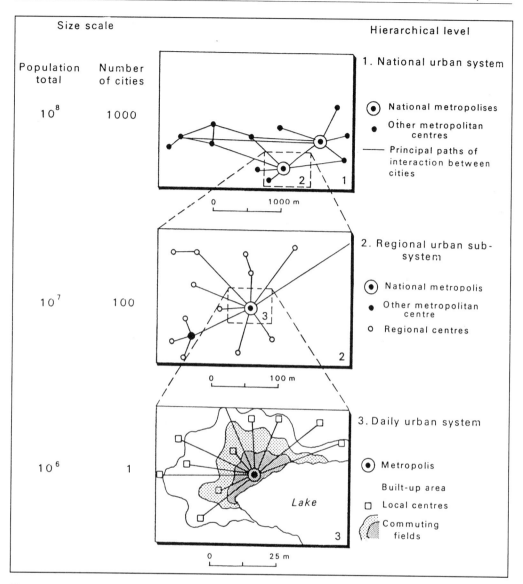

Figure 4.1 Urban system at urban, regional and national scales

has been closely related to complex global economic, social, political and technological changes affecting the 'modes of production' and 'social relations' associated with the concepts of the post-industrial society and post-Fordism. Consequently, a discussion of the global dimension is developed within the more explicitly economic analysis of Chapter 5.

Theories of the urban system

The law of the primate city

One of the earliest generalizations concerning the size and distribution of cities in a country was the 'law of the primate city' (Jefferson 1939). This was based upon the observation that a country's leading city is usually disproportionately larger than any other in the system; London was seven times the size of Liverpool, Copenhagen nine times larger than Aarhus, and Mexico City five times the size of Guadalajara. Jefferson argued that in the early stages of a country's urban development the city which emerges as larger than the rest develops an impetus for self-sustaining growth. It becomes an expression of national identity and for this reason tends to attract the political functions of a capital city. This results in the gravitation of all the 'superlatives' of a nation's life towards it which ensures self-sustaining growth. While such a distribution persists, regional imbalances in economic opportunity can never be entirely redressed.

Jefferson admitted that extreme primacy was not universal. Some states incorporated more than one national identity, often coinciding with regional concentrations of identifiable ethnic minority groups. This may result in one or more cities of comparable size rather than a single primate city. In Spain, for example, Madrid is the centre of Castilian nationalism, but Barcelona, central to the Catalan group, has comparable size and influence. On a smaller scale, Bilbao acts as the centre for the Basques. Similar patterns may also arise from the effects of size and distance. In the USA, for example, New York dominates the north-eastern seaboard, but there are several other regional clusters of settlement, dominated by urban centres such as Los Angeles and Chicago. Both the former USSR and China similarly demonstrate evidence for the emergence of more than one very large city as a result of both historical and modern forces.

Thus, the concept of the primate city has some limited significance if applied selectively to distinct regions defined in terms of cultural identity or geographical distinctiveness. With population growth and economic development, however, other cities emerge as alternative major growth points and erode the status of the primate city by creating a more complex city-size distribution. For this reason, primacy is most relevant to countries which have a relatively simple economic and spatial structure, a small area and population, low incomes, economic dependence upon agriculture and a colonial history. For the developed world, however, other more comprehensive concepts have been developed.

The rank-size rule

The rank-size rule is the best known alternative proposition. Zipf (1949) suggested that the city-size distribution in integrated systems of cities in economically advanced countries is expressed by the simple formula:

$$Pr = \frac{Pi}{r}$$

where Pr is the population of a city ranked r, Pi is the population of the largest city, and r is the rank of city Pr.

Thus, the second ranking city of a country has one-half of the population of the largest city, the third ranking city one-third of the largest, and so on down the scale. The graphical plot of the rank-size distribution approximates to the log-normal statistical distribution. When represented on a double logarithmic graph this becomes transformed into a straight

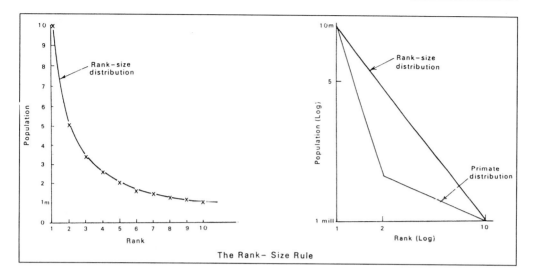

Figure 4.2 Rank-size rule

line (Figure 4.2). This is useful for comparative purposes since by plotting a country's city-size distribution on double logarithmic graph paper, the degree to which the distribution conforms to the rank-size rule is visually expressed by its deviation from a straight line. In addition, if the city-size distribution of a country with a 'primate' distribution is plotted, the resulting curve deviates considerably from the rank-size norm, indicating the domination of one very large city, the absence of cities of intermediate size and a relative profusion of small cities. This is represented by an initial steep incline away from the rank-size norm (Figure 4.2).

The association of primacy with the early stages of economic development and the rank-size with advanced, economically integrated countries, led to the hypothesis that a country's actual city-size distribution is a direct function of its level of economic development. Underdeveloped countries in the early stages of urbanization demonstrate a near primate distribution and highly urbanized, economically advanced countries a rank-size distribution.

This contention was refuted in Berry's (1961) analysis of the city-size distribution of 38 countries at varying levels of development. Rank-size distributions were found in advanced industrial countries, but were also evident in Third World countries with a long history of urban development such as India and China, and in large developing nations such as Brazil which have a proliferation of large resource-based cities. On the other hand, primacy is expected to be associated with a few simple strong forces. This may typify the urban system of newly developing countries where the primate city may be associated with an emerging capital; but such a condition can also be found in small countries such as Denmark where the forces of economic centralization create a tendency towards primacy; or in countries which have been developed under colonial influences and which have a relatively short urban history, such as Australia and New Zealand.

Thus, the progression from a primate to a rank-size distribution can be used as a framework within which descriptive generalizations relating to the urban system of a country may be made. However, the progression is not simply a reflection of levels of economic development and urbanization but is as much related to the length and degree of complexity of the urban development forces. This has considerable empirical validity as well as intuitive appeal. Consequently, the progression from primacy to the rank-size distribution remains a neat framework within which to view variations in the city-size distribution of countries, albeit of descriptive rather than of explanatory or predictive value.

Central place theory

Spatial analysis *per se* was of only secondary interest to studies of city-size distributions. Central place theory, however, introduced an explicitly spatial dimension into the study of settlement systems. Much of this work has been based upon the seminal study of Walter Christaller (1933, translated 1966) in southern Germany and focuses on the attempt to develop a deductive theory to explain the distribution and sizes of towns in terms of the services they performed for surrounding hinterlands, i.e. in terms of their centrality. Thus, the theory is most applicable to an understanding of urban systems which have developed principally as centres of tertiary activity, although it should be noted that the subsequent application of the theory was not restricted to such systems. Most towns, even if based initially upon specialized primary, secondary or quaternary functions, develop a service function for their resident population and a surrounding hinterland. Thus, their service status reflects a broader nodality. Consequently, the concepts and methodologies developed within the context of central place theory can be used to provide insights into the origins and nature of urban systems in general and their changes over time.

Christaller's central place theory

Christaller observed order in the spacing and sizes of service centres in southern Germany. Few large centres, spaced relatively far apart, provided specialized goods and services to large complementary regions (hinterlands). These were termed high-order central places. Conversely, more numerous smaller centres were found at a number of different levels. These were located close together, provided less specialized goods and services to geographically more localized populations, and were termed low-order central places. Christaller's theory sought to explain the principles which determined the nature of such a system.

The theory was based upon an idealized landscape. In this landscape each point had an equal chance of receiving a central place, and the relative accessibility of one point to any other was a direct function of distance, irrespective of direction – in other words there was a uniform transportation surface. This degree of abstraction is not, however, as comprehensive as that included in the concept of the isotropic plain which many subsequent commentaries have assumed to be associated with Christaller's theory. Isotropism assumes the existence of a homogeneous surface and an even distribution of population and consumer purchasing power. Christaller's scheme does not depend upon the latter elements of isotropism; spatial variations in these factors would merely result in minor variations in the deductively derived idealized settlement system. This consideration will be examined further following the discussion of the derivation of Christaller's theory.

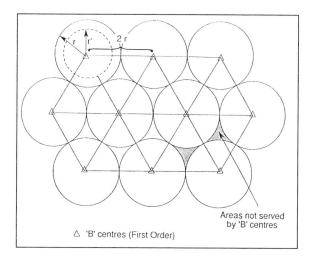

Areas not served by 'B' centres

△ 'B' centres (First Order)

Figure 4.3 B centres in central place theory and the derivation of regular triangular lattices

At the next stage of theory derivation, Christaller considered that every good or service provided from a central place has a range with an upper and a lower limit. The upper limit of the range is the maximum distance a consumer will travel to a centre to obtain the goods, beyond which he/she is more likely to travel to an alternative nearer centre or, if there is no nearer centre, will go without the good altogether. This notion can be measured in terms of the distance (r) over which the good with the strongest degree of attraction (highest-order good) can be provided from that centre. Consequently, the maximum area to be served from a centre will be a circular complementary region around the centre of radius (r), given the uniform transportation surface of the idealized landscape. The lower limit of the range (r′) is the minimum distance necessary to circumscribe a service area with sufficient population to generate enough consumer demand to make the offering of the good just economically viable from a centre.

The relationship between the upper and lower limit of the range of a good is significant to the next stage of the analysis. If the lower limit of the range (r′) is greater than the upper limit (r), then clearly such a good cannot be economically provided at a fixed location in the area. This provides the rationale for the emergence of periodic markets whereby traders will move from place to place, outside their immediate hinterlands to accumulate sufficient revenue to be economically viable. If the upper limit (r) of the good is equal to the lower limit (r′), then that good can just be provided profitably. In addition, if the upper limit of the range (r) is greater than the lower limit (r′), then the good can be provided and the trader can potentially earn excess profits by serving the population in the area between the two circles (Figure 4.3).

The goods and services required by the population of the idealized landscape will obviously comprise an array from high order to low order. High-order goods were considered to be those, such as large items of furniture or fashion clothing, which are relatively costly and tend to be required at infrequent intervals. Thus, consumers are usually willing to travel relatively long distance to high-order centres, which are likely to offer the greatest range of choice. Clearly, the upper and lower limits of the range of such goods are likely to be relatively distant. Conversely, low-order goods are those such as groceries which may be perishable or required in relatively large amounts at frequent intervals. Thus,

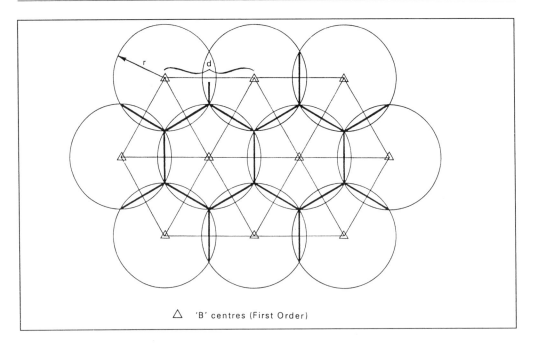

'B' centres (First Order)

Figure 4.4 Ideal circular hinterlands and their generalization into hexagons

consumers will tend to be unwilling to travel far to obtain them and a wide range of product choice will not normally be demanded. The ranges of such goods are consequently likely to be small. An array of goods and services with consumer characteristics intermediate to these two extremes can also be envisaged.

From these initial observations Christaller deduced a model of settlement distribution for the idealized landscape. However, since he was initially concerned to develop a theory to explain the characteristics of a settlement system which was based upon the evolution of rural-market service centres over a long period of time, he suggested two organizing constraints on his system which comprised the marketing principle. These were that first, there should be a minimum number of points of supply of all sizes so that trader profits could be maximized, and second, the whole population of the area should be supplied with each good and service. The relevance of these constraints will become clear in the ensuing discussion.

To satisfy the first constraint, the most important element in the generation of the settlement model is the upper limit of the range of a good supplied from a centre. This is necessary if the number of centres of any size is to be minimized. Accordingly, as a first step, Christaller assumed the existence of a series of settlements ranked 'B'. The upper limit of the range of the highest order good provided in such a centre is designated (r) and notionally the area can be covered with B-centres spaced at distances of 2r and arranged on a regular equilateral triangle lattice (Figure 4.3). However, such a system does not satisfy the second constraint, since there are limited areas between any three circular hinterlands which cannot be served with the highest-order good offered at the B-centres. Thus, a slightly modified structure of overlapping circles becomes necessary to conform to the marketing principle, although the fundamental spatial geometry of the system is largely maintained (Figure 4.4).

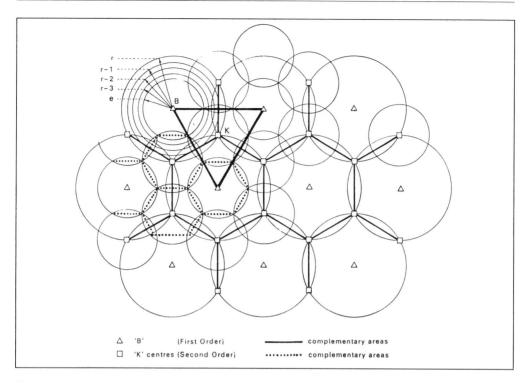

Figure 4.5 Derivation of the second lower order of centres

The B-centres are still arranged according to a regular equilateral triangular lattice spaced slightly more closely together at distance (d), which is a direct function of the upper range of the B-centres. In addition, the hinterlands of the B-centres can be generalized to give exclusive regular hexagonal *areas* rather than the overlapping circles, the rationale for which is that consumers will tend to use the nearest centre to them if each offers the same goods and services. Since, by definition, sufficient consumers can be attracted to each B-centre to make its highest-order function economically viable, it follows that all goods and services with less extensive lower limits to their ranges can also be provided at B-centres, since sufficient people visit them to make such functions economically viable.

Proceeding to the next stage, the outer limits of the ranges of successively lower-order functions can be diagrammatically represented as having radii of r-1, r-2, r-3, etc. (Figure 4.5). Any function supplied from a B-place which has an outer range of less than (r) cannot be supplied to all parts of its complementary area without some consumers undertaking excessively long journeys, or by obtaining the lower order functions while visiting the B-place for its highest order functions. This consideration provides the logical basis for the formation of a lower grade of central places, designated 'K' by Christaller, which will be located at some distance from the B-centres, in the centre of the peripheral parts of their hinterlands. To be most competitive with the B-grade centres, and at the same time central to the peripheral areas, the K-centres will be located in the centre of the equilateral triangles subtended by three B-grade centres. This coincides with the point at which the hexagons defining the hinterlands of the B-centres intersect. The highest order function which can be provided by the K-centres is geometrically determined by radius (e) which defines the outer

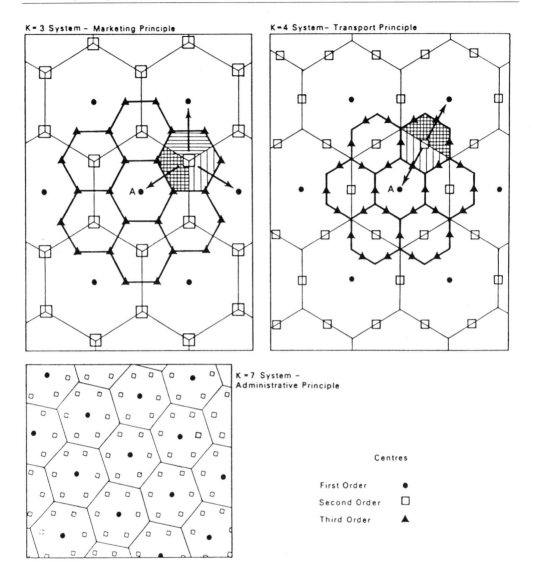

Figure 4.6 K = 3, K = 4 and K = 7: the marketing, transport and administrative principles

limit of its range. Consumers requiring functions which have outer limits to their ranges of greater than radius (e) but less than radius (r) will, therefore, have to obtain them when travelling to the B-centres for their highest-order functions.

For the same reasons as noted for B-centres, the K-centres can provide all the functions with less extensive lower limits to their ranges than the outer range of the highest-order function provided in the K-centres. In addition, in a similar manner to that described in the previous paragraphs, successively lower order centres can be generated. The resulting system of central places derived by Christaller according to the marketing principle is represented in hexagonal form in Figure 4.6.

The settlement system derived in this manner according to the marketing principle was termed the K = 3 framework. This expresses the number of hexagonal trade areas of one order which are contained within a hexagon of the next highest order (Figure 4.6). In this illustration the centrally located first-order centre marked 'A' is taken to transact the whole of the first-order trade for the second-order hexagonal trade area immediately adjacent to it, as well as a third of the first-order trade of the six second-order hexagons surrounding it. In addition, there will be three times as many centres at each successively lower order. Note also that according to the system the first-order centre 'A' will also transact the second-order trade for the second-order hexagonal area adjacent to it.

However, Christaller recognized the fact that systems of settlements did not all necessarily develop based upon the evolution of rural market centres over a long period of time. Two major variants were noted: the transportation principle and the administrative principle. These represent inductive modifications to the original theory. In the first case, he considered that many settlement systems do not develop in areas which have a uniform transportation surface. Historically, early established routeways are very persistent in their effect upon the development of settlement nodes, while the relatively rapid colonization of new territory in the nineteenth and twentieth centuries has been markedly influenced by the development of railways and roads. In these circumstances the development of B-grade centres was envisaged as occurring in much the same manner as that already described, although the centres will be orientated along lines of transportation rather than placed initially at random in a more idealized landscape. However, the development of a next lower order of centres is not expected to gravitate to a median position between three higher-order centres to maximize competitive impact as is expected to occur in the K = 3 system. Such a location would clearly be off the main transportation links between the higher-order centres and, for this reason, would not have the competitive advantages of accessibility associated with a routeway location. Thus, the K-grade centres would be expected to develop on the routeway, at a midpoint between any two B-centres, and successively lower-order centres would be expected to develop in a similar manner. This results in the development of the K = 4 framework illustrated in Figure 4.6. In this case the hexagonal trade area of any one order contains within it the equivalent of four trade areas of the next lower-order centre. Also, the relationship between the number of centres of successively lower orders tends to be represented by a factor of four.

The deviation of the framework associated with the administrative principle tends even more strongly towards empiricism. Again, in this instance the development of the B-centres is expected in the manner already described. However, the settlement pattern of the area is now assumed to have been developed primarily within the context of stronger administrative or political control. Thus, the complementary regions of the successively lower-order centres have to be completely contained within the boundaries of a higher-order centre in order to eradicate the administrative ambiguity which might be associated with the 'border' locations of centres of successively lower order in the K = 3 and K = 4 arrangements. The resulting system is termed the K = 7 framework since the complementary region of any one order of centres contains within it the equivalent of seven regions of the next lower order, although for geometrical reasons these cannot now be regular hexagonal arrangements. This underlines Christaller's attempt to move away from the initial deductive theory towards real-world settlement systems (Figure 4.6). In this case, the number of centres of successively lower orders tends towards the much higher factor of seven, while the much smaller hinterlands of successively lower orders suggests that the actual size of the settlements declines precipitously. The resulting arrangement of few high-order centres exerting an element of control over relatively numerous small low-order centres suggests a much stronger element of primacy than that associated with the alternative frameworks. Thus, it is anticipated that this system is most likely to be found in the very early stages of development or in areas which have been developed based upon a strong element of administrative or political control.

The conceptual value of central place theory

The central place hierarchy

The principal value of central place theory is considered to be the insights it provides into the origins of the structural and behavioural characteristics of systems of settlements and service centres. Systems of service centres are expected to approximate spatially and functionally to a hierarchical structure:

- There are a relatively small number of the highest-order centres serving the widest hinterlands with the highest order goods and services. They will also serve their own local hinterlands with all the lower-order functions.
- There are larger numbers of smaller centres of successively lower orders. These orders will be distinguished from each other by marked discontinuities in the population size and range of functions offered.
- Successively lower order centres will provide a smaller range of goods and services to increasingly localized trade areas. The population living in or near such centres will, conversely, depend upon the higher order centres for more specialized goods and services (a 'nesting' relationship).
- It is assumed that consumers will tend to use the nearest centre offering the goods and services they require (nearest centre assumption).
- The entry of suppliers of goods and services into the system occurs so that the number of establishments and centres is minimized (profit maximization assumption). This assumes that the system develops in conditions of perfect competition.

The early empirical tests of the theory in the 1950s and 1960s were unable to determine whether settlement systems conformed more closely to the stepped hierarchy or tended towards a continuum (Herbert and Thomas 1982). This is not too surprising since Christaller had anticipated a number of factors which would create deviations from a stepped hierarchical structure. Spatial variations in population density or purchasing power, and the tendency for consumers to maximize their total travel effort by combining trips for high and low-order goods, were both considered likely to transform an idealized stepped hierarchy into a continuum. Physiographic variations and deviations from a uniform transportation surface typical of real-world situations were similarly likely to result in deviations from the expected norm. Consequently, interest in the detailed theoretical aspects of central place theory has declined in recent years.

Indices of centrality

Nevertheless, an extensive body of literature generated by central place theory has provided many methodologies and concepts which have been used widely in the study of urban systems, irrespective of whether they clarify aspects of the original formulation. The search for hierarchical and spatial order in systems of cities has, for example, resulted in the derivation of a large number of indices of centrality of varying degrees of statistical sophistication, designed to describe the relative status of centres in a region. Christaller devised a measure of centrality based upon the relative concentration of the telephones in the centres of a region:

$$\text{Centrality} = Tz - \frac{Ez.Tg}{Eg}$$

where Tz is the number of telephones in a particular centre, Ez is the population of the centre, Tg is the number of telephones in the region, and Eg is the population of the region. The functional index derived by Davies (1967) is a similarly derived quantitative measure of centrality. This was based upon the location coefficient of a single establishment of each defined functional type in a specified area:

$$c = \frac{t}{T} \times 100$$

where c was the location coefficient of function t; t was one outlet of function t; and T was the total number of outlets of t in the whole system. The multiplication of the location coefficient of a particular function by the number of establishments of that function in a centre gave the centrality value of that function for the centre. The addition of the centrality values of each function used in the study then gave the functional index of the centre. A comparison of the functional indices of different centres provided a measure of their relative service status.

Less sophisticated, but none the less effective, key criteria measures were based upon the number and/or types of retail and services facilities provided in a centre. Hillier Parker Research (1996), for example, derived a hierarchy of shopping centres for Great Britain based on the number of the 324 principal specialist non-food multiple retailers they contained in 1995 (Table 4.1). In the absence of refined information relating to turnover, floor-space and numbers of employees of shopping centres in the UK since the discontinuation of the Census of Distribution after 1971, this classification provides a useful alternative indication of retail status of the 1,396 largest centres in Britain (Figure 4.7), while equivalent data for 1984, 1989 and 1991 allow for the analysis of changing hierarchical status over time. In fact, despite the difficulties involved in obtaining data sufficiently refined to be indicative of the urban status of a centre or settlement, measures of centrality are widely used in contemporary urban geography to indicate the commercial vitality of centres at national, regional or intra-urban scales of analysis. This is often considered an essential prerequisite for a more detailed analysis of some specific aspect of the urban system.

Table 4.1 Classification of shopping centres of Great Britain, 1995

Grade of centre	Multiple branch score	Number of centres
National e.g. London-West End	252	1
Metropolitan e.g. Manchester	131–17	46
Major Regional e.g. York	75–115	41
Regional e.g. Luton	50–74	61
Minor Regional e.g. Wimbledon	35–49	63
District e.g. Pontypridd	3–346	86

Source: Based on Hillier Parker Research 1996

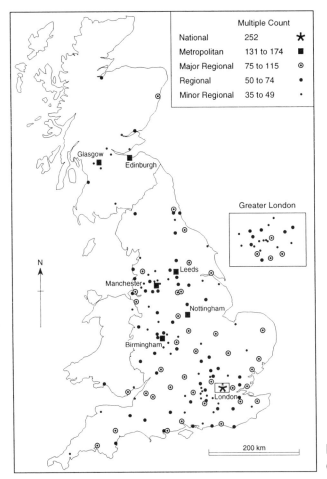

Figure 4.7 The hierarchy of shopping centres in mainland Britain, 1995

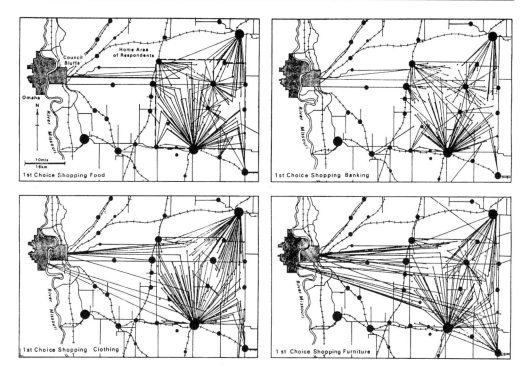

Figure 4.8 Consumer flows near Omaha for food, banking, clothing and furniture

Consumer behaviour

Analyses of the behavioural aspects of central place theory have similarly resulted in a fuller understanding of the determinants of consumer behaviour and the complex nature of the functional interrelationships between urban centres. Consumer behaviour in classical central place theory is considered to be determined by the nearest centre assumption, by which the time-cost budget of journeys for particular goods and services are minimized. An early consumer behavioural study by Berry *et al.* (1962) in south-western Iowa demonstrated the expected relatively localized hinterlands of centres for the provision of low-order functions such as food shopping and banking (Figure 4.8). By contrast, shopping for higher-order goods such as clothing and furniture was much more highly concentrated on the higher-order centres, as anticipated by central place theory. However, the hinterlands of the centres for the different functions overlapped to a significant degree since consumer behaviour patterns only roughly approximated the nearest centre assumption. Similar doubts as to the simplicity of the expected patterns of behaviour have been a recurring theme in investigations of consumer behaviour. In fact, consumer behaviour has been shown to be related to a complex, and as yet not entirely explained, trade-off between the attractions of increasing centre size and the disincentive associated with longer journeys. Nevertheless, a rich methodological heritage has been added to urban geographical analysis. Questionnaire survey techniques have been enhanced and spatial interaction theory has been developed to investigate the functional relationships between centres, all of which have had significant practical application for planning by both public agencies and commercial organizations (see Chapter 11).

Prediction

It is a fundamental tenet of central place theory that the service system which develops in an area tends to be in a state of adjustment (equilibrium) with the societal characteristics which existed during its initial development:

- Of central importance is the **density distribution** of the population. Clearly, the denser the distribution of the population, the greater the potential consumer expenditure contained within an area of unit distance from any location. Hence, the greater the potential number of levels in the hierarchy and the greater the degree of functional specialization of the highest-order centre.

- Of similar note is the effect of variations in the amount of **consumer expenditure** available, usually in association with variations in the degree of sophistication of consumer demand. In a peasant society, barely above subsistence level, expenditure will be low and demand will only exist for very basic requirements. Thus, a hierarchy of few levels with a low level of specialization of functions available in even the highest level is likely. By contrast, the opposite hierarchical characteristics are likely to typify a prosperous society with highly sophisticated consumer demands.

- The **transportation technology** available to the society will also be of considerable importance. Slow or high-cost transport facilities will increase the friction of distance and promote a large number of levels in the hierarchy because of the importance attached to the demand for local offerings of goods and services. Conversely, convenient rapid low-cost forms of transport reduce the importance of local low-order centres relative to the enhanced significance of relatively more distance, highly specialized centres.

Since all three factors vary considerably in societies over time and space, it can be anticipated that the detailed characteristics of central place systems will change to adjust to new circumstances. For this reason the theory is not simply a static description of hierarchical structures but can provide dynamic predictive insights into the nature of change in systems of settlements and service centres. Changes in the density of population, in relative levels of affluence, and in the personal mobility of the population are all capable of precipitating change in various levels of the central place hierarchy. The problem of prediction is, of course, that all three factors may be changing at the same time and may be interrelated. Nevertheless, the theory has predictive value, even if only at a conceptual level, and has been used widely in this manner over the years, particularly in the context of rural settlement systems.

Fundamental changes have, for example, occurred extensively throughout the Great Plains of the western USA and Canada for all three factors mentioned above. Increases in the mechanization of agriculture and the associated amalgamation of farms into fewer, larger units have resulted in a decline in the rural population. For the remaining farmers, however, there has been a concomitant increase in their income. This created a decline in demand for low-order convenience goods, but an increase in demand for the more specialized, expensive goods and services normally found in higher-order service centres. At the same time, the growth in car ownership resulted in a greater personal mobility which made the rural population less dependent upon their local low-order service centres for the provision of goods and services. The combined influences of these changes pointed in the same direction: towards the decline, or even demise, of the lower-order service centres and the increased status of the larger centres. Comparable circumstances have occurred in some of the peripheral regions of the UK such as the industrial valleys of South Wales and extensive parts of Northumberland and Durham. These areas have been subject to population decline associated with deindustrialization since the early 1970s, while the remaining population has become increasingly mobile in recent years. Consequently, most of the smaller service centres have declined dramatically in status and metropolitan concentration of service facilities of all types has been the norm, to a degree that a significant proportion of the less mobile residents of these areas can be characterized as disadvantaged consumers (Thomas and Bromley 1995).

The analysis of such trends can be used to formulate settlement planning strategies, incorporating the stimulation of growth nodes at locations designed to redress unacceptable declines in the availability of local services such as schools, health care, local government and public transport. The use of central place theory in this manner continues to be widely used in urban geography and regional planning.

Periodic markets

The incorporation of a time element and the notion of change over time in central place systems has also been an important element in the context of research into periodic markets. In many Third World countries where low levels of consumer demand and mobility generate insufficient expenditure to support fixed service centres, periodic markets continue to be a major component of the retailing and wholesaling system. Such markets, because of their periodicity and the fact that they occur only on specific days of the week in a given location, means that traders will migrate in well-defined ways from one market location to another. Analysis must therefore be undertaken in a temporal as well as a spatial setting. In terms of the settlement hierarchy within less developed countries, periodic markets are most significant in rural areas and small towns but are still found in large cities, though it is there that they are most subject to pressures of modernization.

In a typical market situation, a basic daily market will function each day of the week but will be augmented considerably on one or two days. Evidence suggests that as a city develops or 'modernizes', the differences between the peaks and lows of activity will gradually diminish as the transformation towards a permanently established market takes place. The length of weeks is a critical feature in the periodicity of markets and will vary with cultural norms from one society to another. While the most common Christian and Muslim week is seven days, in China it is ten or twelve days, in Java five, and in various parts of West Africa it ranges from two to eight days. The length of a week will determine the cycle as the market, or more accurately the market traders, move around. Figure 4.9A idealizes the distribution of market locations and the main days of activity in such a system. Traders circulate around several markets on a regular schedule to accumulate enough trade to remain profitable. In effect, there is a time-space system of rotation rather than fixed central place functions. Such systems are, however, not entirely determined by economic considerations since in the Third World trading is normally much more than a commercial activity; it has religious connotations and provides the opportunities for recreation, social and business contacts (Bromley 1980).

Other attempts to measure spatio-temporal integration in systems of periodic markets have used Smith's trader and consumer hypotheses (Figure 4.9B) (Bromley 1980). While the

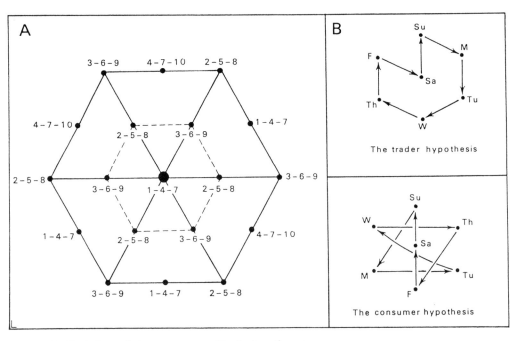

Figure 4.9 Periodic markets: consumer and trader hypotheses

trader hypothesis suggests that markets are synchronized to enable traders to follow routes which minimize their weekly travel costs, the consumer hypothesis suggests that the synchronization is designed to enable dispersed rural populations to have easy access to markets through the week. Neither of these has been shown to have general validity and the commodity hypothesis which suggests that market schedules will be synchronized so that adjacent market-places that supply different types of goods would meet on different days, and that these will normally be at different levels of the market-place hierarchy, may well provide a more appropriate concept (Skinner 1985).

Such theoretical concepts have been reviewed extensively elsewhere (Bromley 1980) and cannot be adequately discussed here. It is clear that periodic markets raise time-space relationships into central focus in the study of central place systems. It is also clear that such markets are still of considerable economic and social significance in many parts of the world despite the evidence that 'modernization' is diminishing their roles. In fact, Skinner (1985) indicates that with the reinstitution of competitive market trading in post-Maoist China since 1977 and an associated increase in demand and efficiency of transport, periodic markets have become daily events in the more populous central parts of most major rural regions. Thus, he suggests that the '*beginning of the end of traditional periodic marketing is at hand*' (Skinner 1985: 41), and the process is predicted to reach fruition in China by the year 2000.

Urban systems in the modern world

The various theories of the urban system offer insights into the relationship between the city size-distribution and the process of development, as well as into the dynamic spatial interrelationships between cities and their hinterlands. For many types of analyses, however, the city has also to be viewed in the context of the more 'urbanized region' of which it is part. This section is concerned with attempts to characterize and classify urbanized regions. Initially, these will be placed in an evolutionary context since their development is intimately related to the historical process of urbanization. The simplest evolutionary framework is that of the three stage 'industrial' model, each stage of which has a typical population size, spatial form and level of interconnectedness. While the universality of these stages remains questionable, in advanced societies they, at least, tend to reflect particular levels of technological development in transport and communication. The three-stage model used as a framework is briefly summarized and attention is focused primarily on its implications for city-hinterland relationships.

Stages of urban systems development

The pre-industrial stage: an urban nucleus

The great majority of pre-industrial cities were small. Most had populations of less than 50,000 and a rudimentary form of economic, social and political organization which was reasonably typical of the period prior to large-scale industrialization. Only in primate cities, usually capitals of more powerful states, did populations exceed 100,000. The transport technology associated with the development of these cities was equally rudimentary. Communications depended upon the pedestrian or on draught animals. Thus, the urban fabric tended to be arranged so that journeys within the city could be kept relatively short. Consequently, despite the continuing debate relating to the variety of reasons for the development of pre-industrial cities and their internal patterns of socio-spatial differentiation, most authorities are agreed upon their characteristically compact form (see Chapter 2). Similarly, because of the limitations of transport facilities, the spheres of influence of such cities were either restricted to the provision of urban services for a relatively localized population living within the area of a day's 'round trip', or, if the city also provided commercial, religious, social or political functions for a wider hinterland, then the frequency of visits by long-distance travellers and the associated functional interrelationships between the city and the outer limits of its hinterland tended to be relatively low. In either case, the city tended to be a distinct urban nucleus loosely related to a wider rural area and to other cities (Figure 4.10A).

The industrial stage: urbanized area

In the early stages of industrialization, town growth was usually associated with the localization of particular resources, and many towns increased considerably in size in relation to the natural advantages which they possessed. Canals and railways provided more efficient means of intercity transport, principally for the conveyance of industrial materials and finished products, and this increased the economic interlinkages between towns with complementary industrial structures and also between industrial towns and major market areas. However, since a town's prosperity tended to be related to the processing of raw materials, the early relationship between neighbours was as often competitive as it was complementary and economic linkages were frequently stronger between relatively distant markets than between near neighbours. In effect, despite the steady increase in economic

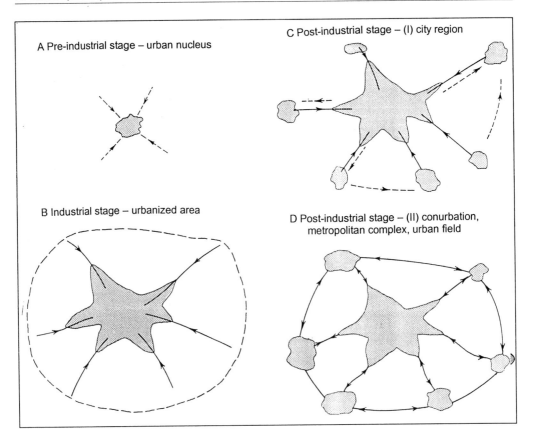

Figure 4.10 Types of urban regions with stylized functional inter-relationships

linkages over space, individual towns still tended to retain a distinct and separate functional identity to a significant degree. Nevertheless, towns became much larger than their pre-industrial counterparts, although they retained their relatively compact form. Intra-city mobility for the most part depended upon public transport. However, the relatively long hours and low wages of the industrial workers necessitated the avoidance of the time and cost associated with a significant journey to work and this gradually became linked with increasing residential differentiation on social class lines. Thus, low-status housing gravitated markedly to areas of industrial employment, while new industrial areas and higher status residential suburbs tended to develop along the public transport routes of the major arterial roads radiating outward from the city centres, creating a distinctly tentacular urban form. This process of development resulted in the 'urbanized area' of the industrial period, characterized by larger, but still relatively compact cities, and weak functional linkages beyond the city boundaries (Figure 4.10B).

The post-industrial stage

The post-industrial period is characterized by a considerable increase in the speed and efficiency of communications. Of particular note was the development in the late nineteenth century of the telephone which initiated the growth of improved forms of electronic communication. Similarly, the rapid growth in importance of motor vehicles from the early years of the twentieth century, and particularly in the period since 1945, has changed the emphasis of inter-urban transport from canal and rail to road, while inter-city personal mobility has shifted from public transport to the private car. These changes have reduced the constraint of distance on the development of economic and social linkages both between and within cities. Thus, spatial dispersal has become an increasingly important element of the urban system. The distinction between urban and rural and the functional separateness of individual cities has been reduced drastically as communicative efficiency has increased. Also, ease of communications has allowed amenity considerations to influence the locational characteristics of urban systems. A significant section of the more mobile labour force has gravitated to residential areas in more attractive areas at greater distances from their work. This has resulted in the suburbanization of vast tracts of land around most major cities. Similarly, industries which have high inputs of skill and labour relative to raw materials have been able to gravitate to formerly smaller settlements in the more attractive regions of a country. (See also counter-urbanization, Chapter 5.) In effect, more dispersed forms of the 'urbanized region' have become more dominant features of the urban system (Figure 4.10C and D).

A typology of 'urbanized regions'

A typology of urbanized regions can now be suggested. While the types discussed can be taken broadly to represent evolutionary stages, they are not necessarily mutually exclusive, and there is a transition from one stage to the next rather than sharp discontinuities. Furthermore, irrespective of the sophistication of communications technology, the more extensive types of urbanized region tend to be confined to the larger, more populous areas.

The city region

The term 'city region' has generally been applied to an area focusing on the major employment centre of a region along with the surrounding areas for which it acts as the primary high-order service centre. Its development represents the first stage in the functional integration of urbanized regions. H. J. Mackinder, in *Britain and the British Seas* (1902), was one of the first writers to use the term in this manner to convey the view that the city region of London already encompassed the greater part of south-eastern England. The essential functional relationship between city and region is considered to be one of dependence and for this reason functional relationships are nodal, focusing on the major city (Figure 4.10C). The delimitation of the city and its hinterland (complementary) region has subsequently been an important theme in urban geographical investigation. It was an important element of Christaller's (1933) work, which stimulated the development of a number of methods designed to define the spheres of influence of cities. Davies (1972), for example, used the concept to define the city region of Greater Swansea based upon an investigation of high-order shopping trips. It was suggested that the 33 per cent line provided a reasonable indication of the limits of the city region and encompassed an area just in excess of 500,000 population (Figure 4.11).

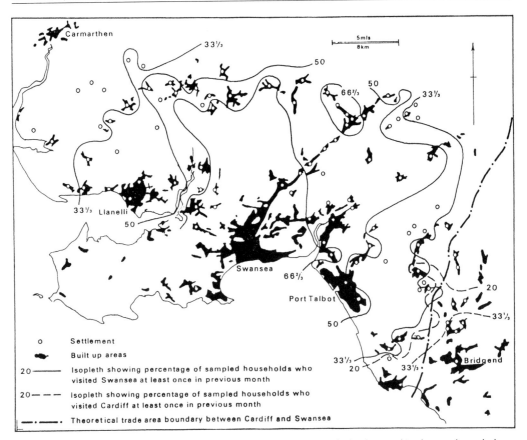

Figure 4.11 Greater Swansea as a city region: generalized consumer behaviour and trade area boundaries.

Evidence of this kind suggests that the city region remains an appropriate concept to describe uni-centred urban regions of less than 750,000 population found in the less populous parts of even the most highly urbanized countries. In fact, it is interesting to note that investigations of the structure of large urban concentrations frequently use variants of the city-region concept based upon employment nodes and associated commuter fields as the basic statistical building block for the purposes of comparative analysis. In the USA, for example, the Standard Metropolitan Statistical Area continues to be used widely in the reports of the US Bureau of the Census. Similarly, in Europe the extensive surveys of Cheshire and Hay (1989) relate their comparative investigations to nodal regions comprising an urban centre or core and contiguous areas comprising a bounded hinterland or ring. These were termed Functional Urban Regions (see Chapter 1).

Conurbation, metropolitan region or urban field

In the more populous, rapidly growing parts of a country, urban development rarely produces a single urban centre. Instead, from the fortuitous circumstances which promote growth, a number of important cities may develop in relatively close proximity. Such a situation developed in Britain during the industrialization of the nineteenth century. Largely based upon the location of coal reserves and associated port facilities, a multicentred form emerged which initiated the development of large urban agglomerations centred on Birmingham and the Black Country, Liverpool and Manchester, Clydeside, Tyneside and the West Riding of Yorkshire. The growth of these initially separate, but close-packed, centres resulted in the physical coalescence of the cities of these areas, although each major centre tended to retain a partially separate identity despite the strong functional linkages which often developed. The resulting urban form was described by Patrick Geddes in 1915 as a conurbation, a term which stressed the characteristic feature of physical agglomeration. Subsequently, with the improvement of communication and transport the functional influence of the conurbations has spread throughout a wider surrounding hinterland, well beyond the limits of their built-up areas, so that the term is now widely used in the British literature to describe not merely physical spread but also multinodal functional units. Usually the most advantageously located centre in the conurbation grows larger than its neighbours and exerts a degree of economic, social and cultural dominance over the whole unit. Birmingham, Manchester, Glasgow, Newcastle upon Tyne and Leeds have assumed this role in their respective British conurbations. However, the functional relationships within the conurbation have some special features and are essentially different from those of the city region. There is, for example, an element of dominance by the largest unit, but the other relatively large specialized cities have many functional linkages of their own; there is no exclusive focus on the major city.

Elsewhere, in areas of population growth which have developed in relation to the locational advantages of centrality to a national or regional service hinterland rather than the localization of natural resources, a similar type of urban form has tended to develop which might be termed a metropolitan region. Early growth is concentrated at the most advantageous location so that, initially, the urban form is similar to the city region. However, as the forces promoting growth gather momentum, increased land costs, congestion and the associated deterioration of the urban environment stimulate an element of decentralization of development to the surrounding region. Many of the small towns in such areas accumulate increased economic significance and develop into moderately sized cities which usually have close functional linkages with the major centre but again retain significant degrees of economic independence. Thus, while the central city tends to retain an element of dominance, the functional complexity is more typical of the conurbation than of the city region. In Britain, the increasing functional linkages of London with towns throughout the south-east of England, as far afield as Southend-on-Sea, Luton, Reading, Southampton, Portsmouth and Brighton, have stimulated a number of regional planning proposals. The strategy of the early 1960s considered the south-east of England, with a population of upwards of 17 million, a metropolitan region for practical planning purposes. Similar units with populations in excess of 10 million can be identified, focusing on New York, Los Angeles and Tokyo, as well as Mexico City, São Paulo, Rio de Janeiro and Shanghai in the developing world.

Metropolitan growth in the economic centre of the Netherlands has resulted in an interesting variant of the conurbation form, termed Randstad Holland (Shachar 1994). This has a population of approximately 5 million and differs significantly from the other metropolitan complexes discussed above in that it incorporates a much stronger element of functional polycentrism. It comprises the three major cities of Amsterdam, Rotterdam and The Hague with populations of between 500,000 and 1 million, Utrecht of approximately

250,000 and Haarlem and Leiden, both larger than 100,000 population. In addition, a number of smaller towns and suburban developments create a significant element of urban continuity between the larger cities. The conurbation has a pseudo-circular shape of approximately 176 km (110 miles) in length, open towards the south-east with a relatively undeveloped centre, hence the term 'Randstad' (ring city) or the alternative 'greenheart metropolis'.

This particular urban form is the result of a combination of physical geographical, historical and economic factors, all of which have tended to promote urban dispersal. Of particular note were the early land-drainage problems associated with the central delta region. Similarly, in the latter half of the nineteenth century the developmental pressures associated with the growth of governmental administrative functions encouraged decentralization from the traditional commercial and cultural centre of Amsterdam to The Hague, while the attraction of port installations to the increasingly economically significant mouth of the Rhine promoted the expansion of Rotterdam. The resulting tripartite urban form exhibits a stronger degree of functional decentralization and specialization than is typical of most other conurbations. In fact, it might be suggested that an approximation to the dispersed city concept exists in Randstad-Holland, albeit on a much larger scale than originally envisaged by Burton in 1963.

In the USA a unit similar to the conurbation, described as the urban field, has been characterized as the basic urban territorial unit of post-industrial society:

> The urban field may be described as a vast multi-centred region having relatively low density, whose form evolves from a finely articulated network of social and economic linkages. Its many centres are set in large areas of green space of which much is given over to agricultural and recreational use. The core city from which the urban field evolved is beginning to loose its traditional dominance: it is becoming merely one of many specialized centres in a region.
>
> (Friedmann 1978: 42)

Friedmann does not define urban fields with any precision, but they are regarded as core areas and hinterlands of at least 300,000 population, with an outer limit of two hours' driving time, which relates to an assumed limit of intermittent recreational trips. The urban fields defined in this manner range in population size from half a million to as many as 20 million and cover the third of the USA in which 90 per cent of the population lives (Figure 4.12). Urban fields are more spatially extensive than the European conurbations and metropolitan complexes since they are based upon higher levels of personal mobility. Thus, urban fields tend to include more extensive areas of low population density. Nevertheless, the concept of the urban field may well become increasingly relevant to an understanding of the functional realities of urbanized regions outside the USA as improvements in communications and transport of a similar kind occur elsewhere.

Megalopolis

As the outer limits of the urban fields of the USA coalesce the emergence of higher order, but more loosely articulated urbanized region have been suggested. Gottmann first introduced the term 'megalopolis' in 1961 to describe the major urbanized areas of the north-eastern

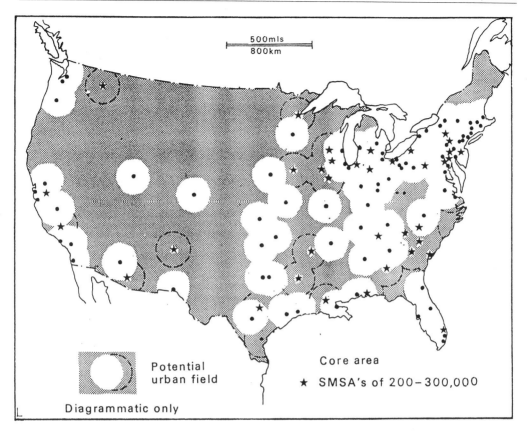

Figure 4.12 The urban field of the USA

seaboard of the USA extending from southern New Hampshire, 800 km south to northern Virginia; and from the Atlantic an average 240 km inland to the foothills of the Appalachians. The population of this area was 38 million, oriented around the major urban centres of Boston, New York, Philadelphia, Baltimore and Washington. Based upon this initial analysis, Gottmann (1976) subsequently defined the characteristic features of megalopolitan urban systems. The term was reserved for very large urban units with a suggested minimum population of 25 million. The emergence of such a unit would be significantly related to its potential for performing an important international exchange function for trade, technology, population and culture for the state in which it was located (cf. world cities, Chapter 5). Consequently, transactional activities would be the central element of economic structure, and they would also tend to be located at major international transportation breakpoints. In addition, because of the scale they would typically have a distinctly polynuclear form, but with sufficient internal physical continuity and functional interrelationships for each to be considered a system in itself, and separated from other units by less urbanized areas. Complete physical continuity was not considered a necessary feature of the megalopolitan system. In fact, in the archetypical area of the north-eastern seaboard of the USA a population density of only 250 persons per square kilometre was used to define its outer edge, while as much as 48 per cent of the urbanized region comprised commercial forest. Instead, the cohesiveness of the system depended upon, and was best indicated by, the relative incidence of communication facilities such as highways, railways, waterways, pipelines and telephone lines, along with transaction flows of commodities, traffic, people and messages. Also, due to the importance of communications in the efficient functioning of such units, it was anticipated that they would usually develop along major transport axes. The high levels of economic, political and social interaction typical of such areas was also considered likely to result in a strong element of self-sustaining growth with some adverse effects. The urban and social environmental problems associated with over-congestion at the centres of developing megalopolitan systems create severe management problems for urban planning.

Defined in this way the megalopolitan form is significantly different in both scale and function from the conurbation. It was initially restricted to six cases comprising: the type-area of the US north-eastern seaboard; the Great Lakes area extending from Chicago to Detroit and the southern shores of Lake Erie; the Tokaido area of Japan centred on Tokyo-Yokohama and extending west to include Osaka-Kobe (see Figure 5.11, p.119); the English megalopolis, centred on the south-east and extending north-westwards to include the West Midlands, Manchester, Merseyside and the West Riding of Yorkshire; the megalopolis of north-western Europe considered to be emerging in the area of Amsterdam, Paris and the Ruhr; and a sixth case centred on Shanghai.

Three other areas were also considered to be growing fast enough to be emergent megalopolitan systems. In South America rapid economic development is resulting in a corridor of development between Rio de Janeiro and São Paulo. In Europe, megalopolitan tendencies were considered to be centred on Milan, Turin and Genoa, extending southward to Pisa and Florence and westward to Marseilles and Avignon; while a third case was suggested likely to result from developmental pressures to link the San Francisco Bay Area with the Los Angeles-San Diego complex. A possible additional case was first suggested by Yeates in 1975. This comprises 'Main Street' Canada, a corridor of development extending along Lakes Erie and Ontario and the St Lawrence Valley, reaching from Windsor in the south 1,100 km north-eastward to Quebec City and centred on the urban regions of Toronto, Ottawa and Montreal. This forms the economic and political centre of Canada in which approximately half of the population live, and where three-quarters of manufacturing and three-fifths of Canada's total income were produced. With a population of over 10 million in 1971, distributed over a wider area than that of the north-eastern seaboard of the USA, this area did not strictly conform to the definition of a megalopolis. Nevertheless, its degree of primacy in the Canadian context, its international functional significance and its internal functional cohesion and polynuclear urban form, combined with its physical contiguity and interrelationships with the Great Lakes megalopolis, suggests that it has megalopolitan features despite its relatively small population.

Megalopolis provides a description of the macro-scale urbanized region, but it has only weak physical and functional connotations. Nevertheless, it offers a broad framework for the study of emerging urban systems at a scale which is becoming increasingly relevant to urbanization in the context of the globalization of economic, social and political forces in the contemporary world system (see Chapter 5).

Ecumenopolis

A yet more futuristic urban form, 'ecumenopolis', was suggested by Doxiadis (1968). This was based upon speculative forecasts of world population trends which assume a level of population, approximately ten times the current figure, will be reached towards the end of the twenty-first century. In these circumstances it is envisaged that a massive increase in functional linkages will occur among separate urbanized regions and there will be a related increase in the physical continuity of urban settlement. This continuous urban system which could emerge in the inhabitable world has been termed the 'universal city' or 'ecumenopolis'. Its spatial limits will be determined by the existence of reasonably flat land and climatic conditions suitable to support human settlement in the future.

Obviously, long-term forecasts of this kind involve numerous imponderables so that the population levels upon which such a structure is based must be considered highly speculative. Nevertheless, the concept of the ecumenopolis is not without value. The 'population explosion' continues to be an important facet of the demography of many countries of the Developing World, while intermittent population growth – though at much lower rates – is also a feature of the great majority of developed countries. Thus, the increased significance of megalopolitan structures and a tendency towards the development of something resembling ecumenopolis might be anticipated. Since such eventualities are considered likely to be accompanied by an accentuation of the urban and social environmental problems associated with overcongestion, the concept of the ecumenopolis serves to underline the potential dangers of unconstrained urban growth. In fact, in North America the physical and functional divisions between the urbanized regions of the north-eastern seaboard, the Great Lakes and 'Main Street' Canada are already becoming blurred. Indeed, should the degree of functional coalescence of the 'urban fields' of the USA be followed by an increased element of physical integration, the North American element of the ecumenopolis might soon be considered more than a futuristic notion (Figure 4.13).

Similarly, in western Europe with the development of the European Union, international developmental pressures have increased in the area comprising the Eurocore or Golden Rectangle, bounded by Birmingham, Paris, Frankfurt and Dortmund (Hall 1994). This area covers 13 per cent of the land of the EU, yet accommodates 25 per cent of the population, while the principal urban concentrations centred on London (12 million), Paris (11 million), Randstad-Holland (5 million) and Rhine-Ruhr (10 million) alone contain a total population of 38 million. The opening of the Channel Tunnel in 1994 and the enhancement of high-speed rail linkages within the 'Eurocore' have increased the developmental potential of these areas. Lille in north-west France, for example, is advantageously located near the Channel Tunnel on the TGV (*Train de Grande Vitesse*) rail network, at a focal point between London, Paris and the Ruhr. This has acted as a stimulus for the initiation in 1994 of the major business and high-tech industrial concentration of Euralille focusing on the construction of a TGV station capable of handling 15,000 passengers a day. This will adjoin the existing Lille-Flandres station which accommodates 70,000 passengers a day (Ampe 1995). Similar development pressures are anticipated for the rail corridor between London and the Channel Tunnel. In addition, since the mid-1970s extensive motorway construction and the development of high speed inter-city rail services have also increased the physical linkages between the core areas and their wider European orbits. The British InterCity 125 rail system and the French TGV services are typical of

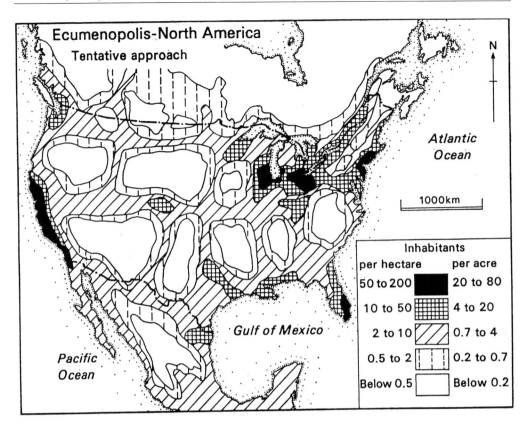

Figure 4.13 The North American ecumenopolis

systems which have also been developed in Germany, Sweden, Italy and Spain (Hall 1995). Thus, as further improvements are made to the transport infrastructure, it is anticipated that the Eurocore will become progressively subject to increasing physical articulation, both within its centre and between the centre and the larger out-lying cities of the EU. A possible scenario has been suggested by Dunford and Perrons (1994). They predict that development pressures in Europe will focus on a 'vital axis' of the core economic region comprising the more favourably located major international cities and their hinterlands in the 'Eurocore', and this will extend from London, through Germany and Switzerland to northern Italy (see Figure 5.8, p.110). This is likely to exhibit strong megalopolitan qualities, not unlike those of the Tokaido corridor in Japan.

Summary

The literature relating to the theories of the urban system has provided much of conceptual and methodological value to assist in the investigation of the characteristics of urban systems in general. Of particular note are the methods developed which provide useful descriptions of the size-distribution and hierarchical ordering of systems of cities. Similarly, techniques have been developed by which it is possible to illustrate the functional interrelationships of centres, while concepts have also been introduced which are capable of providing additional insights into the process of development and change within urban systems. The more specifically physical and functional characteristics of modern urban systems directly reflect temporal change and the impact upon urban form of changing economic forces and of the technology of transport and communications. The compact industrial city has given way to the more spatially diffuse post-industrial metropolitan forms as deconcentration and decentralization have come to increasingly dominate urban life in the western city. The typology of 'urbanized regions' used here accurately reflects the scale of these new 'cities' and suggests the need to view the city, at one and the same time, in a combination of regional, national and international contexts. This reflects a complex array of contemporary economic, social and political changes which are occurring within the context of the emergence of a global economy. It follows that increasing attention needs to be paid to the economic dimension of urban development and the manner in which it manifests itself at a variety of spatial scales. This forms the basis of Chapter 5.

CHAPTER 5

The urban economy

At a general level the nature of urbanization and its associated urban forms in a country are related to the characteristics and extent of economic development. This chapter examines the relationship between economic change and urban development more closely and, in particular, its spatial expression and associated problems at a variety of geographic scales. The historic and contemporary place of a country in the international economic system is obviously likely to influence its economic development and urban system. Countries with strong economies at the forefront of economic advance are likely to have urban systems and problems dominated by the need to accommodate growth, while attempting to maintain the quality of the urban environment. Alternatively, areas with a heritage of outmoded forms of production face problems of economic restructuring and environmental regeneration, while those in the early stages of economic development need to develop a physical and social infrastructure capable of generating self-sustaining growth. Such features are also likely to vary regionally within countries in relation to the nature and relative health of the local economy. Thus, an explicitly economic perspective is considered fundamental to an appreciation of the functional characteristics of urban areas at spatial scales ranging from the global to the intra-urban.

Traditional patterns of regional economic imbalance

Until as recently as the late 1960s, the situation of a country in relation to the international economic system was perceived of in terms of centre-periphery relationships. Either a country formed part of the industrialized centre of the world economy, characterized by the countries of North America and western Europe, or it was part of the developing (Third World) periphery, relying upon the export of natural resources to the centre and exhibiting the characteristics of a dependent economy. The nature of the national urban systems in the countries of the centre, consequently, to varying degrees exhibited strongly articulated hierarchical structures, while the countries of the periphery demonstrated stronger elements of externally oriented primacy.

Within this broad framework, the great majority of the more detailed analyses of the economic context of urban development were undertaken largely from the perspective of individual countries. Attention focused on explanations for regional inequalities in levels of economic development and their findings provide some understanding of spatial variations of the incidence of the variety of urbanized regions discussed in Chapter 4. Inter-regional variations in levels of economic development were generally considered to reflect temporary maladjustments in the economic system. It was assumed that if labour and capital were relatively mobile and reasonable information existed on the availability of economic opportunities, then eventually movement of the factors of production would bring about a regional equalization of economic development. However, the development of such a state of spatial equilibrium clearly did not accord with the pervasiveness of regional economic inequalities evident in most parts of the world.

The inability of the mechanisms promoting spatial equilibrium to account for the persistence of regional inequalities resulted in the formulation of new conceptual models. Of these, Myrdal's (1957) 'cumulative causation' model continues to have considerable significance for the understanding of centre-periphery economic imbalances. During the earliest stage of economic development it was proposed that economic development would focus on the region which has some initial advantage, while the remaining regions of the country would lag behind. With subsequent economic development, rather than the emergence of counterbalancing forces promoting spatial equilibrium, the initial economic advantages of the 'core' region were considered more likely to result in the accumulation of 'derived advantages' which would maintain its pre-eminent economic position. These advantages include a concentration of skilled labour; the availability of capital and enterprise; a good economic and social infrastructure resulting from past development; access to government agencies; and the opportunity to develop ancillary and service industries. The interaction of these factors were considered to create cumulative economic growth in the core region of a country (Figure 5.1)

However, once economic growth had been initiated in a core region, it attracted both capital investment and the in-migration of skilled labour from the peripheral regions of a country. The concentration of the provision of goods and services in the core is also likely to stunt the development of similar economic activities in the periphery. In addition, the relative poverty of the periphery might well result in the provision of a less adequate level of public services than is offered in the core region, and this deflates further the attractions of the periphery. This combination of features, termed by Myrdal the 'backwash effect', was considered likely to accentuate significantly the economic concentration associated with the cumulative causation mechanism.

The opposite, 'spread effect', by which growth in the core area might ultimately result in the stimulation of development in the peripheral regions was also postulated by Myrdal. The core area was considered likely to stimulate demand at the periphery for such things as agricultural produce and raw materials. If the effects of this were sufficiently great, it was considered possible that this could initiate the mechanism of cumulative causation in the periphery with sufficient impetus to promote self-sustaining economic growth. However, it was considered that such a 'spread effect' was likely to occur only in the most highly developed economies, usually with the assistance of positive government policies, and even then the level of economic development was considered unlikely to rival that of the core.

Empirical evidence tends to support the importance of the cumulative causation mechanism, and the backwash or polarization effects have been widely accepted as an explanation for economic and urban concentration in the earlier stages of economic

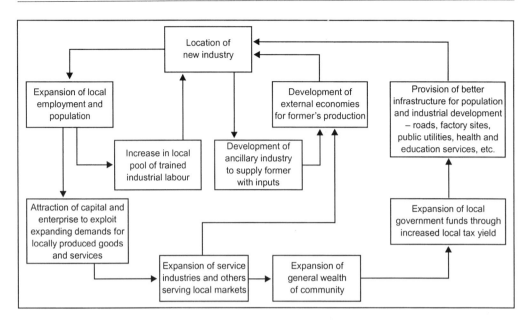

Figure 5.1 Myrdal's cumulative causation model

development. However, evidence for the spontaneous operation of the spread or trickling-down effects to create a measure of regional equalization in the long term is sparse. It appears that the forces of concentration are much stronger than was initially thought by Myrdal, and this suggests the need for strong directive action by national governments or international agencies if a degree of regional equalization is to be achieved. Nevertheless, Myrdal's model provides a strong rationale for the emergence and persistence of inter-regional inequality in levels of economic development and associated urban concentration, and it continues to provide a useful introductory framework in which to view the emergence of regional inequalities in the nation-state. This is illustrated for the British experience in Figure 5.2. In fact, subsequent debate concerning the importance of 'agglomeration economies' for an understanding of continued economic concentration in core regions of the world continues to be based largely on the factors and concepts associated with the cumulative causation model.

Globalization and the urban economy

Centre-periphery relationships continue to be broadly applicable to an understanding of the regional space economy of individual nation-states. However, fundamental changes in the nature of the international capitalist system since 1945 have transformed most western economies in recent years. Cross-border flows of goods, services, capital and information have grown prodigiously, particularly between the advanced economies, but also between the developed and developing world. The term 'globalization' has been widely used to describe the multifaceted, but not entirely understood, process of global economic integration and the emergence of a global economy (Daniels and Lever 1996). A large

Urban Pattern	Population	Economic development
Pre-industrial stage, before 1700 Small towns serving local rural hinterlands. Exception: London as a private city; smaller port cities, such as Bristol, Liverpool	Low and fluctuating, slow growth, mostly rural	Reflects the relative prosperity of local agriculture: commercial development in London and ports
Transitional stage 1700–1850 New urban concentrations, principally in the coalfields. London continues its growth by the 'cumulative causation' mechanism; already a million city by 1801. A centre periphery structure more evident *within* the separate regions than at a national scale	Acceleration of growth; rural-to-urban migration. In England and Wales population increased from 8.8 million in 1801 to 17.9 million in 1851 - urban population from 33.8 per cent in 1801 to 54 per ent in 1801	Early industrial development based upon coal and steam: iron, steel textiles and shipbuilding become the vast industries
Industrial stage 1850-1950 London added 5.5 million to its population 1801 – 1911; Birmingham, Liverpool and Manchester grew up by only c.1 million each in the sae period. Cities of the peripheral regions grew even more slowly. The north and west began to display downward transitional characteristics and a *national* centre periphery structure emerged	Population growth (England and Wales) 17.9 million in 1851 to 36.0 million in 1911; 78.9 per cent of the population lived in cities by 1911. Slower growth in the interwar depression years; larger cities grew more slowly as innovations ceased to enter the urban system.	Emergence of international competition. Basic industries face international competition. Increasing importance of secondary manufacturing; development of cheap efficient transport; eonomic advantages of a centralized market loation for light industrial development are emphasized. Conversely, industrial decline in the north and western peripheral region
Post-industrial stage 1950–1980 As economic forces and environmental planning policies spread, London's urban development, the 'Centre' gradually expands to include the South East, the Midlands and south east Lancashire. Amelioration of urban decline on the periphery by decentralization policies, but regional disparities persist	Stabilization of the population, with a tendency to grow slowly except in times of economic growth. Birth rates fluctuate at a low level	Emergence of service employment as the growth sector of the economy. The attraction of a centralized urban location re-emphasized for such development. New economic element added with exploitation of oil and natural gas in the North Sea in the 1960s and 1970s. Marginal regions and inner cities remain problem areas

Figure 5.2 Stages in the development of the British urban system

number of factors have contributed to the process of global change and they are linked in a complex interactive manner which defies easy analysis. Among these, the importance of the growth of multinational corporations; the deregulation of international finance; increased international flows of trade, financial direct investment and labour migration; the development of post-Fordist modes of production and regulation; the expansion of post-industrial service activities; and the underlying contribution of the complex amalgam of information technology, advanced telecommunications, knowledge and innovation, are all fundamental to an understanding of the processes involved. However, since the early 1970s, these factors have jointly precipitated significant spatial shifts in patterns of economic growth and decline at scales ranging from the international to the local. Such shifts have had fundamental consequences for associated patterns and processes of urban change throughout the world.

Multinational corporations

At the forefront of the process of globalization has been the remarkable growth of multinational corporations (MNCs) since the early 1970s. These firms organize the acquisition of raw materials, the processes of manufacture, the provision of services, and the development of markets in ways which are largely independent of state boundaries and associated national political policy controls. In fact, the turnover of some of the largest multinational corporations rivals the gross domestic products of all but the largest national economies and they are widely considered to be the most important forces generating global shifts in manufacturing and service activities. Among the 50 highest value multinational enterprises in the developed countries, for example, three Japanese banks were valued at greater than $400,000 million in 1993 (Clegg 1996). The highest valued resource-intensive industry was the US-based Exxon petroleum corporation, valued at nearly $80,000 million in 1993, a figure which was far exceeded by General Motors ($121,000 million). In fact, by the early 1990s multinational corporations were reported to control three-quarters of world trade in goods and services (Nilsson *et al.* 1996).

International financial deregulation

International investment in the early postwar years was constrained by the regulation of international financial markets. Regulation was introduced at the Bretton Woods conference of 1944 to maintain stability in world markets in order to assist the restructuring of national economies in the aftermath of the war (Swyngedouw 1996). However, since the late 1960s the gradual dismantling of the international regulatory apparatus, combined with the growth in international agreements to foster trade has resulted in an upsurge in international financial direct investment (FDI) and the prodigious growth of multinational corporations in manufacturing and service provision. This has been accompanied by a gradual decline in the influence of national governments over economic forces affecting locational issues within their countries (Daniels and Lever 1996). This has changed the national economic regulatory regimes in most developed countries. In the UK, for example, the development of the 'Keynesian' style of economic state management and 'state welfarism' to direct the economy and to reconcile the problems of social and spatial disparities in the distribution of well-being in the late industrial period has drastically diminished. The international competitive forces have reduced the opportunities for the government to influence economic trends, while the need for global competitiveness has curtailed welfare expenditure. Thus, economic regulation has moved in a 'neoliberal' direction in which market forces and the strength of private capital are fundamental to an understanding of the national space economy (Tickell and Peck 1995).

Information technology and technologic innovation

The rapid improvement and increasing convergence of telecommunications, computing and information technology have greatly facilitated the development of the international organizational linkages needed for the efficient functioning of multinational enterprises and the globalization of financial markets. Without the necessary 'transactional' infrastructure it is unlikely that the scale and pace of such change could have occurred. In addition, technologic innovation has been at the forefront of the research and development dimension of all new forms of high technology manufacture involving microelectronics, computers, lasers, bioengineering and robotics (Holly 1996). The aerospace and defence industries have often been in a leading position in the process of change, but innovative technology has also been closely associated with the burgeoning growth of new forms of consumer electronic products and automobile manufacture.

Post-Fordist modes of production

Technological innovation in consumer electronics has generated new markets for high-value, low-weight goods such as more sophisticated television and telephonic facilities, personal computers, digital music systems, and kitchen and leisure equipment. At the same time, technologic advances in methods of production based on robotics and flexible systems of computerized production control have initiated fundamental changes in the modes of production throughout the manufacturing sector. New computerized microelectronic technologies have reduced the need for the rigidities of production methods and the necessity to produce large quantities of single standardized items to achieve economies of scale associated with 'Fordist' production line processing. Similarly, the need for close vertical integration of production from raw materials, via component production to finished products, has declined in significance in the new circumstances. Instead, more 'flexible' post-Fordist methods based on the new technologies allow for the production of smaller quantities of products which can be geared more precisely to the changing needs of an increasingly segmented consumer market (Holly 1996). Such methods have been applied throughout the manufacturing sector for the production of goods ranging from car manufacture and consumer electronics to clothing and foodstuffs. The US based clothing retailer 'The Firm', for example, has been able to change rapidly the styles and range of the product mix of its manufacturing capacity in Hong Kong in accordance with information on current sales trends. The San Francisco based clothing retailer, 'The Gap', operates in a similar way. The new methods have resulted in the establishment of looser 'horizontal networks' of production based upon component suppliers rather than strongly vertically integrated firms. Thus, the various components required to be assembled into final products need not necessarily be located in close proximity to each other. This feature has been accentuated further by technical improvements in all modes of transport which have resulted in a reduction in the relative cost of bulk, long distance transport.

These changes have a number of implications for the location of manufacturing. Decentralization has been a common response, precipitated by the search for cheap labour or resources, while escaping the costs of congestion and unionized labour of the older-established industrial concentrations (Holly 1996). For products needing only low levels of skill associated with routine production methods or assembly such as car manufacturing, consumer electronics and clothing manufacture, dispersal has incorporated a truly global dimension. Development has focused particularly in the newly industrializing countries (NICs) of South-east Asia such as Hong Kong, Singapore, South Korea and Taiwan – the so-called 'Asian tiger' or 'four dragon' economies – while similar effects have been noted in Brazil and on the European periphery in Portugal, Greece and Ireland. At the same time, however, within these countries industrial clusters have emerged to benefit from the agglomeration economies associated with proximity to 'lead firms' while sharing infrastructure provision and the advantages of concentrated labour pools. However, the competitive impact of this trend has resulted in the steady deindustrialization of the older developed industrial countries, particularly in the regions dominated by concentrations of extractive industry and traditional and heavy manufacturing activities. This has been most marked since the worldwide economic recession from the early 1970s, particularly in the countries and regions exhibiting high costs of production and outmoded working practices.

Clustering, however, has also characterized activities such as the aerospace industry, microelectronics firms and the research and development function of large multinational organizations which require a highly skilled labour force. In such cases, concentration has tended to be retained in the most advanced industrial economies and, more specifically, in the areas offering particular advantages for innovative industrial activities. Some of the older core industrial regions (such as London, Tokyo and Paris) have continued to provide such attractions, although new concentrations such as Silicon Valley in California, Bavaria in southern Germany and the north-eastern 'Third Italy' have also entered the arena.

The expansion of service activities

In most western economies the importance of manufacturing reached a peak in the late 1960s and early 1970s. However, global economic integration has also been accompanied by a gradual expansion of service employment since the late 1960s to a degree that tertiary activities now dominate all advanced post-industrial economies. Since that time service employment has grown typically by rates of 40–80 per cent so that by 1990 service employment averaged 62 per cent for the countries of the Organization for Economic Cooperation and Development (OECD) (Marshall and Wood 1995). Services now dominate employment in the USA and Canada to the greatest degree (71 per cent), and the UK, Australia, Norway, Belgium and the Netherlands are not far behind (69 per cent) (Table 5.1). This has been accompanied by a higher proportion of females in the labour forces. The female share of the labour force in the countries of the developed world has increased from around a quarter to a third in 1960 to over 40 per cent, while in the service sector the proportion is typically more than 75 per cent (Marshall and Wood 1995).

In part, this reflects the declining importance of the traditional manufacturing sector. Of greater significance, however, is the wide range of specialized producer services needed to support both the processes involved in economic globalization and the development of high technology industry. Foremost among these are finance and banking, insurance, legal advice, communications, research and development, market research and advertising. The internationalization of the financial markets, manufacture, and the trading of goods and services has created heavy demands for professional skills in transactional activities throughout the business arena. At the same time, modern manufacturing requires heavy inputs of specialized research and development skills, marketing and advertising expertise, and sales personnel. Consequently, while employment in the USA grew by nearly 19 per cent in the period 1979–89, producer service employment grew by nearly 59 per cent. For the same period in the UK, overall employment fell by 3.5 per cent, but producer service employment expanded dramatically by 66 per cent (Marhall and Wood 1995). In fact, the importance, scale and range of producer services which have emerged since the late 1960s prompted Gottmann (1983) to suggest the emergence of two service sectors elaborating upon the 'tertiary' definition. The quaternary sector was used to define the transactional activities, while the quinary services were those which focused on innovation.

The increase in producer service employment in the advanced economies is now

Table 5.1 Service employment in OECD countries, 1970–90

	1970 absolute (000)	Civilian employment (%)	1990 absolute (000)	Civilian employment (%)	1970–90 growth (%)
USA	48,083	61	83,658	71	74
Canada	4,866	61	8,947	71	84
North America	52,949	61	92,605	71	75
Japan	23,890	47	36,700	59	54
Australia	2,964	55	5,418	69	83
New Zealand	523	49	954	65	82
Denmark	1,173	51	1,765	67	51
Finalnd	906	43	1,489	61	64
Iceland	38	47	75	60	97
Norway	731	49	1,370	69	87
Sweden	2,060	54	3,045	68	48
Austria	1,342	44	1,886	55	41
Belgium	1,892	53	2,570	69	36
France	8,602	47	13,904	64	45
Germany	10,999	42	15,874	57	44
Ireland	450	43	629	56	40
Luxembourg	65	46	125	66	92
Netherlands	2,569	55	4,333	69	69
Switzerland	1,428	45	2,119	60	48
UK	12,686	52	18,305	69	44
Turkey	2,251	18	6,202	32	176
Greece	1,072	34	1,771	48	65
Italy	7,749	40	12,383	58	60
Portugal	1,240	37	2,120	47	71
Spain	5,575	36	6,890	55	51
EC	54,072	45	86,669	61	60
OECD	143,154	49	232,533	62	62

Services: major divisions 6, 7, 8, 9, 0 of the ISC
Source: Marshall and Wood 1995: 10 (based on OECD data 1992)

considered to represent a fundamental economic restructuring which has blurred the former distinction between manufacturing and services. Modern manufacturing is integrally dependent upon specialized services to function efficiently and to retain its innovative competitive edge, while the service activities generate further demands for ever more sophisticated applications of computer and microelectronic information technology to function effectively in the global economy. In effect, the traditional characterization of manufacture as 'wealth creating' with services confined to 'distribution and wealth consumption' is an outmoded representation of economic realities. Instead, Marshall and Wood's (1995) view that all analyses of urban and regional economic development processes in the modern world should be 'service-informed' finds ready support.

However, while the 'tertiarization' of the advanced economies has been led by the producer services, intermittent, but less dramatic, growth has also characterized the 'traditional' service sector. This reflects the demands, albeit halting in some cases, of economic development and affluence in many western countries. The consumer *services* sector has been moderately buoyant, reflecting developments in retailing and the growth of tourism, leisure, sport and cultural activities. Similarly, the distributive services of wholesaling and transport have kept pace with economic development, as have the public services such as government administration, education and health (Marshall and Wood 1995).

The growth of the service sector in developed economies has, however, not been without negative social consequences. Sassen (1991), particularly, has highlighted the emergence of deep divisions in the labour force in the global cities between the highly skilled and highly waged technical and managerial functions and those involved in routine clerical and consumer service occupations. The latter are poorly paid, have little security of tenure, are often part-time, with a characteristically large proportion of women. At the lowest levels, the growth of menial occupations associated with the catering trade or office cleaning has tended to create an 'underclass' undertaking 'casualized' jobs. This polarization of the labour force is now widely recognized as a fundamental element of the post-industrial service economy. Crang and Martin (1991), for example, note that the 'Cambridge phenomenon' of modern innovatory economic expansion has been accompanied locally by a widening of social disparities, and a substantial problem of low paid, casual employment and unemployment among the unskilled. However, while there is little doubt that the growth of the service economy has been accompanied by a growing polarization of occupational and income structures, Hamnett (1994) has suggested that this division is not as 'pathologic' everywhere as the early commentators imply. Focusing on the experience of Randstad-Holland, he argues that in cities which have retained a significant manufacturing base and lack high levels of immigration a broader 'professionalization' in the workforce serves to reduce the divides.

Globalization: the spatial implications for urban development processes

Together, the ongoing processes of global economic change are resulting in a new, but still uneven, international restructuring of economic activity based upon spatial variations in the potential profitability of capitalist production of the new world economic order. The influence of the 'friction of distance' for the location of economic activity has declined with improvements in transport technology, but even more markedly due to the revolutionary changes in electronic forms of communication and data transfer. However, while there has been a decline in the importance of distance, the specificity of location or territoriality are widely accredited to have achieved fundamental significance for an explanation of the spatial distribution of economic concentration and uneven development in the context of the changing global economy. The characteristics of places which support an innovatory 'business culture', and provide ease of access to information, transport and government agencies, while offering an amenable quality of life, are 'comparative advantages' which are considered particularly conducive to development in the new economic circumstances (Daniels and Lever 1996). In effect, the new economies of agglomeration appear to favour metropolitan concentration in those 'core' locations in the global economy which offer advantages for the newer forms of technologically based economic activities. A favourable positioning on the looser global economic networks of the multinational corporations is considered particularly advantageous for economic development (Graham 1995). By contrast, formerly favourable locations within the integrated national urban economies characteristic of the Fordist era have declined in significance, particularly in the less attractive peripheral regions of countries. In effect, the areas characterized by the more traditional forms of manufacture have experienced economic stagnation or decline, structural unemployment, and out-migration.

Global concentration

The principal motive force in economic globalization is considered to be financial direct investment (FDI) by multinational enterprises (MNEs) involved in manufacture, trade and services. Their activities, however, are highly concentrated within and between the major markets of the developed countries. Of an estimated 35,000 existing in the early 1990s, 30,900 were centred in the USA, Japan, UK, France, Germany, Switzerland and Canada (Daniels 1996). Concentration is even greater among the largest industrial corporations. Of the top 500 in 1991, the USA (157) and Japan (119) head the list, while a substantial European dimension is also represented by the UK (45), Germany (33) and France (32) (Drennan 1996). In fact, through the 1980s the developed countries accounted for 97 per cent of world outflows of FDI and 75 per cent of inflows, and these were dominated by the activities of the countries of the so-called 'Triad' of the European Union, the USA and Japan (81 per cent of outflows and 71 per cent of inflows) (Clegg 1996: 103).

To a substantial degree the economic concentration of the activities of the MNEs has been assisted and 'institutionalized' by the creation of multinational government blocs established with the primary aim of maintaining the economic interests of the member states. Lever (1996) identifies the most important as the European Union (EU) with the emergence of the Single European Market; the North American Free Trade Association of the USA, Canada and Mexico (NAFTA); and Japan and its association with the newly industrializing countries of South-east Asia. Together these associations of countries accounted for 85 per cent of world trade by the late 1980s, 46 per cent between themselves and 39 per cent with other countries. These organizations have added a powerful political dimension to the economic forces of globalization which has served to maintain a concentration of economic activity in the context of globalization.

Clearly, the activities of the largest multinational corporation are, to date, focused primarily on the market opportunities and more stable economic circumstances presented by the developed economies. This has maintained a strong centre-periphery pattern of global economic relations in which major world regions are largely excluded from the process of global capital accumulation while being maintained by a subsistence economy. Friedmann (1995) estimates that the global economic system excludes two-thirds of the world's population, and this has severe implications for global political stability should the periphery become destabilized, or if migrant labour to the core is too large to be assimilated peacefully. In effect, a dystopian image of the future world order is envisaged if the problems of an increasingly fragmented and marginalized periphery are not redressed.

Financial cores: the global cities

Within the global core areas, however, the three major cities of London, New York and Tokyo have risen to dominate the global pattern of specialized 'transactional activities' in financial and related producer services. The money markets and associated financial, investment, insurance and legal services display a degree of worldwide dominance in these cities that has led to their characterization as 'global cities', at the pinnacle of the world financial hierarchy (Sassen 1991; 1994). In part, this reflects historical inertia, in the case of London dating back to its imperial heritage, and to New York's financial dominance during the industrialization of the USA. More recently, the national concentration of the headquarters of the multinational corporations centred in the UK, the USA and Japan has been a major contributor to the dominance of these cities due to the demands they generate for specialized producer services. The contribution of producer services to employment in Greater London, for example, increased from 13 per cent to 23 per cent in the period 1971–89, while the equivalent figures increased from 18 per cent to 30 per cent in New York between 1968 and 1994, the latter being three times the figure for manufacture (Drennan 1996).

The importance of agglomeration economies are, however, considered to be of even greater explanatory significance for the emergence and maintained financial dominance of the global cities. The operation of the specialized financial markets requires the concentration of expert advice necessary for the provision of customized services in information-intensive activities. Such concentration also offers the opportunity for meetings at short notice, while face-to-face contacts are still considered necessary to maximize trust during complex financial and legal negotiations, despite the availability of increasingly sophisticated telecommunications. Together, these advantages are considered to reduce 'uncertainty' in the context of a complex decision-making environment (Drennan 1996). Consequently, each of these cities exhibits a considerable degree of global and national primacy for the distribution of financial and related business services. In 1989, for example, 60 per cent of the British financial service sector was concentrated in London, and this was fifteen times greater than the second tier cities of Birmingham and Manchester (Marshall and Wood 1995). Not surprisingly, service activities tend to dominate the employment structure of these cities (e.g. Frost and Spence, 1993).

The global cities generate undoubted benefits for the economies of their parent countries through 'invisible earnings' and the generation of service employment,while the presence of international finance and the availability of expert financial advice are also of potential value for the generation of other service and innovatory manufacturing activities. However, to a significant degree, the specialized financial, insurance and legal activities are linked more strongly with global economic networks than with the local national economies in which they are located (Drennan 1996). Evidently, these activities are substantially divorced from the local economies and are not subject to strong national political control.

The global concentration of international financial transactions and the global investment activities of the multinational corporations into the three dominant global cities attests to the continued potency of the cumulative causation mechanism for the world economic order. However, the question arises: are they likely to retain this dominance into the foreseeable future? Doubts have been raised by Drennan (1996) which are suggestive of possible outcomes rather than indicative of likely trends. The financial markets of Japan, for example, retain a degree of regulatory control which might offer opportunities to alternative centres such as Hong Kong, although the future of the latter seems equally imponderable due to its recent (1997) return to Chinese control. Equally, development and the expansion of the markets of China, Brazil and India could offer attractions for the relocation of multinational corporations to these countries, while in the USA the expansion of Pacific trading linkages might offer added impetus to the already buoyant economies of San Francisco and Los Angeles. Diseconomies of agglomeration are also having adverse effects on the efficiency of the urban infrastructure and environmental amenity of the global cities. All are affected by urban decay, traffic congestion, air pollution, and the social divisions between rich and poor to a degree that the attractions of alternative cities could be heightened (Sassen 1991). London and New York are considered to be increasingly adversely affected by the operation of a national 'neoliberal regulatory environment', characterized by a weak local government planning regime and limited integration of public utility services such as transportation planning and welfare provision for the economically and socially indigent. It is equally possible, however, that the global cities will respond to the challenges presented by these changes and retain their pre-eminence in the financial arena. In the short term the continued primacy of the global cities appears assured but their long-term dominance is not guaranteed.

Control centres: the world cities

However, despite the domination of the distribution of specialized financial services by the global cities, it has long been argued that economic globalization has introduced a substantially broader global dimension into the world urban system. Friedmann and Wolff (1982), for example, suggested that the internationalization of production and markets by transnational corporations has created a network of world cities located in the principal urban regions in which most of the world's active capital is concentrated. They are characterized as control centres in which corporate decision-making and finance are concentrated, and they provide the function of integrating national economies with the world system. Their economies are strongly oriented towards post-industrial transactional activities and they tend to contain population concentrations of 5 million to 15 million, foremost among which are the three global cities along with other major centres such as Los Angeles, San Francisco, Chicago, Miami, Paris, Randstad, Frankfurt, Zurich, Hong Kong, Singapore, Bangkok, Cairo, Mexico City and São Paulo.

However, while there is now wide agreement on the recognition of the importance of world cities to the global economic order, a precise definition of which cities qualify for this status continues to be debateable. The importance of global economic 'command' is a recurring theme, and was central to Friedmann's (1995) re-examination of the concept. In this, a more precise hierarchy of world cities was defined in accordance with the estimate of the spatial spread of economic power they exerted in the global system (Figure 5.3). The global command role was confined to the three major financial nodes, while five other cities were seen as having a significant international influence (Table 5.2). The national and subnational centres dominated their respective economies and served as a link with the international capitalist system.

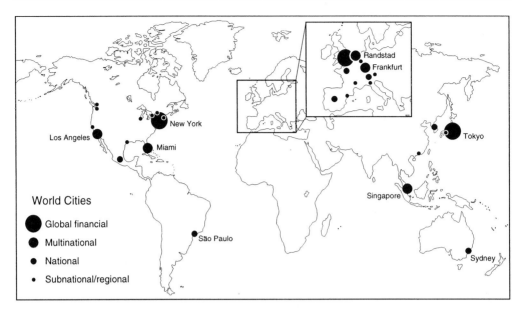

Figure 5.3 World cities in the 1990s

Table 5.2 World cities in the 1990s

Global financial centre	Subnational/regional centres
London	Osaka-Kobe
New York	San Francisco
Tokyo	Seattle
	Houston
Multinational centres	Chicago
	Boston
Miami (Caribbean, Latin America)	Vancouver
Los Angeles (Pacific RIm)	Toronto
Frankfurt (Western Europe)	Montreal
Randstad (Western Europe)	Hong Kong
Singapore (South-east Asia)	Milan
	Lyon
National centres	Barcelona
	Munich
Paris	Düsseldorf-Köln-Essen-Dortmund (Rhine-
Zurich	Ruhr)
Madrid	
Mexico City	
São Paulo	
Seoul	
Sydney	

Source: Based on Friedmann 1995

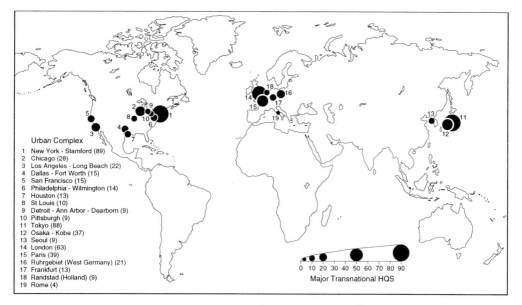

Urban Complex
1   New York - Stamford (89)
2   Chicago (28)
3   Los Angeles - Long Beach (22)
4   Dallas - Fort Worth (15)
5   San Francisco (15)
6   Philadelphia - Wilmington (14)
7   Houston (13)
8   St Louis (10)
9   Detroit - Ann Arbor - Dearborn (9)
10 Pittsburgh (9)
11 Tokyo (88)
12 Osaka - Kobe (37)
13 Seoul (9)
14 London (63)
15 Paris (39)
16 Ruhrgebiet (West Germany) (21)
17 Frankfurt (13)
18 Randstad (Holland) (9)
19 Rome (4)

0 10 20 30 40 50 60 70 80 90
Major Transnational HQS

Figure 5.4 World cities as concentrations of transnational head-quarter offices, 1990

Table 5.3 Headquarters of major transnational firms: major urban complexes of the world, 1990

Region	Urban complex	Major transnational headquarters
North America	New York-Stamford	89
	Chicago	28
	Los Angeles-Long Beach	22
	Dallas-Fort Worth	15
	San Francisco	15
	Philadelphia-Wilmington	14
	Houston	13
	St Louis	10
	Detroit-Ann Arbor-Dearborn	9
	Pittsburgh	9
Asia	Tokyo	88
	Osaka-Kobe	37
	Seroul	9
Europe	London	63
	Paris	39
	Ruhrgebiet (West Germany)	21
	Frankfurt	13
	Randstad (Holland)	9
	Rome	4

Source: Hicks and Nivin 1996; 26, based on information from the Burton Center for Development Studies

The designation of the 'major urban complexes of the world' portrays a narrower view (Figure 5.4). Hicks and Nivin (1996) suggest that the global economy is anchored by approximately 500 transnational firms, the headquarters of which are highly concentrated into only 19 urban complexes (Table 5.3). These are again dominated by the Triad of the USA, Japan and the European Union. In each case, however, the attractions of locations offering advantages for agglomeration in the emerging global economic environment are reflected in the emergence of an increasing number of world cities which are beginning to erode the exclusivity of the global city status.

Core regions

The development of the world cities is closely associated with the emergence of economic core regions which offer an innovatory business culture consistent with the information revolution and the more flexible post-Fordist manufacturing and service environment. Corporate headquarters and producer services have been attracted particularly to the traditional centres of finance, business and government. These are the areas which offer the contacts with financial institutions and government, the markets, specialized labour and communications most conducive to economic success in the new circumstances. Such situations are also attractive to high technology and related defence-oriented growth industries. It is likely that the interactive relationships which emerge between producer services and high-technology industry contribute a multiplier effect which accentuates the developmental attractions of the economic core areas. Concentrations of both forms of activities also generate high incomes which support the additional attractions of high order specialized retail, leisure and entertainment facilities. This array of factors lends continued support to the strong regional centralization tendencies associated with the cumulative causation process, and goes a long way to explain the emergence of a 'milieu of innovation' in many of the older concentrations of economic activity (Castells and Hall 1994). London, New York, Tokyo, and Paris have all benefited from the operation of these forces in recent years. The economy of London has been diversifying steadily with the expansion of high-tech industry and research and development activities along the M4 motorway corridor and the 'western crescent' (Figure 5.5). The emergence of a similar concentration in the orbit of Cambridge has added a significant 'northern' component to this trend. A comparable phenomenon has been suggested for south Paris centred on the Cité Scientifique in the Île de France Sud (Castells and Hall 1994). In all these cases, the historical advantages have been adapted to the new circumstances, although the transition has not been entirely spontaneous. In the cases of London and Paris, for example, government defence expenditure has acted as a significant stimulus for high-tech and research and development activities, while in Japan, government coordination of national technologic development via the Ministry of International Trade and Industry (MITI) has been of fundamental importance (Castells and Hall 1994).

Innovatory business activities have also served to accentuate the world city and core region status of locations, which for a variety of reasons, have adapted best to the new economic conditions. This can be best illustrated for the USA. The size and historical evolution of the country predisposed it towards an economic multipolarity, indicated by the status of New York, Chicago, Los Angeles and San Francisco. Recent economic changes, however, have added substantially to the complexity of the situation. Foremost among these

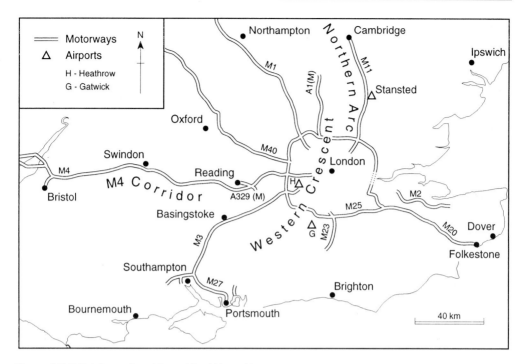

Figure 5.5 Britain's sunrise strip and the M4 corridor

has been the importance of technologic innovation, epitomized by the growth of 'Silicon Valley' south of San Francisco, between Palo Alto and San José. The juxtaposition of scientific knowledge focused on Stanford University and the universities of the Bay area combined with an entrepreneurial environment resulted in the emergence of a concentration of microelectronic and computer based industries employing over 330,000 in 1989 (Castells and Hall 1996). Again, however, government investment in high technology and defence oriented industries, partly reflecting the historical-strategic Pacific location, has been a contributory factor. Similar circumstances have contributed to the economic regeneration of the Boston area in the vicinity of Highway 128 in the period 1975–85, a situation which also has close parallels with the experiences of southern California.

The emergence of smaller core regions and cities claiming world status have also developed elsewhere in the 'Sunbelt'. Initially, this reflected the exploitation of large oil and gas resources assisted by a heritage of low wages, non-unionized labour, low taxation, less government control, and favourable climatic and associated recreational considerations. However, the transition to a broader innovatory economic environment has been accomplished in a number of cases, exemplified by Dallas-Fort Worth and Houston (Figure 5.4). In fact, the Dallas-Fort Worth metropolitan complex had a population of 3.9 million in 1990, with the fourth highest concentration of the headquarters of transnational firms in the USA (Hicks and Nivin 1996).

Comparable trends can be recognized in Europe. Some traditional core regions have accumulated concentrations of the newer forms of economic activities sufficient to sustain cities with claims to a world status. The case of Paris has already been mentioned, while Brussels, Randstad, Milan, Rome, Frankfurt and the cities of the Ruhr also have strong claims to world city status (e.g. Shachar 1994).

Secondary regions and internationalized cities

Other areas which are less favourably located in relation to the global economic networks can, however, benefit from international growth impulses reflecting the global orientation of the national economy in which they are set. They may not accumulate a principal role with respect to international investment and trade, but factors such as their location or availability of trained labour might well prove attractive to the newer forms of manufacture and service employment associated with the post-industrial economy. Such development can have a significant spread effect, modifying the characteristic centralization tendencies within the core areas of the global economy. Again, examples drawn from the USA are illustrative of this effect.

Metropolitan Miami, for example, with a population of 2 million, is not characterized as an international command centre (Nijman 1996). Its peripherality and restricted hinterland limits its international potential. Yet, Miami is increasingly being drawn into the global economy as a financial centre linked to Latin America and as a focus of international tourism. Similarly, the twin cities metropolitan area of Minneapolis-St Paul, originally developed with respect to the regional forestry, agriculture and iron ore resource bases, has substantially diversified its economy in recent years to support a population of 1.8 million (Kaplan and Schwartz 1996). Foreign direct investment from Canada, the Netherlands, the UK, Japan and Germany has reoriented the economy towards high-technology manufacture, particularly of computers and electronic circuits, which accounts for over 50 per cent of the employment. A comparable situation has emerged on the Pacific north-west. Foreign direct investment and international trade is growing in the vicinity of Seattle (2.5 million) and Portland (1.5 million) and the emergence of a 'Cascadia conurbation' extending north to encompass Vancouver appears a distinct possibility (Harvey 1996).

Other examples of increasingly 'internationalized cities' are evident in the European arena. American defence expenditure combined with scientific education and research are considered to underlie the emergence of a concentration of high-technology activities focusing on the Bavarian cities of München and Nürnberg (Castells and Hall 1996), while the southern German province of Baden Würtemberg is developing in a similar manner. The development of 'Third Italy' in the north-eastern province of Emilia-Romagna centred on Bologna has emerged as a comparable growth area. In the UK, a combination of attractions such as good access, skilled labour and environmental amenities have attracted high technology and related service activities to 'Silicon Glen' south of Glasgow and to the Cambridge region ('Silicon Fen'), although the latter is also part of the London economic area.

Newly industrializing countries and the global periphery

From at least the early industrial period, the centre-periphery model has characterized the relationship between the economies of the developed and less developed countries. A combination of imperialism, colonialism and industrialization established an exploitative relationship between the developed and the underdeveloped world based on the acquisition of raw materials, on the development of export market opportunities, and on the aquisition of cheap foodstuffs and labour. Economic development in the developing countries was, therefore, narrowly based and focused on port cities and localized concentrations of natural resources, the characteristic features of a dependent economy.

Since the early 1970s, however, global economic forces have also generated industrialization in parts of the developing world economies of the global periphery. Competition between multinational enterprises increased following the rise in fuel prices associated with the assertion of the strength of the Organization of Petroleum Exporting Countries (OPEC) in 1973. This accentuated the advantages of locations offering lower costs of production and distribution. Subsequent industrial development in the Middle East, focused particularly on the Gulf States and Saudi Arabia, is based largely upon the increase in oil revenues, while a shift of both manufacturing and service activities to countries such as China, India, Brazil and Mexico also reflects the attractions of ease of access to their large domestic markets. In China, for example, considerable urban development has taken place since 1978 as a result of economic restructuring designed to supply the large domestic markets and to develop a stronger involvement in world markets (Xu *et al.* 1995). This has been focused primarily on the east coastal region and the principal metropolitan centres of Shanghai (*c.*12 million) and Beijing (*c.*9 million), reflecting the comparative advantages of a combination of major domestic markets and the opportunity to develop foreign trade.

Development, however, has been attracted particularly to areas offering concentrations of low-cost labour in countries in which the political and social circumstances were perceived as attractive to international investors. The initial focus of activity was on the manufacture of products based on relatively routine production methods requiring low levels of skill such as metal and plastic domestic products, and clothing, but the steady acquisition of improved skills has generated diversification into auto-related manufacture and increasingly sophisticated consumer electronics. Such development, however, has not been widespread, but has been highly concentrated in Hong Kong, Singapore, Taiwan and South Korea, each of which has unusual political circumstances which have assisted their development. Hong Kong and Singapore were largely 'insulated' from potential problems of a developing world situation due to their almost 'city-state' status, although each in recent years has increasingly been linked with adjacent territories to extend their access to low-cost labour reserves. The Shenzhen Economic Zone on mainland China near to Hong Kong has grown to accommodate 3 million people since the mid-1970s, while Singapore is following a 'growth triangle' policy with Malaysia extending over a radius of 50 km. Similarly, the western and Japanese governments have encouraged investment in Taiwan and South Korea due to their international strategic significance. Economic development in Hong Kong, Singapore and Seoul has consequently attracted a significant degree of financial and related service activities, and each has a sufficient regional 'control' function in South-east Asia to have claims for world city status (Friedmann 1995), while the urban concentration of Taipei has a marked degree of primacy in Taiwan. In fact, the level of development in these countries suggests that the term 'rapidly industrializing economies' (RIE) is more appropriate than newly industrializing countries (Drakakis-Smith 1996). Elsewhere, in South-east Asia development has been slower, although development in Thailand and Malaysia are beginning to display the characteristics of newly industrializing countries.

However, most recent analysts suggest that economic development in the NICs has not radically altered the centre-periphery characteristics of the global economy, and a neocolonial dependency situation requiring the intervention of international agencies such as the International Monetary Fund and the World Bank persists for the most part. Trade flows out of the developing countries as a whole are still dominated by primary products and in-flows by manufactured goods. In 1991, for example, manufactured goods to OECD countries from the developing world was still less than 20 per cent, despite an increase from 2 per cent in the early 1970s (Drakakis-Smith 1996). Economic development in most of the developing world countries continued to focus on import substitution industries (ISIs), and domestic markets were still insufficiently large to generate self-sustaining economic growth. Thus, Gwynne (1996b) suggests that if the experiences of Taiwan and South Korea are to be emulated elsewhere, outward-oriented industrialization will need to be stimulated by a combination of strong government economic and infrastructural planning in partnership with free-market investment. However, the prospects of a major transformation is not regarded optimistically in most places in the short term. Thus, while many of the 'mega-cities' of the world, such as Beijing, Shanghai, Bombay, Calcutta, Lagos and Nairobi, have achieved a large degree of primacy in their own countries, their current low degree of global articulation precludes a world city status. Elsewhere, in some of the more developed economies of Latin America and the former 'eastern bloc', economic development based upon home demand and narrower trading links has also resulted in large urban concentrations such as Rio de Janeiro, Buenos Aires and Moscow. Again, they have yet to be firmly integrated into the global economy, although development in China and Latin America, and changes in the former communist bloc could well change this situation in the foreseeable future.

De-industrialization and national peripheries

De-industrialization of the economic peripheries has also been a marked feature of most western industrialized countries since the early 1970s. This reflects a combination of the international competition of the newly industrializing countries in manufacturing and the worldwide economic recession. This has resulted in job losses reflecting a reduction in demand along with the need for greater productivity in the remaining plants. In the British context Massey and Meegan (1982) highlighted the explanatory significance of the interrelated processes of intensification of labour productivity, investment and technical change designed to reduce labour inputs, and the rationalization of production by disinvestment in plant. This has resulted in the gradual collapse of the traditional economies of the older industrial conurbations of the North East, North West, Scotland and Wales, while problems have also been felt intermittently in the formerly prosperous region of the West Midlands. Between the early 1970s and early 1990s manufacturing employment in Britain declined from 7.5 million to 4.3 million, with the job losses occurring primarily in the peripheral older industrial regions (Martin 1993).

These losses have not been compensated by the growth of the new high-tech and related service activities which have been concentrated strongly in the core region of the south and east. Employment in computer software and information technology (IT) services, activities considered to be at the forefront of economic restructuring, exhibited a substantial expansion of 169 per cent in the UK from 54,800 to 147,500 between 1981 and 1991 (Coe 1996). This demonstrated a marked concentration throughout the south-east, with primary foci on the 'western crescent', Cambridge and the M4 corridor. However, an element of regional 'spread' is suggested by the concentration of 'branch' activity in the vicinity of Warrington (Figure 5.6). The growth of these and related service and high-tech employment

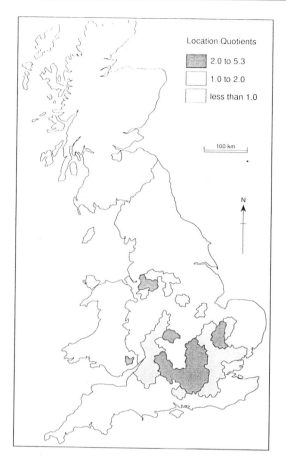

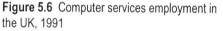

Figure 5.6 Computer services employment in the UK, 1991

is reflected in the period 1979–90 when the number of employees in the south increased by 1.35 million compared with continued losses of 0.2 million in the north (Martin 1993). As a result, the economic health of Britain continues to exhibit a north-south divide, with all but the south and eastern regions suffering the negative effects of stagnation and economic restructuring (Marshall and Wood 1995). The 'north' consequently has all the problems associated with a decaying urban infrastructure and has been able for the most part to attract only weak forms of economic development largely confined to routinized branch plants, usually externally controlled by multinational corporations.

However, negative characterization of the 'north' is not necessarily an immutable feature of the economic geography of the UK. Britain has been increasingly successful since the early 1980s in attracting inward investment in the manufacturing sector. In 1982–3, 133 projects providing over 10,000 jobs were attracted from overseas sources, but this had risen to 434 projects with 88,000 jobs in 1994–5 (Lorenz 1996). In fact, in 1997 the South Korean firm, LG Electronics, initiated its development of a £1.7 billion micro-chip and consumer electronics complex in Newport in South Wales. This will provide over 6,000 jobs and constitutes the largest-ever inward investment into Europe. Subsequently, Hyundai, also based in South Korea, intends to develop an even larger project of two electronics factories in Fife in Scotland (£2.4 billion). Such activity, initiated by the establishment of the Sony plant in South Wales in 1976, has added a significant consumer electronics industry to

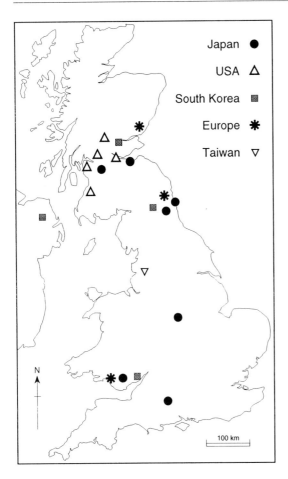

Figure 5.7 Twenty largest overseas investments in manufacturing in the UK, 1975–96

the economy, while Japanese investment has partially regenerated car manufacturing via the activities of Nissan, Honda and Toyota.

Overall, much of this investment has come from Japan, the USA and Europe, along with an interesting reverse flow from the rapidly industrializing South Korea. However, it is notable that much of the largest foreign investments have focused on the peripheral areas of Scotland, the north-east and Wales, in part reflecting a combination of the availability of suitable labour and the activities of the government inward investment agencies, respectively Scottish Enterprise, the Northern Development Company and the Welsh Development Agency (Figure 5.7). While the fundamental north-south economic divide has not yet been redressed, these events at least suggest the potential for reducing regional imbalances, a situation that the regional inward investment agencies are seeking to extend by strengthening local supply chains. However, the degree to which 'local agencies' can manipulate global economic forces remains a highly debatable issue which will be addressed more fully in the next section.

In any event, it may be that the regional regenerative activities will result in a different kind of north-south divide, reflecting differential emphases on manufacture and service employment. However, the end result may, nevertheless, reduce the differentials in standards of living, and create buoyant 'secondary regions' similar to those noted earlier for the USA and Europe. Certainly, Edinburgh, Glasgow and Cardiff already demonstrate strong elements of regional primacy, partly based on their partially separate political identities in Scotland and Wales; equivalent status also exists in Newcastle upon Tyne, Leeds and Sheffield.

However, the problem of peripherality in Britain is considered to continue to act as an obstacle to the reduction of regional imbalances. In effect, it is widely considered that the free market economic ethos espoused by the former Conservative government had maintained the traditional centre-periphery economic divisions and socio-economic inequalities, and has accumulated a heightened political division between an increasingly Conservative south and a Labour north. The commitment of the incoming Labour government (in May 1997) to a 'devolutionist' perspective and to regional economic regeneration may ultimately serve to reduce the divide.

The same trend is also recognized throughout western Europe. The decline of the traditional manufacturing areas combined with the weak development of the tertiary sector has resulted in a familiar pattern of population loss, in association with economic, social and urban environmental problems. This was most evident in north-west Italy centred on Turin and Genoa, in eastern and northern France (Valenciennes), the Saarland and parts of the Ruhr (Duisburg and Essen) of western Germany and throughout southern Belgium (Charleroi) (Cheshire and Hay 1989). The ports within the economic peripheries were considered particularly vulnerable since the development of containerization and roll-on/roll-off facilities has resulted in the loss of trans-shipment functions and processing associated with former breaks-of-bulk. In more recent years, the international competitive effects of globalization have increased the disadvantages of the peripheral areas and accentuated the significance of a non-interventionist neoliberal regulatory environment throughout Europe (Dunford and Perrons 1994). Consequently, a strong pattern of regional inequality has been identified (Figure 5.8). This comprises a 'vital axis' of a 'core' economic region focusing on the more favourably located major international cities and their hinterlands which extends from London, through Germany and Switzerland to northern Italy. By contrast, underdeveloped regions characterize the Atlantic, Mediterranean and 'Ottoman' peripheries, the reduction of uneven development within which is considered to require major planned programmes of public expenditure and decentralization of power to the regional level – both of which eventualities are considered unlikely in the prevailing political climate.

A similar feature is exhibited in the older manufacturing areas of the 'Frostbelt' (Snowbelt, Rustbelt) of the north-east and mid-west of the USA. From the early 1970s to the mid-1980s most of the larger cities lost substantial proportions of their employment in manufacturing, wholesaling and retailing, while the growth of service employment did not compensate for the losses. The situation was particularly problematic in Detroit and St Louis where significant losses were also recorded in the service sector. Employment decline was, however, the general pattern, with substantial net losses evident in Chicago, Newark, Philadelphia, Cleveland and Baltimore. However, more recently, the spread effect associated with the globalization of the US economy has served to reaffirm the status of the cities able to exert a significant regional function in the new economic situation. Chicago, Philadelphia, St Louis and Detroit have been most notable in this respect (Hicks and Nivin 1996).

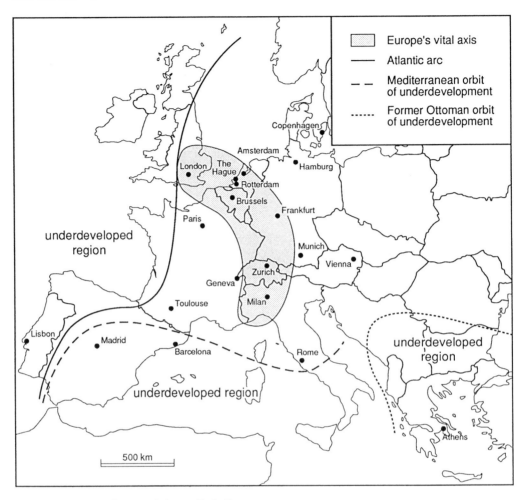

Figure 5.8 Regional economic inequality in Europe

Europe demonstrates an additional dimension of urban deterioration, paradoxically associated with population growth, but still within a general context of economic peripherality. Agricultural restructuring in the poorer rural areas of southern Italy, central Spain, Portugal and Greece has stimulated a rural-urban migration without the development of an equivalent urban employment base. This has created overcrowding and the proliferation for unplanned and under-serviced housing around the edges of cities such as Lisbon, Athens, Salonika, Cagliari, Naples and Palermo, reminiscent of a Third World situation (Cheshire and Hay 1989).

Core regions and counterurbanization

The diseconomies of urban concentration associated with rising land prices, the costs of transport and traffic congestion, competition for labour and the reduction of environmental amenity have for many years asserted the advantages of decentralization within the core regions. The site constraints and transportation considerations have been important to extensive manufacturing space users since the interwar period, while in more recent years the labour availability and amenity factors have proved appealing to routine office functions and high technology industry. The initial response was a suburbanization of industrial employment to free-standing sites or to industrial estates on the fringes of most cities, while office employment gravitated initially to suburban shopping centres and, more latterly, to office parks. The pressures for decentralization have, however, been so great that these intra-urban responses have been succeeded by more marked intra-regional and inter-regional expressions of decentralization termed counter-urbanization. The early definition of counter-urbanization, based on the experiences of the USA in the 1970s, stressed the importance of individual preferences for the environmental attractions of a semi-rural lifestyle and the avoidance of the problems associated with life in big cities (Berry 1976).

Subsequently, counter-urbanization has resulted from the operation of a more complex combination of factors. Among these, the lack of suitable space for the expansion and development of the new forms of employment in the older cities; the attraction of suitable labour; and the availability of lower rents, rates and wage levels in rural areas have been most prominent. In the European context, these forces have been interpreted from a structuralist perspective by Fielding (1982) to reflect the 'logic of capital accumulation'. The migration of jobs is considered to reflect attempts to maximize profits by minimizing labour costs within smaller (compliant) labour pools. Within economic core regions this has resulted in the faster growth of the smaller towns and sub-regional centres in the vicinity of the large conurbations, and often involves migration flows from the central cities and deindustrializing peripheries. Ironically, the migration tends to be socially selective and primarily involves intermediate white-collar and technical operatives, not the semi-skilled and unskilled manual workers displaced from the declining industrial sectors. Characteristically, the largest cities demonstrate net population losses, while gains are highest in the medium and smaller settlements in the growth regions (Champion 1992). The process was a well-established feature of urbanization in the USA in the 1970s, and a similar decentralization of service employment and high technology industry was also identified widely throughout western Europe in the same period. This has been particularly marked in Britain since the mid-1970s, and was closely associated with the gravitation of new high technology and defence-related industries to the small and medium-sized towns of the South East, South West, the East Midlands and East Anglia. In the south-east of England the resulting 'dispersed city' form, extending from Southampton-Portsmouth, through Surrey and Berkshire, north-westward to Hertfordshire, Northampton and Cambridge has been described as Britain's Sunbelt (Figure 5.5), with close parallels drawn with California's Silicon Valley (Boddy *et al.* 1986).

However, by the 1980s, counter-urbanization was already emerging as a far more complex phenomenon than had at first been imagined. In some countries it had declined in significance by the early to mid-1980s as the attractions of core regions had begun to reassert themselves, sometimes as a reflection of government regenerative policies. This was the situation in the USA, while Japan, Norway, Sweden, Finland, Spain and Italy also exhibited this trend (Champion 1992), although counter-urbanization had beeen reasserted in the USA by the late 1980s and early 1990s. By contrast, counter-urbanization has continued in south-east England, France, Germany, the Netherlands and Denmark to the late 1990s. Evidently, the tendency towards deconcentration promoted by the array of factors noted above can be redressed by countervailing forces. While, for example, the areas outside the influence of the larger cities might retain amenable lifestyle advantages, the availability of suitable labour and space is not as easily predictable; while public policy can improve the diseconomies of urban concentration by infrastructural and regenerative environmental initiatives. Similarly, the growth of the 'information economy' has reasserted the attractions of core areas, while the larger cities are usually the primary focus of migrants to those countries with significant elements of international immigration. Furthermore, other complex demographic trends can create intra-regional and inter-regional changes in population concentration which have little to do with counter-urbanization *per se*. Variations in fertility reflecting differential age structures between urban and rural areas, for example, can result in population changes which do not reflect economically induced migration flows. Likewise, migration to retirement locations can create important demographic changes, but these have little to do with counter-urbanization as defined above.

Thus, while there may be underlying tendencies towards counter-urbanization in many countries, this may not be expressed everywhere as net migration flows from the older central cities to more attractive peripheral areas within growing economic regions. The demographic changes and associated changes in population concentration in the developed economies are, therefore, likely to be far more complex due to the variety of factors involved, and the relative importance of these factors are likely to vary significantly in relation to the economic and societal specifics of particular countries. For these reasons, Sant and Simons (1993) have argued that counter-urbanization should no longer be examined as a simple pattern, but treated as a process of regional restructuring, the causes and consequences of which can be both complex and variable. In effect, while there may be an underlying tendency towards population deconcentration in wealthy urbanized countries, its strength, the reasons for it, and the particular way in which it manifests itself require more detailed examination of the economic and social forces involved. In fact, it may well be that there will be a retreat from the strictures imposed by concept of counter-urbanization towards a wider investigation of the causes of population redistribution, probably reflecting complex combinations of economic 'job-led' and environmental ('people-led') attractions (Champion 1997). A significant move in this direction is indicated by a refocusing of analysis upon the theories and issues associated with migration into rural areas throughout the developed world rather than the narrower conception of counter-urbanization (Boyle and Halfacree 1997).

The intra-urban dimension of economic change

Economic changes has also been reflected in the land-use patterns and the social geography of the city. Concentrations of employment are an important element of the urban fabric, and these have been subject to substantial physical and functional change. The distribution of manufacturing in the industrial city reflected the importance of historical influences (Figure 5.9). Early industrialization, based upon bulky raw materials and fuels, asserted the locational advantages of sites suitable for river transport, canals and railways, outside the already congested pre-industrial city. In such locations relatively large amounts of cheap land were usually available which offered advantages for ease of assembly of raw materials and the distribution of manufactured products, as well as access to water for use in the production processes and for waste disposal. Inner city industrial concentrations such as these were a

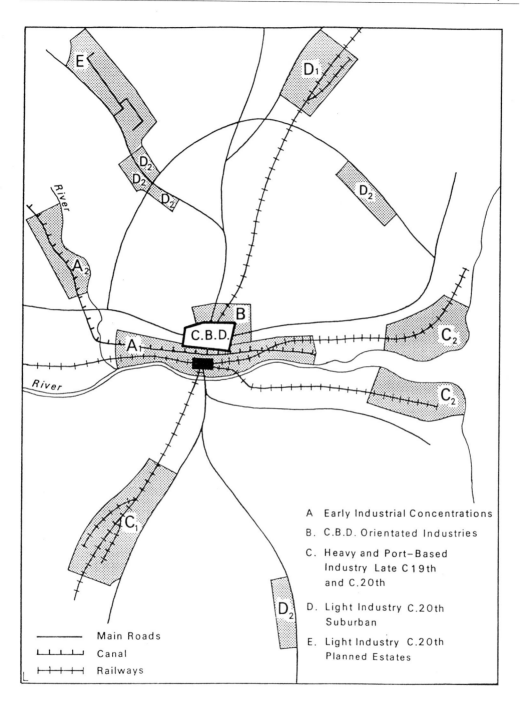

Figure 5.9 A generalized model of manufacturing areas in cities

well-marked feature of most major British cities (A). At the same time, the expanding central business districts attracted a variety of associated functions such as wholesaling, warehousing and business machine maintenance, while the early concentration of newspaper offices often attracted printing and publishing to city centre sites (B). The availability of cheap immigrant or itinerant labour in the low-status 'transition zones' which developed around the expanding city centres also encouraged the development of small-scale manufacturing. The garment trades of New York, London and Paris are well known examples of this phenomenon.

Subsequently, with the growth in scale of heavy industry towards the end of the nineteenth century the need emerged for large railway-based sites on the peripheries of cities (C1), while the use of larger ocean-going vessels necessitated the migration of port-based industries from early waterfront sites to large estuarine or reclaimed coastal locations (C2). In Britain the decline of the London docks and the development of the Thames estuary was indicative of this trend, as was the concentration of heavy engineering and chemicals on Teesside; the postwar development of Europoort, Rotterdam is a spectacular example of the same process.

With the expansion of road transport and electrical power in the twentieth century, the newly developing light industries gravitated to the less congested and environmentally more attractive suburban peripheries (D). Nevertheless, the process of dispersal was not entirely unconstrained since the need for communications and public utilities promoted a degree of centralization within the suburbs. Later, to offset the environmental disadvantages of uncoordinated dispersal, the planning of industrial estates by public authorities in Britain and the zoning of land for industrial parks in the USA had a similar effect (E). To this pattern has been added the development of office employment. The initial concentration of offices in the central business districts has been followed by a decentralization of many routine operations to the vicinity of the major suburban shopping centres of the largest cities and, ultimately, to the development of office parks and suburban downtowns (see Chapter 8).

This pattern of employment opportunities has been modified substantially by the economic changes since the early 1970s. The shift towards a service-dominated economy has generated a considerable demand for office space for corporate headquarters, related producer services and government administration in all major cities. This has created a buoyant demand for office space in the traditional concentrations in the central business districts, sometimes displacing some of their traditional functions. In London, the decentralization of newspaper printing and publishing from Fleet Street to the Docklands, and fruit and vegetable wholesaling from Covent Garden to Nine Elms, has been accompanied by an increased concentration of finance and business services in these areas. A similar trend has generated a substantial commercial revival in the CBDs of many of the cities in the USA which have attracted the headquarters of transnational firms (Hicks and Nivin 1996). At the same time, office expansion has been a continuing feature in the established suburban nodes of the largest cities and in the wider regional context of counter-urbanization noted earlier.

At the intra-urban scale, however, the adverse effects of de-industrialization have also been widespread. Employment in manufacturing has been lost on a prodigious scale in most major industrial cities, and particularly in the principal conurbations. This has been exacerbated in port cities by the loss of goods-handling activities associated with technological changes and rationalization in bulk goods-handling. These changes have not been confined to the peripheral regions of countries. Inner London lost 45 per cent of its manufacturing employment in the period 1971–81, while Birmingham, Liverpool and Glasgow exhibited similar situations. In the USA the situation was substantially the same. St Louis, for example, suffered a prolonged period of urban decline and a central city population loss of 47 per cent between 1950 and 1980 (Cheshire and Hay 1989), while the decline of the Chicago stockyards was a spectacular example of the same effect. This has resulted in the widespread abandonment of the large former industrial sites in inner cities and in the obsolete docklands.

In most of the older industrial cities, and particularly in the 'peripheral' economic regions, this has resulted in the creation of industrial dereliction over extensive parts of the inner cities. The poor urban environment and high rates of unemployment among the relatively immobile semi-skilled and unskilled former industrial workers have combined to create disadvantageous economic and social conditions which have been associated with social problems such as delinquency, criminality, alcoholism and drug abuse; in short, the inner city problem. In the USA and UK this has been accentuated by the ethnic minority dimension. The low levels of social and physical mobility, particularly of the black and Hispanic groups, associated with discriminatory practices in employment and house sales have served to heighten the poor conditions of such areas.

In recent years, however, in the older industrial cities which have benefited from the pressures of post-industrial economic growth many of the formerly derelict sites have been subject to regeneration resulting in a positive transformation of the urban environment. The Quincy Market redevelopment of central Boston is a small-scale example of this effect, similar to Covent Garden in London and the Les Halles redevelopment into the Forum and Pompidou Centre in Paris. On a larger scale the Harbour Place redevelopment of the Baltimore waterfront has created a shopping and hotel 'festival market-place' which is estimated to attract over 20 million visitors per year. This has its counterpart in the Harbourside scheme in Sydney and its extension into the Darling Harbour shopping, convention and exhibition centre complex, including a monorail rapid transit link to the central business district. In Canada every major city has developed similar schemes in inner city locations, particularly where 'waterfront' development opportunities have presented themselves (Hoyle 1996).

The redevelopment of the London Docklands is an even more extensive example of the same effect. Pressures for central area development have been channelled eastward from the traditional commercial core of the 'City' to the adjacent 40 square kilometres of former dockland. The redevelopment of such an extensive area required coordination so the former Conservative government established an Enterprise Zone incentive scheme in 1980 to stimulate development in the Isle of Dogs, while the commercially orientated London Docklands Development Corporation was appointed for the remaining area in 1981 (Figure 5.10). This has resulted in a redevelopment programme which includes extensive areas of housing, the relocation of most of the national newspapers from Fleet Street, the development of office complexes, and a small airport. A major office complex of around 0.8 million square metres, designed to employ in excess of 60,000 people, has been constructed at Canary Wharf. A heritage of urban decay and an obsolete dock system are being transformed into a prestigious commercial, residential and recreational environment. Physically and socially 'secure' residential development predominates, characterized by 'postmodernist bunker architecture' symptomatic of the social polarization noted earlier in

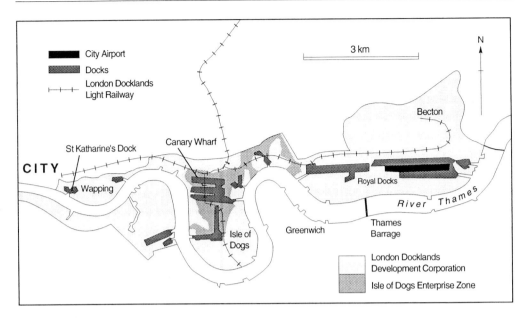

Figure 5.10 Urban redevelopment: the London Docklands

modern world cities; this is the natural habitat of the yuppies (young upwardly mobile professionals) working in the financial and related service sector (Short 1989).

The regeneration of extensive derelict sites has not, however, solved the social problems of the inner city; quite the contrary. The majority of the new job opportunities are in professional occupations, while most of the new residential development is oriented towards the middle to upper status market, as is the gentrification of the old. The immobile, unemployed, semi-skilled and unskilled population in the inner city are largely unable to benefit from the process of change ('yuffies' – young urban failures). Apart from a minority of inner city residents involved in the more menial domestic and cleaning occupations associated with the growth in hotels, restaurants and high-status housing, the economic opportunities available to the resident population are not significantly improved. This constitutes a 'mismatch' between job types and employee types in the context of an increasingly service-oriented economy. Thus, social polarization is increased in the inner city, particularly if the resident population is predominantly composed of ethnic minority groups (Sassen 1991). In these circumstances, it is not surprising that alienation and demoralization are features of inner city life and civil disorder has been an intermittent feature of the US city since the late 1960s. In Britain, the emergence of similar situations in Toxteth (Liverpool), Birmingham, Bristol, and the London districts of Hackney and Brixton in the 1980s and 1990s are based upon broadly comparable conditions.

In the peripheral areas which have not benefited from economic growth, the adverse environmental impact of urban dereliction also continues to be problematic. This is particularly evident in Britain where little redevelopment has occurred without government policy initiatives:

- Inner city partnerships of local authorities and government departments were established under the Inner Urban Areas Act 1978, for Liverpool, Manchester-Salford,

Birmingham, Newcastle-Gateshead, Hackney-Islington and Lambeth.

- Urban development corporations were created in 1980 for the London and Merseyside docklands and similar schemes have been initiated subsequently in all the major conurbations. These have adopted a commercial orientation and aim to work closely with the private sector.
- Enterprise zones were also established in 1980 in derelict inner city sites throughout the country, offering a relaxed planning regime and financial incentives designed to attract new employment. In the peripheral regions they appear to have mainly redistributed development rather than attracted significant new investment, while, in the absence of investment in manufacturing, retail development has been a common response (see also Chapters 8 and 11).

These measures have been supplemented by the redevelopment of relatively restricted sites which are sufficiently advantageously located to attract private investment for residential, leisure or commercial users. Usually, such schemes are oriented towards a niche in the local market rather than reflecting economic regeneration. The transformation of part of the former Swansea docklands into the residential Marina Quarter and the redevelopment of Salford Quays are typical examples.

Despite this array of activity and the associated environmental improvement of some inner city locations, the adverse economic and social consequences of deindustrialization in the cities of the north and west have not been substantially redressed by these essentially local urban initiatives. In the absence of comprehensive central government intervention to redistribute the economic growth impulses to the disadvantaged regions it seems unlikely that the existing policy instruments can have more than a local 'cosmetic' effect on the inner city problem.

Globalism, localism and the regional question

The economic restructuring associated with contemporary world economic changes are clearly capable of generating complex spatial changes at the global and regional scales. However, much of the literature in urban political economy relating to globalization implies an economically deterministic explanation for the great majority of the associated social, geographical and political transformations of cities (Graham 1995). The essence of the globalist view is that contemporary levels of economic success of countries, regions or cities is a direct reflection of a favourable positioning on the global network of multinational corporations, irrespective of location in a national economy. In such a situation any particular locale or region is powerless to stimulate substantial economic development, and is largely reduced to marketing the locale ('place marketing') to ameliorate rather than resolve economic, social, or political problems. The opportunity for 'planning' at global, national regional or local scales, therefore, to ameliorate the problems of uneven development is severely restricted.

The alternative localist view has, however, been gaining considerable ground in recent years. This asserts that due to the 'footloose' characteristics of many of the new forms of high-technology industry and associated service activities, and the reduction of the 'friction of distance' associated with innovations in information technology, the specific characteristics of localities can exert a significant influence on the economic development process (Cooke 1989). Features such as the characteristics of the workforce, the existence of an entrepreneurial milieu, the creation of suitable promotional agencies and a conducive regulatory regime, or the existence of a particularly amenable environment, are considered capable of modifying the global forces for local advantage. Amin and Thrift (1995) stress the local developmental importance of interaction between economic factors and a wide array of social networks of firms, financial institutions, chambers of commerce and trade, training agencies, local and national government agencies, development agencies, innovation centres and marketing boards. The synergy necessary to promote local development was termed 'institutional thickness'. In essence, despite the undoubted strength of the forces associated with globalization, there is an increased potential for local policy-makers to improve the economic fortunes of their cities through appropriate local strategies. The development of secondary core regions and the regeneration of some of the older industrial areas noted in earlier sections conform with this view.

However, while these authors suggest that individual locales or cities are capable of creating a milieu capable of stimulating development, they also imply that the development impulses are more likely to be successful if mobilized via subnational agencies of governance, articulated at the regional level. Cooke (1996), for example, stresses the need to interlink local and regional institutions as agents of redevelopment, expressed in terms of a 'networked regional innovation architecture' drawn from a combination of the public and private sector agencies. Older industrial areas are seen as requiring the development of innovative infrastructure based on vertical and lateral networks between large and small firms, supported by research institutions promoting technology transfer. The German example of Baden Würtemberg and the Emilia-Romagna scheme in Italy are presented as models for regional regeneration, while redevelopment in Wales, the Spanish provinces of Catalonia, Valencia and the Basque country, North Rhine-Westphalia, and the peripheral parts of Pennsylvania are all considered to be assisted by the same mechanisms. Support for the importance of the regional dimension and regional agencies in the regeneration of older industrial areas is also suggested for the countries of the European Union. Lever (1996) indicates that the establishment of the European Regional Development Fund in 1975 and the progressive expansion of regional agencies and strategies in ensuing years has initiated a significant convergence between centres and peripheries.

However, despite the euphoric claims of the localist and regionalists, the extent to which local institutions are able to redress the uneven spatial distribution of economic advantages associated with globalization remains debateable. Doubts have been expressed for the British situation by Lovering (1995) in an evocatively entitled article: 'Creating discourses rather than jobs: the crisis in the cities and the transitional fantasies of intellectuals and policy makers'.

The view is taken that the reliance of the 'new localist' outlook on entrepreneurial initiative rather than a stronger traditional 'welfarist' focus is a significant weakness. In the UK, financial controls and broad economic policy strategies remain centralized. In these circumstances, it is suggested that there is little real evidence of 'local' regeneration. Instead, the activities of the plethora of economic development departments in local authorities, the regional redevelopment agencies, the Urban Development Corporations designed to harness private investment, and the Training and Enterprise Councils are 'creating discourses rather than jobs', and are more active in 'place marketing' and the 'management of social distress' than in instituting fundamental economic restructuring. A substantial centre-periphery economic polarization is portrayed as an enduring feature of the space economy which will require a much stronger (probably governmental) apparatus to redress.

However, the wider international perspective adopted by Castells and Hall (1994) is more cautiously optimistic of the potential redistributive effects of 'local' intervention. They also subscribe to the view that contemporary economic health reflects a favourable positioning in relation to the agglomerative advantages of global economic forces. The developmental potential of a 'milieu of innovation' based on the synergetic links between the headquarters of multinational enterprises, research and development, high-technology manufacture, and access to expertise and information technology is particularly stressed.

Primarily, these forces are seen as confirming the dominant status of the core regions comprising the older major metropolitan areas such as London, Tokyo, New York and Paris which have adapted previous advantage to the new circumstances. However, they are also seen as responsible for the development of the other smaller complexes which have managed to create an active 'milieu of innovation' and assume a commanding position in the new world order. Silicon Valley is presented as the archetypal case, while the experiences of Los Angeles, Boston and Cambridge are considered to reflect a similar array of forces. The

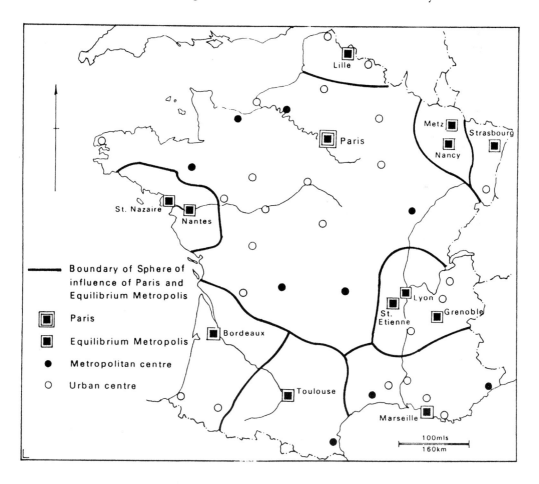

Figure 5.11 Equilibrium metropoles and metropolitan centres in France

Figure 5.12 The Tokaido corridor and technopoles in Japan

experiences of Bavaria, Baden Würtemberg and Emilia-Romagna are smaller scale examples of a similar effect, while in the rapidly industrializing countries, developments in Singapore, Hong Kong, Seoul and Taipei are broadly comparable cases.

The redistributive logic of these cases is presented as the need to replicate similar 'milieux of innovation' in less spontaneously advantaged locations to 'spread' the generative influences more widely. These ideas are a natural progression from the traditional regional planning principle of 'comparative advantage' whereby decentralization policies should focus on those locations and resources which are most likely to attract new development. In effect, the development of new 'technopoles' to regenerate industrial peripheries or to spread development to reduce the 'diseconomies' of congestion in the core regions is an updated extension of the 'growth poles', epitomized by the French *métropoles d'équilibre*, into the modern idiom (Figure 5.11). The development of technopoles of Sophia-Antipolis near Nice and Meylan near Grenoble are indicative of this trend, continuing the interventionist central government role in regional redistributive policy (Fielding 1994).

To date, however, Japan is the only country which has comprehensively applied the technopolis concept as an instrument for regional development, and the examination of this case has yielded instructive results (Castells and Hall 1994). In the early 1980s one-half of the population of Japan was concentrated in the 300 mile Tokaido corridor connecting Tokyo with Nagoya and Osaka, while one-half of the employment in manufacturing was located in Greater Tokyo. Thus, the technopolis programme was initiated to reduce congestion in this area and to promote development in the peripheral regions. Since 1979, 26 technopoles have been designated (Figure 5.12) by the Ministry of International Trade and Industry based on regional centres with existing populations of over 150,000. In these cities, government investment in research universities, industrial parks and the training in engineering skills has been combined with the encouragement of private investment to develop alternative growth nodes. Evidence of decentralization exists, but the policy has not been entirely successful. The technopoles achieving most growth were the eight closest to Tokyo, suggesting an intra-regional rather than a national impact. Furthermore, much of the decentralization was of 'branch plants' in search of cheap sites, while inter-industry linkages and leading-edge research and development service activities were conspicuously absent. In effect, a partial modification of the forces of decentralization are evident rather than a radical restructuring of the uneven distribution of development.

It appears that a favourable positioning in relation to the global economic forces is fundamental to the potential for regional development. By contrast, the redistributive manipulation of these forces to reduce the strong tendencies towards uneven development appears to require considerable 'governmental' intervention, and even then the likelihood of success continues to be debatable. This suggests the continued persistence of centre-periphery economic relations within countries, particularly in the context of a neoliberal regulatory environment in which state interventionist policies are at a minimum.

Summary

The central theme of the preceding discussion has been the effect of economic changes on the patterns and problems of urban development at a variety of spatial scales. It was particularly apparent that international economic considerations have become increasingly important since the mid-1970s, to a degree that, without an appreciation of economic globalization, it is not possible to understand the complex nature of worldwide urban change and the manner in which it affects particular countries, or indeed particular cities. The concentration of investment and trade in the developed economies, focusing on the Triad of the European Union, USA and Japan has been a marked feature of the development process. The economic impact of globalization has tended to concentrate development in a relatively small number of global cities, world cities and core regions, which play a 'commanding' role in global economic development. New core regions have also developed in areas which either are favourably situated on the global economic networks, or have been able to create an innovatory business environment. An element of 'spread' can be detected in secondary regions which have been able to adapt to the new conditions. This lends support to the potential redistributive effects of 'local' initiatives, particularly when articulated at the regional scale and supported by active regional 'agencies'.

However, redistribution of growth impulses, particularly to declining older industrial peripheries and inner cities, continues to require strong government initiatives both to provide infrastructural support and to stimulate private investment. Precise blueprints for effective urban and regional regeneration strategies have not yet been developed.

At the same time, most of the developing countries of the global periphery have remained marginal to and 'dependent' upon the mainstream of world economic development. The experiences of the newly industrializing countries have been viewed as exceptions rather than the rule, although more optimistic commentators regard these examples as prototypes for the future development of the countries of the global periphery. In the short term, however, the prospects for the global economic integration of the periphery appear both slight and politically problematic. In this situation, the growth of 'mega-cities', largely divorced from the economic development process, are more likely to exacerbate than resolve the problems of global economic polarization.

CHAPTER 6

The system of control: local government, local governance and the local state

In Chapter 3 it was demonstrated that the intra-urban spatial structure of cities reflects a combination of the specifics of their historical origins and evolution, along with the level of economic development and political ethos of the surrounding society. In all societies, however, the process of urban growth has necessitated a degree of coordinated control to minimize the potentially adverse impacts of conflicting land-uses, and to ensure the efficient functioning of the economic and social life of the city. Historically, the maintenance of the health of the city by the abolition of infectious diseases often precipitated the development of legislative controls and the provision of public utility services such as pure water supplies and efficient sewage disposal systems. The steadily increasing spatial concentration and spread of cities has served to confirm the need for the control and organization of an ever-widening range of services designed to preserve the efficiency and quality of urban life. In most countries, however, the size of the state and its associated bureaucracy is too large for the control of urban areas and the representation of local issues to be undertaken by a central organization. Central governments are concerned primarily with national and international issues and are usually too remote from local issues to be sufficiently responsive to local needs. This provides the basic reason for the development of local government or the local state. Since such organizations have increasingly influenced the details of the processes and patterns of urban growth throughout the twentieth century a consideration of their impact is opportune at this point.

The functions of local government and the local state

There are alternative views on the functions of the local state. The pragmatic basis of local government has been explored by Sharpe (1976) who identified its three major functions as promoting liberty, participation and efficient service provision. Local forms of organization provide liberty by acting as a counter to the lack of local responsiveness usually associated with overcentralization. Participation in the process of government was also considered likely to be enhanced by some form of local electoral accountability and control. Similarly, local organizations were considered most likely to maximize the efficiency of service provision since they were well placed close to the point of service delivery to assess local needs. This rationale of local government represents a consensus perspective emanating from a liberal-democratic tradition. Emphasis is placed on the maintenance of the status quo by making central government responsive to local problems by a system of local organizations operating in a functionalist manner through a series of balances and checks.

In the early 1980s, however, an alternative conflict or dissensus view of local government gained considerable support. This had its origins in the Marxist interpretation of the capitalist state and has now evolved to offer a materialist-structuralist dimension or political economy perspective on the nature and functioning of local government and the local state. The local state is seen as a natural but dependent extension of the central state, and is developed to further the aims of the state. In the capitalist state Saunders (1980) identified three principal functions of the local state. It assists the promotion of private production and capital accumulation by providing the infrastructure of transport, land-use planning, and the wide array of public utility services necessary to sustain the local economy. It provides for the reproduction of labour by providing services designed, for example, to educate and train the labour force; to house in public sector accommodation those who cannot afford a home of their own; and to provide for the cultural and recreational needs commensurate with the maintenance of a 'contented' (compliant) workforce. At the same time, the local state is responsible for the maintenance of social order by providing policing and social welfare functions. Thus, the essence of the argument is that the local state is supportive of the capitalist state by promoting economic efficiency and ensuring that potential conflicts between capital and labour are minimized.

Johnston (1982a) subscribes to the latter view of the local state and offers additional supportive speculations. It is, for example, convenient for infrastructural facilities to be provided in accordance with local needs. This has the additional advantage of deflecting complaints or diffusing conflict away from the central state, while the involvement of local decision-making adds to the legitimation of the central state. Moreover, the establishment of a competitive relationship between spatially fragmented local states, for example, for the attraction of employment opportunities by offering infrastructural inducements, diverts additional finance towards capital accumulation, while automatically reducing expenditure on social forms of 'non-productive' collective consumption.

However, both these perspectives were developed largely in the context of western industrial societies in which local government had a strong 'managerial' role in controlling land-use planning and providing a wide range of urban services. This reflected a liberal-democratic and welfarist tradition associated with strong Keynesian state controls over national economies (see also Chapter 5). Since the mid-1980s, with the post-industrial growth of global competition, the economic sovereignty of the nation-state has declined and most western governments have had to be more mindful of market forces. Most have moved towards a neoliberal mode of economic regulation whereby 'unproductive' public service expenditure has been cut in order to make more capital available for private investment. In effect, much greater precedence has been afforded to private enterprise in the process of capital accumulation. This has been reflected in the reduction in welfare state expenditure and the gradual privatization of many services formerly provided by local government. Thus, local government is being replaced by a broader conception of 'local governance' in which a fragmented combination of public, private and voluntary agencies deliver services once provided by the local state. In this situation, local government becomes only one of many forces affecting the local environment and local service delivery system, and local development in the post-industrial city is increasingly influenced by market forces and quangos (quasi-autonomous non-governmental organizations).

In these complex new and changing conditions relatively little is known empirically about the precise way in which the new forms of local governance are functioning. However, concepts emerging from the discourses of 'regulation theory', which aim to understand the complex manner in which macro-economic changes are related to social and political change in the local state, are beginning to enlighten the debate (Mayer 1995). The function of local government has been characterized as changing from 'provider' to 'enabler', while the 'managerialism' of the industrial era is being replaced by a post-industrial 'entrepreneurialism' (Davoudi 1995).

In most western countries it is not possible to distinguish clearly whether the consensus, conflict or neoliberal interpretation of the local state is more appropriate to an understanding of the manner in which it currently functions. Does local governance serve a purely pragmatic function designed to enhance the overall quality of life by providing services and reconciling conflicting local aims? Is it an agent operating primarily to promote the aims of capitalist accumulation? Or is it a much more complex combination of these situations? These questions cannot be answered with any degree of precision since they require an intimate knowledge of the motives of, and pressures upon, central governments. Furthermore, the relative significance of the interpretations is likely to vary over time and between countries. Nevertheless, it is likely that under most forms of modern capitalism each has some relevance. Thus, the alternative perspectives on the functions of the local state provide a useful contextual framework offering insights into the potential effects of local government agencies on the nature of urban life.

The spatial structure of local government

Whatever the broad societal functions of the local state, the influence of the agencies of local government on the geography of the city reflects a combination of its degree of executive independent power, its spatial structure and the specific activities which it can perform. Local government is most usually characterized by a hierarchical form of organization as the central government operates in a 'diffusive' way downwards through a number of increasingly localized levels. Within this general framework, however, there is scope for considerable variation. The levels can vary with respect to their degree of financial and political autonomy. The elected state legislatures of the USA, for example, have considerable independence from Federal government control for the provision of a wide range of services such as highways and social security. This far exceeds the powers of the second tier of county councils (and emerging unitary authorities) in the UK. Similarly, despite tendencies towards tiered hierarchical structures comprising regional, metropolitan and community levels, the precise number of levels as well as their relative spatial extents and population sizes can be subject to marked variations, even within a single country. Likewise, substantial variations exist between countries in the range of functions performed by broadly comparable units; while the situation can be complicated further, as in the USA, by the creation of special district jurisdictions frequently performing single functions. Such variations tend to reflect the political-historical development of a country in combination with the range of local services to be provided and the nature of the problems to be resolved.

Thus, in western cities, despite a degree of underlying communality of issues and problems, the nature of the local government administrative system and the manner in which it affects the geography of the city can vary widely. The local government system of the USA is, for example, characterized by considerable spatial and functional fragmentation. At the opposite extreme, the system in the UK has for most of the twentieth century conformed to a neatly hierarchical spatial structure, with only limited variations throughout the country. Most other western countries fall between these two extremes. Sharpe (1995), for example, has suggested for Europe a 'napoleonic' group comprising Spain, France, Italy, Belgium, Portugal and Greece, where fragmentation of power at the local municipal level is still marked, although various 'regional' forms have been inserted in an intermediate position. By contrast a northern European group of Sweden, Norway, Denmark and Germany have undertaken significant reforms which veer more towards the British experience. Evidence from the USA and the UK forms the basis of the ensuing discussion since they represent 'polar' types on the continuum between administrative fragmentation and hierarchical order. Consequently, they provide insights into the effects of these markedly contrasting local political systems on the processes of urban growth, elements of which are present to varying degrees in most other western countries. However, examples from parts of the world will also be introduced to develop broader comparisons.

The local government system of the USA: spatial and functional fragmentation

From its earliest political origins the development of the local government system of the USA has maintained a premium on the importance of local democracy. This has been manifest in a strong tradition supporting the decentralization of political authority which was accentuated by a history of gradual colonization. Thus, local autonomy, the associated importance of property ownership interests, and a political ethos which has incorporated only a weak element of directive-compulsion from government at all levels, are basic to an understanding of the nature of the local government system and the manner in which it has influenced urban development. The local government system reflects directly these considerations. The individual **states** are, for example, of considerable importance to the political life of the country. They are more important spenders on service provision than the Federal government and retain control over transport, housing, health, safety and welfare. The Federal government has only an indirect control over these functions by offering grants or inducements to act in accordance with wider Federal policies. Below this level the **county** was initially the basic unit of political devolution for the rural areas, with the range of services provided related to their populations (Johnston 1982b). In counties without substantial clusters of settlements the legal minimum of services provided are policing, road maintenance and public welfare, but more populous units offer a broader base of public utilities such as sewage disposal and refuse collection.

In the nineteenth century, however, the growth of large cities necessitated the incorporation of urban **municipalities** for the control of service provision independent of the counties. This accentuated the spatial fragmentation of the local government system since relatively small suburban concentrations often comprising as few as 500 residents were able to petition for incorporation as separate municipalities. This also resulted in a functional fragmentation because the range of powers devolved from the counties varied relative to the population of the new units. Initially, the problem of coordinating service provision between municipalities in the growing metropolitan areas was resolved by state support for the annexation of the smaller units by the larger central cities.

By 1900, however, states had become nervous of the growth of the potential political influence of the largest cities. This combined with suburban preferences to avoid the financial burdens associated with the management of the inner areas of modern industrial metropoli, and was exacerbated in the postwar period by the increasing ghettoization of the inner city. Together, these forces ensured widespread state support for the preservation of the autonomy of the suburban interests. Thus, annexation has virtually ceased for much of the twentieth century and the fragmented administrative structure illustrated by Figure 6.1 and characterized by Johnston (1982b) as 'municipal balkanisation' is the usual result.

The problems of coordinating service provision resulting from this process introduced further complexity with the incorporation of ad hoc **special districts**. These were designed to offer a single service such as policing, fire services or transportation planning to a specified area by overriding municipal boundaries. The majority, however, are the school districts, established usually to include areas of relatively homogenous social character in order to retain a degree of social and ethnic exclusivity. The potential complexity of a bewildering array of local administrations, each with the power to raise and spend money, is illustrated graphically by the 1,500 units operating in the New York Metropolitan Region. This has resulted in a fundamental political and social dualism between central cities and suburbs, which is frequently compounded by divisions between one suburb and another. The resulting segregation is basic to an understanding of many of the urban conflicts within the US city in the twentieth century, graphically illustrated for Los Angeles by Davis (1990).

Administrative fragmentation has had major implications for the spatial structure of cities

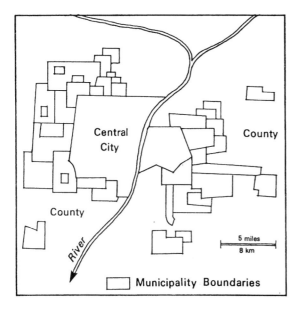

Figure 6.1 The local government structure of the USA

and for the degree of social segregation of residential areas. Most municipalities have zoning powers to control land-use. In practice exclusionary zoning has been the typical response, designed to retain the residential status and environmental quality of an area. This has been accomplished by discouraging high-density developments likely to attract low-income groups and ethnic minorities. Noxious and costly-to-service industrial development has similarly been excluded, while revenue-generating light industry or shopping malls have sometimes been encouraged by financial inducements to locate in non-intrusive locations to enhance the local tax base. In effect, policies have aimed consistently to minimize 'negative externalities' and maximize 'positive externalities' offered by the opportunities provided by the 'jurisdictional partitioning'.

The application of such policies across metropolitan regions has produced recurring geographical results. The larger and older central cities tend to retain only the least attractive industrial development. Here also will be concentrated the lowest status white and ethnic minority groups whose unemployment levels will be accentuated by the migration of the newer opportunities to suburban locations beyond their travel limits. Both the industrial and social areas of such central cities are costly to service, particularly since they are located at the hub of the intra-city transportation network. This necessitates high rates of property taxation on a usually declining tax base. By contrast, the administrative fragmentation combined with the greater mobility of the middle classes and the attractions of suburban life have encouraged suburbanization by allowing them to 'vote with their feet'. The higher status suburbs are also less costly to service and can consequently offer the additional incentive of low levels of property taxation. The resulting fiscal dislocation between central city and suburbs acts to the continued disadvantage of the centre and has precipitated a spiral decline in the quality of the environment and its efficient functioning. This is summed up in the notion of the urban crisis. In extreme situations some central city administrations have become virtually bankrupt, the most spectacular example of which was the case of New York in October 1975 (Johnston 1982a). This was not an isolated incident. New York suffered a similar budget deficit of $3.5 billion in 1991, which seriously undermined the political credibility of the then mayor, David Dinkins. Washington DC also approached a comparable situation in December 1994. The smaller city (c.575,000) reported a likely budget deficit of $500 million, while major concerns at a rising crime rate and declining quality of a wide range of services fuelled speculation of mismanagement and corruption in city administration.

Paradoxically, however, many suburban residents continue to work in the concentrations of business activities in the CBD and use the associated historical concentrations of cultural, entertainment and recreational facilities. This indicates the existence of an exploitative relationship between suburbs and central cities, and the characterization of the suburban residents as 'free-riders'.

The intermittent financial crises suffered by central city administrations have, however, not resulted in radical 'structural changes' to the local government system. Instead, financial aid has been obtained from lending institutions or from state and Federal agencies, all of whom have tended to impose budgetary restraint to 'solve' the problem rather than substantially improve the situation of the inner cities. This represents a veiled movement in the direction of increased political centralization. This reflects the unwillingness of the suburban communities to voluntarily relinquish their entrenched financial, social and racial advantages, while state governments have been loth to alienate their political strength. In practice, the ideal of local democratic control has been synonomous with the selfish interests of suburban USA rather than reflecting 'democracy' in a literal sense.

Thus, for the most part, change has been gradual, involving 'procedural adjustments' rather than radical reform. Exclusionary zoning, for example, has been attacked in state legislatures by resorting to the fourteenth Amendment of the US Constitution whereby 'No State shall make or enforce any law which shall abridge the privileges or immunities of citizens of the United States'.

Zoning ordinances might be seen as restrictive, but legal battles have been long and complex and little success has been achieved. Similarly, the desegregation of schools by amalgamating school boards and instituting busing to ensure racial integration has found support in state and Federal courts, but not without considerable opposition and real progress has been slow. In recent years the situation has been complicated further by opposition to reform from central cities such as Detroit, Los Angeles and Washington DC where the black population are a majority and have obtained, and wish to retain, effective political control (Johnston 1982b).

Elsewhere, 'voluntary cooperations' and 'service agreements' have been established between closely related municipalities to assist the coordination of services such as policing, sewage disposal, water provision and land-use planning for economically viable units. Such devices have the appeal of resolving the immediate problems of service provision without relinquishing local control. As such, they constitute defence mechanisms against re-organization. This frequently has the effect of increasing social polarization in a metropolitan region since socially similar units are those most likely to be involved.

Of wider significance are the metropolitan councils initiated with the aid of state and Federal support grants in Detroit in 1954, and later developed for New York, Philadelphia and San Francisco. The Twin Cities Metropolitan Council, covering the seven counties of the Minneapolis-St Paul urban area, has since 1967 been notably successful in the coordination of land-use planning, economic development, transportation, water provision and waste disposal (Crosby and Bryson 1995). These are multipurpose advisory bodies designed to enhance cooperation and the coordination of service provision, ideally at a city-regional scale. However, efforts to give these bodies directive powers have been resisted strongly by the constituent municipalities, and cooperation rather than control remains the central operative mechanism. Consequently, their achievements, while variable, tend towards the modest, and instability is an inherent feature of their functioning.

Examples of structural reform at the scale of the metropolitan region, designed to achieve economies of scale and efficiency of service provision, while aiming to reduce the worst effects of socio-spatial segregation do, however, exist in the USA, particularly if overall white political control is likely to be maintained. Integration occurred in Nashville, Tennessee, in 1965, while Dade County, Florida, encompassing the Miami Metropolitan Area followed in 1971. Of similar type is the 'Unigov' administration initiated in 1969 for the city of Indianapolis and the outlying areas of Marion County, Indiana. Some successes have been achieved in strategic planning and service provision, but as in the cases of most of the other examples, the continued strength of 50 lower tier 'municipal' authorities continues to curtail the activities of the 'metropolitan' government (Blomquist and Parks 1995). The Montreal Urban Community in Canada functions in much the same way (Sancton 1995). The unit has been in existence since 1970 and covers an area containing a population of just over 3 million. It has achieved some success in the redistribution of tax receipts on an equitable basis across the metropolitan region. However, its role in strategic planning control and service provision has been weakened by the fact that it is composed of delegates from the lower tier municipal authorities, rather than having the stronger element of independent power seen in other Canadian cities, notably Toronto.

To achieve similar results, some states have instituted legislation to curtail the balkanization process and encourage metropolitan forms of government. Texas and Missouri have positively encouraged annexation in the vicinity of large cities, while Ohio, Georgia, Arizona and North Carolina do not allow the incorporation of new municipalities within specified distances of existing large towns. For the most part, however, the essence of a spatially fragmented local government system, consistent with a neoliberalist interpretation of local governance, remains throughout the USA.

The fragmentation of local government has clearly served to emphasize social and spatial segregative tendencies and to accentuate the central city-suburban dichotomy. In effect, Soja's notion that

> there is no doubt that the maze of counties, cities, townships and special districts, many tending to pursue narrow local interests at the expense of the larger functional community, both directly and indirectly exacerbate some of the major problems facing predominantly urban America
>
> (Soja 1971: 45)

continues to be relevant, and change tends to conform more to evolutionary reform than to a radical restructuring.

The local government system of the UK: hierarchical structures

The local government system of the UK is fundamentally different from that of the USA. Its early development reflected the practical need for forms of local control rather than being related to ideals of local democracy, and major changes in its subsequent development have been largely imposed by central government rather than reflecting local pressures. Central control has consequently been stronger throughout its evolution and a neater hierarchical ordering has resulted.

Prior to 1974 the system was dominated by the structure established in the late nineteenth century. The Local Government Act 1888 established the county councils and county boroughs as a top tier, while the Local Government Act 1894 established a lower, second tier within the county council areas comprising municipal boroughs, urban districts and rural districts (Figure 6.2). This was a radical reorganization necessitated by the rapid urban expansion in Britain following the Industrial Revolution. The earlier system, comprising a multitude of local health boards and sanitary authorities, conceptually similar to the fragmented structure emerging in the USA, often pursued independent and conflicting policies, occasionally with dire results for the health of the urban and rural areas

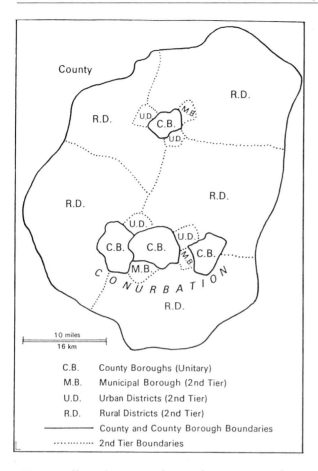

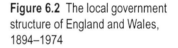

Figure 6.2 The local government structure of England and Wales, 1894–1974

alike. In effect, the county boroughs were created as unitary authorities for the largest towns to replace a confused structure based upon the medieval charter boroughs and their subsequent appendages. The county councils were to control the areas remaining outside the major towns, while a degree of local autonomy was to be given to the smaller urban units (the municipal boroughs and urban districts) and to the rural districts. The structure gave belated recognition to the functional interrelationships of the Victorian era rather than being appropriate for urban expansion in the twentieth century. The division between the county boroughs and county councils gave credence to the persistence of a functional distinction between town and country, while the lower tier authorities paradoxically recognized the spread of urban influences into the country margins.

In the twentieth century this structure became increasingly irrelevant to the efficient operation of the rapidly developing range of local government activities. The process of suburbanization overrode administrative boundaries and established strong functional linkages between separate administrative units. The county borough/county council division became particularly unreal, while in the large conurbations a number of county boroughs had physically merged (Figure 6.2). Problems were most apparent for land-use planning. The great majority of county boroughs had restricted administrative boundaries throughout the period of rapid urban growth. At the same time, they had to provide substantial numbers of public sector council houses for the needs of the lower status groups and for slum clearance schemes. Large-scale boundary extensions to undertake imaginative urban planning were the exception and usually involved protracted legal disputes due to the conflicting interests of the urban-oriented county boroughs and the rurally oriented county councils. Thus in most of the larger cities, urban planning schemes were constrained by restrictive boundaries and dominated by local authority housing estates. This had the additional effect of accentuating social polarization between the lower status inner cities and the higher status suburban margins.

In fact, by the late 1950s there was widespread agreement at central and local government levels that radical structural reform was long overdue. Reform focused on the need to promote the dual aims of 'administrative efficiency', while preserving 'local democracy' in a period of rapid change. Fewer, but larger, units were envisaged to achieve economies of scale. These were to reflect the functional realities of a 'city regional' ideal to facilitate coordinated strategic planning, and to enhance a sense of social identity in order to promote 'participation' in local government affairs.

These aims were consistent with the wider recognition in planning debate in Europe and North America that some form of 'city or metropolitan regional' scale of local government was necessary to promote the efficient functioning of urban areas in a period of continuing urban growth (Barlow 1991; Sharpe 1995). Ideally, such units would be defined as discrete economic entities based upon functioning labour market areas. They would be responsible for the major 'strategic' planning functions including physical planning, economic development, transportation policy and environmental enhancement, and have powers independent of any lower tier authorities. Lower tier authorities might continue to be responsible for more localized services such as education, housing and recreation, but these would be provided within the strategy defined at the metropolitan level.

In Britain, however, central government is the dominating influence over local government change. Thus, the actual process of change reflected political rather than planning ideals (see also Chapter 7). The Redcliffe-Maud Commission, set up by the Labour government in 1966, presented proposals in1969 comprising alternative 'unitary' or 'two-tier' authorities based on the city regional concept. Both would have radically altered the existing local government structure. Whether either of these alternatives would have achieved the accredited aims of the reform is, however, debatable since both the boundaries and the powers of the new units were subject to widespread critical scrutiny by planners.

In the event, the decision to adopt the unitary version of the proposals met with the obstacle of a change of government in 1970. The incoming Conservative government did not consider that large unitary authorities would provide administrative efficiency and local democracy. Instead, a system comprising a top tier of 38 county councils and 6 metropolitan counties, the latter modelled on the experimental Greater London Council initiated in 1964, was proposed in 1971 and became operative in April 1974 (Figure 6.3). These authorities were to be complemented by a lower level of around 370 district councils. The counties were to be responsible for broad 'strategic' functions such a structure planning, transport and education, while the district authorities retained substantial powers such as the formulation of local plans and the provision of public sector housing.

The precedence given to the pre-existing counties was considered to reflect traditional Conservative support, while the restricted boundaries for the large conurbations have been seen as a mechanism designed to contain the areas of traditional Labour control.

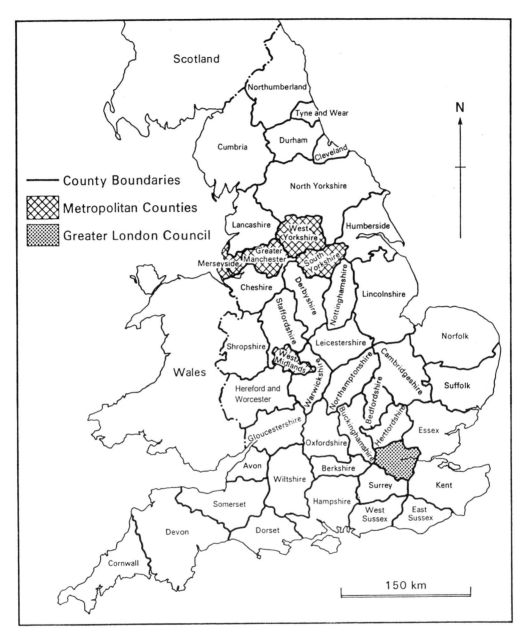

Figure 6.3 English counties after the 1974 reorganization

Paradoxically, however, the city regional concept was promoted with the creation of the new counties of Avon, Cleveland and Humberside (Figure 6.3).

While the 1974 reforms constituted a significant rationalization of the earlier structure, in subsequent years problems inherent in the new system became increasingly evident. The metropolitan counties, for example, were seen as too spatially restricted for strategic planning purposes and characterized as major urban units 'embedded' in broader economic regions. Similarly, the widespread adherence to pre-existing county boundaries was inconsistent with emerging functional entities, particularly in the south-east of England. The two-tier structure also proved problematic. The ideal of the lower tier operating policies consistent with the broader strategic aims of the counties has been largely illusory. Instead, the strength of the districts has frequently allowed local interests to confound wider strategic aims. This has generated costly conflicts between the levels which has a detrimental effect on the image of local government to the public. In fact, even by the early 1970s the inherent weakness of the two-tier system in Greater London had marginalized the strategic planning potential of the Greater London Council, a reflection of insufficient independent power.

The dependence of the local state upon central government in Britain is demonstrated further by recent events. Since 1979, the promotion of efficient planning in a context of strong city regional administrative structures was not a primary interest of the Conservative government. Instead, attention focused on anti-inflationary, monetarist policies designed to resolve the economic crises of post-industrial capitalism (see also Chapters 7 and 8). The reduction of public expenditure has been a central issue and has involved curtailing local government spending by exerting firmer central control. This coincided with a deterioration of the quality of life in the early 1980s in the inner cities most adversely affected by economic recession, and brought the usually Labour controlled metropolitan county and district councils into direct conflict with central government over levels of expenditure. This culminated in the 'rate-capping' legislation of 1984 designed to curb the activities of high-spending local authorities. Ostensibly to cut the cost of local government bureaucracy, the government subsequently abolished the Greater London Council in 1986 and the remaining six metropolitan counties in 1987.

At the same time, to effect improvements to urban areas, while avoiding the inefficiencies considered inherent in local government action, the government increased administrative fragmentation by establishing a number of special purpose organizations since the mid-1970s, reminiscent of the US system. Urban Development Corporations, Housing Action Trusts, Training and Enterprise Councils, devolved management in schools, and the privatization of many public services are all typical of this trend. The increasing significance of 'quangos' and the increase of 'government by appointees' has been considered to reflect a new conception of 'community governance', characterized by the gradual dismantling of local government and the creation of a 'democratic deficit' (Clarke and Stewart 1994). This is consistent with the neoliberal regulatory basis of contemporary local government in the UK.

In short, by 1990 the Conservative government considered local government throughout the UK to be inefficient, costly and conflict-provoking, and in need of another radical review. Fundamental to this review has been the aim to promote efficiency by abolishing the two-tier structure in favour of a reassertion of the unitary principle. Ideally, the new unitary authorities were to be based on areas with a 'community of identity', larger than the existing districts, but not as extensive as the counties. Following a period of debate, the new structures were initiated in Wales and Scotland in 1996. Typically, for the urban areas of South Wales the new districts are unlikely to be capable of promoting efficient strategic planning for the twenty-first century (Figure 6.4). The former county of West Glamorgan, which approximated to the city region of Greater Swansea, was divided into two districts, despite their strong economic functional integration. Similarly, Cardiff and Newport are separated, and restricted by closely defined boundaries. Such units will not be sufficiently

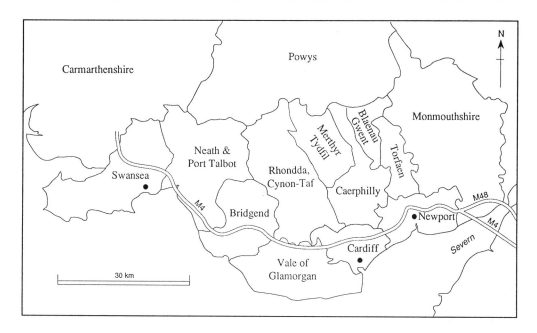

Figure 6.4 Unitary authorities in South Wales, 1996

extensive in most areas to perform the classic strategic planning coordination role associated with the ideals of metropolitan government (Harris and Tewdwr-Jones 1995).

For England, however, the situation is much more problematic. The reform is being undertaken by a Local Government Commission for each county via a consultation process designed to evaluate alternatives and 'reflect the identities and interests of local communities'. Not unexpectedly, consultation has not resulted in the emergence of a country-wide consensus on the form of the new structure. For some counties such as Oxfordshire, Cambridgeshire, Cheshire and Lancashire, the Commission reported insufficient support to warrant a change. By contrast, for Bedfordshire and Buckinghamshire there was genuine support for the new unitary structure. However, unitary authorities have been proposed for many urban areas, although most of these are little larger than the county boroughs which were abolished in 1974, such as Southampton and Portsmouth. In addition, for many of the rural areas surrounding the larger cities, the retention of two-tier structures has been proposed (Johnston and Pattie 1996). It is not currently clear whether these complex variations will be introduced at the target date of 1997. However, even if a greater degree of unity is imposed similar to the situations in Wales and Scotland, the resulting fragmentary system seems unlikely to provide a solution which assists the efficient provision of the strategic planning functions for land-use coordination, transportation and economic development. In fact, Leach (1994) already envisages the need for formal joint organizations with executive powers to coordinate such activities in the conurbations and larger city regions. Thus, the development of a system based on a 'unitary myth' rather than a 'unity reality' is anticipated. In effect, the system appears to be moving in the direction of the US system rather than towards the kinds of 'city-regional' forms favoured by most of the planning fraternity.

The trend in Britain is clear. The period since the early 1980s has witnessed a significant shift in political control towards increased centralization combined with a lower level of financial responsibility at the local level. Whether this will be reflected in a more cost-effective and efficient provision of local services, while ensuring the coordination of planning and transportation strategies is, however, highly debatable. The scale and spread of the functional interrelationships associated with modern urban development suggests the need for at least a city-regional form of strategic control rather than a polarization between central government and localized units. However, the experiences of the USA and the UK suggest that the future form and function of local government will be determined as much by the vagaries of national political change in combination with wider economic imperatives and pressures, as by the needs of planning.

Discussion

Despite fundamental differences between the local governance systems of the USA and the UK, both have had a significant effect on the process of urban growth. In the USA, the tradition of local democratic control has allowed both socially and spatially defined interest groups to accentuate segregation in the city and has presented major obstacles to the development of reforms necessary to institute effective metropolitan planning. In the UK, integrated urban development policies have also been restrained for much of the twentieth century due to the entrenched heritage of the Victorian local government reforms. Positive planning has been restricted by the location of administrative boundaries, although adverse social segregative tendencies equivalent to those in US cities did not reflect the local government structure. The potential for radical restructuring has been much greater in the UK, yet the key position of central government in the process of administrative change has progressively compromised the needs of urban planning. In recent years, however, it is notable that in both cases fiscal issues have instituted a shift towards a greater degree of centralization and reduced the immediate prospects for the emergence of city-regional forms of government.

In fact, Sharpe (1995) suggests common obstacles to the development of metropolitan forms of local government occur in many western countries. Hostility to strong metropolitan government is considered to emanate from two principal quarters. Central governments (or state governments in federal systems) rarely wish their authority to be undermined by major urban units, particularly if there are party political differences between the two levels. At the same time, existing lower level municipal authorities tend to guard their traditional powers and privileges jealously. They usually stress their advantages for recognizing and responding to local community issues, while metropolitan authorities are characterized as expensive and impersonal entities. This is a close approximation to the US situation. Similarly, in the UK the abolition of the GLC and the other metropolitan counties in the 1980s reflected central government misgivings, while the continued avoidance of the city regional form also reflects central government economic imperatives. Again, little support for change has come from the lower tier authorities.

Comparable situations have been recognized throughout Europe. Since the mid-1980s experiments with metropolitan government in Barcelona, Rotterdam and Copenhagen have been abolished (Sharpe 1995). While a reduction in enthusiasm for 'master planning' in the context of a slow-down of economic growth is recognized as a contributory factor, in each case the central and local forces noted above were of major significance (Barlow 1991). In Barcelona, for example, tensions between the right-wing autonomous government of Catalonia and the socialist metropolitan government were central to the return to 'municipal' local government (Grimaldos and Ferrer 1995).

However, examples of metropolitan government which appear to be providing efficient strategic planning and associated services continue to exist. The case of Metro Toronto, initiated in 1954, has evolved into a form which is widely considered to offer an efficient system of service provision for a population of over 2 million (Barlow 1991; Feldman 1995). Likewise, the government of the Tokyo Metropolitan Region has emerged to act as the strategic planning authority for an area accommodating over 11 million people. Currently, this authority is developing strategies designed to avoid the problems of excessive centralization by initiating policies designed to create an efficiently functioning multi-centred metropolis (Togo 1995). Also in the etherlands, the abolition of the Rijnmond Authority, based on metropolitan Rotterdam, is being reconsidered. It appears that such an organization is necessary to coordinate development pressures in this physically and functionally complex estuarine area (Hendriks and Toonen 1995). Likewise, in 1990 the Italian government proposed to establish metropolitan governments for the major cities, together accommodating between a quarter and a third of the population (Angotti 1993). Thus, it may well be that the functional logic of metropolitan government will in future be re-asserted in the light of the continuing development pressures associated with urban growth in western countries. However, this message will need to be appreciated by central governments if 'parochial' interests are to be overcome.

CHAPTER 7

Transport issues in the city

In all cities there is a close interactive relationship between the transportation network, the urban morphology and the spatial patterns of urban functions. Behaviour in the city, such as journeys to work, shopping trips, visits to health centres and to leisure facilities, is also closely related to the system of urban transport. In fact, the efficient functioning of the city is directly dependent upon the efficiency of the components of the urban transportation system. During the process of economic development the evolving system both connects the various functional elements of the urban fabric and directs the pattern of urban growth. A generalized evolutionary sequence is portrayed for the western city (Figure 7.1), and this is closely associated with innovations in transport technology (Figure 7.2).

This evolutionary sequence is most relevant to medium-sized cities in which development was initiated in the nineteenth century and has resulted in strongly centralized urban systems. However, variations in the scale of cities and the societal context of the urban development process are responsible for significant deviations from the general model. A number of examples will serve to illustrate the potential variability.

Urban transport systems

Western cities: centralized systems

The most marked deviations occurred in cities that experienced high and rapid rates of urban development in the nineteenth century. London, for example, reached a population of 6 million by 1900 and, to a lesser extent, a similar situation occurred in the smaller British conurbations. In these circumstances, the pressure for urban growth could not be accommodated by the relatively inefficient, road-based public transport system, and railways, which had been introduced initially for the inter-city transportation, became a much more active agent of urban growth. Thus, from 1860 to 1914 the London Underground system and suburban railway lines were basic formative influences; they allowed extensive suburbanization and the development of commuter settlements well beyond the city centre. Access to stations was critical as the railway became a much more important element in the intra-urban transportation network. The process had social consequences since the higher status groups were those financially most able to benefit from the pleasant environment of the suburbs and social polarization between the inner city and

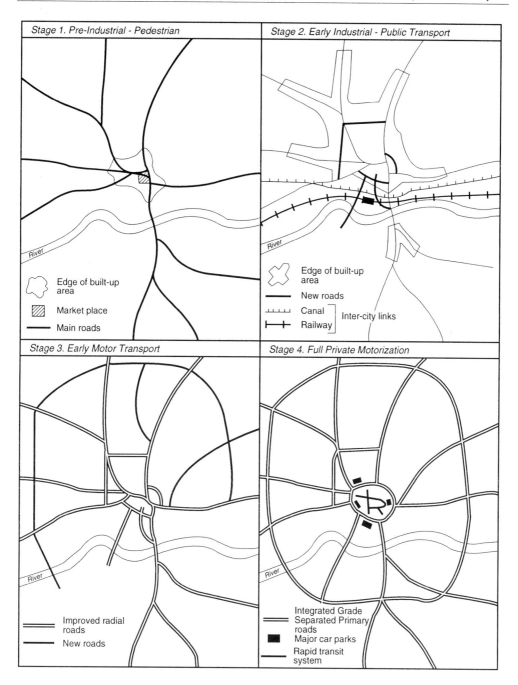

Figure 7.1 Stages in the evolution of urban transport systems

the outer suburbs was initiated during this period.

Paris exhibits a different variant. Residential densities in the inner city were nearly three times those of London due to the constraining influence of successive historical fortifications, a feature which Paris has in common with many European cities. The high

	Urban functions	Transport technology	Transportation system	Urban form
Stage 1 **Pre-** **industrial**	defence, marketing, political-symbolic, craft industry	pedestrian, draught-animal	route convergence, radial	compact
Stage 2 **Early** **industrial**	basic indsutries, secondary, manufacturing	electric tram, streetcar, public transport	radial improvements, incremental additions	high density suburbanization, stellate form
Stage 3 **Industrial**	broadening industry, tertiary service expansion	otor bus, publi transport, early ars	additional radials, initiation of 'ring' roads (incomplete)	lower density suburbanization, industrial deentralization
Stage 4 **Post-** **industrial**	addition of uaternary activities	towards universal car ownership	integrated radial and circumferential road network	low density suburbanization, widespread functional decentralization

Figure 7.2 Evolution of the transport system of western cities

density allowed urban growth to occur without the necessity for an intra-urban railway system, although the resulting traffic congestion provided the impetus for the urgent construction of the Metro after 1900. Thus, the Paris Metro did not direct suburban growth but was designed to integrate the existing parts of the inner city and remains confined largely to that area in the late 1990s. As such, it has the form of a 'modern' inner-city rapid transit system and the subsequent process of suburbanization in Paris in the late nineteenth and early twentieth centuries had a simpler form, related to the original radial road system.

With the postwar growth of the Paris agglomeration to 8.5 million by the early 1960s and the expectation of continued development, a drastic re-evaluation of the transport network was made. In 1961 the French government approved a new regional metro system to provide a rapid suburban rail service for the whole agglomeration (RER – *Réseau Express Régional*). This was designed to complement, and was integrated with, the inner-city Metro by the mid-1980s. The subsequent urban planning strategies dating from the *Schema Directeur d'Amènagement et d'Urbanisme de la Région de Paris* of 1965, initiated the improvement of the radial road system, the development of circumferential routes starting with the inner ring *Boulevard Périphérique* along the line of the outermost fortification, and the development of east-west routes both north and south of the Seine along the lines of the preferred axes of urban development (Figure 7.3). Thus, despite the initial deviation of the Parisian transport network, recent modifications have brought it closer to the suggested western model (Hall 1995).

Other variations characterize the rapidly growing metropolitan centres of the developing world. Here, urban growth is more closely related to the 'population explosion', and to the strong rural-urban migration flows. By 1985 Mexico City had reached a population of 16.7

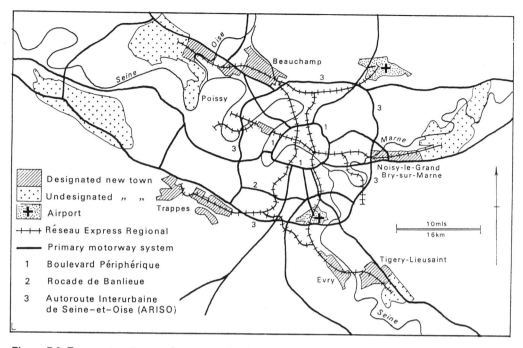

Figure 7.3 Transport systems and new town development in Paris

million, Calcutta 10.3 million, while Lagos is currently estimated at 5.8 million (Devas and Rakodi 1993). In fact, they indicate that seven of the ten largest cities in the world are located in the developing world. In total, there are 25 cities with populations exceeding 4 million, twice the number that existed in 1970.

In most of these cities, where poverty is endemic, there is a lack of finance to develop adequate public controls over the structure and quality of the urban environment. High density and low quality residential developments predominate and are served by rudimentary improvements and extensions to the early radial road networks. Public transport normally consists of an inadequate bus or tram system, largely confined to the radial routes which are frequently the only roads sufficiently wide for this purpose; traffic congestion of pedestrians and vehicles is usually considerable. The resulting urban structure tends to be highly centralized and inefficient, while the possibility of developing a more sophisticated transport system based on radically improved roads and railways is usually far too costly to be contemplated in anything other than a partial and piecemeal manner (Figure 7.4A). A similar transportation system has been illustrated for Jakarta, serving an urban agglomeration of 7.8 million people (Devas and Rakodi 1993).

Evidence also suggests that in the long term it is not necessarily only the lack of finance which will be the principal obstacle to improvement in developing world cities. The rapidly growing economy of the greater Bangkok Metropolitan Region, containing an estimated population already in excess of 10 million in 1992, provides the finance and expertise available to substantially improve the highway network (Daniere 1995). Yet traffic problems are gradually deteriorating, and peak hour traffic flows are typically of the order of 3–8 km per hour. The source of the problem is considered to reflect the lack of integration between

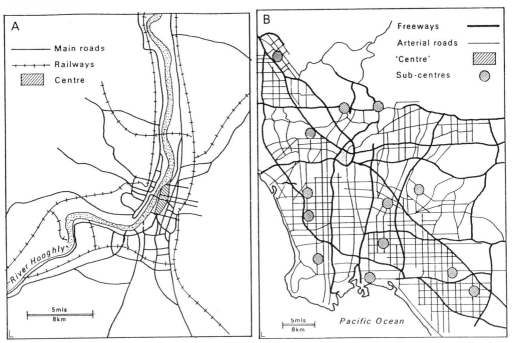

Figure 7.4 Two city transport systems: A Calcutta and centralization; B Los Angeles and de-centralization

the many institutions responsible for building and managing the network. Of equal significance were obstacles presented by the interests of the traditional political elites whose concerns focused on economic development rather than the development of the necessary supportive infrastructure. Similar constraints characterize urban management and service provision in most developing world countries (Devas and Rakodi 1993).

Western cities: decentralized systems

A radically different transport network evolves in situations typified by the development of high levels of private car ownership. This has been particularly widespread in more recently urbanized parts of the USA, Canada and Australia, and is epitomized by the case of Los Angeles where a metropolis of 10 million people had developed by 1970, almost entirely within the era of mass car ownerships. The combined influence of high levels of personal mobility, affluence and the absence of significant space constraints on urban growth encouraged low density suburbanization. This in turn had a fundamental influence upon the functional structure of the urban system and the closely associated transport network. The dispersed population and high levels of personal mobility have positively encouraged the decentralization of employment and service activities throughout the urban system on a scale much larger than that experienced in cities more reliant upon public transportation. As a result, in 1990 85 per cent of journeys to work in the 50 largest metropolitan areas in the USA were undertaken by car (Cervero and Landis 1995). At the same time, the cost of providing unrestricted car access to the traditional central business districts has acted as a significant constraint upon the development of a strongly centralized urban structure. In fact, it has been suggested that whatever the scale of a metropolitan area the largest central business district can provide for a maximum of only 150,000–180,000 car commuters, and even then significant peak-hour traffic congestion is likely to result (Thomson 1977).

Thus, the initial centre of Los Angeles has not dominated the intra-urban system of central places and a number of alternative functional nodes have emerged. This is reflected in a transport network in which the radial component of the road system centred on Los Angeles is only very weakly developed (Figure 7.4B). Instead, by the early 1940s the demands of a highly motorized society had necessitated the extensive development of urban motorways or freeways with their characteristic grade-separated intersections at potential points of congestion (cloverleaves). These were supplemented by the construction of a rectilinear grid system of secondary arterial roads designed to incorporate the expanding suburbs into the loosely knit urban structure. In such a system, the influence of public transport has been minimal.

However, concern for the environmental impacts of fully decentralized urban systems has been growing since the late 1950s. Attention has focused on the considerable amounts of land taken for highway construction, and associated concerns for energy conservation and air pollution. Consequently, moves away from highway solutions towards a firmer commitment to public transit systems have occurred in many cities. This culminated in the Intermodal Surface Transport Efficiency Act 1991 (ISTEA). This offers Federal aid for innovations integrating land-use with improvements to transit and highway infrastructure designed to enhance both urban transport and the environment (Paaswell 1995). To date, the overall effect of this legislation has not been great due to the considerable operational problems which need to be overcome. However, a shift towards a more comprehensive approach to urban transport issues is signalled.

Nevertheless, urban development in the motor age has been characterized by the archetypical 'suburban city' of Los Angeles. Whereas these features are particularly well marked in cities of the western USA developed in the postwar period, such as Denver and Salt Lake City, they have increasingly been superimposed upon the urban fabric of cities originally developed in earlier technological conditions.

The urban transportation problem

Transportation problems are virtually universal facets of urban growth whatever the detailed characteristics of the transport system in specific areas. They take the form of peak-hour congestion of public and private transport particularly in city centres and at other nodal points on the transport network; parking difficulties; noise and atmospheric pollution; and pedestrian and vehicular accidents. This reflects the fact that the growth of traffic demand, whether for public or private transport in a developed or developing world context tends to be faster than the development of either public controls or of the finance necessary to provide an efficiently functioning system.

More specifically, the number of vehicles, both public transport and private cars, can respond rapidly to the growth in demand, in the absence of public controls on levels of vehicle ownership typical of most countries. This process has been aided by the vigorous development of a car-manufacturing industry throughout most of the developed world. By contrast, the provision of a system capable of accommodating the increasing traffic levels

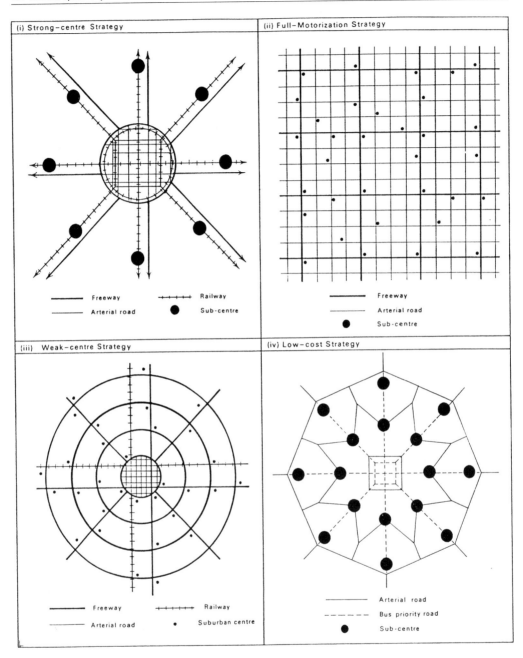

Figure 7.5 Urban transport planning strategies

requires, in the long term, comprehensive planning and control and high levels of investment in transport infrastructure.

The essentially economic basis of the problem is now widely appreciated, and the concept of 'pricing deficiencies' is central to the debate. The greater part of the cost of supplying transport facilities is seen, with the partial exception of public transport, not to be borne directly by the user. The provision of adequate roads and parking and the minimization of

(i)	**Strong-centre strategy: centralized cities**
Aim	To maintain economic advantages of centralization and iniise central city congestion.
Policy	1. Efficient public transport, suburbs to entre and within the city centre.
	2. Decentralization of functions to nodal points to spread traffic loads.
Problems	Tends to create peak-hour congestion.
(ii)	**Full-motorisation strategy: decentralized cities**
Aim	To retain high levels of car accessibility throuhout the syste.
Policy	Decentralized functional structure based upon the extension of urban freeways.
Problems	Land and construction costs, long distances travelled, energy costs' environmental impacts, lack of social identity, possible nodal congestion.
(iii)	**Weak-centre strategy: inner centralized and outer decentralized cities**
Aim	To retain coercial and social advantages of a city centre and ease of mobility throughout the suburbs.
Policy	1. Integrated system of radial and cirumferential roads.
	2. Supplementary commuter rail services to the centre.
Problems	Tends towards decentralization in the absence of sufficient investment in public transport and central redevelopment.
(iv)	**Low-cost strategy: Third World cities**
Aim	To alleviate congestion and assist economic development.
Policy	1. Improveent of the radial roads and public transport syste.
	2. Controls on central development and the encouragement of decentralization to peripheral nodes.
Problems	City growth tends to be faster than levels of investment in transport infrastructure.

After Thompson, 1977. Reproduced by permission of J.M. Thompson)

Figure 7.6 Urban transport planning strategies

environmental problems have been perceived traditionally as publicly provided activities, serving the community at large rather than specific groups of transport users. Thus, the system has been funded from the general pool of central and local government expenditure, in which transport has to compete with the financing of the whole range of additional public service facilities, usually from an inadequate overall budget. As a result, 'underinvestment' is an almost universal characteristic of the transport infrastructure of cities due to the failure to apply strict economic principles to the development and rearrangement of urban transport over a long period of time. Nevertheless, at a broad conceptual level Thomson (1977) identifies four main physical strategies designed to improve a particular type of transport network (Figures 7.5 and 7.6). These were proposed as 'ideal types' rather than offering specific solutions to urban transport problems, and as such are of continuing interest for policy formulation.

Private transport versus public transport

Whatever the transport planning strategy adopted in a city, the steadily continuing growth in levels of private car ownership in most societies in relation to alternative modes of public transport has tended to confound solutions to the urban transportation problem. This reflects a combination of the economic problems of public transport and the behavioural attractions of the private car. Public transport systems are usually designed to cope with peak-hour journeys to and from workplaces. In the interim periods considerable investment in capital equipment and labour is underutilized and involves costs which have to be covered by a combination of relatively high fares and cuts in off-peak services. Usually, these measures have a detrimental effect on demand, which further compounds the financial problem and frequently leads to a decline in the quality and financial viability of the services offered.

The nature of the problem, which is strongly supported in the academic literature, can be illustrated by anecdotal evidence from two widely different areas. An irate correspondent writing to the local newspaper in Swansea, South Wales, articulated a series of complaints relating to the local bus service typical of the British situation (*South Wales Evening Post* 1 October 1992). The last bus to a relatively populous rural area only 12 miles from the city centre left as early as 5.40 pm; the bus station was considered to offer poor facilities, with seating for only the first 4 people in a queue; 14 passengers on the bus had to stand for the 40 minute journey which would have taken 15 minutes by car, while the fare was equivalent to the cost of 1 gallon of petrol. A similar 'downward spiral' was evident in Toronto in the early 1990s (Barber 1993). The Toronto Transit Commission, which is considered a model for public transport in North America, reported a decline in passenger numbers from 464 million in 1988 to an estimated 393 million in 1993, despite a steady increase in subsidy to 40 per cent over the previous 25 years.

By contrast, apart from peak-hour journeys to city centres in the larger highly centralized cities, the private car is usually a more flexible and convenient means of travel. The pervasive strength of this force is suggested by the following, and not untypical, response of a car owner:

> I live about two kilometres from work, a 25–minute walk in fine weather. There is a bus stop a few hundred yards from my front door, and the bus that stops there stops about seven minutes later at the front door of The Globe and Mail's Toronto office.
>
> This morning, I drove to work.
>
> I could reel off the usual excuses. . . but all lame. The real reason I drove was that driving was easiest, and flesh is weak.
>
> (Barber 1993: 2).

Also, car journeys are perceived as less costly since the marginal cost of a specific trip is usually compared with the public transport fare. Thus, increasing road traffic has created pressures for more highways and this has tended to increase costs and exacerbate environmental problems.

The early response to the emerging problem of urban traffic congestion has usually aimed to combine car accommodation with environmental preservation. Typically, this involved the provision of a comprehensively upgraded road network comprising the main radial routes, an inner ring road surrounding the CBD and one or more suburban ring roads (Figure 7.1, stage 4). Ideally, major intersections are 'grade-separated' with flyovers, while the creation of pedestrian precincts and other traffic-free 'environmental areas' has been given some priority. The provision of car-parking facilities and their integration with major trip destination points is also of central importance. For the central business districts various traffic limitation and management schemes in association with public transport strategies have been the usual response. Such strategies were epitomized in the mid-1960s by the Buchanan Report for British cities (Ministry of Transport 1963).

However, since the early 1970s a wide official realization of the economic and environmental impact of the unrestricted use of the car in cities has been linked with the 'suppressed demand' argument. This argument, initially introduced into the urban transport debate in Britain in the Buchanan Report, has been reiterated regularly, most notably by Mogridge (1987). In situations of steadily increasing car ownership it is suggested that there is an enormous suppressed demand for car journeys. Thus, any new roads built quickly attract more traffic until a new equilibrium of congestion is reached (around 19 km per hour in central London). In fact, it is considered: 'impossible to improve traffic speed where demand is in excess of any possible supply of road space' (Mogridge 1987: 167).

The near capacity traffic levels and frequent congestion experienced on the M25 London orbital motorway (completed only in 1987) is a classic example of this effect. Already, the number of lanes is being increased in the section under greatest pressure in the vicinity of Heathrow Airport, while even relatively minor accidents or roadworks are capable of initiating 'gridlock' lasting hours in many locations in Greater London.

It follows that journey times can be improved only by improving the quality and speed of public transport systems since they dictate the levels of car use. This constitutes a strong argument for near universal moves towards both traffic limitation strategies and the positive promotion of public transport in western cities of all types. This implies that the current variants of the urban transport system are tending to converge. In centralized systems this involves the decentralization of activities to nodal locations in the suburbs, while in decentralized systems a greater degree of concentration of functions in the central city and a limited number of suburban locations is considered appropriate. In either situation, the siting of urban activities is undertaken with a view to encouraging the use of public transport, and at the same time cars are actively discouraged from situations which would give rise to heavy social costs.

Public transport: public service or commercial service?

The urban transportation literature suggests that in most countries public transport is not commercially viable for the reasons outlined earlier. Public transport systems demonstrate an almost universal inability to meet costs so that their quality and efficiency in cities reflects their degree of subsidization. Thus, for the purposes of transport planning it has been argued that it is better to regard public transport as a publicly provided rather than a commercial service.

The economics and politics of urban transport

The acceptance of this view by governments, however, varies significantly. This is epitomized by the central importance of economic issues and increasing politicization of the transport issue in the UK since the early 1980s. In the mid-1970s, for example, the Labour government made a firm commitment to the promotion of public transport in British cities. Finance was to be directed more strongly to the public sector and coordination of the different modes of transport was a primary aim. A Transport Policy and Programme was to be formulated via the strategic planning function of each county and subject to an annual review by the Department of the Environment (DoE). The official view was that continued increase in car ownership and usage was bound to reduce the commercial viability of public transport, which would accentuate the urban transportation problem and reduce the quality of urban life. This resulted in a number of fare-cutting experiments in the early 1980s based upon local rate subsidies designed to increase the attractions of public transport. Notable examples not only occurred in South Yorkshire but also included the 'Fares Fair' policy of the Greater London Council which included an integrated fare structure covering bus, underground and rail.

Such initiatives, however, were contrary to the commercial orientation of the Conservative government elected in 1979 and committed to a reduction in the public service expenditure (see also Chapters 6 and 8). Rate-capping subsequently abolished local government subsidies to public transport, while the Transport Act 1985 instituted the 'deregulation' of public transport, aiming to promote competition and innovation. The effects of the change in emphasis to a 'commercial' orientation were not initially encouraging. Higher fares and lower levels of use soon characterized bus services in South Yorkshire, with the exception of the profitable routes in the higher density urban areas, while, elsewhere, a general reduction in the quality and reliability of services appeared to become the norm.

Initiatives to ameliorate the urban transport problem since the mid-1980s reflected an uneasy relationship between two principal standpoints held by the then Conservative government. On the one hand, the government recognized the need to develop a stronger public transport sector, while exerting firmer controls over car usage. On the other hand, these ends needed to be achieved increasingly by privatized 'commercial' solutions rather than by stronger public intervention. Policy was, therefore, seen in terms of more efficient privately financed public transport involving bus, light rail and conventional railways; road pricing via permits or metering systems; and privatized toll roads.

The debate has been complicated further in the early 1990s by the gradual strengthening throughout most western countries of the need to reduce the energy consumption and environmental pollution associated with steadily rising levels of private vehicle ownership and usage. This trend was formalized by the European Commission's (CEC 1992) promotion of the 'compact city' in the context of 'sustainable' urban development. A compact urban form was to be the principal means of reducing the number and length of journeys in urban areas, while maximizing the opportunities for providing viable systems of public transport. This concept has been integrated into British transport policy (DoE 1994a), and has received considerable support in Europe, the USA and Australia (Breheny 1994). Despite widespread international support, the questions of whether substantial increases in urban densities can be achieved and whether this will result in significant reductions in energy consumption and pollution remain debatable issues (Breheny 1994; Hall 1995). Nevertheless, irrespective of environmental considerations, there is little doubt that the more compact the city, the more viable public transport is likely to be.

Additional impetus was given to the environmental dimension of transport policy in the UK with the report of the Royal Commission on Environmental Pollution in October 1994 (DoE 1994c). Recommendations were made to reduce the £19 million road-building programme by 50 per cent, the savings being diverted to finance public transport improvements. At the same time, car usage was to be discouraged by doubling petrol costs, introducing graduated taxes with increasing car size, and by generally reducing speed limits.

This climate of opinion provided the framework for the so-called 'great transport debate' of 1994–5, the prelude to the publication of guidelines for a future national transport policy by the Department of Transport (DoT 1996). In the event, very little is likely to change in the near future. The Green Paper reaffirmed a commitment to the promotion of public transport and the reduction of dependence on the car in towns. In principle, support is also given for measures to discourage the use of the car in cities such as road pricing, and the taxing of non-residential parking spaces in city centres. However, private finance continued to be seen as the principal mechanism to effect public transport improvements; while local authorities were to be responsible for schemes designed to reduce car usage, no additional public funding appeared likely to be available for this purpose.

Not surprisingly, the proposals were widely criticized by the road and environmental lobbies alike, on the grounds that they lacked substance and did not define firm targets. No clear mechanisms were specified to control traffic levels or to develop integrated transport strategies for urban areas, while the absence of a firm financial commitment to reform was not reassuring. Serious doubts were also expressed that private finance will be attracted to invest in public transport at a scale necessary to instigate significant improvements due to the substantial scale of investment and high levels of perceived risk associated with such schemes. Partnerships of public and private funding are considered to have greater potential (Banister 1995). In effect, there appeared to be a clear credibility gap between the Conservative government's recognition of necessary objectives and the economic commitment required for associated action. This is perhaps not surprising in a period prior to a general election, given the political capital which would result from a shift in policy on public expenditure and its related tax implications. The likely political unpopularity of introducing strong policies of constraint on motorists also could be discounted. However, notwithstanding the complexity of the issues involved in the public transport debate, a firmer commitment to public transport initiatives combined with controls over car use are likely outcomes of the election of the Labour government in May 1997.

A closely parallel situation has also been illustrated for Toronto with equally pessimistic conclusions (Filion 1996). From the mid-1960s the Toronto Transit Commission relied partly on subsidies to promote a rapid transit system in the central city integrated with suburban rail and bus services. This resulted in a steady increase in journeys to work by transit to a high of 22 per cent in 1988 for the Census Metropolitan Area (1991 population, 3.9 million). Also, there was at this time widespread public authority support for policies consistent with the further enhancement of public transport. These included the characteristic post-modern planning values noted in most other advanced capitalist societies. Strategy focused on the promotion of environmental conservation through compact nodal forms of urban expansion along transit 'corridors', combined with a reurbanization of inner city sites abandoned during the process of deindustrialization. Together these policies aimed to reduce car journeys and encourage the use of public transport. However, since the late 1980s these policies have been increasingly at odds with the global economic competitive pressures felt in many post-industrial western societies which have precipitated public expenditure cut-backs. The consequent abrupt end of subsidies to the Transit Commission in 1988 resulted in the familiar sequence of fare increases and declines in quality of services, resulting in a 15 per cent decline in ridership by

1993. Filion (1996) suggests that the continuing divergence of the environmentally oriented planning ideals and the increasing importance of economic forces over urban development are likely to result in more low density peripheral development and increases in car use, despite an official commitment to the contrary.

The recent events concerning urban transport planning in western countries illustrate the fact that planning requirements and economic and political priorities do not necessarily coincide. In most circumstances urban transport policy will be a compromise between the economic, political and planning perspectives. However, due to the considerable costs and substantial powers necessary to develop an effective system of urban transport in modern society, the attitudes adopted by government will be central to policy formulation in most countries, albeit in a context of strong economic and social obstacles to the development of effective systems of public transport. The prospects for the immediate future do not appear promising.

The promotion of public transport

Irrespective of political philosophy, policies designed to increase the importance of public transport in cities incorporate a number of common elements. To be most effective, strategies must both enhance the attractions of public transport, while at the same time restrict the use of private cars. Also, such policies need to be related to journeys between suburbs and destinations, and within major destinations such as city centres or concentrations of employment. A wide range of strategies exists.

Enhancing the attraction of public transport

For public transport to appeal to the public at large a number of general issues are of fundamental importance. Ease of access at both origins and destinations is critical and a five-minute or 450 metre trip is accepted widely as an outer limit. Similarly, a cost or time advantage is important, especially if assisted by a frequent, reliable service offered over a dense route coverage.

A number of methods have been adopted to achieve these aims, most notably in the context of bus travel. Since the early 1970s restricted bus lanes have been introduced widely in Britain for both central city and selected suburban routes, while express bus services to city centres from collecting points in the outer suburbs are common. Conceptually similar park and ride schemes have been adopted with varying degrees of enthusiasm, some such as the Oxford and Bath examples with a significant measure of success. Demand responsive dial-a-ride minibus services have also been tried. For the most part, however, all these devices have been introduced in a piecemeal fashion as 'curative' rather than 'preventive' action so that their full potential has been difficult to assess. The exceptions, however, are the new town experiments such as the bus priority Superbus system in Stevenage and the largely segregated Busways as the basis of the urban fabric of Runcorn. The relative success of these schemes is encouraging but the opportunity to introduce similarly comprehensive systems into large towns with established routeways and travel patterns is both economically and behaviourally problematic.

In recent years, however, attempts to enhance the attractions of public transport have recognized the need in virtually all the largest cities to develop comprehensive systems integrating heavy rail-based rapid transit with urban services (50,000–60,000 passengers per hour compared with 10,000 for buses). Stockholm has, for example, since the early 1950s integrated urban expansion with rail transport via a system of satellite new towns. As a result, in 1990 38 per cent of residents and 53 per cent of workers living in the rail-served new towns commuted by rail (Cervero and Landis, 1995). The Bay Area Rapid Transit System (BART) completed in the early 1970s in San Francisco introduced these principles to avoid the financial and environmental costs of urban motorways, while at the same time maintaining the advantages of a recognizable 'city centre' in a rapidly decentralizing urban structure. As a result, the CBD of San Francisco continues to flourish, and 3.7 million square metres of new office space was constructed there in the period 1975–92 (Cervero and Landis 1995). However, the system has not been without difficulties. These reflected a combination of problems with the high degree of new technology used and an underestimation of the difficulty of effecting behavioural shifts from the car to public transport for people living further than a quarter of a mile from a station. Such problems, however, are not inevitable and the Metropolitan Atlanta Rapid Transit Authority (MARTA) has been operating a more conventional system since the late 1970s with a considerable measure of success.

In the UK the most recent comprehensive public transport system is the Tyneside Metro. Learning from North American and European experience the network was based upon proven technology and, apart from the underground section between Newcastle upon Tyne and Gateshead, the majority of the 55 km, 47–station system uses upgraded British Rail tracks. Nevertheless, the £70 million cost projected in 1974 escalated to £300 million by its opening in 1981, and the system has been heavily subsidized ever since. The system is now integrated with bus services, and park and ride facilities at a number of stations. The Passenger Transport Executive claims that the Metro has proven a cost-effective means of improving mobility and supporting economic regeneration, and hopes to extend it to the whole of the urban agglomeration of Tyne and Wear. It is unlikely that a similar network will be developed elsewhere in the UK in the near future due to the change in government attitude in the 1980s towards the subsidization of public transport. However, the election of the 'new' Labour government in May 1997 may well lead to a re-evaluation of the situation.

The advantages of comprehensive integrated public transport have, nevertheless, been accepted and a number of major cities are now planning conceptually similar systems, albeit with the intention of using electric trams along existing roads to limit costs, and by attempting to attract a substantial proportion of private investment. These have been modelled on modern European systems exemplified by cities such as Grenoble and Hanover. The Metrolink network for greater Manchester is now well under way (Figure 7.7), while an even more extensive system of 200 km is being developed for the Birmingham conurbation. The South Yorkshire Passenger Transport Executive also completed a 29 km system for the smaller city of Sheffield (population *c.* 500,00) in 1995 (Townroe 1995). Lines focus on the city centre and extend in three directions into the suburbs, including links with the Meadowhall shopping complex in the Don Valley redevelopment area. The potential for such developments, however, is heavily dependent upon the availability of sufficient finance if they are to have a substantial impact upon the urban transportation problem.

Rapid transit rail systems have also been used to maintain accessibility between the

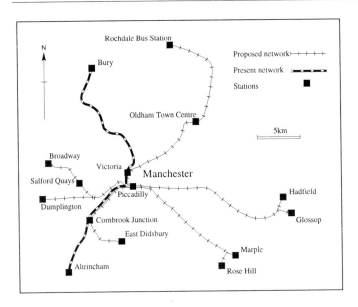

Figure 7.7 The Metrolink light rail network in Manchester

component parts of the largest city centres. The underground systems of London, Paris and New York are obvious early examples. However, as the scale of business activities and the traffic demands upon the central areas have continued to increase, incremental improvements have had to be made. In London the Victoria Line (1972), the Jubilee Line (1979) and its extension, and the proposed Mainline express route between Heathrow Airport and Paddington, are indicative of the pressures; while in Paris the construction of the Metro link between the Gare du Nord and the Gare de Lyon is the result of similar pressures. Elsewhere, in many western cities of greater than 1 million population, the development of inner city rapid transit systems to facilitate internal integration has been a frequent response as exemplified by Toronto, Montreal and Glasgow. On a smaller scale, the Loop-and-Link underground railway system designed to join the mainline rail termini in the centre of Liverpool with the suburban systems of Merseyside and the Wirral has a counterpart in the recently completed Windsor Link in Manchester. In fact, even in the next tier of smaller provincial cities, the need to maintain the competitive position of the city centres in the face of the competitive forces of decentralization has stimulated the development of light rail transit lines. The C-Train system in Calgary (c. 750,000 population) links the city centre with the more populous suburbs, via a number of major traffic generators such as the university campus (Figure 7.8). A slightly less extensive system also operates in Edmonton for much the same reasons. Both are similar to the system introduced in Sheffield.

A more piecemeal approach has also used high capacity rail systems to solve the transport problems presented by specific routes in major cities. Frequently, these are based upon new technology such as the monorail service between Tokyo International Airport and the city centre, although the extension of conventional systems such as the London Underground to Heathrow Airport are not uncommon.

Light rail systems have also been used to stimulate economic development in particular parts of cities. A Light Rapid Rail Transit route (LRRT) forming a 10 km corridor from the city centre of Buffalo through the declining inner suburbs was constructed to revitalize

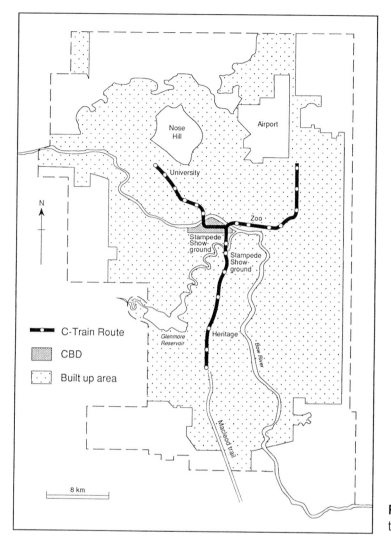

Figure 7.8 Light rail transit system in Calgary

retailing and employment in the city centre and adjacent suburbs. In London the Docklands Light Railway (LDLR), built in the late 1980s from the eastern edge of the City to the Isle of Dogs, was designed to assist the early stages of the redevelopment, most notably in the major office concentration at Canary Wharf (Figure 7.9). Half of the capital costs was financed by the development company, and its subsequent extension to the Royal Docks and Becton was also intended to stimulate the regeneration process in the docklands. In fact, from the outset the LDLR had insufficient capacity to serve adequately a development on the scale of Canary Wharf. Along with the economic recession, this is considered to be a major factor contributing to the financial difficulties of the development. This example stands in stark contrast with the comparable major office decentralization of La Défense in Paris which was closely integrated with the high capacity express underground railway (RER) and the bus and urban motorway networks (see also Chapter 8). The experience of Canary Wharf is an object lesson in the need for major development projects to be fully integrated with an adequate transportation planning infrastructure if their potential is to be

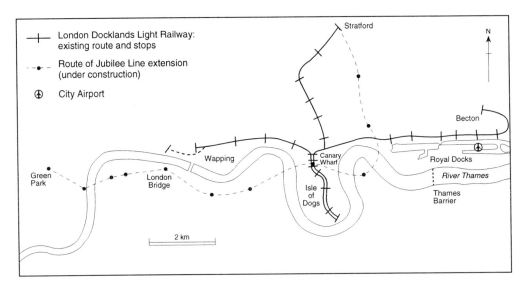

Figure 7.9 London Docklands light railway

maximized. In fact, it is anticipated that the fortunes of the Canary Wharf project will not substantially improve prior to the completion of the £2.5 billion extension of the Jubilee Line of the London underground system in 1998–9 (Figure 7.9).

Restricting the use of private cars

To promote public transport effectively, it is not enough to increase its attractions. Such policies have to be complemented by restraints on the use of private cars. Again a wide range of devices has been used to achieve this end and these have been aimed principally at the areas of greatest congestion in city centres. Policies generally involve the motorist paying for access in order for public authorities to recover at least part of the costs imposed by the high levels of traffic. In most western countries, however, the restriction of the private motorist is a politically sensitive issue. Consequently, a gradual introduction of increasingly Draconian measures, as the scale of the problem increases, is the more usual sequence of events.

The initial response is the introduction of traffic management schemes comprising a combination of parking restrictions, car-parking charges, one-way systems and exclusive bus lanes. Apart from the smallest towns, such policies usually do no more than partially contain a deteriorating situation and often exacerbate conflicts between pedestrians and vehicular traffic. This necessitates the introduction of more comprehensive policies based upon directive forms of parking control in combination with pedestrianization and traffic calming in commercially or environmentally sensitive areas. Leeds introduced a particularly innovative example of such policies in the early 1970s. Long-stay low-cost parking, designed to attract commuters, was concentrated around the periphery of the central area. This was complemented by the provision of short-stay high-cost parking within the centre for shoppers and business visitors, while bus stops were located adjacent to all main destinations in the city centre. This model has been adopted widely in British cities in recent years.

Stronger measures involving road pricing and traffic restraint are gradually achieving wider acceptance. An experimental road pricing scheme was introduced in Singapore in the

1970s in conjunction with parking controls, public transport provision and infrastructural improvements. Since 1975, motorists without a full complement of passengers must buy an entry licence before making a peak-period journey to the city centre. This had the effect of reducing the number of cars entering the centre during the morning peak period by a third. The more technically sophisticated Hong Kong experiment involving electronic meters attached to cars which were activated by sensors in the roads has now been discontinued due to implementation problems. However, road pricing for vehicles entering the central city was introduced in the Norwegian cities of Oslo, Bergen and Trondheim in the early 1990s, while a similar scheme was initiated in Stockholm in 1996 (Hall 1995). While such devices have until recently been considered exotic or fanciful, it is notable that the general idea of road pricing, the use of entry permits for central London and a wider use of toll roads are becoming increasingly common elements in the debate on urban transport in Britain. Politically, however, such initiatives are considered problematic due to the constraints they would impose upon private motorists. Thus, they remain a marginal element of national transport policy (DoT 1996)

In practice, traffic restraint has been the more usual response. This has been particularly evident in western Europe and the experiences of cities such as Bonn, Stuttgart, Vienna, Bologna and Copenhagen have demonstrated that traffic restraint in the city centres combined with improved public transport and extensive pedestrianization have distinct commercial and environmental advantages. In Florence, this has involved comprehensive restrictions on motor vehicles within the area of the former city walls, with residents' passes restricted to one per family. Parking has been concentrated on the periphery and the centre is served by shuttle bus services.

On a note of caution, however, it is evident that policies of traffic restraint in city centres must be considered in the context of broader land-use planning and public transport strategies in the city region. Pressures for suburbanization and functional decentralization are fundamental tendencies associated with rising levels of private car ownership in the post-industrial city. Consequently, undue restrictions imposed on city centres are likely to channel developmental pressures to more accessible suburban nodes. This can be used to advantage to spread traffic loads but care has to be taken if the demise of the traditional city centre is not to result.

Summary

Clearly, there is no shortage of possible solutions to the urban transportation problem. A number of important issues, however, remain to be resolved and are likely to be central to the continuing debate. Of primary significance is the governmental attitude to public transport. Its potential is likely to be closely related to the degree to which it is considered a publicly subsidized or commercially viable service. In either event, radical improvements will incorporate substantial financial implications. In practice, it is also apparent that policies designed to enhance the attractions of public transport have to be integrated with both restraints on private vehicle usage and wider issues of land-use planning. The national planning strategy for the Netherlands for the period 1990–2015 represents a strong move in this direction (Hall 1995). Similarly, to be most effective the various modes of public and private transport need to be coordinated with one another. Finally, it is evident that the 'choice' of transport mode used is as much a behavioural as an economically based decision. The existing literature pays scant regard to the detailed determinants of modal choice. Thus, to maximize the effectiveness of the wide array of urban transport strategies, additional insights into this issue are necessary.

CHAPTER 8

Urban services

The city as a service centre

The physical expansion and increasing functional complexity of urban life in western cities in the twentieth century has resulted in a proliferation of the quantity and variety of services needed by the urban population. The resulting range of services is provided by a variety of commercial and governmental agencies so that their spatial distributions, associated functional characteristics and patterns of usage also vary significantly. Nevertheless, five centrally distinct but overlapping categories can be suggested for preliminary analysis: shopping, wholesaling and warehousing, offices, medical services, and public utilities.

Shopping

The most widely evident services are the those normally associated with shopping. These comprise retail outlets; personal services such as hairdressers, dry cleaners and photographers; professional services such as banks, building societies, solicitors and estate agents; and a range of catering and entertainment facilities. Their unity derives from the fact that they are provided usually for individual customers drawn from relatively local urban hinterlands. Their traditional locational patterns have in the past resulted from the competitive decisions taken by a large number of small suppliers aiming to maximize the commercial advantages of accessibility to the perceived distribution of consumer demand. However, rapid and radical change has characterized the retail environment since the mid-1960s. Many retail firms have grown to national and international significance; retailer-manufacturer-supplier power relationships have changed in favour of retailers; while increasingly affluent and mobile consumers have generated demands for ever more specialized and sophisticated goods and services from steadily improving shopping environments (Bromley and Thomas 1993b; Wrigley and Lowe 1996). In these circumstances, the resulting pattern of shopping opportunities varies between western countries, and reflects a complex negotiation between the commercial priorities of the retail business and property development sectors; changing consumer demands in relation to growing affluence, personal mobility and temporal opportunities; mediated by planning and other legal controls instigated by central and local government to provide for public concerns (Guy 1994a). Nevertheless, trends towards decentralization, combined with concentration into larger but fewer shopping opportunities, are recognized throughout most western societies.

Wholesaling and warehousing

The wholesaling function and associated warehousing activities comprise a second category which traditionally has had close functional and geographical associations with shopping. In its simplest form the wholesaling activity aims to serve retailing, consumer services, office activities, public utilities and industry by providing them with goods which are subsequently sold to the public, consumed by the recipient organization or used to produce a profit. The emphasis is, therefore, on the distribution function. The service is performed mainly for users who are companies and institutions of varying sizes rather than individuals. However, improvements in information technology have offered the opportunity to retailers and manufacturers to maintain only a minimal stock level, distributed from a relatively small number of distribution depots on the system of major roads in most countries (McKinnon 1989). Spatial concentration is also beginning to characterize the wholesaling and warehousing functions.

Offices

Offices concerned with transactional and administrative activities associated with the collection, processing and exchange of information comprise a third category of service. Notable among these are the international, national and regional headquarters of organizations involved in finance, insurance, commerce, industry and government. The 'consumers' of the services in this instance are the business organizations and administrative institutions involved in all sections of economic, social and political life rather than individual customers. Thus, the locational patterns of offices tend to demonstrate a greater degree of concentration in larger centres at both national and intra-urban scale than in the case of shopping centres. Traditionally, this has been considered to reflect the stronger forces of centralization associated with the need to maintain close communication linkages between the different office functions and maximum access to a highly diversified labour market. Nevertheless, due to the problems of access to the centres of the largest cities in recent years, the opportunities offered by advanced forms of communications technology have resulted in a substantial degree of suburbanization of office activities, particularly for the more routine functions. This has been a steady trend in Greater London since the mid-1970s, and the La Défense development in Paris is a spectacular example of the same trend. Similarly in the USA, the emergence of concentrations of retail and office activities at nodal locations in the suburbs have been defined as 'suburban downtowns' (Hartshorn and Muller 1989), while a great variety of types of office concentration have been identified in suburban locations (Matthew 1993).

Medical services

A fourth category of medical services comprising hospitals, general practitioners, dental surgeries, pharmacies and ambulance services can be suggested. These services are closely connected functionally and are significantly different from the previous groups since in most countries they are subject to a stronger degree of public control. The locational decisions of, for example, general practitioners and dentists are restricted usually by a combination of professional or governmental licensing controls. In the case of hospitals, the individual units tend to be larger relative to the scale of the system as a whole and, therefore, less responsive to changes in the nature and location of user demand, while their location policies are usually subject to a greater degree of public control than shopping facilities.

Public utilities

The fifth category comprises public utilities such as schools, public libraries, museums, leisure centres, local government administration offices and police and fire services. Their location policies are subject to public control in most countries and have little dependence upon a competitive market mechanism.

In summary, it is clear that while the five categories of activities outlined above have been introduced under the general heading of 'urban services', this title subsumes considerable variability. Thus, it must be stressed at the outset that due to the differences in the nature of, and controls over, the specific categories of services, both the locational decisions – which determined their spatial patterns – and the associated user decisions – which relate to their use – exhibit considerable variation in detail both between and within the categories suggested.

The changing role of the city centre

In the early stages of city development rudimentary versions of the urban services noted above became concentrated near to the city centre in order to serve the relatively compact urban area. In the context of the growing city the particular locational requirements of the various services tended to result in the emergence of a spatial segregation by function over a wider area. However, with the development of lower density suburbanization in the postwar period, the opportunities offered to serve a decentralizing population, combined with the problem of maintaining accessibility to the city centre for an increasingly car-oriented society, has asserted the attractions of functional decentralization for most of the traditional city centre activities. Competition, therefore, has emerged as the typical relationship between the city centre and suburbs for the development of most urban services. This competition found the earliest and most graphic expression in many of the cities of the USA where catastrophic city centre decline was not uncommon (Jacobs 1961). Nevertheless, most central areas continue to contain concentrations of urban service activities, partly because the location of the central area continues to allow it to provide services performing a city-wide or wider regional function, and partly because the forces of inertia have maintained elements of the original pattern. In most western countries, however, the historic commercial dominance of the city centre has now been called into question, and the need for ameliorative planning strategies is widely recognized as imperative to its future survival. Consequently, the early academic concern to delimit the central business district and achieve a comprehensive understanding of its internal spatial structure, while of continuing contextual value, has given way to analyses of the detailed relationships between its physical form and functioning. Much of the latter work has the ultimate aim of contributing to policy initiatives designed to retain the city centre as the major commercial, social and cultural focus of urban life.

However, at present, the city centre frequently remains as a primary focus of many urban service facilities, around which the subsequently developed intra-urban service systems are arranged. For this reason it will be instructive to consider the distribution of urban services in the city centre as a first stage in the development of an understanding of the spatial patterns of service facilities in the city.

The central business district

Much of the early urban geographical interest in the city centre focused on the central business district (CBD), particularly through the pioneering work of Murphy, Vance and Epstein in the USA (Murphy 1972). The CBD was characterized as the functional core of the city around which activities requiring an accessible location for their economic viability or functional efficiency tended to gravitate. Typically, it comprised concentrations of retailing and associated consumer services, commercial and public office activities, wholesaling and warehousing and an array of entertainment and cultural activities. A method of CBD delimitation was developed based on detailed land-use surveys of the functions attracted by the commercial potential of centrality: retail and consumer services, including restaurants, entertainment facilities and hotels; and commercial office activities. Subsequently, variants of the technique have been used widely in a number of countries in the initial stage of analyses of the CBD, comprehensive reviews of which are available elsewhere (Murphy 1972; Herbert and Thomas 1982; 1990).

However, the enduring heritage of the early literature is its contribution to an understanding of the internal structure of the CBD. The spatial differentiation of functions was related to the 'bid rent' value per unit area of sites, itself a reflection of accessibility. Thus, the extent to which an activity can profit from exploiting the commercial advantages of accessibility will determine land value, and this will be reflected in the spatial arrangement of business activities. This suggested the likelihood of a broad concentricity of similar retail types reflecting their hierarchical status. However, this relationship holds true only at a highly generalized level. Relative accessibility within the city centre is rarely a function merely of distance from the peak land value intersection (PLVI). Morphological complexity associated with physical site constraints and historical factors superimposes strong segregative effects upon any tendency towards concentric zonation. The conflict between the need to gravitate to the central point to maximize the commercial advantages of accessibility, and the geometric limitations of space at this point associated with the demands of city growth, served to accentuate further the tendency to functional segregation. Consequently, functional segregation has come to dominate the spatial structure of most modern city centres (Figure 8.1). In the largest 'world cities' such as London, New York and Paris it was considered that these same segregative forces initiated the development of a characteristically fragmented spatial structure (Figure 8.2). Some similarities are evident in these cities but detailed differences in spatial structure reflect the local physiographic and historical constraints, and the socio-economic variations in which such cities need to be viewed.

The microspatial regularities within the CBD identified in the exploratory work of Nelson (1958) also continue to retain credence. The detailed decisions of both businesses and individuals were considered to result in a degree of spatial ordering amongst retailers. The theory of cumulative attraction was based on the premise that a number of stores dealing in similar or complementary types of goods will attract more business if they are

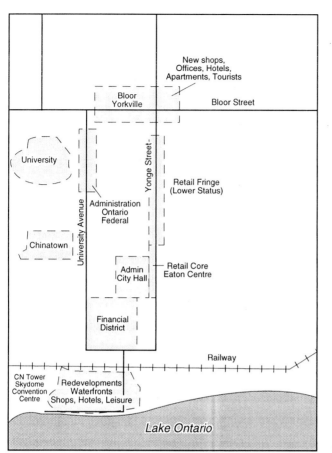

Figure 8.1 Commercial developments in downtown Toronto

clustered. This results from an increase in shared business because shoppers can compare quality and prices, or because customer inter-change is encouraged between stores offering complementary goods and services. Together, these tendencies constitute the rule of retail compatibility. Conversely, stores selling standardized convenience products may well be mutually repelled to minimize competitive hazard. These ideas initiated an interest in the recognition of regularities in the distribution of shop types, and extensive evidence suggests that high-order or quality comparison goods retailers tend to cluster into particular sections of a centre, while low-order goods outlets are significantly more dispersed often at the margins of a centre (Brown 1992). The behaviour of shoppers demonstrates consistent findings. Strong comparison shopping linkages between large department stores in city centres is widely apparent, while a functional complementarity between clothing and footwear stores, and furniture and furnishings has a comparable effect (see also Chapter 11).

The CBD: contemporary issues

Since the mid-1950s the character, internal structure and problems of city centres in North America and western Europe have been transformed by a number of major modifying influences. These vary in their degrees of importance between countries but reflect a combination of pressures associated with the competitive impact of functional

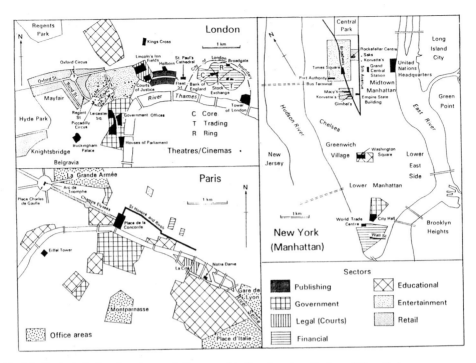

Table 8.2 Central city functional areas in three world cities: London, Paris and New York

decentralization, particularly of retail and office activities; problems of accessibility associated with increases in private car ownership; and economic and social changes resulting from deindustrialization and ethnic ghettoization. The city centres, consequently, tend to present fewer attractions for shoppers and employers, and the process of decline is exacerbated further by the fears for the personal safety and security of those that continue to have to use the area. Commonly, however, the segregation and fragmentation of functions has tended to increase significantly.

The adverse commercial impacts of such changes first became markedly apparent in the USA, and was characterized by Berry *et al.* (1963) as 'commercial blight'. Urban decentralization was generated by a rapid increase in car ownership and associated improvements of urban highways, which considerably improved intra-city mobility. This initiated a decentralization of employment opportunities from the restrictions of a city centre location, while at the same time an increased desire for spacious living encouraged residential suburbanization which resulted in the reduction of residential densities by a factor of between 4 and 8. These trends favoured the development of planned car-oriented shopping facilities in the outer suburbs which were also encouraged by the lack of effective planning controls. The availability of suitably large, relatively cheap suburban sites resulted in the proliferation of planned suburban shopping malls, at nodal locations on rapid transit routes. By contrast, the ease of access to the city centres was reduced, while the replacement of the middle-class white population of the inner suburbs by low status groups (usually ethnic minorities) undermined the spending power of the inner city market. Inevitably, the combination of the attractions of the new suburban centres along with the deterioration of the commercial environment of the city centre, exacerbated by fears generated by social and

DEMOGRAPHIC SHIFTS

Suburbanization of population
and buying power
Depopulation of inner city areas
Change in the socio-economic
composition of the inner city population

NEW COMPETITION IN RETAILING

Regional malls
Smaller Shopping centers
Ribbon developments

CHARACTERISTICS OF THE
DOWNTOWN AREAS

Traffic and parking problems
Negative image
Obsolete physical plant
Fragmentation of land-use

Source: After Lord 1988

Figure 8.3 Causes of the decline of downtown retailing in the USA

racial problems, has resulted in the widespread decline of the CBD in the USA since the mid-1950s (Lord 1988). The causes of decline in retail and associated functions in the downtowns of US cities is schematically represented in Figure 8.3, and a graphic illustration of the decline of the CBD of Charlotte, North Carolina, through into the early 1990s is provided by Guy and Lord (1993).

In fact, Lord (1988) suggests that the traditional city centre in the USA has become less of a retail-commercial district and more of an office-commercial and cultural-entertainment complex. Its weakness as a retail centre results from its increasing dependence on 'internal markets' comprising CBD employees, tourists and city centre residents, rather than its traditional orientation towards the metropolitan area shoppers now intercepted by the profusion of suburban shopping opportunities.

However, these adverse circumstances have not led to the inexorable decline of the CBD everywhere, since many city centres have retained significant advantages for the provision of specialist shopping activities. Potentially, they are still at the point of maximum accessibility to the whole city region in comparison with the sectoral accessibility of the suburban regional centres. Again, due to historical inertia, the CBD retains concentrations of office employment, governmental activities, entertainment, medical, and cultural facilities which bring significant numbers of people regularly to the city centre. Many city centres have also developed an important and expanding tourist and convention trade function. In addition, a significant demand by selective groups – the unmarried, childless, mobile sections of the higher-income categories and the affluent elderly – for middle and high-cost apartments in central locations has resulted in the residential regeneration of formerly socially declining districts in some of the environmentally more attractive city centres. In Chicago, for example, this trend has brought over 20,000 residents back to the central city (Mazur 1991),

---

HISTORIC ADVANTAGES

    Access to the city region
    Government Administration
        local and federal
    Office concentration
    Historic buildings - tourism

DEVELOPMENT OPPORTUNITIES

    Gentrification of older enclaves
    Redevelopment of former industrial sites
        waterfronts, dockyards, railways

REORIENTATION TO 'INTERNAL MARKETS'

    High status residents of gentrified areas
    White collar office workers
    Festival - leisure shoppers - visitors/tourists
    Convention visitors

Figure 8.4 Commercial regeneration of retailing in city centres in the USA

and this has the effect of enhancing the potential retail expenditure of the inner city population and contributes to a safer and more attractive city centre environment. Likewise, the deindustrialization of the inner city has provided developmental opportunities on waterfronts, and former dockyards and railyards for offices, housing, convention centres, leisure and associated 'festival' shopping opportunities, all of which have strengthened the 'internal markets' of the downtown (Figure 8.4).

Since the mid-1970s, therefore, the declining centres of a significant number of cities in the USA have witnessed, at least, a partial revitalization. A number of mixed office, hotel convention centres and shopping complexes exemplified by the Prudential Centre in Boston and the Renaissance Centre in Detroit have added distinct but separate commercial precincts to traditional city areas. Similarly, a number of large shopping malls have been added to North Michigan Avenue in Chicago to transform it into the area known as the 'Magnificent Mile'. This is now a 24-hour zone catering for residents, shoppers, office workers and tourists, and is accredited as one of the safest areas in the city (Oc and Trench 1993). Speciality, theme or festival centres have also been developed in a number of city centres. Faneuil Hall and Quincy Market in Central Boston, the Ghiardelli Square on the San Francisco waterfront, Harbour Place in Baltimore and the Trumps Centre in New York are notable early examples of a trend which is now virtually nationwide. In fact, a large number of redevelopment strategies have been used in recent years, and these have been comprehensively reviewed by Robertson (1995) (Figure 8.5).

However, the process of downtown regeneration has rarely entirely offset the competitive impact of functional decentralization, and the CBD, in most cases, continues to occupy a commercially secondary and environmentally problematic status. In fact, in many instances the process of regeneration has itself added problems of spatial fragmentation to the efficient functioning of the city centre. The redevelopment process has normally involved joint ventures, initiated by public authority enthusiasm, but requiring major elements of private

PEDESTRIANIZATION
Traffic free streets
Transit malls
Skywalks
Subways

INDOOR CENTRES
Regional shopping malls
Mixed use complexes
shopping, residential office
Festival market places

HISTORIC PRESERVATION
Adaptive reuse of old buildings

WATERFRONT DEVELOPMENT
Water-dependent - marinas
water related - restaurants, aquaria
water enhanced - hotels, housing

OFFICE DEVELOPMENT
Corporate headquarter complexes
Mixed office,
residential shopping complexes

SPECIAL ACTIVITY GENERATORS
Convention centres
Sports stadia

TRANSPORTATION ENHANCEMENT
Mass transit improvement
Light rail transit
Car parking improvement

(After Robertson, 1995)

Figure 8.5 Downtown redevelopment strategies in the USA

investment to bring the schemes to fruition. For this reason, the public sector has normally occupied an 'enabling' role rather than a strongly 'directive' function, so that there has been a strong tendency for private finance to favour 'secure and segregated' developments in the frequently problematic environmental circumstances of the central city. Thus, commercial interests are the fulcrum of the regeneration process, with a focus on luxury retail consumption, exclusive residential development, and office precincts which are separated from the other elements of the urban fabric. In effect, regeneration is essentially a process of re-commercialization, insulated from the poor and ethnic minorities, and resulting in the increased 'privatization of public space' in the post-modern city. This process has been illustrated for New Orleans by Brooks and Young (1993), while similar considerations underlie the shift of the CBD core of Los Angeles west to Bunker Hill away from the historic downtown, left to serve an ethnic mix of poor Asians, Mexicans and Central Americans (Loukaitou-Sideris 1993). In fact, the latter study suggests that a combination of commercial and security considerations has fundamentally transformed the character of urban design. High walls, blank façades, limited access to parking areas and the streets are portrayed as separating functions from the wider urban fabric, while excluding the less affluent. Attractive areas of 'open space' are largely contained within building complexes, and form sanitized 'oases of nostalgic imagery'; all of which detract from the spontaneous character of city centre life.

Since the mid-1980s, partly a reflection of a slowdown in economic development and partly in an attempt to reduce fragmentation and segregation in the city centre, large-scale redevelopment is being replaced by more subtle attempts to reintegrate the component parts of the city centre and return to a truly 'living city'. At the forefront of this activity has been the Business Improvement District (BIDs) policy, of which there are already over 1,000 examples in the USA (Mallett 1994). Local referenda empower business leaders to levy local taxes to improve the quality of the environment. This involves a combination of activities focusing on the improvement of the cleanliness, security, and aesthetic quality of the street environment in order to enhance the image of the city centre and to 'soften' the edges of the fragmentation associated with large-scale redevelopment.

However, in Canada, while subject to similar competitive pressures, the situation of the city centres is far less problematic. This reflects, until recently, sustained urban population growth, combined with firmer planning constraints on the development of decentralized regional shopping centres and the absence of a substantial inner city racial problem (Jones and Simmons 1990). Thus, development and redevelopment strategies aiming to retain the attractions of the downtowns by promoting modern retail facilities, environmental improvements, festival shopping centres and enhanced public transport systems have been widely undertaken. Large city centre shopping complexes, usually focusing on an Eaton's department store, have been developed in most major Canadian cities, the largest of which in Toronto offers in excess of 186,000 square metres of shopping floorspace. Even in Edmonton, with the competition of what is accredited as the world's largest mega-regional shopping mall, the West Edmonton Mall containing over 376,000 square metres located 5 miles west of the downtown, active redevelopment has retained a vibrant city centre (Canadian Geographer 1991). In fact, the Canadian situation suggests that a degree of accommodation between the old and the new is possible even in a situation of substantial decentralization.

In western Europe the impact of retail decentralization has been generally less marked than in North America, due principally to more restrictive planning regimes. This has been particularly evident in the UK, where prior to the 1980s central and local government faith in the efficiency of the traditional hierarchy of shopping centres to serve urban areas was the basis of retail planning policy. This found strongest expression in a commitment to the maintenance of the city centre as the commercial and social hub of urban life. Thus, large-scale retail redevelopments were initiated in the 1950s and a number of recurrent elements have come to increasingly characterize the spatial structure of the central areas of British cities (Figure 8.6). Inner ring roads with associated car-parking facilities usually surround the CBD; pedestrianized retail concentrations, separate office districts, civic centres, and entertainment districts are more easily distinguishable within the CBD, while conservation areas to preserve historic elements of city centres are frequent. Thus, like the North American city, spatial segregation and functional fragmentation have become increasingly characteristic features of British city centres, although reflecting town planning ideals rather than market forces.

This phase has been followed by the construction of covered malls from the mid-1960s. Between 1965 and 1989, 8.9 million square metres of retail floorspace has been provided in 604 town centre shopping schemes of 4,650 square metres or more (DoE 1992). However, in many cases this activity has not been accompanied by sufficient investment in the

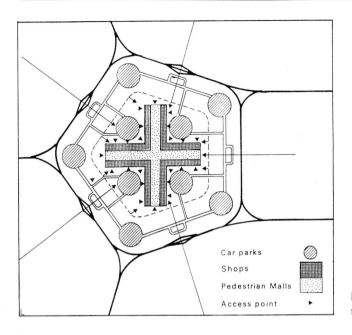

Car parks

Shops

Pedestrian Malls

Access point

Figure 8.6 An idealized central area structure for Coventry

infrastructure necessary to enhance public transport facilities, road access, and the quantity and quality of car-parking facilities demanded by the more affluent, mobile segment of the market. Ease of access to the city centre has rarely been improved for users of public transport, and has been reduced for the car-borne shopper (DoE 1994b). At the same time, the decline of inner city industry and the redevelopment of some of the densely occupied inner suburbs by lower density housing, usually occupied by relatively poor and often ethnically concentrated communities, has reduced the captive market of many city centres and inner suburban shopping centres.

However, despite an official commitment to the traditional shopping hierarchy, gradual decentralization has taken place since the mid-1960s (Thomas and Bromley 1993). This was accentuated for much of the 1980s, contingent upon a stronger government commitment to a market philosophy. This, along with a nationwide growth in car ownership and the associated redistribution of the population to suburban and rural locations, has had a negative competitive impact on the traditional city centres and inner suburban centres. Consequently, the process of decentralization appears to have curtailed the growth of the central shopping areas of the older industrial towns and cities and initiated a 'compaction' process at their margins. Deterioration of the city centres of Sheffield and Dudley has, for example, been linked with the development of nearby regional shopping centres (DoE 1993; Rowley 1993), and, in Swansea, with the vigorous growth of the retail warehousing sector (Thomas and Bromley 1993). Thus, many city centres in the UK, particularly in the larger industrial towns, now display evidence of commercial decline indicated by long-term vacancies, lower status stores replacing market leaders, the emergence of charity shops, and the development of a general air of dilapidation, most evident in locations peripheral to a centre. This process reduces the overall attractiveness of the centre and is analogous to the process of decline already noted in the USA. In fact, widespread concern is now being expressed on the future of the city centre, and the notional ideal of a complementarity between city centre and suburban shopping is giving way to a recognition of the growing competitive impact of unrestrained decentralization.

However, a commitment to the long-term 'vitality and viability' of the city centre in the UK has been strongly reasserted by central government at regular intervals since 1988 (DoE, 1992; 1994b; HOC (House of Commons), 1994). The favoured mechanism for regeneration is seen as a partnership between public sector initiation and direction, combined with private sector finance. This reflected the market orientation of the former Conservative government, and closely mirrors the experience of the USA. More specifically, town centre management to promote active development, firm management and positive promotion is regarded as a vital ingredient of the regeneration process, and 89 town or city centre managers have been appointed (HOC 1994). However, the issues of funding of town centre management and the status of town centre managers remain unresolved. Boots and Marks & Spencer have provided considerable support for town centre management schemes, but additional private sector funding has been low and sporadic, while the 'managers' generally occupy middle-management rather than top-executive posts. Clearly, the potential contribution of town centre management to the revitalization process still requires the firm and urgent resolution of the outstanding questions.

However, retail decentralization continues in the UK at present (see pp.174–181), albeit at a constrained pace. Consequently, despite an apparent official commitment to the future vitality of the city centres, there is an urgent need for vigorous public and private sector regenerative activity if the situation is not to deteriorate further.

A substantial element of constraint on retail decentralization has also characterized the situation in the rest of western Europe, a comprehensive review of which has been provided by Davies (1995). Following the less restrictive attitudes to retail decentralization of the 1960s and early 1970s, the recognition of the competitive impact of retail decentralization on the city centres led to the widespread introduction of stricter controls. This was initiated with the French *Loi Royer* in 1973 and strongly reaffirmed in 1993. A similar trend in former West Germany was reflected in the gradual strengthening of the *Baunutzungsverordnung* legislation since 1977 (Reynolds 1993). Control has been the particular hallmark of the German experience where concerted efforts have been directed at the revitalization of the city centre with an emphasis on comprehensive pedestrianization programmes instituted under the *Verkehrberuhigung* concept (traffic calming), environmental enhancement strategies, and public transport improvement policies. At the same time, except where decentralization is seen as advantageous to the reduction of inner city congestion, the new retail forces have been severely restricted in the emerging strategies. In both cases, however, more imaginative pedestrianization and car-parking schemes are generally considered to have maintained better access along with a more amenable shopping environment than characterized the British situation. Likewise, in central Copenhagen the problems of commercial decline associated with retail decentralization resulted in the formulation of 'Ideplan 77', comprising a wide range of environmental improvements focusing on enhanced pedestrianization, improved car-parking, and the functional segregation of a variety of speciality retail and leisure precincts.

The case of the Netherlands was initially portrayed less optimistically. Borchert's (1988) review suggested that legislation formalized in 1976 was largely ineffective, and this precipitated major problems, particularly for the smaller shopping centres. Inner city decline, particularly in the largest centres of Amsterdam, Rotterdam, The Hague, Utrecht and Eindhoven was also apparent in the late 1980s, although more recent revitalization initiatives by city authorities appear to be retrieving the situation. The completion of a new City Hall and library complex in The Hague in 1995 is seen as the first step in the creation of the revitalized 'New Center'. This is intended to encourage private sector investment in a major office complex (600,000 square metres) designed to link the main railway station with the City Hall to form a new 'heart' for the city centre (de Pater 1996).

In general, however, the European evidence promotes the value of firm direction, designed to reduce uncertainties and to accommodate commercial innovation. In all countries, however, it seems that the critical issue for the continued strength of retailing in city centres is the vexed question of access. The location of city centres at the hub of the urban transport network has obvious advantages for attracting a significant proportion of the users of public transport. The ease of access for car-borne shoppers offered by most suburban shopping centres is still, however, nowhere nearly matched by city centres. In an increasingly motorized society, whatever the improvements undertaken in the traditional city centres, the continued commitment of the large magnet stores and investment in new retail facilities is still critically dependent upon car-borne shoppers being able to park with ease; in close proximity to the major retail concentrations; at minimal cost; and in safe and amenable surroundings. The failure to grasp this particular nettle is likely, in the absence of severe restraints on continued decentralization, to result in the progressive decline of city centre retailing in European cities.

The experience of the largest international centres such as London and Paris are an exception to this generalization. Despite the scale of traffic congestion, in both cases the strength of the 'internal market' support provided by the international office and governmental functions, the associated residential gentrification, as well as thriving tourist industries have combined to avoid widespread commercial blight. In London, the buoyancy of retailing in the Knightsbridge area, and the development of 'festival' retailing exemplified by the redevelopment of the Covent Garden wholesale market, are indicative of this situation. In Paris, the maintained exclusivity of the Rue Faubourg St Honoré and the redevelopment of the three-level Forum shopping centre at *Les Halles* are of equivalent significance. Even so, the tendency towards commercial decline intermittently noted in Oxford Street, London, is symptomatic of the loss of the metropolitan area trade and the environmental deterioration associated with traffic congestion.

The dispersal of urban services

The suburbanization of shopping facilities

With the physical expansion of urban areas well beyond the original city centres a point is soon reached when significant numbers of people are located too far away from the CBD to be supplied conveniently with the most frequently required goods and services. New suppliers of the most frequently required, lowest order functions respond to this situation by establishing premises in locations accessible to the increasingly dispersed population. If dispersion of demand continues, it becomes feasible for increasingly more specialized functions to decentralize. Usually, these additional functions will gravitate to the most

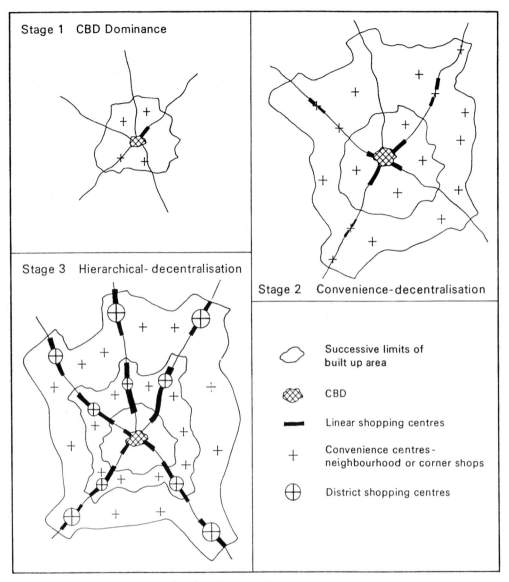

Figure 8.7 Schematic representation of retail decentralization

accessible of the original non-central locations and, in the process, create a series of second-order service centres. This process is schematically illustrated in Figure 8.7. These centres will not normally achieve the degree of specialization found in the CBD because they will be less accessible to the city-wide population necessary to support the highest-order functions. The remainder of the original non-central service locations will continue to provide lower-order functions in positions interstitial to the highest-order centres. These form a series of lower-order centres. This process ideally leads to a nested hierarchical spatial pattern of service centres in cities, similar to the central place system conceptualized by Christaller (1933).

The application of these concepts to the study of intra-urban service centres was first developed in the North American literature. Berry *et al.* (1963) indicated that Chicago demonstrated a central commercial dominance until 1910, but by 1935, 75 per cent of business establishments were located beyond the CBD. Commercial land-use extended in ribbons along most grid and arterial routeways and at the busiest intersections outlying business centres developed which could be differentiated into neighbourhood, community and regional hierarchical orders, in proportion to their size and degree of centrality to the surrounding population. The essentially linear pattern was related to the dependence of the population on public transport routes in the densely populated inner suburbs.

Since 1950 the strong forces promoting retail decentralization noted in the previous section have resulted in the transformation of the intra-urban system of shopping centres in US cities. Planned car-oriented shopping centres have been developed at a profusion of accessible locations on the intra-urban highway network. Lord (1988) records that between 1950 and 1980 the number of such centres increased from 100 to 22,000 by a process characterized as the 'malling of the American landscape'. The newly developed centres have tended to increase in size from neighbourhood to regional status as personal mobility has increased. In the process the enhanced sophistication of design and the degree of specialization of the centres has developed from parades of small shops with forecourt parking facilities providing essentially convenience items, through larger parades including superstores and junior department stores, to the enclosed regional shopping malls including superstores and department stores set in vast car parks. Lord (1988) records that in the Baltimore metropolitan area alone (population 2.2 million) there were ten regional shopping centres of greater than 46,500 square metres, two of which exceeded 92,900 square metres, while even larger examples such as the City Post Oak area in suburban Houston (185,750 square metres) are not uncommon.

Currently, however, the most spectacular example is the West Edmonton Mall in Canada, to which the term 'mega-regional centre' has been applied. This centre, developed by the Triple Five Corporation, comprises a comprehensive shopping and leisure centre of 376,000 square metres, including the 46,500 square metres Fantasyland indoor amusement park and around 14,000 car-parking spaces. Five major department stores are represented in the two-level centre, along with an ice skating rink, indoor lake and over 400 shops, effectively forming an alternative city centre, offering twice the retail floorspace of the downtown (Figure 8.8). A second combined retail-leisure complex, the Mall of America (390,000 square metres) was opened by the same company in 1992 in Bloomington, 8 miles south of the city centre of Minneapolis. This provides over 400 shops, including four department stores on three shopping levels, and at the heart of the mall is a 7 acre amusement park called Knott's Camp Snoopy (Figure 8.8). The fact that only two centres of this scale have been developed raises the question that perhaps the limiting size of the planned shopping centre phenomenon has been reached? Certainly, recent reports of the proposal of a third retail-leisure complex by Triple Five for Silver Spring, Maryland, north of Washington DC, appears to be more specifically leisure-tourist orientated, and to be of a significantly smaller scale (116,000 square metres).

However, there is little doubt that the North American city has moved away from the traditional monocentric form organized around the CBD towards a distinctly polycentric structure. In the USA, Lord (1988) notes that by as early as 1982 there were already 14 metropolitan areas in which a total of 25 major suburban retail concentrations exceeded the

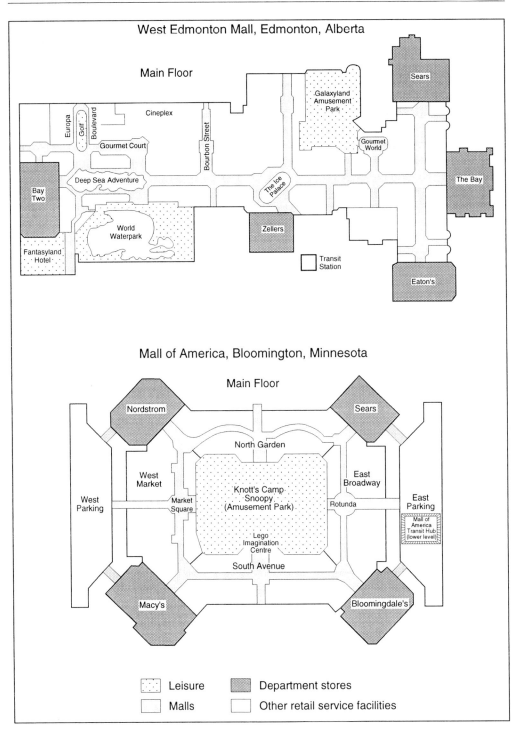

Figure 8.8 Two North American mega-malls: Edmonton and Bloomington

retail sales levels of the CBD, the trend being particularly marked in Atlanta (3) and Indianapolis (6). In many instances, however, the more rudimentary early centres of all sizes are now suffering from the competition of the larger, more attractive recent developments and many require extensive refurbishment.

The system of shopping facilities in North American cities has also demonstrated increased spatial fragmentation since improved personal mobility has allowed the locational specialization of retail conformations to take place. Specialization has occurred by product, particularly for infrequently purchased goods such as automobiles and furniture, and also by social class, leading to both high-status fashion centres and low-status discount stores. In addition, highway-oriented functions such as service stations, restaurants, drive-ins and motels have accentuated the linear pattern of commercial land-use. In addition, the commercial blight evident in the CBD has also afflicted the inner suburbs. Decline has been substantial and prolonged. Retailers of the higher-order goods traders have gone out of business. Vacancy rates of one-third to one-half are not uncommon as the residential areas have declined in status.

The outcome of this overall process of change, unmitigated by planning intervention, is what Berry *et al.* (1963) have termed 'spatial anarchy'. In situations of this kind, it is recognized that some semblance of order based upon a hierarchical arrangement of shopping centres remains. Indeed, Morrill (1987) presented the case that the largest 34 of the 400 'shopping areas' in Metropolitan Seattle transacted 75 per cent of the business in a clearly recognizable hierarchical structure. Nevertheless, ribbon developments of various kinds were recognized along with the emergence of specialized functional areas, while the imminent transition to a four centre metropolitan structure was predicted. Thus, the appropriateness of the concepts derived from central place theory as a basis for the analysis of the system of shopping centres in North American cities has become increasingly questionable. In fact, the continuing anarchic quality of the resulting system is suggested by Jones and Simmons' (1990) typology of retail clusters (Figure 8.9).

The pressures for change noted for the North American situation have emerged in most other western countries. However, the growth in personal mobility and affluence, and the associated decentralization and suburbanization, have not proceeded as rapidly elsewhere, while urban planning controls have exerted a variable influence. This is reflected in international variations in the process of adjustment.

In the Australian and European intra-urban systems the process of change is well advanced. As early as the mid-1960s there were already six large planned centres in suburban Melbourne, one of which was of regional significance. In addition, the initiation of a process of commercial blight had occurred in the inner suburbs in which recent southern European immigrants were concentrated. The familiar North American pattern of central area decline was also apparent for the six Australian state capitals by the late 1970s (Alexander and Dawson 1979).

Similar tendencies have emerged throughout western Europe. However, the scale and nature of decentralization varies substantially between countries, and it is difficult to discern a detailed comparability of trends between countries due to variations in the retail business environment, data definitions and planning regimes (Reynolds 1993). Nevertheless, it is evident that there has been a widespread development of superstores and hypermarkets (ranging between 2,325 and 23,250 square metres). Reynolds (1993) notes that in France

Figure 8.9 Morphologies of metropolitan retail clusters

The varying morphology of the metropolitan retail cluster

Unplanned nodes	Strips	Planned centres
Metropolitan (a) Central business district (b) Specialized produt area	(a) Downtown pedestrian mall (b) Speiality retail strip (b) Ethnic shopping street	(a) Super-regional (b) Downtown fashion mall (c) Theme mall
Regional (a) Arterial intersetion (a) Downtown of older suburb	(b) Automobile row (b) Furniture strip	(a) Regional mall (a) Pedestrian mall at major intersection (b) Superstore (b) Discount mall
Community (a) Street intersection	(a) Shopping Street (a) Fast-food strip	(a) Community mall
Neighbourhood (a) Corner cluster	(a) Suburban strip mall	(a) Neighbourhood plaza

Note: Items marked (a) serve spatial markets, (b) serve specialized markets.
Source: K. Jones and Simmons 1990

there were 450 *centres intercommunaux* of greater than 5000 square metres, usually comprising a hypermarket and a number of specialist stores. The development of planned suburban shopping centres of all sizes has also been important. In the former West Germany there were 500 new centres by 1977, 57 of which achieved regional status; while in Paris alone 15 new regional shopping centres were designated in conjunction with a strategy for planned suburban growth which included 5 new towns (Davies 1984). The recognition of the competitive impact of retail decentralization, however, led to moves towards the stricter controls noted earlier for France and the former West Germany, and also developed in Belgium, the Netherlands and Scandinavia (Reynolds 1993; Davies 1995). Nevertheless, retail decentralization has continued to be a widespread feature of retail change in western Europe, and Reynolds offers an exploratory typology of 19 types of new planned retail clusters which have emerged (Figure 8.10).

A cautious attitude to retail decentralization, supported by restrictive planning controls, is also characteristic of the British experience. Throughout the period 1960–80 central and local government was committed to the retention of the traditional shopping hierarchy focused on the city centre and complemented by a range of district centres, neighbourhood parades and a range of more localized facilities. This is schematically represented in Figure 8.11. Retail planning policy focused on the encouragement of investment in CBD redevelopment, along with the improvement of the shopping, traffic and parking environment of the smaller unplanned centres. A limited number of planned district centres, such as Seacroft in Leeds and Cowley in Oxford, were developed to ensure equality of access to services throughout a city region. Below this level, a series of neighbourhood or corner store facilities were considered necessary to provide convenience goods for the less mobile sections of the community, while also serving a supplementary convenience function for the population at large.

Figure 8.10 Typology of planned shopping centres in Europe

I: Regional Shopping Centre (30,000 m² +) (322,900 sq ft) *
(Centres commerciaux régionaux, grandes centros periféricos, regionaen Shopping-Center)
(Two or more anchors)

Locational variants	--central area in traditional core	Eldon Square, Newcastle, UK
	--entral area adjacent traditional core	La Part-Dieu, Lyon, France
	--non-central suburban growth pole	Vélizy 2, Versailles, France
	--green field site/transport node	Curno, Bergame, Italy
Compositional variants	--hypermarket-dominated	A6, Jönköping, Sweden
	--department & variety store-dominated	Lakeside, Thurrock, UK
	--foood, non-food and leisure anchors	Parquesur, Madrid, Spain

II: Intermediate Centres (10,000 m² -- 30,000 m²) (107,600 -- 322,900 sq ft)
(Centres intercommunaux, centros intermedios)
(at least one anchor, integrated)

Locational variants	--non central suburban community	Auchan, Torino, Italy
	--greenfield site/transport node	Caeron Toll, Edinburgh, UK
Compositional variants	--hypermarket-anchored	Euromarché,
	--specialty non-food anchored	BHV, Cergy, France

III: Retail Parks (5,000 m² --20,000 m²) (53,800 -- 215,300 sq ft)
(Centres de magasins d'usine ou parc des entrepôts, parques comerciales, retail warehouse parks)
(Not obviously anchored; not wholly integrated centres)

Locational variants	--non-central suburban community	Various, UK
	--greenfield site/transport node	Lakeside Retail Park, UK
Compositional variants	--retail warehouse tenant mix	Fairacres Retail Park, Abingdon, UK
	--factory outlet tenant mix	Direct Usines, Nancy, France
	--hybrid tenant mix	Fosse Park, Leicester, UK

III: Speciality centres (1,000m² +) (18,800 s ft)
(arcades, galeries marchandes, galerías comerciales, Galerien)

Locational variants	--central area in traditional core	Arcades, Lille, France
Compositional variants	--non-food specialist traders	Powerscourt Town House, Dublin, Eire
	--department store conversion	Centre Point, Braunschweig, Germany.

---

* – Floorspace figures are indicative only.
Note: Centre providing for loal or neighbourhood needs are excluded.
Source: Reynolds 1993

Despite the constraints of decentralization imposed by most structure plans, steady commercial pressure in the period 1965–79 initiated the process of retail decentralization at this time. Since the early 1980s the increasingly 'free-market' orientation of central government resulted in the relaxation of restrictions on such developments for much of the 1980s. This operated primarily through the appeals procedure rather than by the formulation of a comprehensive new strategy. The situation was exacerbated by the Enterprise Zone Policy announced in 1980 which encouraged retail developments in the many enterprise zones where investment in new manufacturing was considered unlikely. The changes have substantially modified the traditionally hierarchy over the last thirty years, to a degree that they could be considered to constitute a 'retail revolution'.

The development of superstores and hypermarkets (over 2,325 square metres) from the

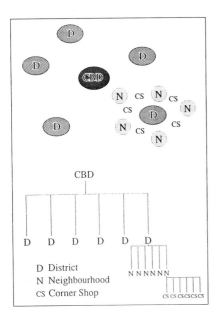

Figure 8.11 Urban retail system in the UK pre-1965

mid-1960s constituted the 'first wave' of retail decentralization (Schiller, 1986). By 1993 Verdict Market Research reported that the existing 868 superstores transacted near to 50 per cent of the grocery shopping trade, and the top five retail corporations (Sainsbury's, Tesco, Argyll-Safeway, Asda, Dee-Gateway) controlled an estimated 61.4 per cent of the British grocery market, with their activities focused primarily on the larger superstores.

This was followed in the mid-1970s by a 'second wave' characterized by retail warehouses (930–18,600 square metres), initially selling DIY (do-it-yourself) products and garden centres ('roofrack' trade) and bulky durable goods such as furniture, carpets and electricals. More recently, the range of goods offered in retail warehouses has expanded to include clothing, footwear and toys. Consequently, by the early 1990s around 2,000 retail warehouses and 250 retail parks accounted for 14 per cent of non-food retailing (DoE 1992). To these have recently been added the warehouse club format, introduced by Costco from the USA, and developed by Matalan, Makro and Cargo Club. These offer bulk purchasing, a customer loyalty scheme and marked price-cutting as their principal attractions.

The locational requirements of most superstores, hypermarkets and retail warehouses have similarly stressed the need for ease of access and parking, along with the financial advantages of low site costs. Consequently, large accessible sites adjacent to major intersections, central to newly developing residential areas, on the edges of cities, or on the fringes of industrial estates have been favoured. Also, as a result of ad hoc planning decision, individual stores have often been developed in isolated free-standing locations. Initially, these developments added a distinct element of spatial fragmentation to the system of shopping centres in many towns.

With the increasing scale of retail decentralization, planning authorities have directed development to industrial estate or enterprise zone sites. This has resulted in the emergence of loose agglomerations, or occasionally planned concentrations of retail warehouses, in industrial estate locations or articulated along main arterial roads. Such developments have been termed 'retail warehouse parks'. Where such developments incorporate superstores, a more balanced shopping environment results, with a potentially greater impact on the local or even regional shopping facilities. These have been termed 'retail parks'. The retail park has become a distinctive new element in the retail structure of most British cities, the largest of which are to be found in enterprise zones. The unplanned Swansea enterprise zone retail park, for example, included 2 superstores and 24 retail warehouses by 1988. These total 39,000 square metres, a scale fast approaching the threshold for a small regional centre (46,500 square metres).

The forces generating retail decentralization have gathered even greater momentum in recent years. In fact, Schiller identified a 'third wave' dating from the proposal by Marks & Spencer in May 1984 to open out-of-town stores. All the major high street chain stores have followed this lead, so that the third wave is distinguished by the decentralization of the full range of quality comparison goods shopping and supporting specialist services. The spatial form of the new wave and its status in the retail system is of critical significance to the process of retail change. The logical conclusion of the decentralization of quality comparison goods retailing was the development of regional out-of-town shopping centres. The opening of the MetroCentre in the Gateshead Enterprise Zone in 1986, planned as an integrated regional shopping and leisure complex, was the first major example of the new phase (Figure 8.12). This has been followed by a plethora of similar applications and reflects the recognition of the potential commercial importance of the third wave (Figure 8.13).

In practice, however, central government caution on the potential impact of the new centres on the traditional town and city centres, supported by the larger high street retailers with large property investment portfolios in the city centres, has curtailed the number of new regional shopping centres (Guy 1994). In fact, by 1996 only four had been built, and these appear to reflect a variety of factors rather than a direct commercial response to market opportunities. The first three – the MetroCentre, Gateshead (136,430 square metres), Merry Hill, Dudley (148,000 square metres) and Meadowhall, Sheffield (116,250 square metres) were all built in enterprise zones, and were intended to rehabilitate derelict former-industrial sites, while providing areas of economic opportunity in areas of high unemployment. The Lakeside Centre in Thurrock (116,250 square metres) was, in part, similarly designed to rehabilitate a derelict chalk quarry, while providing improved shopping opportunities in an area deemed to be under-served with high-order retailing. From the government perspective, they are regarded as experimental, and the impact of each is being investigated to determine future policy for the development of centres of this scale. Evidence to date suggests that such centres can have serious negative effects on nearby centres of similar or smaller sizes (Thomas and Bromley 1993). The impact of Merry Hill on Dudley (DoE 1993; Perkins 1996) and of Meadowhall on Sheffield and Rotherham (Rowley, 1993) are cases in point. However, each has enhanced the shopping facilities for the population in their trade areas, while providing opportunities for economic regeneration and improving the images of the areas in which they are located (Williams 1992).

The critical issue for retail impact is the overall number of such centres to be built. As indicated earlier, central government remains supportive of the commercial and social significance of existing city centres. However, a degree of continued ambivalence is suggested by recent decisions to support a further phase of regional centres (Figure 8.13). In addition, in the absence of a definitive policy of the future place of regional shopping

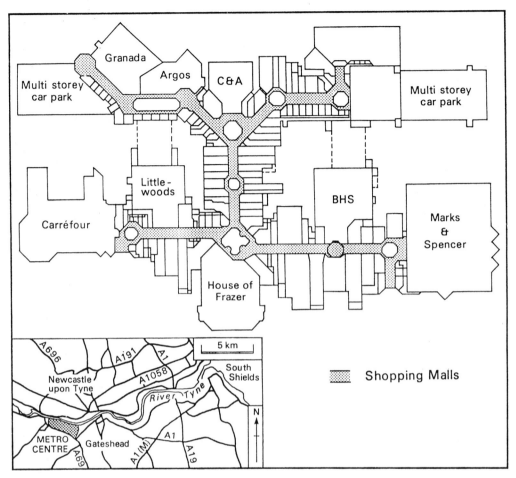

Figure 8.12 Metrocentre, Gateshead: a regional shopping centre

centres, permission has been granted for a number of sub-regional centres (under 46,500 square metres), typically comprising a Marks & Spencer store, a superstore and a small number of retail warehouses. Culverhouse Cross outside Cardiff, and Fosse Park adjacent to the M1 outside Leicester, are examples of this type. Similarly, the Merry Hill centre is to be expanded by one-third, while a development company has obtained approval for a shopping and leisure complex at White City in inner London.

However, Schiller's (1986) view that the development of new regional centres is likely to be limited in number and largely confined to the edges of the major conurbations due to site constraints continues to have some force. There are few locations with sufficiently good road access to serve catchment populations in excess of 250,000, which would not generate unacceptably high levels of local traffic on or near to major inter-regional traffic arteries, and which at the same time would be large enough to accommodate such developments. The dangers, therefore, suggested by Schiller of the gradual addition of quality comparison goods retailing to existing retail parks are worthy of reiteration. This could result in the creation of a large number of 'hybrid centres', which if developed in excess of 46,500 square metres will form unplanned or *de facto* regional centres, with potentially explosive impact on the existing retail system.

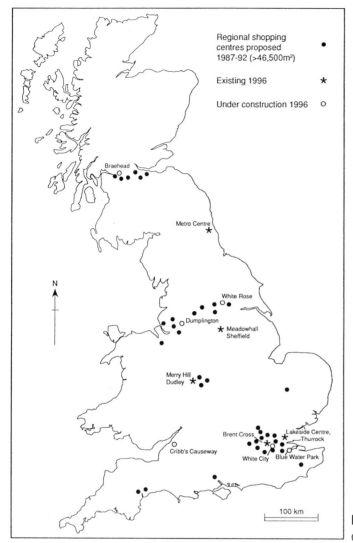

Figure 8.13 Regional shopping centres in the UK, 1996

Retail change in the UK has been subject to two powerful and conflicting sets of forces. On the one hand, the commitment of local government planners to the assumption of the commercial and social efficiency of a traditional hierarchical system of urban shopping centres has tended to retain a strong element of centralization and inertia in the system. By contrast, the commercial pressures, for large decentralized facilities, increasingly supported by central government, reflects the combined influence of deep-seated forces affecting both social lifestyles and the economic organization of retailing. The relationship between these two sets of forces has not at any stage been accommodated by a comprehensive retail planning strategy. Consequently, the cities of Britain demonstrate a combination of evolutionary and revolutionary features, epitomized by 'hierarchic' and 'anarchic' retail forms. This is illustrated for Greater Swansea (Figure 8.14). Clearly, the spatially anarchic retail system which developed in the cities of the USA in the postwar period has not emerged in the UK, while the traditional centres have not yet had to contend with the unfettered forces of decentralization. The regular reassertion of central government caution on the issue

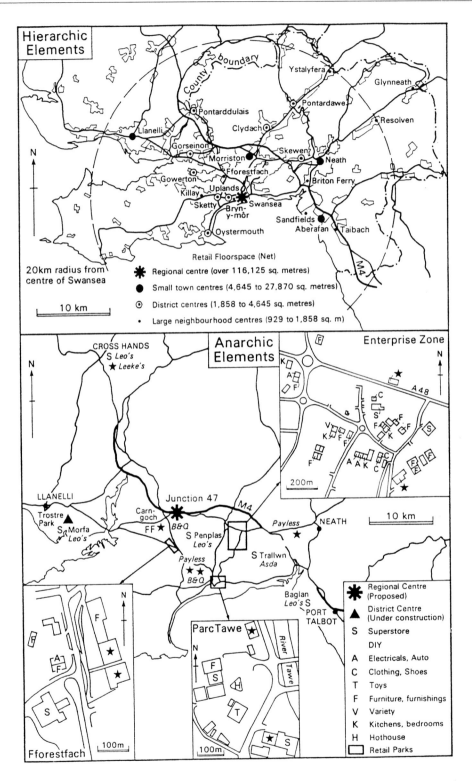

Figure 8.14 Hierarchic and anarchic elements of a retail system, Swansea

of retail decentralization following the profusion of applications for regional centres has provided a temporary respite to evaluate the situation. However, the pressures for continued decentralization, combined with the evidence of the impacts of the process to date, suggest the urgency of the need for formulating a firm retail planning strategy capable of maintaining a complementary relationship between the old centres and the new commercial pressures; and for retaining the city centre as a commercial and social focus of urban life. The changes associated with the 'retail revolution' are continuing to unfold. Nevertheless, at the moment, Brown's (1993: 191) contention that in Britain 'the intra-urban hierarchy is alive and, if not exactly well, is certainly in better shape than the critics of the central place model might lead one to expect' continues to find support.

Wholesaling and warehousing

The essence of the wholesaling and warehousing functions is that they provide a distribution and supply service for other business and industrial functions and thus gravitate towards these 'primary' activities. With the increasing demand for larger modern premises on extensive sites, the improvement in the intra-urban communications networks and the decentralization of the activities which wholesaling and warehousing have served since 1945, pressures for decentralization have also affected these functions.

There have, however, been few geographical analyses of wholesaling and warehousing. Early work recognized a variety of traditional wholesaling districts on the edges of city centres to supply the business community of the surrounding hinterland, along with produce districts serving small-scale customers such as hotels, restaurants and produce retailers; while stockholders of speciality office equipment gravitated to similar sites to service the business community of the CBD.

Changes in transport technology, particularly associated with the increased importance of road haulage, have prompted general wholesaling functions to migrate to a variety of peripheral urban locations which offer convenient road access. Again, the general increase in city centre traffic congestion and site costs, with associated growth in both the scale of operations and the service areas, has produced major difficulties in central city sites. Consequently, planners have encouraged suburban relocations such as the Covent Garden market from central London to Nine Elms and the Les Halles produce market to Rungis in suburban Paris.

More recently, however, the emergence of large organizations in all facets of economic life has resulted in both producers and retailers becoming more directly involved in distribution to improve all aspects of operational efficiency. However, improvements in information technology, characterized in retailing by Electronic Point of Sale (EPOS) Systems for in-store stock control and Electronic Data Interchange (EDI) for automatic ordering from suppliers, has led to the concepts of 'just-in-time' (JIT) stock replenishment and the ultimate ideal of the 'stockless' distribution chain. The economic advantages to retailers and manufacturers of the need to maintain only a minimal stock level, distributed from a relatively small number of distribution depots, strategically located in relation to their network of outlets, is clear. This has resulted in Britain in the emergence of a relatively small number of large concentrations of distributional depots near to the larger centres of

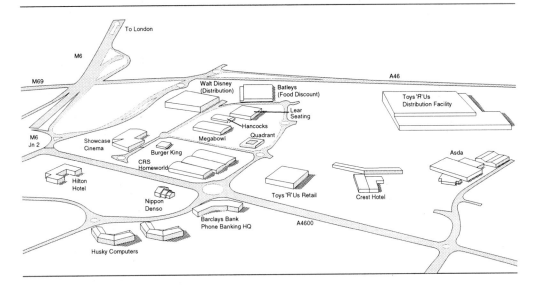

Figure 8.15 Intersection city: Cross Point business park, Coventry

population, closely associated with the motorway network (McKinnon 1989). The close relationship between concentrations of the wholesaling and warehousing function and the full range of levels of the urban hierarchy has, therefore, declined. Instead, large modern distribution centres are becoming a marked new feature of the wholesaling and warehousing scene in accessible locations along the main motorway corridors, particularly near all the major conurbations. These are beginning to form substantial employment concentrations which are likely to have regional significance as 'poles' of economic development, and are often intermingled with the 'anarchic' warehouse elements of retail decentralization. One such concentration, located at junction 2 of the M6 near Coventry, comprises a complex amalgam of retail, distribution, office and manufacturing functions (Figure 8.15). This has been described disparagingly as an 'intersection city', due to its mundane design and sense of 'placelessness' (Pearman 1994). The emerging functional concentration is beginning to bear a close resemblance to the 'hybrid' regional centres predicted by Schiller (1986). However, for food products the pattern remains more regionally dispersed, reflecting the wider spatial dispersion of outlets offering convenience good, although increasing concentration at nodal points in the most populous parts of the country is the dominating trend.

Offices in the suburbs

Offices are concerned primarily with transactional and administrative activities serving business organizations and administrative institutions involved in all sections of the life of a country or region. Consequently, office location patterns reflect the need for access to, and intercommunications between, the broad economic, social and political forces central to the life of the country. This expresses itself in a greater degree of concentrations of office activities into a relatively small number of the largest cities in the centrally significant or rapidly growing regions of developed countries than occurs for the services previously considered. In the UK, London dominates the distribution of the headquarters of the top industrial companies, while Paris with 90 per cent of the headquarters of major national companies and nearly half of the civil service jobs dominates the French pattern. The only exception is the USA, where the scale of the space economy combined with the location of areas of rapid growth has resulted in the emergence of secondary nodes in Chicago, the industrial cities of the mid-west, Los Angeles and San Francisco, although none rivals the concentration in New York and the associated cities of the north-east seaboard.

Similarly, at the intra-urban scale there has until relatively recently been a characteristic dominance of office clusters in the CBD and its periphery. This reflects the pervasive influence of the agglomeration economies associated with the need for access; for direct contact between decision-makers; for access to the investment and money markets; to government agencies; and to expert consultation in the professions and higher educational establishments. Even following developments in telecommunications technology, the so-called external economies of a city centre location, based upon the complex network of local linkages, often requiring face-to-face contact, has to a significant degree maintained the importance of a city centre location. The combined influence of these centralization forces was reflected directly in the postwar office building booms in the centres of the largest western cities such as New York, London, Tokyo and Toronto, while the same forces are still reflected in the presence of distinct office-commercial concentrations of tower blocks in the centres of most 'transactional' cities of global, world and regional economic significance (see also Chapter 5).

However, the scale of centralization has contributed to locational diseconomies in city centres associated with the familiar problems of traffic congestion and rising site costs. This has resulted since the 1970s in a reappraisal of city centre locations as advances in telecommunications technology have reduced some of the advantages of centralization, particularly for routine operations. At the same time, suburban locations usually offer lower site costs, the opportunity to provide more car-parking and the flexibility to allow incremental increases in floorspace. Also suburban locations might offer shorter journeys to work and an attractive suburban working environment.

Thus, clustering of office activities has emerged in North American cities in the inner suburban service centres of the larger metropolitan areas, at nodal points on the interstate highway network, near to airports, and more recently, in the vicinity of regional shopping centres. Lord (1988) notes that the latter locations, now termed suburban business centres, have been particularly favoured, and the City Post Oak regional shopping centre in suburban Houston has attracted a concentration of 1.9 million square metres of office development. Hartshorn and Muller (1989) have suggested that this form of suburban clustering could well be at the forefront of the radical restructuring of the North American 'metropolitan space economy'. Using evidence from Atlanta, they predict the emergence of a number of 'suburban downtowns' on the edges of the US city which will 'rearticulate' the city structure in accordance with an 'urban realms model', replacing a formless suburban sprawl (Figure 8.16). The suburban downtown is defined as a cluster of activities focused on a regional shopping centre, and including a concentration of at least 465,000 square metres of office floorspace incorporating the headquarters of one of the top thousand American companies, together employing around 50,000 persons. The clear emergence of such a

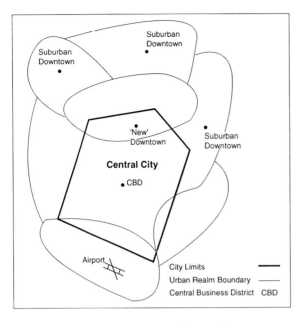

Suburban
Downtown

Suburban
Downtown

'New'
Downtown

Suburban
Downtown

Central City

• CBD

Airport

City Limits ———

Urban Realm Boundary ———

Central Business District   CBD

Figure 8.16 Urban realms model and Atlanta polycentric metropolis

structure will probably require firmer planning control and direction than is often currently exerted, while Matthew (1993) suggests that many US and Canadian cities exhibit significant deviations from this norm. However, Garreau (1991) graphically illustrates the development in most major North American cities of embryonic suburban downtowns, which he terms 'edge cities'. In fact, he asserts that these areas already include two-thirds of all North American office activities.

In the western European cities office decentralization has been weaker and more fundamentally affected by central and local government controls. In the UK by the mid-1960s London was the only city where a limited dispersal had occurred spontaneously. This initially took the form of an uncoordinated speculative scatter, with more organized exceptions in Croydon, Ealing and Wembley. The Greater London Development Plan of 1969 attempted to assert a greater degree of order by directing development to the largest 28 shopping centres to minimize potential problems of traffic congestion and service coordination, while maximizing external economies of concentration and public transport provision. The policy achieved a measure of success and large urban office concentrations such as Croydon emerged, although the relative autonomy of the London boroughs resulted in local deviations from the overall strategy.

The relaxation of government control in the 1980s, however, combined with advances in telecommunications and a buoyant demand for office accommodation, introduced significant spatial changes. Redevelopment proposals for the formerly blighted sites near the main railway stations involved integrated office, shopping and residential complexes. Notable examples in London include the Broadgate development near Liverpool Street Station, the Holborn Viaduct Site and the King's Cross redevelopment scheme. At the same time, government encouragement of the commercial redevelopment of the London Docklands resulted in a large new office complex at Canary Wharf on the Isle of Dogs, although economic problems associated with the recession of the 1990s has curtailed its progress (see also Chapter 5). Nevertheless, the functional fragmentation of the largest cities noted earlier is likely to continue in London (Figure 8.2)

Elsewhere in western Europe and North America there are similar trends and policies. In Paris development pressures in the 1970s resulted in new office concentrations in the inner city at the Avenue de la Grande Armée in the west, Montparnasse in the south, the Gare du Lyon in the east, and the Place d'Italie in the south-east. Office development has also been directed increasingly to nodal suburban sites, and to the system of regional shopping centres and new towns. Of these the most spectacular development has emerged at La Défense in the inner suburbs only 2 miles north-west of the Arc de Triomphe. The site of 300 ha. offers excellent access with its own railway station, bus terminus, extensive car-parking and direct links to central Paris via the new express underground (RER) and the urban motorway network. It comprises 10 per cent of the office floorspace of central Paris and provides for 100,000 jobs in an integrated retail, leisure and residential complex (HOC 1994). The City Nord office park located 6 km north of the city centre of Hamburg was developed for similar reasons. The scheme was used to divert development pressures away from the city centre and now provides for 30,000 jobs in an accessible and attractive suburban location. Similarly, in the San Francisco area the East Bay office complex developed in the 1980s provides 1.9 milliom square metres of office floorspace which has acted as an alternative to concentration in the downtown (Walker 1996).

The suburban decentralization of offices is now a well-established feature of most western cities and in most cases urban planners are attempting to control the process of relocation. The most favoured solution has been to concentrate the dispersal at a limited number of nodal locations on the urban transport system, while integrating office employment with the suburban provision of shopping facilities, leisure activities and housing. The rationale behind this policy has been the need to avoid the diseconomies of central area congestion, while at the same time maximizing the attractions of the agglomeration advantages of concentration in non-central locations.

The medical services system

Like shopping centres, the medical services system has been viewed by geographers broadly within the conceptual framework of central place theory. The upper hierarchical levels are characterized by large specialized medical centres and teaching hospitals, while at the lowest levels a more ubiquitous distribution of partnerships of general practitioners, individual physicians or paramedical personnel located in health centres or home based situations provides a less specialized entry to the system. Similarly, the number of levels in the hierarchy are considered to reflect a combination of the density of population, levels of personal mobility, the varying degree of specialization and frequency of treatment required, and the finance available to provide the service.

However, the 'commercial' analogy cannot be taken too far. General practitioners are not market oriented to the same degree as retailers, but are usually restricted by professional codes – which, for example, discourage advertising – or government licensing controls – which aim at a socially equitable spatial distribution of surgeries. Similarly, for hospitals the individual units tend to be larger relative to the scale of the system as a whole compared with an individual retail outlet and, therefore, are less responsive to changes in the nature and location of demand, while in many countries hospital location policies are becoming subject to direct governmental control.

Nevertheless, in the USA the fee-for-service basis of the health care delivery system is sufficiently strong for central place theory and the methodology of retail studies to have been used initially as an analytical framework. Market considerations of profitability and the ability of the patient to pay have strongly influenced the spatial structure of the system, and are reflected in the locational behaviour of physicians. Most are located in commercial centres and their levels of specialization are related to the hierarchical status of the centres. Similarly, changes in the locations of physicians over time closely follow the changing pattern of demand of their middle and high status patients in a process closely analogous to that associated with commercial blight. De Vise's (1971) early study illustrated the catastrophic decline in the number of physicians in the inner suburbs of Chicago 1950–70 from 475 to 76 contingent upon a transition from middle-class white to low-status negro communities. More recently, Shannon and Cutchin (1994) suggest that this process is characteristic of most developed countries, noting evidence from Detroit, Pittsburgh, New York and Phoenix, along with studies undertaken in the UK and New Zealand. Their investigation of Munich between 1950 and 1990 similarly indicated the avoidance by general practitioners of inner city concentrations of poor ethnically segregated populations.

The locational determinants of hospitals are even more complex. Hospitals vary with respect to the type of care and the degree of specialization offered. There may also be variations in hospital type according to their religious affiliation and to the degree to which they will accept charity patients, and this is paralleled by variations in demand for their services. The relationship between the supply and demand criteria results in a hierarchy of hospitals, conceptually similar to the hierarchy of shopping centres (Figure 8.17). In general, the largest, most specialized hospitals are found in the central city, while the lower-order district and community hospitals are more frequently located in suburban and urban peripheral sites. Locational inertia is, however, characteristic of the specialized hospitals located in city centres. Imbalances in the location of supply and demand are overcome in the short term by suburban patients undertaking relatively long journeys, but this situation need not necessarily operate in favour of the inner city concentrations of low-status communities. Their access to hospitals is still via a physician, frequently in a suburban practice, and in any event is restricted to the relatively small number of hospitals admitting charity patients wherever they are located.

The commercial orientation of service provision results in a socially and spatially regressive pattern of service provision. The financially stable sections of the community secure the best quality of health care, while poor people, elderly people and ethnic minorities, and particularly those living in deteriorating inner cities or remote rural areas, are typically most adversely affected. The ameliorative policies associated with the Federal Medicare and Medicaid programmes, designed to assist aged and poor people respectively, have since 1966 attempted to redress these imbalances, despite an unenthusiastic commitment to 'socialized' medicine. However, policies designed to reduce expenditure on public welfare programmes associated with economic recession and the 'austerity capitalism' of the Reagan and Bush administrations of the 1980s and early 1990s have exacerbated the situation for the economically indigent. Consequently, an 'underclass' of the low-waged and unemployed comprising near to 25 per cent of the population has only limited access to the

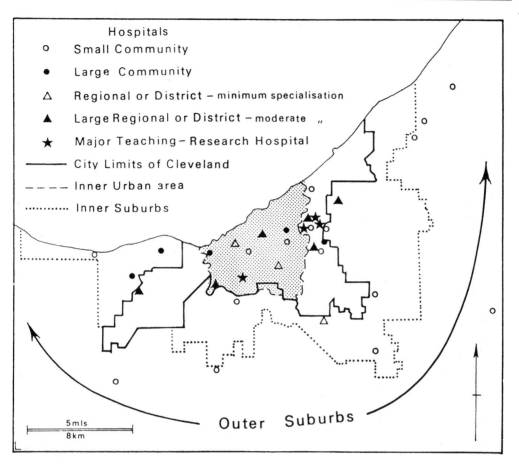

Figure 8.17 Hierarchy of hospitals in Cleveland, Ohio

quality of health care considered typical of a developed country (Bodenheimer 1989).

It is now widely recognized that the commercial basis of the system underlies many of its problems. The fact that finance 'drives' the system may well promote more capital intensive medical tests and procedures than are perhaps clinically necessary – a tendency which is accentuated by the 'defensive' stance adopted by medics by fears of litigation. At the same time, the high costs of continuing care associated with an ageing population, along with the high cost of administration related to the organizational complexity of the system, have similar inflationary effects. These trends have resulted in the emergence of a new disadvantaged group estimated in 1992 to comprise 34 million people or 12 per cent of the population: those with insufficient incomes to provide health insurance for themselves, and yet earn too much to qualify for Federal assistance.

Thus, despite the fact that medical services in the USA account for 13 per cent of the GNP, a figure of approximately double that for the UK, substantial imbalances in access to health care persist. Consequently, the socially divisive potential of unequal access to care has attracted renewed policy initiatives since the mid-1980s (Mayer 1986). Characteristically, these focused on financial issues rather than the instigation of a radical reform. The central dilemma of the Republicans was to devise a system of cost-cutting without reducing the quality of service to the fee-payers, while at the same time reducing the imbalances in the system.

In the public sector economies have involved the introduction of maximum payments based on ailment diagnosis rather than the cost of care (Diagnosis Related Groups or DRGs). This has the potential for increasing the division between public and private medical care. The private sector has, by contrast, witnessed the emergency of Health Maintenance Organizations (HMOs) which contract with employers or individuals to provide fixed-fee medical services in order to contain escalating costs. The government was supportive of such 'preferred provider organizations' with their focus on financial viability at minimum cost, a trend which is leading to the 'corporatization of American health care' (Mayer 1986). It was anticipated that the competition offered by these organizations will have a general deflationary effect on the cost of health care.

However, there was little evidence that the social and spatial inequalities of access inherent in the system had declined by the early 1990s. This, along with the enduring financial crises in the system, has under the Democratic Clinton administration threatened to precipitate more radical changes. Nevertheless, muted public support for a 'welfarist' policy, along with the 'conservative' stance of the entrenched financial interests in the health care system, resulted in proposals falling far short of a 'National Health' initiative. Hillary Clinton was appointed policy coordinator in 1993, and the scheme sought to curtail expenditure along the lines of the existing financial strategies, while extending health insurance to uninsured people. The strategy was promoted as 'managed competition' rather than 'socialized medicine'. Even so, the scheme did not achieve widespread popular or political support, and the system remains substantially unchanged. In effect, it appears that the nature of the existing system is highly resistant to radical reform, and the social and spatial inequalities of access seem set to persist into the foreseeable future.

The medical service systems of the UK and USA have in the past been placed virtually at opposite extremes of the continuum between public and private organizational control. The British National Health Service (NHS) introduced in 1948 continues to be primarily financed and controlled by the government, and traditionally services have been provided with minimal direct charge. The NHS replaced a variety of private and voluntary general hospitals and private medical practitioners, reminiscent of the system in the USA, by a less complex organizational structure based upon a hierarchical ordering of services. This has been subject to intermittent change but the principles of coordinating control and planning at the upper levels of the hierarchy, along with the devolution of service provision to the local level to maximize responsiveness, has been maintained in successive administrative restructurings in 1974 and 1982 (Figure 8.18).

In terms of service provision, since 1962 increasing centralization has characterized the system. For hospital services, a general hospital of 1,500–2,000 beds with associated ancillary convalescent and special care units for the integration of facilities in each health district of 200,000–300,000 population has been the administrative and medical ideal. Below this level, primary care has been provided by general practitioners (GPs), each serving approximately 2,000–2,500 persons, although significant and persistent imbalances have been apparent in the peripheral regions of the UK and in the less attractive parts of the major cities. General practitioners have, however, also been encouraged to centralize into large group practices to serve 10,000–15,000 people. Ideally, these were to operate from

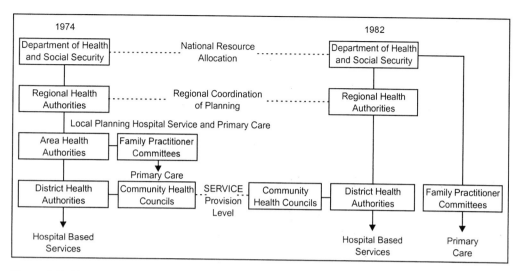

Figure 8.18 National Health Service delivery system in the UK, 1974 and 1982

health centres, providing a wider range of more specialized diagnostic and therapeutic out-patient facilities than the smaller practices, and were designed to allow hospitals to concentrate on more serious ailments. This is reflected in the rapid increase in the number of group practices, irrespective of whether they operate from fully fledged health centres. In 1961, only 17 per cent of general practitioners functioned in group practices of four or more, but this had increased to 60 per cent by 1994, comprising a total of 15,881 practices in England alone (Figure 8.19) (Department of Health (DoH) 1995).

The publicly funded NHS, organized via a neat administrative structure and incorporating service provision ideals, appeared more likely to offer administrative efficiency, combined with a social and spatial equality of access to health care than the US

Figure 8.19 General medical practitioners in England and the rise of the group practice

Type of Practitioner	1961	%	1981	%	1991	%	1994	%
One doctor	5377	28.3	2990	13.4	2923	11.4	2824	10.6
Two doctors	6344	33.8	4004	18.0	3707	14.4	3644	13.7
Three doctors	4008	21.2	5132	23.0	4521	17.6	4218	15.9
Four doctors	1984	10.5	4255	19.1	4671	18.2	4700	17.7
Five doctors	715	3.8	2940	13.2	4060	15.8	4275	16.1
Six or more	450	2.4	2983	13.4	5804	22.6	6906	26.0
Total	**18878**	**100**	**22304**	**100**	**25686**	**100**	**26567**	**100**

Sources: DHSS Health and Personal Social Services Statistics for England (1980, 1988)London: HMSO; DoH Health and Personal Social Services. Statistics for England (1995) London: HMSO

system. Nevertheless, a wide array of problems have emerged and remain to be resolved. Accusations from medics and politicians that too high a proportion of resources are spent on administration rather than treatment have been a persistent component of the health debate. Thus, in 1982 the area health authorities were abolished and their functions devolved to the district level to reduce costs and enhance responsiveness to public needs (Figure 8.18).

Throughout its history the NHS has also been considered to reflect the managerial and bureaucratic viewpoints. The needs expressed by patients or consumers of the service (consumer sovereignty) have always occupied a secondary role. Until 1974, the consumer was represented by the lay appointees to the various administrative committees, and their loyalties were usually divided ambiguously between managerial responsibility and community representation. The major decisions to develop district general hospitals, and to amalgamate general practitioners into health centres and group practices, did not necessarily represent the best interests of the consumer. Both decisions reduced the accessibility of medical services to the patient, with scant attention given to the social implications of these actions. Obviously, professional medical considerations, managerial decisions and financial limitations have to be accommodated, but a socially optimal spatial allocation of medical services must take account of the needs of both the supply system and the users.

To redress this imbalance, since 1974 the control of service provision has been devolved to the most local level. In addition, community health councils (CHCs) were created to represent public opinion, but these are still largely composed of representatives nominated by local authorities, health group interests and medics and, as currently constituted, have very limited representative power. CHCs thus tend to adopt one of two roles, depending upon a combination of the nature of local issues and the personalities of their members. Either there is a general compliance with official NHS proposals, or a conflict on issues involving controversial change. In either event, the status of the CHCs is not conducive to a constructive dialogue between service providers and the public. The situation was exacerbated further by the changes of 1982 (Figure 8.18). Since that date the eminently local family practitioner committees (FPCs), reconstituted into family health service authorities (FHSAs) in 1990, responsible for the organization of general practitioner services, dentists, opticians and pharmacies, became responsible directly to the Department of Health rather than to the district health authorities. This also had the effect of reducing the formal links between CHCs and the FPCs (and FHSAs) along with the consumer viewpoint.

Also, despite the existence of the NHS since 1948, with its accredited aims of reducing social and spatial inequalities of access to health care facilities, significant imbalances remain. The typically high geographical concentrations of ill-health and premature death characteristic of the lower status groups in the declining industrial regions, the deteriorating inner cities and the poorer suburbs have been demonstrated to persist in a wide range of studies (e.g. King's Fund 1995). In part, this is considered still to reflect the 'inverse care law' by which the availability of good medical care varies inversely with the needs of those served, although the influence of past working conditions and contemporary lifestyles are also contributory factors. Policies initiated in the mid-1970s to redress these imbalances, such as the regional redistribution of finance via the Resource Allocation Working Party (RAWP), or the provision of financial incentives to attract general practitioners to under-provided areas, are indicative of an official recognition of the geographical dimension of the problem.

However, since the mid-1980s the political ideals of the Conservative Government have began to alter fundamentally health care delivery in the UK. The need to introduce economies associated with the recession of the early 1980s has been succeeded by a financial philosophy designed to contain expenditure on public services like the NHS. Eyles and Woods' (1983) structuralist interpretation of this trend stressed a government commitment to 'reduce unproductive social expenditure' and a shift in 'systemic imperatives' from social issues to economic considerations. This has close parallels with the period of 'austerity capitalism' in the USA, and has promoted a significant acceleration of the private medical sector as an alternative service.

The trend was given formal direction and added impetus in the government White Paper *Working for Patients* (DoH, 1989). The two principal cornerstones of policy were reaffirmed as the need to maintain a cost-effective and consumer-responsive system. The main emphasis, however, was focused on the need to exercise economy in order to improve the system. The importance of financial management and accountability have been asserted along with the aim of promoting competition between service providers. The resulting policy instruments introduced radical changes into the character of the NHS. Already, over half the population of England and Wales are served by GP practices with independent 'fundholding' status. They have the duty to manage budgets, ultimately set by the Department of Health, by controlling the costs of prescriptions and diagnostic tests, as well as directing patients to hospitals offering cost-efficient care. Savings effected in these ways are then available to finance better appointed health centres, including a wider range of diagnostic and therapeutic services.

At the same time, the former general district hospitals are being transformed into 'National Health Service Trust Hospitals'. They, also, are charged with managing their own budgets, and provide services under contract to the district health authorities. Ideally, each hospital competes for the provision of particular medical procedures, and any savings effected are intended to improve both the quantity and quality of hospital care.

Clearly, the emerging system was poised to become a closer approximation to the epithet, 'managed competition', than its US counterpart. However, the effectiveness of the changes in providing an effective health care delivery system are, as yet, difficult to gauge. It may well be that GP services are improving, but patient fears that cost considerations might delay expensive investigations or treatments, or that potentially 'expensive' patients find greater difficulty registering with a practice of their choice, are raised regularly. Concern has also focused on the possibility that an 'internal market' is emerging whereby patients from fundholding practices are obtaining preferential referral for hospital treatment. The medical and social implications of consortia of GP practices providing 'night treatment centres', often adjacent to hospital casualty units, for out-of hours' consultation, are also not yet evident. Associated with this trend is the vexed question of the future of home visits by GPs. Similarly, in the hospital sector, disquiet has been expressed that a tendency of hospital specialization by function is resulting in longer distances having to be travelled, particularly by out-patients and visitors. Inefficient competition between hospitals is also a possibility, while concern is expressed throughout the service that too much effort is being deflected into financial management rather than into the provision of health care.

By contrast, the 'consumer responsive' dimension of reform has not commanded commensurate government attention. However, *The Patient's Charter* was formalized in 1992 (DoH 1992). This largely reaffirmed the 'Charter Rights' established at the inception of the NHS, although they were strengthened by the addition of a number of precise quality standards concerning features such as referral and treatment waiting times, and anticipated arrival times of emergency services. For the most part, however, an independent 'consumer' voice in the decision-making processes has not been substantially strengthened. In fact, there appears to have been a tendency for the areas and extent to which community health councils have the right to be involved in the deliberations of FHSAs and NHS Trusts to have declined, while in some areas the CHCs have been under pressure to reduce their membership to reduce costs. Likewise, in November 1994 the National Consumer Council called for a Royal Commission to review social and spatial equity of service delivery in the NHS.

Detailed investigation needs to be undertaken to assess adequately the costs and benefits of the changes. A report, for example, on GP fundholding practices by the Audit Commission (J. Laurance, *The Times* 22 May 1996) indicated that fewer than 10 per cent achieved significant benefits for patients, while most had only 'modest ambitions'. Evidence from the hospital sector currently tends to the anecdotal, but reports expressing concerns at the apparently adverse effects of competition between institutions are widespread. There is also no shortage of reports of hospital ward closures, or the intermittent lack of sufficient beds to cater for demand. However, precise evaluations of the changes present considerable difficulties due to the complexity of the current transitionary situation. Additional difficulties are presented by the problem of disentangling the effects of the organizational changes from the effects of the absolute level of funding provided by government in a context of escalating costs of medical technology, and a political climate of financial stringency in public service investment (Maynard 1994). Suffice it to say that comprehensively 'informed' debate is well nigh impossible, although experience to date suggests that it is likely that future changes will reflect a combination of economic evaluations and political attitudes. Clearly, the working of the system is highly susceptible to changes in government attitude, and substantial modification is anticipated by the return of a Labour government in 1997.

Thus, despite the fact that the health care delivery systems of the USA and the UK are being progressively modified by economic forces, they are still very different. The system in the USA continues to be influenced fundamentally by commercial factors. Similarly, in the UK, despite the rapid increase in the influence of market forces in recent years, public intervention is still central to its understanding. In effect, each continues to demonstrate archetypical features respectively of private and public control, albeit in a rapidly changing, and potentially converging, modern situation. Clearly, a variety of intermediate or alternative systems characterize other countries, but usually the determining variations are related to a combination of economic and political considerations. This avenue has been pursued in greater detail by Curtis and Taket (1996).

However, whatever the detailed nature of the health care delivery system, there are a number of lines of investigation to which urban geographical research can be directed. Of particular interest is the spatial structure of the systems of supply of hospital facilities, primary medical care and associated pharmaceutical services. Investigation is needed of the spatial imbalances of accessibility to the various services enjoyed by the different communities of an urban region. Alternatively, the demand side of the system can be investigated in a manner analogous to the consumer behaviour studies of retail geography. A considerable amount of research has in fact already been undertaken under the general heading of health care utilization behaviour. In either situation, however, the bulk of the literature suggests a need for a synthesis of social and organizational approaches along with the traditional spatial perspective for the continued investigation of medical service systems.

Public utility services

By definition, the locational and operating policies of the public utility services are subject to direct public control, usually via a local government organization. With the concentration of the population of developed countries into urban areas such services, particularly in the spheres of education, welfare, recreation and the provision of emergency facilities, have become increasingly important facets of urban life. These have been termed 'collectivized public services' by Pinch (1985). Urban geographical interest in these services focuses on three major themes.

First, and of primary interest is the size of the facilities, their relative spatial locations and the extent of the areas they serve. Choices have to be made between a relatively small number of large units located far apart and a larger number of small units spaced closer together. The former tend to maximize accessibility, while the latter can offer higher degrees of specialization. Arguments have been widely raised against the development of a small number of units, particularly for sports and informal recreational facilities, because these disadvantaged the 'low mobility' younger age groups and those without a car.

A second line of interest centres on the operational implications of the alternative strategies in terms of the 'efficiency' with which the service is provided. Fire fighting and ambulance services, for example, need locations which allow them to reach the outer limits of their service areas within acceptable time limits. Access and the related issue of the 'distance decay' of efficiency are of critical importance.

Third, the social implications of alternative strategies are also worthy of investigation. In the case of educational facilities, for example, interest has focused upon the effects of alternative catchment-area strategies. Herbert (1976) drew attention to the adverse social repercussions felt by US black urban communities of defining neighbourhood catchment areas for secondary schools and the development of policies designed to redress the disadvantages such as redrawing catchment-area boundaries, busing and compensatory education. Similar misgivings relating to social disadvantage have given rise to the definition of Educational Priority Areas in British cities (see also chapter 12).

Clearly, the geographical analysis of public utility services has proceeded rapidly in recent years. A number of reviews demonstrate the wide literature in the social sciences relating to the provision and evaluation of public utility services and offer an assessment of the contemporary theoretical concepts of methodologies. They stress the need to integrate the social and spatial perspectives to maximize future geographical investigations of these services. Notable in this respect is Massam's (1993) presentation of both the conceptual ideas and technical procedures used in the evaluation of alternative locations for public utility services. The complexity of the decision-making process is examined in the context of a complex trade-off between alternative planning strategies, evaluative criteria, and the variety of interest groups which usually have to be satisfied.

Summary

In the nineteenth century the unity of the wide array of commercial and public services was essentially spatial. Concentrations occurred in and around the edges of city centres, and functional segregation emerged both between and within service types in relation to the specifics of the physical and commercial opportunities offered by sites. Retailing gravitated to its various markets, finance retained its early agglomerative advantages of concentration, wholesaling and warehousing responded to changing transport technology, while the public service sector was displaced into peripheral locations. The changing circumstances of twentieth-century urban development has, however, witnessed a major change from the central city concentration of services to a widespread suburban decentralization. The inherent functional differences between the various types of services have been focused in quite different spatial patterns of adjustment. Thus, the spatial unity of the nineteenth century has been replaced by a spatial divergence by function, which is also reflected in the associated patterns of service utilization behaviour. Retailing, for example, has demonstrated both hierarchic and anarchic responses. Traditional wholesaling and warehousing is being replaced by transport-oriented systems of distribution, and rationalized into fewer nodal locations by modern electronic technology. Offices demonstrate the inertial aspects of central city concentration along with a degree of spatial fragmentation and suburbanization, while the public utilities increasingly reflect public controls and considerations of locational optimality. As a consequence, in recent years the various urban services are being analysed in increasingly different ways. The basic methodologies, however, retain a degree of unity, while the analyses of all stress the need to integrate spatial and social considerations for maximum effect.

CHAPTER 9

The residential mosaic

Traditional theories of city as place

The dichotomy of cities in space and city as place is well established in urban geography. Within the traditional set of theories concerned with city as place, some are indigenous to geography, others are derivative. Urban morphology, with its origins in site-situation studies, analyses of the built fabric of the city and change over time, has strong claims to be an indigenous theory and is an example of continuity within urban geography.

Urban morphology

Traditional studies of the sites and situations of urban settlements also considered historical growth phases and their relation to urban form and morphology. During the later 1940s and the 1950s, this type of perspective became known as the urban morphological approach. The first task, during this period, was to introduce a geographical methodology into a type of study which had been dominated by historical approaches. Smailes (1953) developed a typology of morphological divisions which could be applied to British cities, and suggested a model of urban structure. His concept of townscape, with its components of street plan, buildings, design features and land-use, adopted categories, such as 'terrace-ribbing' and 'villa-studding', that were broad and imprecise with only a general descriptive value. Conzen (1960; 1962) developed the technique of town-plan analysis involving a higher order of detail and an emphasis on the need to relate form to process. Discord between form and function occurred as changing land-uses produced the need for functions to adapt to built-forms designed for different purposes. Town plan analysis included concepts such as the burgage cycle, that referred to a specific form of land-holding and its development through a set of stages, and the fixation lines that marked a still-stand period in the urban growth process. Fringe-belts were zones of land, beyond fixation lines, containing functions, such as cemeteries and public utilities, that required large amounts of space and peripherality rather than centrality. Former fringe-belts became relict components of urban land-use.

Urban morphology was severely criticized during the 1960s as being mainly descriptive, lacking in good measurement techniques and failing to develop a general theory, but there have been significant developments seeking to integrate its concepts with other dimensions of the urban system. Whitehand (1967) investigated the outcomes of competition for fringe-belt sites in the context of building cycles and the activities of house-builders and saw urban landscapes as cumulative, though incomplete, records of booms, slumps and innovations. Other studies integrated urban morphology with urban rent theory, city centre change, historico-geographic theories of urban form and especially with the movement for urban conservation. The task was to show greater awareness of urban fabric and to form a stronger theoretical base for urban morphology, and has provided useful conclusions:

- Different elements of the urban landscape change at different speeds.
- There are persistent elements in urban landscape, notably street lines.
- Whereas survival of morphological elements is the most obvious legacy, imprints and influences, the relict features, can remain long after the physical form has gone.
- Development of urban landscapes is uneven: both the extent of change and the form it takes are subject to cycles.

Derivative sources: land economics

Theories of urban land values, rents, costs and accessibility strongly influenced urban geography. Rent was conceptualized as a charge for accessibility, or a saving in transport costs, involving a bidding process to determine the occupancy and use of land. Ratcliff (1949) developed the concept of bid-rent curves and their influence upon land-use patterns within the city, and the model assumed a central point with greatest accessibility, from which location centrality-value would decrease in a regular manner towards the urban peripheries. An efficient land-use pattern emerged as various activities competed for locations by 'bidding' at various rent levels; their bids weighed their needs for centrality against their ability to pay higher rents and the likelihood of increased transport costs with distance removed from the city centre.

> The use that can extract the greatest return from a given site will be the successful bidder . . . from this emerges an orderly pattern of land-use spatially organized to perform most efficiently the economic functions that characterize urban life.
>
> (Ratcliff 1949: 369)

Figure 9.1 illustrates the bid-rent model and the way in which it can be translated into broad concentric bands of land-use within the city. Those retailing functions which have the greatest need for accessibility in order to maximize profits pay the highest rents for the most central locations. This land is normally intensively used and has strong vertical building development. There is a broader industrial/commercial zone containing functions with less need for centrality and residential land-use occupies more peripheral urban space making trade-offs between land and transport costs. The land-value gradient tends to be matched by a density gradient. This type of trade-off model makes assumptions which depart from reality and the actual land-value surface of a city is more variegated than the model suggests, with lesser peaks at locations outside the central city.

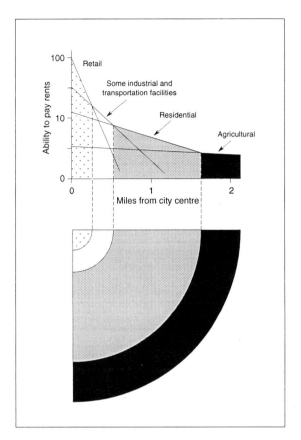

Figure 9.1 Bid-rent curve and urban land-use zones

Derivative sources: social ecology

The Chicago school of social ecology (or urban ecology), most closely associated with Robert Ezra Park, provided a second derivative source of concepts and ideas for urban geography. A great quality of this school was its detailed empirical knowledge of Chicago, based upon intensive field work and involvement, and reflected in their many publications (see Theodorson 1961). Park has been described as an undisciplined empiricist, excited by the patterns and apparent explanations which he saw in city life, but his adoption of a general framework within which to study his patterns led him into a methodology which was committed to theory-building. This framework Park derived from an analogy with the biological world, and the belief that the patterns and relationships evident there could be paralleled by land-use and people within cities. His enthusiasm for a biological analogy reflected the contemporary appeal of Social Darwinism and the guidelines of classical economics. The biological analogy offered a *Gestalt* or total model which was simple and logical and allowed similarities to the biological world to be observed, measured and recorded.

Within the overall framework, there were concepts and a terminology. Symbiosis described the basic set of relationships and the mutual interdependence of the elements of urban life. Park developed symbiosis as an analogy with the example of the humble bee and pollen and their place in the 'web of life'. Closely allied to symbiosis was the concept of competition, translated into economic terms with space being allocated on a competitive basis between users. Community was defined as a population group inhabiting a distinguishable geographical territory and coexisting through a set of symbiotic relationships. The dominance of one particular group was due to its superior competitive power and segregation occurred as the result of a combination of the forces of selection. Invasion and succession described the gradual incursion of one group into the territory of another and eventual displacement as succession took place.

There was always an understanding of the differences between biological and human society, with the latter having the extra dimension of cultural and traditional values. Park suggested that social organization could be studied at two levels, the biotic, in which competition was the guiding process, and the cultural, in which consensus and communication among members of society were the main factors, but still with the assumption that the biotic level could be studied separately. It was the paucity of their treatment of cultural values that proved one of the major points of criticism of social ecologists. They consistently understated distinctively human qualities of the city in a conceptual framework which was essentially mechanistic and generalized.

The critics seized on this as a basic deficiency and questioned the use of a biological analogy. The best known empirical example of this criticism was Firey's (1947) study of *Land Use in Central Boston*. Here ecological laws were insufficient as explanations, and cultural factors, which he described variously as non-rational values, sentiment and symbolism, were the dominant influences in some parts of the city. The motivations of the families who acted to preserve Beacon Hill, an old and prestigious residential district, against the encroachment of commercial functions and lower-status groups, were not economic but were culturally driven. Domosh (1992), in a similar study of the Back Bay area in Boston, came to similar conclusions. She argued that by the late nineteenth century Boston's upper classes were remarkably cohesive and the Boston Association was developed to protect their interests. The Back Bay residential development embodied the ideologies of the elite and allowed them to distance themselves from the new immigrants. Beacon Hill belonged to 'old Boston' but Back Bay offered an opportunity for the newer upper-income groups. Alihan (1938) rejected the biological analogy on more general grounds. She suggested that the Chicago school used terminology inconsistently, thus affecting the interpretation of key concepts such as community and society. This obsession with words was later to evoke cynical rejoinders, such as the claim that human ecology has already inspired a generation of critics too easily irritated by figures of speech, but contemporaneously the defences were few. Wirth (1945), always a less committed ecologist, redefined a position for social ecology as a perspective which focused attention upon localized or territorially defined social structures and phenomena. Ecology provided a perspective on the city, but behaviour could be understood only in the light of habit, custom, institutions, morals, ethics and laws.

Saunders (1981) saw tensions in Park's work arising from the use of the term 'community' to refer to both a physical entity and to a process, including both biotic forces involved in human competition for space, and expressions of consensus in which cultural values prevail. Saunders (1981), however, regarded some of the criticisms of human ecology as misguided:

- Firey's argument on the validity of ecological laws when applied to Boston was misguided because he and Park asked different questions. Firey was interested why Beacon Hill survived, Park in why the rich lived there in the first place.

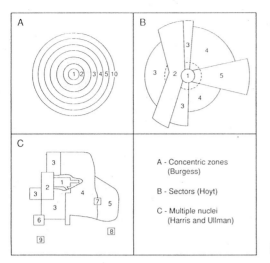

Figure 9.2 Classic models of the city

- Alihan argued that the Chicago monographs failed to distinguish between biotic and cultural forces, but they never intended to. Biotic factors had created natural areas by ecological theory, the monographs sought to examine them as cultural forms.
- Robinson's ecological fallacy argument, individual versus aggregate values was invalid, as Park always emphasized the irreducibility of community as area.

Urban geographers did not take a serious interest in social ecology until the 1960s, when despite its caveats, it still held attractions, including its serious attempt to provide a systematic theory of the city. Again, social ecology had a strong empirical and fieldwork content and there were important land-use models and territorial concepts which had direct appeal to geographical method.

Of the so-called 'classical' models of urban land-use, that proposed by Burgess (1925), Park's principal collaborator, is undoubtedly the best known. The concentric-zonal model (Figure 9.2A) offered a descriptive framework within which to view both the spatial organization of land-use in the city and its change over time. Burgess was aware of the work on urban land values and bid-rents and differences in land values were regarded as the mechanisms by which different functional groups were distributed in space in an orderly and efficient, yet unplanned way.

The model made a number of assumptions including a uniform land surface, universal accessibility to a single centred city and free competition for space. Other assumptions, such as a heterogeneous population, a mixed industrial-commercial base, cheap transit and a capitalist system, were based on contemporary US society. Under these conditions, Burgess suggested that the zonal arrangement of land-uses from centre to periphery would be

1. central business district
2. transition zone
3. zone of workingmen's homes
4. zone of better residences
5. commuters' zone.

Burgess did not claim universality for his model but nevertheless thought that it had some generality within North America. The Burgess model was both a description of urban structure and a framework for urban growth and change, and was essentially concerned with residential structure and change. Invasion and succession gave the dynamic for change as population groups gradually moved outwards from the centre as their status and level of assimilation improved. Change was most pronounced in the transition zone where an expanding CBD forced land-use change and affected land values. As inhabitants abandoned the inner city, migrants replaced them giving high rates of population turnover. This mobility was seen as the main cause of social disorganization and social problems in the transition zone.

Later empirical tests of the zonal model offered a variety of criticisms, including those of its generality. Empirically, researchers argued that gradients were easier to identify than zones and that related concepts such as 'natural areas' emphasized the heterogeneity within zones. Much of the criticism arose from expectations of the zonal model which were never part of its original formulation. It is a model and the search for concentric zones in many empirical studies was one of the less enlightened practices of the 1960s.

Hoyt's (1939) sector model of urban land-use (Figure 9.2B) was the second of the classic models of urban spatial form. Hoyt focused on housing and rent and gathered rental and land value data, which he mapped by blocks, for 142 US cities. His model took the form of a series of sectors emanating from the central business district. The high-grade residential areas pre-empted the most desirable space and were powerful forces affecting the pattern of urban growth. Other residential areas aligned around the high-grade areas, with the lowest-grade areas occupying the least desirable land, often adjacent to manufacturing districts. The various residential areas took the spatial form of sectors, extending from the centre to the periphery, and were thus in apparent contrast with the concentric zones suggested by Burgess. The common elements were the focal nature of the central business district and the presence of a transition-zone which was clearly identifiable in North American cities. Growth occurred in the sector model through a process of neighbourhood change mainly driven by the dynamic characteristics of the high-grade residential areas. These moved towards amenity land, along transport routes, and towards the homes of leaders of the community; production of new housing on the urban periphery could therefore act as a catalyst for change.

The third classic model was that by Harris and Ullman (1945) which they termed the multiple nuclei model (Figure 9.2C). Its main distinctive quality was its abandonment of the central business district as a sole focal point, replacing it by a number of discrete nuclei around which individual land-uses were geared. As the conditions for the location of these nuclei may vary, there was no one generalized spatial form which could be suggested.

The merits of the spatial models of the city, in particular concentric zones and sectors, have been extensively discussed but some summary points can be made.

- Whereas these models are often labelled as land-use models, and refer to commercial and industrial activities, they are essentially concerned with residential structure and change.
- Burgess used the ecological processes of invasion and succession in his explanation, describing these as processes of distribution which sift and sort and relocate individuals and groups by residence and occupation.
- Hoyt focused on a 'filtering' process whereby housing stock was passed down the income hierarchy as the wealthy moved to new homes.
- Burgess explained residential change on the 'demand-side' as new arrivals competed for

space in the inner city and caused ripples to spread outwards. Hoyt, however, saw the stimulus on the 'supply-side' as new housing on the periphery prompted filtering downwards of older housing (Badcock 1984).

- Hoyt had less reliance on accessibility to a centre and introduced the *preferences* of social groups for locations and contiguities, Burgess had more mechanistic assumptions and was closer to the rationale of the bid-rent model.

- Empirical research has tended to support Hoyt rather than Burgess, though a search for spatial forms is not the best test of the 'model's value. Davie was critical of Burgess from his New Haven study, Schnore found that not all US cities showed increased residential status towards the edge of the city, Robson talked of the game of 'hunt the Chicago model' and Saunders (1981) argued that tests of the models inevitably led up a cul-de-sac.

- Although the models take different spatial forms, they should be assessed for the insights they provide into the processes of residential differentiation.

- Spatial forms are useful summaries of urban structure under certain assumptions of underlying conditions. The different forms of zones and sectors are not necessarily contradictory, as they may measure different aspects of urban structure and have complementarity which subsequent research into social areas has revealed.

- As a 'geometry of space', the zonal form has considerable generality and has been used to compare pre-industrial and industrial cities (change over time) as well as modern regional variations.

- The spatial models, especially of zones and sectors, continue to have useful roles in the teaching of urban geography as a means of organizing study of the city, testing more general theories and introducing the theme of functional differentiation in space.

Some progressions

Urban morphology, land economics and human ecology rank as the traditional theories of urban geography and in varying ways were cast in the mould of positive science. Urban morphology has more recently sought to develop models and generalizations, and both land economics and social ecology were linked with general theories and models, even though all contained some exceptions. Several new theories began as reactions to positive science and became significant in their own right. There were the **subjective approaches** developed initially in the humanism perspective. Initially at least their clearest mission was to question the mechanistic, aggregative and 'dehumanizing' qualities of spatial analysis. As Ley (1977) argued, spatial analysts, in their zest to construct models, failed to separate fact from value and reduced place and space to abstract geometries in which people were 'pallid entrepreneurial figures'. With its pre-occupation with generalizations and abstractions from reality, spatial analysis offered a superficial view of human behaviour and no real attempt to understand internal motives and the nature of processes which were at work. Ley (1977: 501) stated the need 'to delve beneath the distribution maps and spatial facts to an examination of social and cognitive processes in their everyday context'.

There was a new emphasis on the subjective meanings of place and space and a sensitivity to the need to make subjective values central to the comprehension of urban environments and socio-spatial behaviour. These could be sentiments and symbolisms, as in Firey's study of a Boston neighbourhood, emphases of the social values attached to place, or on the 'anchoring points' in urban space which are 'stamped by human intention, value and memory' (Buttimer 1976); all marked a renewal of the thrust to understand the subjective qualities of the urban life-world. Relph expressed this well in his study of *Place and Placelessness*:

> Places are fusions of human and natural orders and are significant centres for our immediate experiences of the world. They are defined less by unique locations, landscapes and communities than by the focusing of experiences and intentions onto particular setting.
>
> (Relph 1976: 141)

A second expression of subjectivism in urban geography can be found in **behavioural studies**, though these contained contrasted perspectives. **Behaviourism** had strong links with biological sciences and environmental psychology and rested substantially upon the ideas of stimulus and response developed by psychologists in intensive experimental research, often under laboratory conditions. This type of behaviourism is quantifiable, has the goal of generalization, and belongs squarely in the tradition of positivist science.

Another psychologist introduced concepts with a greater emphasis on subjectivity. H. A. Simon (1957) argued that studies of behaviour made the assumption of economic man, a person endowed with perfect knowledge, the wish to optimize, and the ability to calculate which course of action would achieve the desired optimum. This assumption needed correction and his formulation of bounded rationality suggested that although people strove to be rational, they were hampered by an incomplete knowledge and limited ability to calculate. His concept of 'satisficing' suggested that people work towards levels of attainment which are acceptable, but less than optimal. Satisficer man is a figure much closer to reality than economic man, and behavioural studies adjusted their methods of data collection interpretation to accommodate this more subjective position.

Behaviouralist studies were less interested in the stimulus-response heritage of scientific behaviourism, and more focused on qualitative studies of decision-making at an individual level. The concept of place utility underlined the uncertainty with which people encountered the real world, and there was more awareness of the importance of individual goals, levels of knowledge, and personal preferences. This new emphasis assumed that people had choices and this assumption carried its own caveats, but the immediate benefits were greater concerns with process and a decreasing dependence on aggregate statistics and models.

Other dimensions were the interest in spatial imagery and cognitive mapping. Boulding's (1956) work on the image was a key reference and, in its simplest terms, this was seen as a picture of the world carried around in people's minds and a reference point for their behaviour. The form which the image takes is moulded both by external conditions of socialization, experience and context and, also, by internal factors such as values and prejudices. This concept of image offered a link between phenomenal (objective) and behavioural (subjective) environments but there was no consensus on the nature of this link. For Jackson and Smith (1984), cognitive images were hypothetical constructs whose relation

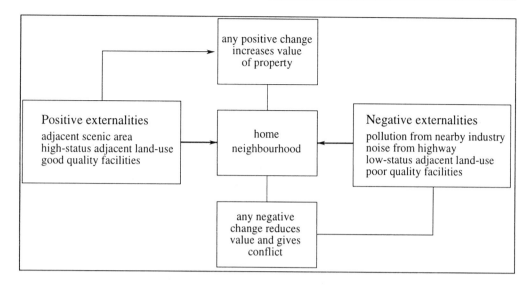

Figure 9.3 Externalities affecting residences and sources of conflict

to actual behaviour was far from clear. This bore directly on the studies of mental maps of the city and raised doubts on the accuracy of cognitive mapping. Downs (1970) had suggested a three-fold typology of cognitive studies in urban geography; structural, which measured awareness of place; evaluative, which recognized the qualities of place; and preference, which expressed levels of desirability for places.

From structuralism came several issues including the **urban question**, which asks whether the city can be theorized as a discrete objective:

> Weber, Durkheim, Marx and Engels all came to very similar conclusions . . . all agreed that the city played an historically specific role in the development of Western capitalism, but they all also argued that, once capitalism had become established, the city ceased to be a theoretically significant category of analysis. The city in other words was not seen as a significant object of study in its own right.
>
> (Saunders 1981: 249)

There was also the issue of resource allocation and **conflict** within the city:

> the outcome of resource allocation is etched or registered in urban space . . . as inquisitiveness about spatial organization must assuredly lead to a questioning of the mechanisms and processes that produce spatial inequalities and uneven urban outcomes.
>
> (Badcock 1984: 55)

Earlier studies on **urban conflicts** (Cox and Johnston 1982) focused on the roles of externality fields of urban activities which could be both positive and negative in their effects (Figure 9.3). In some ways the social geography of the city could be viewed as the outcome of conflicts between unequally endowed groups seeking to gain or avoid an externality effect (Knox 1995). There are many locational conflicts involving issues such as highway construction, school closures, and opening of day-centres for homeless or mentally ill people. The protagonists tend to be locally organized groups versus some authoritative agency such as the municipality or school board. Neighbourhood activism and community action have often sprung from issues of this kind as the priorities of market economies or city government on the one hand differ from those of local residents on the other. Again, the more successful neighbourhood action groups tend to be those who can draw upon professional expertise and commitment. There is renewed interest in the concept of **citizenship** and the ways in which diferent kinds of people can be drawn into processes of decision-making, local initiatives and forms of community actions.

On broader fronts, it was argued that capitalist society – as any other – contains its imperatives. The form of the city is one expression of those imperatives and any view of processes could not be divorced from this wider societal context. The relevant urban question may be one of interpreting the city within society rather than distinguishing the city from society. The city is a microcosm of society and

> is firstly a spatial mirror of society and its historical and organizational principles. That is, it reflects the previous and currently prevailing operating rules – of culture, technology, economy, and social behaviour – of the society within which the city has developed.
>
> (Bourne 1982: 6)

These 'traditional' theories set the context for much of the foundation work in social geography and its concerns with the city. One of the earliest of these was the focus on the city as a social mosaic and the study of the many forms of segregation evident in urban life.

The bases of residential segregation

Residential land-use occupies about 40 per cent of space in the average western city, twice the amount of space occupied by transport, the second largest user. A social geography of the city begins with residential land-use and its strong patterns of segregation. Residential space in the western city is uneven space, reflecting differing levels of advantage or disadvantage and setting the conditions for both interaction and conflict. We need to consider the bases of residential segregation and the processes which 'produce' them.

The bases of residential segregation in western cities have been most commonly identified as socio-economic status, family status or stage-in-life cycle, minority group membership or ethnic status, and, in many cases, migrant status (Figure 9.4). These 'dimensions' emerge most clearly in North American cities where housing is allocated on market principles and the ability to buy or rent a dwelling unit is reflected in a household's position in social space. An orderly social geography emerges as similar households make similar decisions in a housing market that contains a variety of types of dwellings in specific locations. Generally, developers build estates of uniform characteristics designed for, and occupied by, particular groups of people. As older housing is bought, sold or rented, there is a general tendency towards continuity, though change occurs and can be rapid.

The notion of choice must be treated with caution as residential decisions are rarely

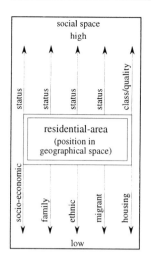

Figure 9.4 Bases of residential segreation

entirely in the hands of individual consumers. Similarly, the view that economic factors produce the residential mosaic is seductive but only partially true. Both individual dwellings and residential areas are imbued with social and symbolic values that sometimes outweigh their economic value in the housing market; 'home' and 'home area' have affective as well as rational meanings. Again, the city as place is 'time-layered', its different areas and districts belong to specific periods of time with their own cultural contexts and histories. Residential segregation is most evident at a neighbourhood scale but residual signs of other forms of separation are still found in parts of Europe. White (1984) showed that in parts of southern Europe, there was occasional middle-class occupancy of the lower floors of apartment blocks with workers on upper floors, giving vertical segregation. Again, in some areas there was segregation between fronts and backs of buildings with richer residents occupying the larger, airy dwellings overlooking the street.

The extent of residential separation

Attempts to establish the actual extent of residential separation have focused on a number of indices of segregation of which the Index of Dissimilarity (ID) is the best known; this is stated as

$$ID = \overset{\frac{1}{2}}{\underset{i=1}{\Sigma}} (x_i - y_i)$$

or one-half the sum of differences between two population groups, x and y, for each of i spatial units in a given city. The two population groups may be minorities, such as blacks compared with Hispanics, or may comprise one minority group compared with the total population. Indices of dissimilarity fall within a range of 0 to 100 and are measures of displacement – the proportion of the total population of one specified group required to move residence in order for no segregation to exist. A score of 100 indicates complete segregation.

Generally, these analyses of ethnic groups reveal high levels of segregation in western cities. A study of cities in the USA (Taeuber and Taeuber 1965) obtained a median index of dissimilarity between blacks and whites of 87.8 at the city block level and of 79.3 at the census tract level; Rees (1979) calculated a segregation index for blacks in twelve American urban areas of 76.2. There are claims (Taeuber 1988) that American black segregation is slowly decreasing over time with changes in ID from 85 in 1940 to 82 in 1970 and 76 by the 1980s. Yet, Massey and Denton (1993) showed that for black Americans there had been little real change over time and a state of hyper-segregation could be said to exist. Areas receiving new migrants, such as Puerto Ricans, Mexicans and Asians, in US cities, consistently reveal IDs of over 60. British analyses of New Commonwealth immigrants suggest that levels of residential segregation were increasing in the 1960s with indices based upon 1971 census data ranging from 38 for Indians to 51 for Caribbeans; in Coventry, the Pakistanis with an index score of 70 proved the most segregated group (Jones 1979). Peach (1996) concluded that US-style ghettos did not exist in British cities although at ED and street level, there were occasionally high concentrations of ethnic minorities. IDs for black British groups were typically in the range 40 to 50; for Indians the ID scores were generally lower, and for Pakistanis, they were generally higher. Highest levels of segregation were found for Bangladeshis and these tended to persist despite the decreasing segregation of other groups as households moved from the inner city to municipal estates. A study of Belfast (Poole and Boal 1973) produced an index score of 70.9 for street-by-street segregation between Catholics and Protestants, and Keane (1985) showed that in Belfast's public sector estates, the index rose from 64 to 92 from 1969 to 1977. Within Belfast, the index ranged from 19.7 in Holywood to 72.8 in West Belfast.

Keane also used an Index of Isolation (P*) which takes account of the composition of the population group and gives some indication of probability of contact. This can be expressed as

$$_xP_y = \sum_{i=1}^{n} \left(\frac{x_i}{x}\right)\left(\frac{y_i}{t_i}\right)$$

where

   x is the total number in group X in the city
   x is the number of group X in a census tract (or small area)
   y is the number of group Y in a census tract
   t_i is the total population of the census tract;

an $_xP^*_y$ value of 0.4983 would mean that an average member of group X lived in an area where 49.83 per cent of the total population belonged to group Y.

Using this index, Keane showed that although the overall ID increased between 1969 to 1977, suggesting greater segregation, the likelihood of Protestant contact with Catholics also marginally increased from 0.13 to 0.17 as a result of a larger number of Protestants in the overall population. Studies of 'transactional' contact have shown that even in situations of complete residential segregation, such as that between Jews and Arabs in Jerusalem, there was still a considerable amount of economic, political and legal interaction through business contacts.

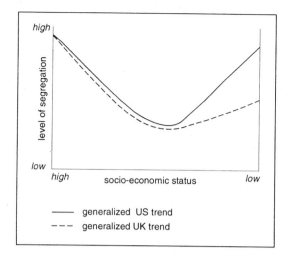

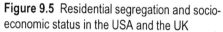

Figure 9.5 Residential segregation and socio-economic status in the USA and the UK

There are other forms of residential segregation which can be measured. In a study of census tract data for eight US cities using occupational groups, Fine *et al.* (1971) found indices of 27 between professional and clerical workers, 50 between professional and unskilled manual workers, and 36 between unskilled manual and clerical workers. These findings indicate greater residential separation with increasing social distance. Duncan and Duncan (1955) brought together a large number of US studies and concluded that socio-economic status segregation was most marked at extremes of the hierarchy; in other words, the very rich and very poor were most clearly segregated, with less clear differentiation in the broad middle band of social classes. This finding has some intuitive appeal but the problems of defining occupations in terms of status are greatest in this middle band. Studies of British cities have produced similar results but showed less marked segregation at the lower end of the socio-economic status scale (see Figure 9.5), a finding that reflected the relative strength of the British welfare system in the 1970s. Socio-economic status segregation was higher in larger British cities, particularly those with high numbers of professionals and managers.

Analyses of demographic segregation have obtained modest results. Most of these studies have focused on segregation of the elderly and the trend towards greater separation. Golant (1980) reported indices of dissimilarity ranging between 10.8 and 37.7 for elderly people (aged 65 years and over) in 72 US cities. For the same subgroup in 241 American SMSAs, Cowgill (1978) obtained a range of index scores from 15.2 to 44.4. Elderly people possess a level of residential segregation, which will increase as residential developments, specifically for older age groups, become more common, but this is not as high as that identified either for ethnic minorities or socio-economic groups. Life cycle stage segregation is a more general concept but has proved difficult to demonstrate empirically. There are problems of data and definition and calculation is difficult because life cycle stage has no necessary close correlation with chronological age. These types of analyses of residential segregation belong to the dissimilarist school of users of the index of dissimilarity. Another approach has been that concerned with the classification of residential areas.

The definition of residential areas

The objective of defining and classifying residential areas has been pursued vigorously in social geography. In some ways this approach has its origins in urban morphology with its studies of sub-regions and their place in historical phases of growth. More properly, however, the early precursor was the natural area concept, a product of the Chicago school of social ecology in the 1920s and 1930s. Natural areas placed the emphasis on people rather than on built environments and on social rather than physical processes. Residential differentiation had a number of objectives. First, it has sought to identify and delimit residential areas within cities; second, to define their qualities; and third, to examine the bases of residential separation and their persistence over time. Earlier studies were largely intuitive and subjective, later studies were more quantitative and with a progression from single indicators to the use of multivariate statistical procedures.

Natural areas

The natural area concept was developed by Robert Park and his associates in Chicago. Although the concentric zonal model stands as the main spatial generalization of the Chicago school, it was the natural area concept that generated the most inspired empirical studies of the city. The natural area was conceived as a geographical unit, distinguished both by its physical individuality and by the social, economic and cultural characteristics of its population; it shares common ground with the concepts of neighbourhood and local community. In contrast to the sub-regions and unpeopled townscapes of the urban morphologists, natural areas were always envisaged as places with both social and physical uniformity. The Chicago school studied the whole city and developed its theory of social ecology at this scale. However, the ethnographic monographs of the Chicago school paid little regard to symbiosis. It was in these ethnographies, such as the *Gold Coast and the Slum* (Zorbaugh 1929) and *The Ghetto* (Wirth 1928), that the natural area concept found its clearest expression.

The natural areas identified by Zorbaugh had *de facto* boundaries such as major roads, railways, parks, lakes and rivers. Each natural area's physical individuality was reflected in land values and rents, but Zorbaugh saw them as products of economic rather than cultural processes that were not necessarily coterminous with community. Zorbaugh is remembered for his vivid portrayal of life in Chicago's Near Northside, a district of some 90,000 people, close to the city centre. Near Northside was an area of diversity but the main contrast was between the high-prestige district of the Gold Coast, along Lake Shore Drive, and the Slum, the low-status district west of State Street (Figure 9.6). This latter district was itself a mosaic, containing the rooming-house district, hobohemia, little Sicily and other ethnic quarters. These natural areas derived part of their individuality from their built environments but much more from their distinctive populations and ways of life. Zorbaugh emphasized their dynamic qualities and, in describing the territorial shifts they experienced, used ecological concepts such as 'invasion – succession'. Wirth's approach to the study of natural areas was reflected in his preface to *The Ghetto* (1928): 'Having started with the study of a geographical area, I found myself, quite unwittingly, examining the natural history of an institution and the psychology of a people'.

In his study, Wirth examined the evolution of Jewish ghettos and described them as

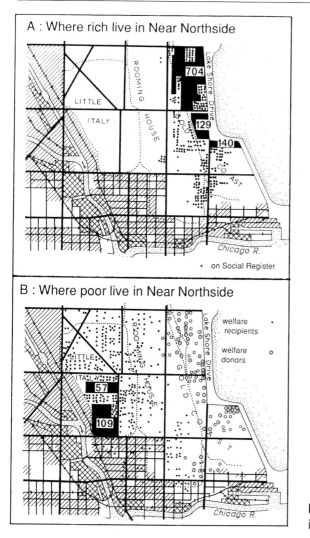

A : Where rich live in Near Northside

704
129
140

• on Social Register

B : Where poor live in Near Northside

welfare recipients •

welfare donors o

57
109

Figure 9.6 The Gold Coast and the Slum in Chicago

communities of interest, motivated by the need to preserve a religion and drawing strength from the inner solidarity of strong family ties. Wirth identified the Chicago ghetto as a territory demarcated from adjacent parts of the city by environmental barriers such as street-car lines and railway tracks. Within these limits was the natural area, a socially cohesive community with a distinctive personality. These natural areas, Gold Coast, Slum and Ghetto, had visible boundaries but were, in the main, identified subjectively. Zorbaugh also used simple indicators such as the addresses of people listed in prestigious directories to locate areas of high social status, and of those receiving welfare payments to show areas of low social status. This procedure involving the use of indicators was widely applied in later research. The variety among natural areas was recognized. Zorbaugh described the ethnic districts as close-knit communities, but other natural areas were, in his view, scarcely communities at all; a feature of the Gold Coast was that 'one does not know one's neighbours'.

The natural area was reassessed when Hatt (1946), in his study of Seattle, suggested that

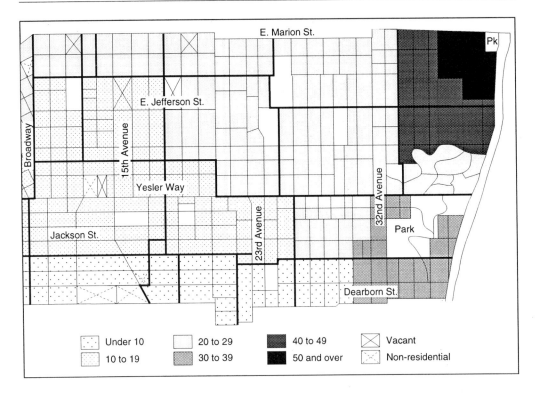

Figure 9.7 Natural areas in central Seattle showing mean rental values in dollars

the natural area concept could be interpreted in two ways. On the one hand was the ethnographic view of the natural area as a spatial unit, limited by natural boundaries, enclosing a homogeneous population with a characteristic moral order; on the other was the ecological view of a territory united on the basis of a set of relationships analogous to the biological world. Hatt concluded that whereas this latter symbiotic interpretation should be rejected, natural areas defined as logical statistical constructs offered excellent frameworks for further analysis. He identified natural areas in Seattle using rental values as indicators (Figure 9.7). This followed Zorbaugh, who had used indicators, but Hatt saw rental values as a more general and diagnostic measure of urban conditions. The qualities of such indicators, based on rents, land values, and rates or local property taxes, are now well established.

Improvements in the quality and availability of census data for cities and their presentation for small territorial units, such as census tracts (CTs) in North America and enumeration districts (EDs) in the UK, have had major impacts upon residential differentiation studies. Census small areas or small area statistics allow a reasonable assumption of internal homogeneity, so that when scores are allocated to such areas they are equivalent to point distributions which may be aggregated to form areal patterns. These assumptions for census small areas need to be qualified. The population size of census small areas varies considerably with census tracts in North American cities varying from under 1,000 to over 10,000 and British enumeration districts from under 100 to over 1500. The assumption of internal homogeneity rests on small size, but it is not normally there by design. Boundaries are defined with the practical needs of census-taking in mind and uniformity may not be a specific criterion. An exception is the Canadian census which states that census tracts are designed to be relatively uniform in area, population, economic status, and living conditions. Finally, the use of census small areas does raise the issues of ecological fallacy and the modifiable unit area. Ecological fallacy arises when individual characteristics are assumed from aggregate information, e.g. a census small area may be classified as 'poor' but may contain individual households that are relatively wealthy. The modifiable unit area problem arises because any change of boundaries, or the amalgamation or separation areal units, will produce different results.

An early example of the use of census small areas in the UK was the study of Belfast (Jones 1960) which included a classification of social regions based on measures of population density, social status and religious affiliations. This approach had self-imposed limitations as it used indicators of specific relevance to Belfast, but provided a useful link between natural area studies and those procedures based exclusively on census data. It was now clear that the national census small area statistics contained a large number of indicators which could be used to classify residential areas, and that these indicators could be used either singly or in combination.

Social area analysis

Social area analysis was a method developed in studies of Los Angeles and San Francisco and involved both empirical classifications of census tracts and a theoretical framework (Shevky and Williams 1949; Shevky and Bell 1955). The classifications used three composite indicators labelled social rank or economic status, urbanization or family status, and segregation or ethnic status. Social area analysis was a multivariate technique, based on census small areas, and was generally successful in North American applications as a methodology to classify residential areas in cities. As a theory of urban development it was far more contentious but the principle of establishing a theory of residential differentiation, before proceeding to a method of classification, set social area analysis apart. The study of natural areas in essence began with the empirical recognition of geographical territories and then moved to the study of their social characteristics and related processes. In other words, whereas social area analysis claimed to begin with a deductive theory and then tested it with empirical data, natural areas could be viewed as beginning with inductive observations and then fitting these to a theory of the city.

For Shevky and Bell (1995) the city was an integral part of society and as such would mirror change over time. They suggested that such societal change, which they described as increasing scale or the change from traditional to modern life styles, had three main expressions (Figure 9.8), labelled constructs, each of which changed over time. Social rank or economic status referred to the tendency for society to become more stratified on the basis of work specialization and social prestige. Urbanization or family status described a weakening of the traditional organization of the family as the society became more urbanized. Segregation or ethnic status suggested that over time the overall population group would tend to separate into distinctive clusters based primarily upon ethnicity. Having derived these constructs as key indicators of societal change, Shevky and Bell sought to measure them from the available census data. Social rank was measured by two key indices. An index of occupation was calculated from the number of operatives, craftsmen

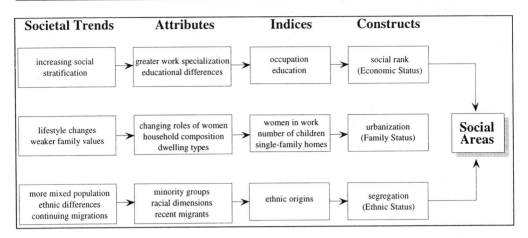

Figure 9.8 The rationale of social area analysis

and labourers per 1,000 employed persons; an index of education was based on the number of persons who had completed no more than grade school (eight years or less of schooling) per 1,000 persons aged 25 years and over. Urbanization was based upon three indices: fertility measured by the number of children aged 0 to 4 years per 1,000 women aged 15 to 44; women at work measured by the number of females employed in relation to the total number of females aged 15 years and over; and single-family detached dwelling units, measured by the number of single-family homes (a term which has a specific meaning in North American censuses) as a proportion of all dwelling units. Social rank and urbanization were the main constructs of social area analysis and a large part of the computational procedure was concerned with their derivation. The third construct, segregation, was calculated as a simple percentage of the numbers in specified minority groups (mainly those of ethnic origins outside north-west Europe) as a proportion of total population.

These constructs of class (economic status), household type (family status) and race (ethnic status) were proposed as dimensions of social space, measured from census data, and combined in stipulated ways to form criteria for the definition of social areas. The operational procedure which leads to the eventual social areas can be briefly summarized:

1. The scores on the individual indices were transformed into standardized ratios to allow more valid comparisons over different ranges of initial index scores. This gave a range of 0 to 100 on each ratio.
2. The constructs were calculated from the means of the ratio scores.
3. The economic status and family status scores were each given a four-fold division to produce sixteen possible social area types.
4. Ethnic status was added to the classification where the proportion of a census tract's total population in specified minority group was above the city average.

For the first applications of social area analysis in Los Angeles and San Francisco, the emphasis was on divisions identified in social space, and census tracts were classified without reference to their spatial location. However, as the census tracts were areas which had spatial locations, a map of social areas in the city could be derived. The case study of Winnipeg shows a typical set of results from an application of social area analysis to a North American city.

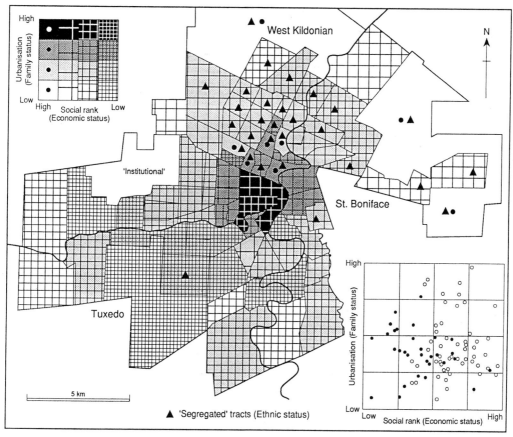

Figure 9.9 Social areas in Winnipeg, Canada

The metropolitan area of Winnipeg had a population in 1961 of 475,989 and was divided into 86 census tracts with an average population of 5,500; over half the census tracts were between 3,000 and 6,000 with only 3 with less than 1,000 and 5 with more than 10,000. The social space diagram for Winnipeg (Figure 9.9) was the classification of census tracts, with each point representing a census tract, the position of which is determined by its scores on social rank and urbanization, together with a separate symbol for tracts which were segregated. All six indices therefore, occupation, education, fertility, women at work, single-family dwellings and ethnicity, affected the classification of each census tract. The census tract in 4D, for example, has high social rank, with few people employed in manual occupations and few without advanced education. It is also high scoring in terms of urbanization, with few children, high numbers of women in employment and a comparative absence of single-family homes. The census tract contains few members of specified ethnic groups, is not classed as segregated and was, in fact, part of a high prestige residential district, predominantly of rented apartments, in a central city location. Figure 9.9 also provided an overall impression of the social structure of the city, showing that 63 per cent of the census tracts were within the two higher social rank categories and 25 per cent are in the two higher urbanization categories; of the 31 tracts which were classed as segregated, only 8 qualified as higher social rank.

Social area analysis specifies a set of relationships among its constructs and ratios which must exist to validate any specific application of the procedure. This set of relationships can be tested by statistical techniques, the most straightforward of which is Spearman's rank order correlation coefficient. The results of these tests in Winnipeg are shown in Table 9.1 together with the set of relationships which the theory postulates. The specified set of relationships requires that the ratios which make up the respective constructs should be dependent on each other. This requires high positive correlations between occupation and education and that the women-at-work ratio should have an inverse relationship with both fertility and single-family homes, but the latter two are positively related. The results for Winnipeg confirmed the specified set of relationships in a way which has been typical of North American studies, and the higher than expected correlation between the occupation and fertility ratios is common.

The social space classification forms the basis for the derivation of social areas in geographical space. Contiguous census tracts with scores in the same categories may be aggregated to form social areas in the sixteen-class typology, with the additional segregation categorization. Figure 9.9 also shows the mosaic of social areas, and studies have detected generalized patterns by plotting the individual constructs. In the southern and western parts of the city are the high-prestige residential areas, with inner city tenements and low-cost suburbs in central, northern and eastern districts. Urbanization scores distinguish between the central city districts of low family status and the outer suburbs of stronger family life, while segregation indices demarcate the French enclave of St Boniface and the Ukrainian districts extending north along Main Street.

Applications of social area analysis in the USA and Canada consistently reveal sectors of economic status, zones of family status and ethnic clusters. In summary, social area analysis, despite its contested theory, provided an important stage in the evolution of residential differentiation studies, principally because its typology of residential areas accurately identified the key bases of residential separation in North American cities. Applications in other parts of the world, especially in Europe, have proved less convincing.

Table 9.1 Correlation scores for Winnipeg

Ratios	Occupation	Education	Fertility	Women at work
Education	+0.84*			
Fertility	+0.53*	+0.34		
Women at work	+0.03	+0.23	−0.53*	
Single-family dwellings	−0.07	−0.33	+0.45	−0.68*

*Significant at the 0.1 per cent level

	Specified set			
	Occupation	Education	Fertility	Women at work
Education	+			
Fertility	0	0		
Women at work	0	0	-	
Single-family dwellings	0	0	+	-

Factorial ecology

The term factorial ecology has been used to describe classifications of residential areas which employ factor analysis as a technique. Factor analysis is a family of multivariate procedures and the results obtained from factorial ecologies may vary according to the particular procedure adopted. Ideally, there is a need to establish the invariant quality of results across a range of factoring techniques. A second consideration is the form of input as this again will strongly influence results. Input usually comprises a set of variables, commonly derived from the census and covering social, economic and demographic characteristics, measured for a set of observations or census small areas (Figure 9.10).

Factor analysis has largely been used as a summarizing device which operates in terms of the interrelationships among the set of input variables and identifies, in the order of their significance, a series of factors which are diagnostic of the input and which account for measurable amounts of the initial variance. Whereas social area analysis selected its dimensions deductively, factor analysis achieves this inductively. Three forms of output – eigen values, loadings and scores – provide the means of interpreting the results obtained. The eigen values indicate the relative strengths of the factors and can be expressed as proportions of the total variance or variability in the initial input; loadings are calculated for each original variable against each factor, range in value from +1.0 to -1.0, and allow the factor to be interpreted. Scores are calculated for each observation on every factor and enable the spatial patterns to be shown. Again, Winnipeg can serve as a case study.

From the Canadian census, 34 variables were calculated for each of the 86 census tracts in the urban area; this particular study used a components model with a varimax rotation. The results (Table 9.2A) are useful in that they closely resemble a large number of studies of North American cities completed in the later 1960s and early 1970s. From the eigen values it is clear that the leading dimension accounts for almost one-third of the initial variance (32.2 per cent), and the leading three dimensions for almost two-thirds. A few leading loadings are shown for each of the main dimensions in order to characterize the factors. Factor 1 is described as a measure of housing style indicative of family status or stage-in-life-cycle, Factor 2 as a measure of economic status and Factors 3 and 6 of ethnic status. These dimensions are the same as the constructs of social area analysis and most North American studies show very similar results. Table 9.2(b) shows similar results from a 1971 analysis of Winnipeg in which migrant status had replaced ethnic status and the family-status dimension was more clearly defined.

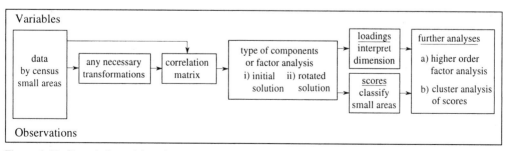

Figure 9.10 Steps in factorial ecology

Table 9.2 Factorial ecology

A Winnipeg (1961): nature of factors

Factor 1 (housing sytle) (32.2%)		Factor 2 (social status) (23.8%)	
Variables	*Loadings*	*Various*	*Loadings*
single-family dwellings	+0.91	high school or university	+0.93
single-person households	-0.89	males in managerial, professional, technical employment	+0.92
owner-occupied households	+0.89	males primary, craftsmen labourers	+0.91
tenant-occupied households	-0.87	males salaries 6,000 or more	+0.88

Factor 3 (ethnicity) (8.6%)	
Variables	*Loadings*
French origins	+0.98
English language only	-0.97
Roman Catholic	+0.89

B Winnipeg (1971)*

Component 1 (family status) (21.5%)		Component 2 (socio-economic) (13.4%)	
Variables	Loadings	Variables	Loadings
small households	+0.90	construction/transport workers	+0.86
apartments	+0.80	manufacturing workers	+0.76
children	-0.98	graduates	-0.91
family size	-0.97	white-collar ratio	-0.88

Component 3 (migrant status) (10.6%)	
Variables	Loadings
middle-aged	+0.86
low inter-municipal movers	+0.84
non-migrants	+0.80
new housing	-0.82
mature adults	-0.66

Note: * 1971 results obtained by Dr W. K. D. Davies

The spatial patterns of scores are shown in Figure 9.11 with Factor 1 scores (9.11A) distinguishing between the central city and the family suburbs; Factor 2 scores (9.11B) between the high-prestige districts of south and west and the low-prestige districts of north and east; Factor 3 (9.11C) identifies the French district of St Boniface and scores from Factor 4 are for the Ukrainian ethnic districts. Spatial generalizations of these scores are zonal for Factor 1, sectoral for Factor 2 and clusters for Factor 3.

The Winnipeg case study produced a set of results which are typical of North American factorial ecologies and confirm the existence of the three main constructs of economic, family and ethnic status. Later studies of Canadian cities often identified a migrant status dimension, showing the importance of continuing inward movement and change; the black ethnic dimension remains strong in North American studies.

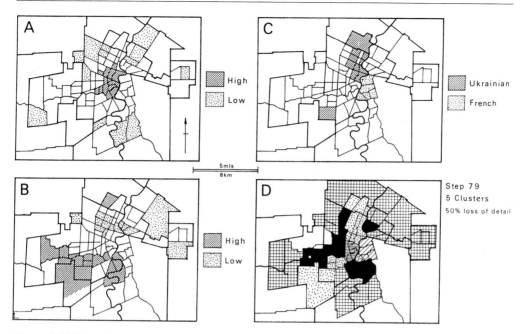

Figure 9.11 Factorial ecology of Winnipeg, Canada A Family status B Social status C Ethnic status
D Generalized clusters

West European cities

White (1984) reviewed the factorial ecologies which have been carried out for west
European cities and although the data inputs vary, some of the main features found in North
American cities continue to appear. Socio-economic status, often linked with housing
quality, is normally the first-ranking dimension. Family status, identified by demographic
and life-cycle stage measures, typifies the second dimension; ethnic status, commonly the
third-ranking dimension, is associated with the presence of foreign migrant workers. A study
of Leuven (Louvain), Belgium, nicely illustrates this kind of European result (see Table 9.3).
Attempts to generalize upon the spatial expressions of these dimensions have proved difficult
and as White (1984: 182) suggested: 'ecological analysis leads to the identification of
complicated patterns of social or residential areas based on the complex interaction of social
class, life-cycle and housing dimensions with urban space.'

The old city core of Vienna, for example, was divided into a business area with many
resident middle-class professionals but also a mixture of population groups, and an
administrative area with many managerial staff. A surrounding inner area was mainly
occupied by older middle-class apartment dwellers with mainly modern working-class areas
on the southern edge of the city. This pattern does not fit easily into any spatial model and
White's generalized model for the west European city retained a historic core of associated
high-status residence (see Figure 9.12B).

The familiar triad of social status, family status and ethnic/migrant status has also been
identified for British cities but the spatial generalization of zones, sectors or clusters, was
strongly distorted by the significant presence of public sector housing. Polish cities in the
pre-socialist form replicated the western dimensions but, as socialist cities, differentiation
along those lines was much less evident. The socio-economic status separation, in particular,

Table 9.3 Nature of components in Leuven (Louvain), Belgium

Component 1 (socio-economic status)	
Variables	*Loadings*
small dwellings	+0.93
labourers	+0.78
businessmen	-0.85
large dwellings	-0.83
Component 2 (minority group)	
Variables	*Loadings*
students	+0.93
foreign-born	+0.85
substandardness	+0.61
Component 3 (family status)	
Variables	*Loadings*
single-person household	+0.93
no children	+0.91
two-person household	-0.94
children	-0.82

was apparent only for specialized groups, but events since the end of the socialist regimes have once again led to modified urban forms. Non-western cities bear little resemblance to the western model; they have less separation of residential and commercial land-use, less social class segregation, strong variations in housing quality, and marked ethnic or cultural divisions of urban space.

Generalizations from factorial ecology

Sufficient factorial ecologies have been completed to allow some generalizations to be made. There is a general confirmation of the three main dimensions of economic, family and ethnic status in North American studies. The ethnic minority may vary in type and dimensions and is occasionally superseded by more general migrant status measures, but this triad remains remarkably consistent and the conditions under which it emerges are of interest. Socio-economic status dimensions occur where there is social stratification in that society and this is matched by corresponding subdivisions of the housing market (each group lives in a particular type of residential area). Similarly, a family status dimension occurs where family types can be linked to specific stages of the life-cycle and each stage is separately provided for by the housing market. Socio-economic status and family might be associated in social space but could still appear as geographically separate where the housing market caters for all life cycle stages within each socio-economic status sector. The necessary conditions for the two leading dimensions are, therefore, ranking by socio-economic status, clear stages of the life cycle, a housing market structured to cater for each possible combination of these characteristics in distinctive sub areas, and a population consisting of independent households mobile enough to use the possibilities. A factorial ecology in which the two dimensions failed to emerge could be explained in terms of the absence or limited

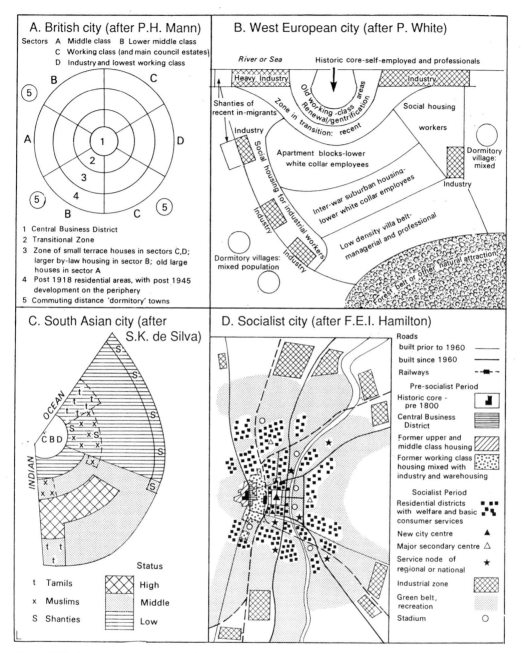

Figure 9.12 Generalization on urban forms and spatial organization

expression of these necessary conditions. Ethnic status emerges where there are identifiable minorities, racially defined or of recent migrant origins, and the persistence of ethnic areas is more a function of constraint than choice though both may be relevant.

Regional variations in the outcomes of factorial ecologies can be related to the idea of a stage model in which cities display particular social geographies at different stages of their development; and to a social formation model which suggests that different types of societies will have contrasted urban factorial ecologies. Free-market capitalism is one type of 'social formation', socialist societies form another, welfare states a third, and less appropriately, the Third World countries can be placed in a very broad fourth category. Generalizations of this kind are clearly sweeping and vulnerable to detailed analyses. Factorial ecologies, however, have produced evidence which gives them some level of credibility; their findings have given insights into the nature of social stratification, its expression as residential segregation in cities, and as a classification of residential areas.

Residential mobility

The term residential mobility refers to the migration of households within the same city. Urban populations have had high levels of mobility but these overall rates disguised significant differences among the various groups. Lawton (1979) compared households between successive census dates in English cities in the later nineteenth century and showed that between 40 and 60 per cent recorded no change. In Liverpool, the highest levels of persistence were in the higher status areas and the lowest levels, or greatest change, were in the low-income districts of the inner city. Moore (1972) found mobility rates of 70 per cent change per year to be typical of rooming house districts of the inner city, 5 per cent in more established suburbs, and a city average of around 25 per cent. British estimates, based on the census, suggest changes of just under 10 per cent a year in modern cities, and North American rates are typically higher. Over half (54 per cent) of these moves had taken place within the same local authority area and gave an indication of the level of residential mobility as opposed to other forms of migration. Where total households had moved, 46 per cent of these were owner-occupiers, 30 per cent were council tenants and 24 per cent were private tenants. Although private renters do not form a large segment of the housing market, they are typically over-represented among movers. High rates of residential mobility are common to the central areas of all west European cities; in Amsterdam the peak turnover rate in 1977 was 334 movers per 1,000 population and occurred in a privately rented area.

Housing markets and residential change

Residential mobility is closely related to the urban housing market. Research has therefore paid close attention to the structure of this housing market and the forces which drive it. A number of strands can be recognized: first, there have been attempts to model the urban housing market using a small number of basic variables and the principles of neoclassical economics.

Second there have been studies of the agencies involved in the housing market. These include agencies concerned with the development and supply of housing and also those involved in housing transactions and exchange. These studies have an explicit concern with the decision-makers in the supply side of the urban housing markets, with the allocative systems and the gatekeepers or managers who control them. Agencies may operate at a range of scales from the investment company, which moves capital from one part of the city to another, to the local banker who takes a decision on an individual loan.

Third, there have been analyses of the consumers in the housing market who, within recognized constraints, make decisions on where to live. Decisions, where they are made, may normally be driven by economic considerations but there is ample evidence for the impact of cultural factors, for tastes and preferences not necessarily derived from the economics of housing. Equally, there is evidence of the inability of significant sections of society to exercise choice at all.

Discussion on each of these three themes is developed below but initially some more general context is necessary. It is now accepted that the development of the urban housing market in Western cities must be viewed against a framework of broader societal change. Vance (1978) examined the emerging housing market as western cities moved from pre-capitalist to capitalist stages and housing became a commodity. He also emphasized the contrasted attitudes of North American and west European governments to the provision of low-cost housing and their effects on housing markets. For Walker (1978), housing in the US city was driven by the structural imperatives of a capitalist system, flows of investment under-pinned the directions of urban growth. Similarly, Badcock (1996) regarded the institutional framework behind housing provision as the key to an understanding of the residential assignment process, and argued that gentrification, or the upgrading of older housing as one part of inner city revitalization, could be theorized in terms of the circuits of capital.

Geographers developed an interest in residential mobility as a means of understanding residential patterns and the urban mosaic. The focus was on processes and the movers, or consumers of housing, whose decisions on where to live were the keys to the mosaic of residential areas. This research initially centred on those limited sections of society who possessed the ability to move and to exercise choice and preference. The balance has since been redressed and emphases have shifted from individual households as decision-makers to the forces and mechanisms within society which influence them. This shift has involved greater recognition of the constraints and limits within society and the fact that many 'consumers' are in no position to exercise choice.

Micro-economic models

Micro-economic models of the housing market rest upon simplifying assumptions and generalize upon the distribution of housing prices, supply and densities over urban areas. The approach has a long history and can be identified, for example, in Hurd's (1903) study of urban land values, and in many analyses associated with the regional science school of urban studies (Alonso 1963; Muth 1969). The methodology has been developed and sustained in more specialized studies of residential vacancy chains (Emmi and Magnusson 1995) and of the impact of financial constraints on the housing market (Bourassa 1995). The working bases of these models are found in the economics of supply and location, the neoclassical theories of household behaviour, and the forming of a general equilibrium framework. Models typically assume perfect competition, a uni-dimensional product, invariant tastes and a single-centred city; the market process is then viewed as mechanistic with individual households maximizing satisfaction and finding residential locations according to income, accessibility, needs and space preferences. Suppliers seek to maximize profits in the manner in which they develop new units for the housing market and resell or rent vacancies as they occur.

Outputs from micro-economic models are typically sets of relatively simple generalizations. It has been found that population density, for example, decreases from centre to periphery, whereas housing-lot size tends to increase, as does income of householder and house-buying ability. This set of models demonstrates the contribution of positive science to an understanding of residential land-use in cities. The basic trade-off mechanism states that each household's utility is a balance between space and travel costs, finding

> its optimal location relative to the centre of the city by trading off travel costs which increase with distance from the centre, with housing costs which decrease with distance from the centre and locating at the point at which total costs are minimised.
>
> (Evans 1973: 7–8).

These models can be refined, though the simplifying assumptions tend to distance them from reality. The validity of the assumption of a single-centred city has been diminished by the process of decentralization which relocated employment opportunities and altered urban spatial structure. Badcock (1984) noted that the heavy reliance of the trade-off model on utility theory with its pretensions of free consumer choice made it an 'ideological sham' in a situation where choice is available only to some consumers in the housing market. Similarly, assumptions about the mobility of capital and perfect competition are confounded in a complex housing market.

Micro-economic models of the urban housing market developed as positive science. Subsequently they have been criticized as mechanistic by failing to recognize human diversity, as ideological by serving to legitimize market capitalism, and as ignoring issues of welfare and social inequality. As positive science, this approach has added considerable technical ability to urban analysis and as a methodology it continues to find many applications. Its scope is limited, however, by its restrictive assumptions and by its levels of abstraction.

Agencies in the housing market

One reaction to the abstractions of micro-economic models was the recognition of the roles of decision-making agencies in the housing market. Studies of these agencies allowed deviations from the simplifying assumptions to be recognized and introduced a stronger empiricism to analyses of the ways in which the housing market worked. This approach can accommodate the idea of structural constraints. Decision-making agencies work within encompassing structures and frameworks; their individual decisions are strongly influenced by external forces and the issue of structure and agency is brought into sharp focus.

The suppliers

For Bourne (1976), the supply side of the housing market was not

> as assumed in most micro-economic models, characterized by optimal decision-making within a uniform and unconstrained environment. The housing industry itself, and the various private and public agents responsible for the provision of housing, are not homogeneous in character or behaviour.
>
> (Bourne 1976: 146)

A hierarchy of decision-makers operates within the framework of any particular society and interacts with broad market trends of supply and demand. Within this hierarchy, there is no necessary uniformity of practice and outcomes, and neither is there any valid assumption of optimizing behaviour, but it is here that some understanding of the main determinants of the changing residential geography of urban areas is to be found.

Land has the unique quality of permanence, it is a resource which cannot be depleted. This quality has particular significance in the role of land as a means of accumulation or wealth-creation, its absolute location gives monopoly privileges on use at that site and a value determined by location and use. Land has both a use and an exchange value. Whereas the former relates to the use to which it is currently put and may be reflected in a form of rent, the latter refers to its value when next it enters the market as a commodity, perhaps with a potentially different use. One of the experiences of western cities is that the land market, and through it the housing market, can be manipulated to create shortages which have short-term effects upon the value of land, and the price and availability of housing. Speculators buying land and 'holding' it for future resale are guided by exchange rather than use values. In those societies where urban planning powers have been strengthened, many of their interventions have been directed at this problem.

The development of land for residential property can be theorized in several ways. First, for Marxists, the geographical configuration of the property market is governed by the laws of capital circulation. Lamarche (1976: 102) suggested that as property capital extended its control over urban space, it was increasingly able to create and dictate the conditions for its own profitability. Extension of this control is opposed by 'inertia and lags' or shortages of social investment capital and class resistance to unacceptable redevelopment; urban space is the arena in which elements of capital, class and state interact. Second, there is a welfare view of residential development in which the state intervenes as a holder of land and developer of property with the broad aim of protecting the interests of the weaker players in the housing market. Third, a behavioural view can be identified in which there is greater emphasis on the decision-makers and the discretion which they are able to exercise. The decision-makers include both the managers and gatekeepers who allocate resources and those consumers in a position to make choices. 'Within the limits of the planning framework, it is the decisions and behaviour of the builders and developers that control the contemporary pattern of residential development within cities.' (Kirby 1983: 29).

Figure 9.13 summarizes the main stages involved in the land-development decision; this decision most typically involves the development of new housing upon virgin land but may also include the clearance of old buildings and their replacement by either new constructions or modifications of existing stock. The model moves through an interest stage in which, for example, agricultural land on the urban fringe is recognized as having development potential in the light of current rates of urban growth; a consideration stage at which the developer begins negotiation with the land-owner on costs and also consolidates an assessment of its future exchange value as residential land; if favourably concluded this stage will end in the transference of the land to the developer. Prior to the programming *stage,* the developer will have researched the likelihood of any constraints upon future use of the land but, at this stage, formal planning permissions, made in the context of zoning ordinances and development control, are obtained. There is some evidence that developers are prepared to buy and hold land in the belief that zoning classifications will be changed,

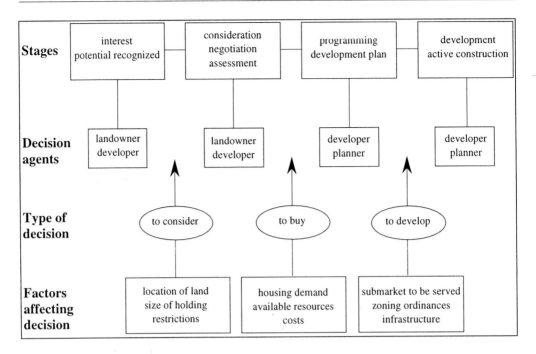

Figure 9.13 Stages in the land development process

but more typically the initial purchase is made with knowledge of favourable development circumstances. Also in the programming stage, the developer has to decide what type of housing and in which price range it is intended to build, a decision most likely to be made by an assessment of the market demand. In the development stage actual construction takes place in which a developer may subcontract part of the holding and phase construction to match the rate at which sales absorb the units which become available. This model has been described in terms of a private developer, but where the public sector, for example a municipality, directly intervenes in the housing market as a developer, it will behave in broadly similar ways. Differences emerge with the possible power of the public sector to acquire land by compulsory purchase and its commitment to build low-cost units to rent or affordable housing to buy, with a welfare rather than a profit motive.

For decision-makers in residential development, the form and extent of state control is a crucial consideration. In much of Europe, government agencies have played major roles for most of the twentieth century; in socialist societies this role was dominant to the extent that there was a virtual state monopoly of housing provision and similar situations existed in other highly centralized states such as Singapore. The most direct forms of intervention involve the building of housing to rent by central or local government but there are numerous other policy instruments. Tax relief subsidies and improvement grants may favour the owner-occupier; rent and rate rebates may help public sector tenants; all of these affect the demand for housing of different types. Fiscal policies are of fundamental importance and Bourassa (1995) has demonstrated that borrowing constraints have major implications for the balance between owning and renting in the housing market.

For land-owners, the steady growth of planning controls, welfare considerations and state intervention has meant a diminution of their powers. Municipal authorities, using powers of development control, may stipulate uses to which land can be put or may use legislative authority to acquire land for its own purposes. Zoning regulations have often adversely affected a land-owner's potential for profit and in general the freedom to act in the land and housing market has been severely restricted. Developers inject new housing into the system and will normally respond to the way in which they perceive the market at any one time and to their current ability to attract or use resources. In this last respect they are vulnerable to prevailing financing conditions, including interest rates and the willingness of banks to lend. Most development is speculative and involves risk; houses are built to be sold so that return on invested capital is not assured until transactions are completed. Private developers have a primary interest in building new houses for middle to high-income groups; their shortcoming has been an unwillingness to provide for the higher risk, lower-profit, cheap housing market. In the USA there has been an assumption that the filtering process, by which housing passes over time from higher- to lower-income occupants, is a sufficient provider for the lower end of the market. The need to ensure a supply of affordable housing is now widely accepted, and elsewhere the public sector has found it necessary to intervene directly in the housing market in the role of both developer and landlord in order to safeguard levels of this kind of provision.

Planners have key interventionist roles in the housing market though their powers vary considerably from one society to another. It can be argued that planners are normally neither initiators of development nor are they major 'redirectors' of urban growth, rather they modify market forces and exercise control over existing trends. At a broad level, strategic plans lay down general allocations of land-use and the main shape of future growth and manage the details of zoning and development control within these established parameters. A key local government responsibility relates to the provision of basic utilities, the stipulation of standards, and quality control.

Managerialism and the 'gatekeepers'

The land development process, involving land-owners, developers and planners, captures one set of agencies in the housing market, those concerned with the supply of housing stock. Additionally, there is a set of agencies concerned with the system of exchange whereby individual dwellings are bought and sold, leased or rented, renovated or renewed. For the consumer, it is this set of agencies with whom interaction is most likely. Managerialism states that between the producer and the consumer there is an intermediate level of decision-makers concerned with the allocation of resources. Pahl (1979) argued that whatever form society took, resources would always be scarce and procedures to distribute them would always be necessary, consequently specific agents – the gatekeepers – would control and allocate such resources.

In the public sector (see Figure 9.14) the key gatekeepers are the local housing manager and the housing committee. They allocate public sector housing and should be driven by welfare principles. Public sector housing was developed as a means of providing affordable housing of good quality for the poorer sections of society and has been a major housing policy in the UK and other European countries. In the USA, the 14 million units of public housing have been described as the basic form of assistance to low-income families (Stegman 1995). The nature of public housing has changed, first with the policy of selling houses at

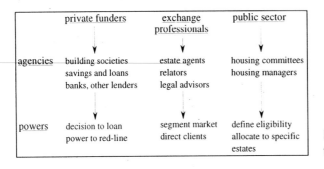

Figure 9.14 Managers (gatekeepers) in the urban housing market

discounts to longer-term tenants, and second, with the changing nature of the client population. In Europe in the last part of the twentieth century, there has been a tendency for tenants to be drawn from the narrow socio-economic range of those dependent on welfare. This reflects not only societal changes, such as the increase in single-parent (usually female-headed) families, persistent unemployment, and a residualized poor, but also overt government policies to reduce its commitment to the provision of low-cost housing to rent. In the UK, the growth of housing associations as separate agencies reflects this changing policy. Public housing allocation has become as much a means of helping the poor in a general way as of solving general housing problems: 'The widespread adoption of housing allowances reflects the fact that housing policy has become primarily an income redistribution issue rather than a shelter issue' (Adams 1990: 122).

The first obstacle for a potential tenant is that of qualifying for public housing. Municipalities often require some years of residence in the area and evidence of housing need. Once qualified, the potential tenant is placed on a waiting list which may be operated in terms of date-order, a points system, special needs or a combination of these. There is competition for desirable estates as public housing estates are differentiated in terms of quality by both consumers and managers. This differentiation often rests on the age of the estate, its level of maintenance and its 'reputation' as suggested by a range of social indicators and inherited 'labels'. Those applicants with the ability to wait have some advantage; in Swansea it was shown that households were prepared to wait up to ten years for attractive estates. Gatekeepers decide who qualifies for public housing and also where they are allocated accommodation within the sector. Difficult-to-let estates are occupied by the losers in this segment of the housing market and polarisation emerges between 'desirable' and 'undesirable' estates. During the 1980s and 1990s, a 'Right to Buy' policy was introduced in the UK which led to 1.5 million public sector dwellings moving into owner-occuppiership in England by 1995; there was a similar trend in the USA. These transactions have tended to involve houses in desirable estates and have had the effect of widening the gaps in the housing market.

In the private sector, prime considerations for the gatekeepers are the market principles of capital assets, credit worthiness and job stability of potential housing consumers. One route to accommodation is offered by the private rental sector, though this is the sector which has experienced dramatic decreases in the stock at its disposal. Private rental, which accounted for 80 to 90 per cent of all housing tenure in the 1920s, is now at levels of 25 to 35 per cent in North America and 10 to 20 per cent in Europe. Its demise is a product of stricter rent controls, higher standards of maintenance, and strong encouragement for home-ownership, though there is some evidence of increased interest in private renting with the fall in house prices and the phenomenon of negative equity, or the plight of home-owners holding loans which are higher than the present-day value of their property. In 1993, 19 per cent of British home-owners who borrowed in 1989 were in negative equity and for London home-owners, the figure was 40 per cent (Dorling and Cornford 1995). Gatekeepers in the private rented sector are the property companies and the landlords. Whereas they are subject to rules on discrimination and fair rents, these are not always easy to control. They often adopt renting practices that favour childless, professional households likely to cause the least management problems. The private rental sector, however, does cover a wide range from high-cost apartments to run-down tenements and row-houses. Many low-income groups such as students, recent migrants and welfare dependents, rely on the diminished private rental sector. In the UK, private renting is dominated by less-desirable properties and members of this 'housing class' are among the least competitive. They have least security, poorest living conditions, and little opportunity to accumulate capital. This picture is not universal. In major world cities, such as London, Paris and New York, the high-quality rental sector has retained its importance. Forms of rental and lease are much more common and favoured in some European countries and a study of Montreal (Choko and Harris 1990) identified low levels of owner-occupance congruent with the values of the local culture.

The quest for home-ownership has been a major feature of many societies during the twentieth century. In the USA, home-ownership rose from 20 per cent in 1920 to 64 per cent in 1992; Stegman (1995) reported that 86 per cent of all US adults would prefer to own their home. In the UK, home-ownership rose from 31 per cent in 1951 to 67 per cent in 1991; in terms of dwellings this was a rise from 3.9 million in 1951 to 15.4 million in 1991 (Hamnett 1992). There is evidence for consumer preference for this form of tenure and there have also been substantial state interventions to enable the change. For the state, home-ownership engenders stability, sense of belonging, pride in place, and a share in the process of capital investment. There is no doubt that British home-owners made substantial financial gains from property purchases before the 1990s. Housing units purchased for £5,000 in 1969 were worth £60,000 in 1989, a rise in real terms of 250% (Hamnett 1992). Government measures to help home-buyers include tax relief on mortgages, subsidies to keep interest rates low, exclusion of homes from capital gains tax, removal of stamp duty, discounts of up to 60 per cent for public housing tenants who wished to purchase, and a role for municipalities as mortgage finance lenders. By the 1990s, state subsidies to owner-occupiers were 40 per cent higher than those to social (public) housing tenants (Knox 1995). During the 1990s in the UK, and earlier elsewhere, the housing market changed and recent buyers were left with negative equities, i.e. their loan was greater than the value of their property and repossessions by lenders who were not being repaid grew rapidly. Economic problems underlie this situation but in the longer term housing has proved a profitable investment and Hamnett (1992) argued that home-ownership had allowed many to share the fruits of economic growth whilst the real losers remained the renters.

The interventionist roles of the state, at both central and local levels, have already been mentioned. Major fiscal moves affecting interest rates and borrowing conditions have major effects; specific policies, such as the right to buy, can bring many properties onto the market; by 1991, 14 per cent of former public housing units had been resold (Forrest *et al.* 1996). Local state as mortgage lender should target the lower end of the market and increase the range of affordable housing. Housing associations have taken over some of the roles of municipalities during the 1980s in serving this segment. Most evidence suggests that affordable housing extends the range of opportunities downwards but not to its lowest limits. Resold public housing remains beyond the reach of the real poor as do local authority mortgages, and Stegman (1995) noted that in the USA 91 per cent of renters could not afford to buy a median-priced home in their area.

Outside the gatekeeping roles of the state, there are key figures in the private sector. Their activities can be described but it is important to note that managerialism as a concept recognizes its limitations. Managers or gatekeepers are decision-makers who allocate resources and to the consumer they are the identifiable points of contact for face-to-face relationships. They rarely, if ever, however, possess complete autonomy. There is variation but generally they serve larger organizations and work within the constraints of policies formed at a higher level of the hierarchy. There will be lending rules, financial limits and risk parameters with which they have to conform. Having said this, the key point is that they have discretion. They interpret rules in an individualistic way and can temper their judgements by personal knowledge and an awareness of local circumstances. There are rationalities to which these gatekeepers must conform but there is also an element of flexibility. Munro (1995) offered some insight into this question with her suggestion that the relationship between lender and borrower may be founded on rationality but is likely also to have a 'moral' dimension.

The managers of financial institutions are key gatekeepers in the housing market. They allocate the funding for house purchase and their decisions, based both upon the credit worthiness of the potential borrower and the quality and location of the prospective property, have a profound effect. Harvey (1977) showed that prospects of home-ownership in Baltimore were strongly affected by the willingness of agencies to lend money and this was reflected by the emergence of a number of sub-markets. In the inner city, only limited and high-cost private finance was available, ethnic areas relied on small community-based, savings and loans societies or federal sources, and only in the affluent white suburbs was there a general availability of private finance (Figure 9.15). These local 'taps and regulators' were important although the wider societal controls were fundamental. Other US studies have highlighted the practices of financial managers which include 'red-lining' or the identification of areas in which any lending would be regarded as high risk. Stegman (1995) reported a 1992 study showing that blacks and Hispanics were 60 per cent more likely to be rejected for mortgage loans than whites, even when financial and employment status, and neighbourhood characteristics were controlled. The Advance Mortgage Corporation noted that red-lining was a 'fact of life' for all 'brownstone communities' (nineteenth-century sandstone row houses) in US cities despite the fact that it had been outlawed in 1977.

British studies of housing finance have shown similar evidence for discriminatory practice; though few building society or bank managers would admit red-lining particular districts, the availability of loans in some inner city areas is only at high rates and short-terms. Back-street finance is a substitute and in Saltley (Birmingham) 93 per cent of borrowers paid above the normal interest rate. Managers are likely to advise buyers against purchasing high-risk properties in certain parts of the city as a surrogate for an overt red-lining policy. It has been argued (Munro 1995) that managers are less likely to be influenced by hard information and a rational assessment than they are by beliefs and values. Profiles of

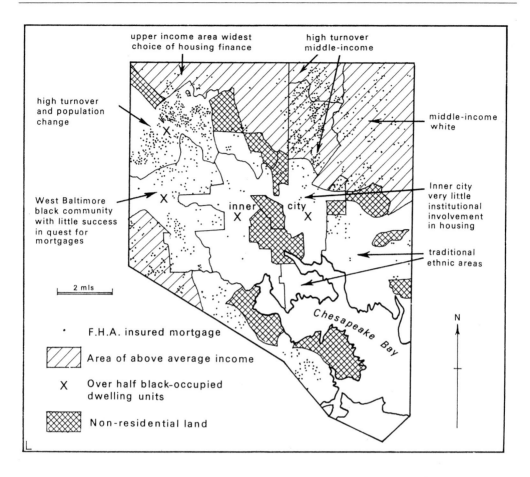

Figure 9.15 Housing finance in Baltimore

successful borrowers reveal a professional, stable job, higher income predominance, and an interest in suburbs or in improving inner city districts. Municipal lending follows a similar pattern but does reach further down the social class range. These decisions by the financial gatekeepers discriminate against particular sections of society and also against specific parts of the city. The effect is to control the social geography; inner city areas will remain depressed until investors decide that it is ripe for inward movements of capital. Gentrification has exemplified this. There are other factors involved but parts of the inner city are selected for upgrading and change as funding for housing change in these areas is forthcoming. In Islington (London) in 1950, almost no housing finance was available and the area was deteriorating; by 1972 the area had been recognized as an investment possibility, funds were available from major lenders and a process of change to renovated, more expensive housing was in full swing.

Real estate agents (realtors) offer another example of gatekeepers. Many estate agents are local, though there is a trend to national organizations. They are housing specialists and act as the intermediaries between buyers and sellers, the brokers of the housing market who liaise with lenders, lawyers, planners, and other professional services. Estate agents seek to match buyers to properties, they flourish when the market is buoyant, they are best rewarded when prices are high. Studies in the USA have often argued that realtors seek to direct the market by guiding black clients away from white areas. Studies of New England in 1953, New Haven in 1968 and Boston in 1983 have shown similar results. Realtors have had key roles in some of the managed processes of rapid residential change, but it must be emphasized that only small minorities are involved in this kind of practice:

- **Blockbusting** has involved the use of scare tactics to encourage whites to move out of chosen areas on the edge of the ghetto. Black families may be moved in and houses can be offered at peppercorn prices.
- **Lily-whiting** is the opposite process and involves steering white buyers away from black areas in order to ensure that the character of the area is unchanged.

More generally, it is in the interests of real estate agents to maintain buoyancy and change in the housing market and many studies have shown practices designed to have these effects. High-income buyers might be directed to areas just below their aspirations and low-income buyers towards areas just above, for example as a mechanism for inducing neighbourhood change. In Islington (London) estate agents were seen as the instigators of the changes which led to gentrification. They saw the possibilities by 'reading' the preferences of their clients for up-market, safe inner-city living, and promoted improvement of housing stock to cater for this demand.

Housing classes

The individual consumer is faced with three main routes into the housing market; renting in the public sector, buying, or renting in the private sector. Which route a household takes is largely determined by its position in 'social space' and it is here that the concept of housing classes is of value. Rex and Moore (1967) used Weberian theory to argue that households fell into distinctive housing classes reflecting their ability to compete in the housing market. Their original seven-fold typology ranged from outright owners of whole houses to tenants of single or shared rooms in lodging houses with no simple alignment of housing class with form of tenure. Both owner occupiers of good quality suburban housing and tenants of expensive inner city apartments are relatively advantaged. Again, the tenant in a desirable public estate may be better off than the owner of a rundown terraced house in the inner city. The typology shown is a modification of that suggested by Cater and Jones (1989):

1A	owner occupiers of legitimate housing (suburban or gentrified)
1B	renters of legitimate public sector housing (usually suburban)
1C	private renters of high-grade property
2A	owner occupiers of low-grade property (usually inner city)
2B	tenants of undesirable public sector housing (often high-rise)
3A	private renters of low-grade property
4	the homeless

The advantage of the housing class idea is that it identifies different sections of society with varying access to the housing market. There is a range from those with greatest choice to those with no choice at all. With the idea of housing class, awareness of constraints and exclusions is brought into much sharper focus. Knox (1995) reported a classification of housing groups, devised by Southwark (London) borough, comprising six groups ranging from upper-income and indigenous middle-income to immigrant lower-income. These

Housing group	Housing type	Supplier
upper-income, professional, managerial	owner-occupiers high cost renters	developers, builders, landlords
middle-income, skilled, mainly white collar	owner-occupiers some renters	developers, builders, landlords
lower-income, semi-skilled unskilled	public sector affordable housing	local authority housing associations
immigrant, lower income, unskilled unemployed	cheap rented difficult-to-let estates	landlords local authority
homeless, unemployed	none or hostels	local authority voluntary agencies

Figure 9.16 Housing groups, types and suppliers

housing groups could be matched with housing types, or different segments of the housing market and there was a parallel range of suppliers. Figure 9.16 draws some of these ideas together. Analyses of this kind have taken the original idea of housing classes forward but have preserved its basic assumptions of groups with differential access to housing, restrictions on the types of housing to which groups can normally aspire, and a housing market which 'serves' different groups in different ways. Housing classes are not static and movements 'up' or 'down' are possible. Buyers of public housing offer an example of upward movement, and repossessed owners now in rented property of downward movement. Housing class was originally argued as an extension of the concept of class with associated ideas of class conflict, this interpretation is contested but the approach remains valuable.

Residential change

Discussion so far has concentrated on the suppliers, the agents and the housing market itself as bases for understanding the emergence of residential areas in cities. Housing also has significant qualities as an item for consumption and the activities of the renters and buyers need to be fitted into the analysis. Earlier research focused on the aggregate scale and the ways in which residential areas changed over time. Hoyt's (1939) sector theory of neighbourhood change was an early example of this kind of study. Using rental values as data, Hoyt plotted the locations of high-grade residential areas in selected US cities at different points in time and showed a tendency for such areas to originate near city centres but to migrate over time to the urban peripheries. This migration of areas tended to occur along specific sectors and some high-grade areas could be initiated outside the city centre. Hoyt's 'laws' sought to explain these patterns. He argued, for example, that high-grade residential areas would pre-empt the most desirable space in the early city, would then migrate out along natural highways, and be directed by proximity to amenity land and the

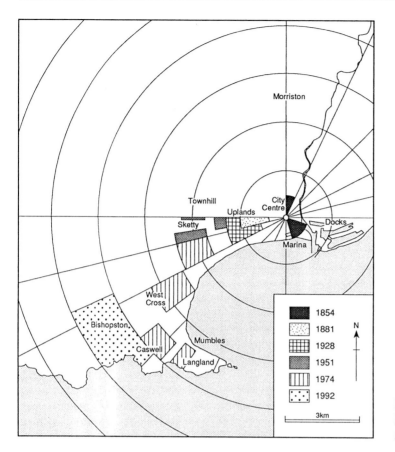

■	1854
▒	1881
▦	1928
▨	1951
⦀	1974
⁘	1992

3km

Figure 9.17 Movement of high-status areas in Swansea

homes of community leaders. Many studies have replicated Hoyt's analysis and have found general confirmation of his ideas. In Swansea, there is a clear progressive migration of the high-grade residential areas from older parts of the inner city to the scenic coastal districts on the western side of the city (Figure 9.17) The model of sectoral growth has also been applied to the expansion of the black ghettos, particularly in newer cities of the southern USA (Ford and Griffin 1979).

The Chicago school acknowledged neighbourhood change both in its use of the invasion-succession model and in the detailed ethnographic studies of specific districts of Chicago. Invasion-succession involved the take-over of a residential area by one social group at the expense of another and was a key process in neighbourhood change. The concentric-zonal model was a model of growth as well as of structure and invasion-succession provided the mechanism of change. Firey (1947), in his study of land-use in central Boston, examined processes of change in a number of inner city districts. Some of these districts showed clear changeover as higher income groups moved out to suburbs and the character of areas was transformed. Beacon Hill was a notable example of the persistence of a high-grade Boston neighbourhood as sentiment and symbolism combined to protect the area against change. Many studies have verified the significance of the cultural values in understanding urban change. In Vancouver, the movement to protect Shaughnessy Heights (Duncan 1992) was promoted by its residents but also by other groups who recognized the symbolic significance of this specific residential area to the city as a whole. A number of general process models have been used to summarize residential area change:

- **Filtering** is a mechanism by which older properties filter down the social scale and become accessible to households of lower incomes than their previous occupants. The downward filtering of property may in some ways be matched by the upward filtering of households seeking improved housing. Properties become available for filtering as new construction creates more attractive alternatives and as obsolescence makes older properties less attractive without major new investment. Filtering remains a major way of providing affordable housing at different levels of the market, though many housing opportunities are taken by new households.

- **Residential vacancy chains** are integral parts of the housing market. Vacancies create mobility as households move within the city and the residential vacancy chain model (Emmi and Magnusson 1995) rests on the assumption that mobility within housing markets is limited to currently available housing opportunities. A single move may set off a chain of vacancies as the filtering process is enacted and obstacles at any one point will have knock-on effects; research has shown that newly constructed dwellings can generate three to four moves and vacancies down the chain.

- **Gentrification** can be placed in this set of processes producing aggregate effects. It has involved the upgrading of older neighbourhoods in the inner city, the movement out of former low-income occupants and the inward movement of higher-income tenants or owners; in this sense, it posits an opposite effect to that suggested by the idea of downward filtering. Gentrification has seemed at times to signal a reaffirmation of the value of urban living and a return to the central city as a reaction to long-running suburbanization. This long-term trend seems unlikely and we are probably entering a post-gentrification era. Hamnett (1991) viewed gentrification as a leading edge in the process of urban restructuring; Van Weesep (1994) thought it was deeply rooted in social dynamics and economic trends and should be regarded as only one component of urban revitalization. Gentrification as a process has attracted a variety of interpretations. For one school of thought (D. M. Smith 1979), the concepts of dis-investment and re-investment are central. Capital abandoned the older properties of the inner city as new suburbs offered better investment opportunities, for the inner city this was dis-investment. As the rent gap and the value gap, or the difference between actual and potential rent or value, grew for older properties, there was a return of capital to the inner city or re-investment. For this school of thought, capital flows, the circulation of capital, and the power-brokers of institutional finance are key players. Gentrification also reflects changing patterns of consumption and the tastes and preferences of middle-income households. Gentrified properties in the inner city appeal to selected buyers or renters, usually younger, non-family households who want a different and more 'urban' lifestyle. Gentrification is one aspect of the 'globalization of culture' (Carpenter and Lees 1995) as the quest for a different lifestyle tends to take similar forms in different parts of the world. Gentrification has occurred in most major cities of the UK and North America; in Australia it has added a new vitality to inner city living with improved local services, better street design, higher valued property and boosted spending power. It has effected neighbourhood change in selective inner city areas. It has positive impacts as described but has the major downside of displacing lower-income residents and reducing the stock of low-cost housing units.

The aggregate scale, with its focus on changing patterns of areas, had its limitations. Obviously areas may change in character in situ but they do not move. All changes are the products of individual households and their residential histories, patterns emerge out of the summary of these individual histories. Behavioural approaches to residential mobility shifted the method to analysis at the scale of the individual household. Initially, the idea of decision-making was central though this was modified with the realisation that many moves were involuntary (up to 40 per cent of moves can be of this kind: Munro 1987) and that many households were in no position to enjoy the privileges of making decisions. Early behavioural work produced variants of a decision-making model for residential mobility and Wolpert's (1965) conceptual statement on decision-making identified a number of derived concepts which could be applied to residential mobility. The concept of place utility referred to the level of satisfaction which a household held for its present residence and this place utility would be affected both by the qualities of the dwelling and by the residential area in which it was located. Changes in place utility could result from household changes, such as an extra child, or from neighbourhood change, such as a rising crime rate; if place utility was seriously affected and led to stress, the household would begin to consider a move (see Figure 9.18). These changes which affect place utility raise the question of why families move and this became a key issue. Rossi (1955), in his original study of Philadelphia, tackled just this question and his results had lasting influence. He found that 39 per cent of moves were involuntary, stemming from reasons such as evictions, urban renewal schemes, loss of job and family break-up, but that there was a set of voluntary moves for which stage-in-life-cycle appeared to be the dominant cause. Households move through a series of stages, from marriage, pre-child, child-bearing to post-child and widowhood. With each stage, housing needs tend to change and although there may be time-lags, the imperatives of more space, less space or different types of space, have a significant impact on place utility. Some stages, such as child-bearing or family-forming and post-child or empty nesters, tend to have particular influence on space needs. Subsequent research has tended to confirm the importance of these life-cycle and space needs reasons in prompting residential moves, though other analyses have questioned the interpretation of space needs as exclusively life-cycle factors. A household may want a larger dwelling for prestige reasons to match a rising level of affluence; a more modern dwelling with up-to-date facilities, especially kitchens and bathrooms, may follow changing tastes and expectations. Moves may be prompted by socio-economic and cultural reasons, though Rossi tended to understate these in his original research. Also relevant is the fact that a move may well be a collective household decision rather than that of an individual. Again, many improvements and modernization can be achieved by modifying an existing property, so moves do not necessarily follow. Given some tendency for inertia, it is unlikely anyway that households will move at all stages of the life cycle and Paris (1995) reminded us of the need to be aware of people's housing opportunities over their life times; there are critical periods when long-term pathways are established and the idea of housing careers, or the longer-term pattern of consumption of housing by a given household, is important.

Other behavioural concepts come into play once the initial decision to seek a move is made. Awareness space refers to those parts of the city of which the household is sufficiently aware to allow them to enter the range of possible locations to be considered. A household

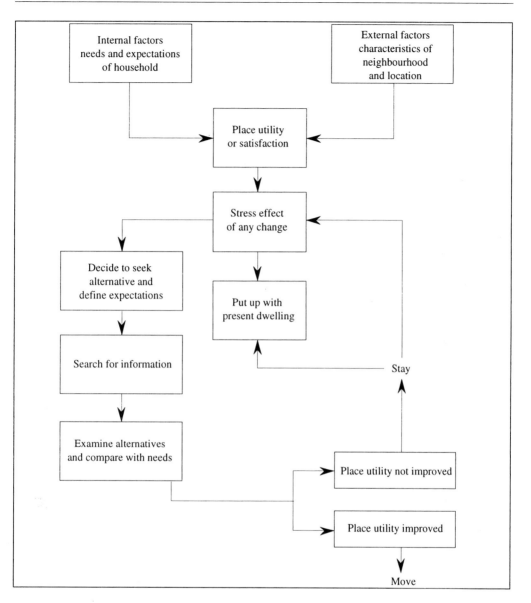

Figure 9.18 Residental mobility: a model of the decision-making process

will have preferences for specific areas based on personal experiences, the advice of others, or some other information source. Search behaviour involves taking steps to scrutinize the housing market and identify opportunities. It is now clear that search behaviour is not optimal, nor exhaustive nor systematic; it has more the character of a broad overview of possibilities and Munro (1995) reported evidence of households making spur-of-the-moment decisions to move after viewing a show-home. Many households rely on casual and informal sources of information about vacancies and will limit their search to segments of the city which interest them and to a small number of options within those segments. Most households tend not to enjoy search and curtail it as much as they can; it is very much a

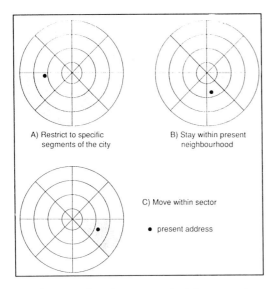

A) Restrict to specific
segments of the city

B) Stay within present
neighbourhood

C) Move within sector

• present address

Figure 9.19 Generalizing residential moves
within the city

satisficing rather than an optimizing experience. Rossi's general finding on search behaviour
was that it was a relatively haphazard process with surprisingly limited use of the formal
sources of information such as newspaper adverts and estate agents. There is variation by
social class groups and low-income movers were likely to consider the fewest options. In the
USA, there are federal policies aimed at providing counselling and funded metro-wide
housing searches for low-income families.

Behavioural studies at the scale of individual households have allowed detailed
verifications of the aggregate models of residential change. It has been found that:

- Movers tend to confine themselves to particular segments of the housing market. They
  will define sub-markets that conform to their needs in terms of costs, access to work,
  suitable neighbours, good facilities and especially schools.
- There is a strong neighbourhood factor, which has some generality but it is more
  relevant to the lower end of the market. This suggests that moves will be made over
  short distances and will allow conditions such as access to work, schools and local
  social networks to remain unchanged while achieving the purpose of a different type of
  dwelling.
- A sectoral factor suggests that movements of higher-income households in particular
  will follow a sectoral path towards the city periphery. Within the overall social
  geography of the city there are established social class or ethnic sectors and movements
  tend to be confined to the most appropriate of these. Figure 9.19 illustrates some of
  these factors.

Summary

This chapter has considered the residential mosaic within the city and has reviewed the ways
in which it has been studied over time. There are patterns to identify and classifications to
form and the literature is rich in examinations of these. Housing markets are major topics in
their own right and concern one of the most basic needs of city dwellers; here, perhaps more

vividly than anywhere else, the structure and agency tensions are clear and well exemplified. Policies developed to cope with housing questions have fundamental impact on planning and governmental strategies. Similarly, residential change is really about the ways people use housing stock as producers, managers, and consumers. These topics are among the most central in any study of the social geography of the city.

CHAPTER 10

Minority groups and segregated areas

The term 'minority' suggests a group of people which is numerically small within a particular society. As will be evident in this chapter, it is difficult to find terms which are not contested and minority or minority group is no exception. It has been applied, for example, in situations where the group actually forms a majority, as in earlier references to the place of women in society, and is often used where it has added meanings which may be racial, ethnic or subordinate. The literature on minority groups is permeated by added meanings in which racial connotations are the most pervasive. A central point is that terms like minority, race and ethnic are socially constructed and are 'the product of specific historical and geographical forces, rather than biologically given ideas whose meaning is dictated by nature' (Jackson and Penrose 1993: 1).

Mason (1995) argued that studies of minority groups often stress the facts of difference when they should recognize diversity. Difference assumes that there is some kind of norm from which minorities diverge and the frequent emphasis on assimilation processes assumes that these divergent groups will adapt to this norm over time but that, in the mean time, they belong to some 'other' category. Diversity, by contrast, has no necessary assumption of a 'merging' or integration, it is more of a 'we and they' rather than an 'us and them' situation. The idea of difference draws in a labelling process whereby minority groups are regarded as unequal, stigmatized and problematic.

When ideas of 'race' appeared in the nineteenth and early twentieth centuries, they were linked with physical variations, especially skin colour, and with personal, social and cultural competencies. Race, however, was always more than human difference, it was a social relationship. As Jackson and Penrose (1993) argued, when the New Commonwealth immigrants began to arrive in Britain in the 1950s, they became labelled as ethnic minorities and did not enter an ideological vacuum but were already racialized as a result of Britain's colonial history. American black migrants to northern cities in the USA in the nineteenth and twentieth centuries carried similar racial labels. Crossing the Mason-Dixon line did have some tangible as well as symbolic meaning for black migrants, but the harsh realities of racial discrimination still awaited them in northern cities. Although race is still alluded to as a physical construct, then, it is not a natural or 'essential' category, but has structural and ideological determinants, set within relations of domination and subordination between sections of society. Racism as a concept refers to attitudes and beliefs, to social actions and structures, and to intergroup hostilities. It summarizes relationships between the 'charter group', or dominant majority, and the minority 'the only legitimate sociological usage (of race) is one which identifies race as a particular kind of social relationship constructed in, and through, racist meaning' (Mason 1995: 12).

'Ethnicity' is different from race and refers to a group which believes that its members share a common descent and cultural heritage and that this perception is held by others. The boundaries that emerge between ethnic groups can be regarded as situational or dependent on time and circumstances. A migrant from south Asia could present him/herself as Gujerati, as Indian, Hindu, or British, depending upon the circumstances in which the question was asked. Place has significance to both race and ethnicity as minority groups often cluster in particular districts of the city. The reasons for this are complex and will be explored below but all the evidence of research employing measures of segregation, indicate that ethnic areas offer the strongest evidence of residential separation. As Peach (1996) noted in his discussion of the meaning of the term 'ghetto', its two conditions of being dominated by a single ethnic or racial group, and containing most members of that group, are really met only in ethnic minority areas.

Ethnic areas

Ethnic residential segregation is the most pronounced form of segregation within urban areas. It is found in many contrasted types of society and can often be detected in an incipient form in the very early stages of city growth. Boal (1978; 1987) reviewed the concept of ethnicity and its manifestations in urban social geography and provided useful definitions and guidelines. The bases for ethnic categorization can be racial, religious or national and its recognition may rest on distinguishing physical characteristics, on cultural traits, such as language or custom, or on a group identity obtaining from common origins or traditions. Greeley (1969) summarized this last characteristic as a 'human collectivity' based on an assumption of common origin, real or imaginary. Most research on ethnic groups has focused upon minorities in any given society. Ethnic minority groups are typically segregated but the extent depends on two key factors. The first relates to the migrant status of the group. Most ethnic minorities are initially immigrants and the recency of migration and their migration history are important considerations. The second feature is the social distance that separates the ethnic minority from the 'charter group' or host society, the dominant matrix into which it is inserted. For those immigrants whose differences with the charter group are small, separate identity may be of only temporary duration, whereas for those whose differences – either real or perceived – are great, separation in both society and space is likely to persist. These two factors clearly interact. New migrants, regardless of ethnic status, will be distinctive at least in social characteristics but long-term migrants, however distinctive they have remained, will have acquired some of the characteristics of the new society.

Assimilation: choice and constraint

The maintenance of the ethnic minority group as a distinctive social and spatial entity will depend on the degree to which assimilation occurs. As already discussed, the assumption behind this assimilation model is that the ideal is to reduce difference and to produce

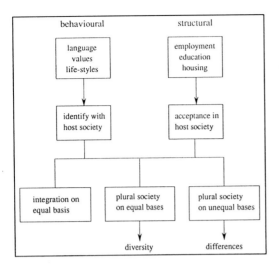

Figure 10.1 Assimilation model

integration, rather than to protect diversity. A distinction is normally made between behavioural and structural assimilation (Figure 10.1). The former describes the process whereby members of a group acquire the attitudes, values and mores of the charter group and are 'acculturated' into the new society. Structural assimilation refers to the ability of migrants to compete successfully in the system of stratification within that society – principally its occupational, educational and housing markets. Both types of assimilation have to be seen in a temporal context but whereas behavioural assimilation is normally attainable by all types of immigrants, structural assimilation is typically much more difficult to achieve. The rate at which behavioural assimilation takes place can vary from one ethnic minority group to another – some groups may purposefully seek to retain their distinctive characteristics and thereby delay assimilation – but a common estimate is that by the third generation a migrant group has substantially acquired the behavioural traits and values of the host society. Time taken to achieve structural assimilation will vary and the type of ethnic minority is again significant with the key factor being the attitude of the charter group. Whereas west European immigrants to the USA, for example, will normally achieve almost immediate structural assimilation, i.e. they will fit into existing systems at a level appropriate to their skills and qualifications, black minorities in US cities continue to occupy lower-paid jobs and low-cost housing after well over a century of in-movement. Most research in the social sciences has been concerned with those ethnic minorities for whom the constraints upon assimilation and levels of discrimination are greatest. These groups are often physically distinct, set apart by inherited biological traits such as colour of skin. Perhaps one of the most powerful arguments for the assimilation model is in these structural terms. It is only through successful structural assimilation that equality of opportunities in these key areas can be realized, though, as Figure 10.1 shows, plural societies on unequal bases and with an emphasis on differences, are the most common outcomes.

These ethnic groups, often disadvantaged and unable to compete effectively in work and housing markets, become residentially segregated into less desirable parts of the urban area. The ethnic areas typical of many cities have often been initiated and maintained by attitudes of a charter group which continues to discriminate and restrict and has the effect of creating

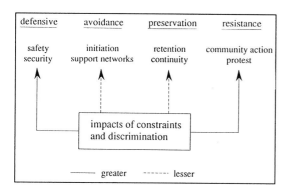

Figure 10.2 Choice functions in segregation

both this separation and disadvantage. Not all of the forces which promote ethnic segregation, however, emanate from the charter group. There is strong evidence that choice operates in the maintenance of ethnic group segregation as, for minorities who wish to retain some level of group cohesion or who have some vision of a plural society, the ethnic area offers an obvious instrument to that end. This idea of a dichotomy between choice and constraint has been challenged. Jackson and Smith (1984) argued that there were no dichotomies of choice/constraint or voluntary/enforced segregation; rather ethnic areas were outcomes of many complex processes emanating from economic, political and ideological structures.

Boal (1978) nominated a number of functions which the ethnic area fulfils (Figure 10.2). The defensive function enables the isolation of individual members of an ethnic minority within the wider society to be reduced and defence to be organized, where needed, within a clearly defined territory. As the term 'ghetto' (from the island of Geto in Venice) was first applied to Jewish compounds in European cities, it had this kind of meaning. An avoidance function emphasized the self-supportive roles of ethnic minorities, particularly in the context of recent migrants. The ethnic area serves as a place of initiation and familiarization, where traditional values, customs and perhaps language are retained and these processes are easier to accomplish. There are often institutions – temple, mosque or community centre – which may be in part designed to provide sustenance at earlier stages of contact with a new society. Chain migration, with earlier migrants maintaining flows of information and aid to those who follow, has frequently been recognized and social networks developed in this way are integral to the avoidance function. Preservation functions are common. Here the aim is to preserve and promote at least the central features of the ethnic group's culture such as language, religion, and marriage customs. Wirth (1928), in his classic study of the ghetto, suggested that for Jews the geographically separated and socially isolated community seemed to offer the best means of preserving the traditional facets of their lifestyle. There is considerable evidence (see Dahya 1974) that Asian communities in the UK place the preservation function very high on their list of priorities. Finally, the resistance function involves the use by an ethnic group of a particular territory as its power-base for action against the wider society. At times during the late 1960s and 1970s, the Black Power movement in the USA used the ghettos for such purposes; some Catholic and Protestant core areas in Northern Ireland have this function and other urban resistance movements have used parts of cities in this way.

These four functions of ethnic areas have been described as choice mechanisms but they could also be regarded as responses to constraint. Wherever choices and constraints operate, they are invariably interwoven and explanations are rarely single-stranded. The social constructions of race and ethnicity encompass many facets of human life and the extent and character of racial segregation summarizes the key characteristics. Whereas choice functions can be identified, few would argue that they act independently of constraints. The ideologies of racism underlie all aspects of the emergence of ethnic areas and these underlying factors can be identified.

First, black minority groups carry the historical connotations of the high points of white supremacy such as slavery and colonialism. The flows of African slaves into the USA placed the origins of the black population into a history of subservience and inferiority with which it remains encumbered. Slavery existed in other parts of the world and in colonial societies the indigenous population, again designated as servile and inferior, was similarly given negative stereotypes. There is a history of labelling and injustice from which ethnic minority groups in North America and Europe have yet to recover. South Africa, the longest survivor of the apartheid tradition, has only in the last part of the twentieth century entered its phase of change.

Second, ethnic minority groups, especially in their earlier days of immigration, but also with remarkable persistence, hold the positions of least advantage in the workplace and the housing markets. Rogers and Uto (1987) emphasized the centrality of work and labour in understanding the disadvantage of ethnic minorities and S. J. Smith (1987) noted that children born in Britain of Caribbean parents were four or five times more likely to be unemployed than their white indigenous counterparts. Mason (1995) stated that ethnic minority members were consistently more likely to be unemployed in the UK and were also vulnerable to hyper-cyclical unemployment or a faster reaction to the ups and downs of economic cycles. This kind of exclusion extends beyond unemployment but members of ethnic minorities are typically unemployed, in less skilled jobs, at lower job levels, and are concentrated in particular sectors of the labour market. British research showed that in comparison with whites, Chinese and Bangladeshis are more likely to work in hotels and catering, Pakistanis and Bangladeshis in textiles and footwear, and Afro-Caribbeans in transport and communication. There are gender differences such as the presence of Afro-Caribbean women in health-care and Asian women in services. Mason (1995) reported some signs of upward job mobility but none the less the unfavourable positions of ethnic minorities in the labour market, for reasons which still basically stem from discrimination, have a fundamental link with their continuing residential segregation.

Perceived social stress is a third reason for the marginalization of ethnic minorities. In large part this derives from racism but there have been events, notably the inner city riots of the 1970s and 1980s, which exacerbated the problem image of these groups. Conflict in housing markets, intergroup rivalries, and the harassment of 'coloured' people by white organizations, ranging from the Ku Klux Klan to the National Front, added to this image of stress, strain and trouble. As Jenkins (1986) showed, these images permeate the labour market and candidates for jobs were being discarded because they were believed to be sources of problems; 'white flight' from housing areas where black in-migration was occurring could be partially explained in the same way.

Fourth, managers and gatekeepers who control and allocate resources can act as sources of discriminatory practice, direct or indirect, which adds to the facts of segregation. S. J. Smith

(1987) pointed to the effects of local government policy and gatekeepers in housing markets; Shah (1979) identified negative roles for the local government policies, other official bodies, the police and the media. The processes involved include exclusion from some areas of resource allocation, or at least from good quality resources, labelling and stereotyping. Some aspects of policing practice, such as the ways in which stop and search policies are implemented, are often seen by black youths to be discriminatory.

If research is concerned with the measurement of segregation, there are several technical aspects to consider. First, the scale of analysis needs to be stated as different levels of spatial resolution will produce different results. Peach (1979) has shown that high levels of segregation can occur where the ethnic minority is numerically very small. In US cities, with proportions of non-white population ranging from 2.1 to 7.0 per cent, indices of dissimilarity still ranged from 60.4 to 98.0. A second issue involves the extent of dominance by one group within an ethnic area. Ford and Griffin (1979) reported that white Americans regarded an area as ethnic if it was 25 per cent black, whereas black Americans would regard it as integrated if it was 25 per cent white. A third issue, concerns the designation of ethnic areas. Most researchers have adopted arbitrary thresholds and Ford and Griffin (1979), for example, defined ghettos as areas with at least 50 per cent black or 70 per cent minority group (blacks, Hispanics, Asians). A problem with the second part of this definition is that separate minority groups may share a general location but will segregate within the ethnic area. Again, ethnic areas are often dynamic and expand or contract over time, so notions of core and periphery may be appropriate.

A typology of ethnic areas

Boal (1978) offered a useful conceptual typology of ethnic areas. A 'colony' is an ethnic area which is temporary in character: its main functions are to provide a foothold for in-migrants who are likely to have little difficulty in achieving either behavioural or structural assimilation and are motivated towards both those ends. An 'enclave' is an ethnic area which persists over time but has a strong element of choice and of the preservation function in particular. The term 'ghetto' is reserved for ethnic areas which persist but are mainly based upon constraints and the discriminatory actions of the charter group. Figure 10.3 suggests ways in which these three spatial forms might emerge. 'Colony' is an initial cluster which disappears over time as the minority group participates successfully in assimilation processes; an example of this is the Dutch immigration into Kalamazoo. 'Enclave' is a more persistent cluster and its institutions, such as temple or mosque, indicate ways in which it functions as a social organization. As Jewish groups in Winnipeg adjusted their spatial positions and migrated to another district of the city, they remained clustered together and moved their cultural institutions to the new locations. The new Jewish enclave met their higher social status aspirations for housing but maintained their cultural cohesion. Less successful Jewish families remained in the older ethnic area and colonized its edges to give some area growth. Ghettos in US cities are best exemplified by black populations. Their relegation to the most substandard and lowest cost inner city districts is a reflection of their inability to achieve upward mobility in the job market. Where black households achieve social mobility, they tend to be restricted to particular sectors of cities as a result of barriers presented by charter group attitudes and discriminatory practice in the housing market. The idea of the ghetto as an internal colony increasingly occupied by an underclass afflicted by disadvantage and

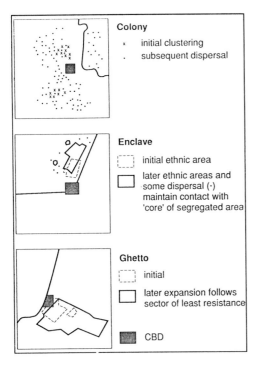

Figure 10.3 Types of ethnic areas

oppression has been used to demonstrate the divisions which appear within the black community as more successful black households achieve outward movement within the ethnic sector.

Ethnic areas in US cities

The subject of ethnic minorities in the USA, and especially of black ethnic groups, has attracted a great deal of research attention. Studies have focused on the early development of immigrant areas (Ward 1971), on the spatial ecology of slave cities (Radford 1976), and on modern processes of ghetto formation. Ford and Griffin (1979) offer a useful typology of black ghettos in the USA (see Figure 10.4). In the early southern ghetto, as found for example in ante-bellum Charleston and New Orleans, blacks typically lived close within white neighbourhoods – for which they served in domestic roles as servants or gardeners – but occupied alleys and back-streets in small dwellings. In the classic southern ghetto the newly freed blacks were placed in purpose-built housing on unwanted land, such as that near railway tracks – 'the other side of the tracks' – or on badly drained areas. As southern states experienced considerable out-migration of blacks, neither of these types of ghettos had potential for growth and tended to stagnate or disappear.

The early northern ghetto was the product of intense competition for space in the early twentieth century. Its tenements and row-houses, especially in large north-eastern cities, were occupied at high density with chronic shortage of space and high levels of poverty and substandardness. Specific districts in the northern cities, such as Chicago's 'south-side' and New York's Harlem, became the destinations of many black migrants. Classic northern ghettos are more recent and much more extensive in scale. As the 'white flight' from the central city gathered force, so large areas of land and housing were left to an expanding black

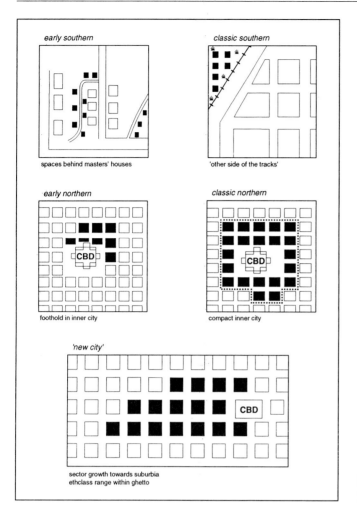

Figure 10.4 Evolution of the black American ghetto

population. The term ghetto has the implication of enforcement and segregation was legally enforceable in the urban north and rural south until a Supreme Court hearing of 1948. Even after legal changes, discriminatory practice continues to have its effect. This type of ghetto, the classic northern, is also found on the west coast in its 'older' large cities. Black south-central Los Angeles, for example, extends 40 km (25 miles) from near Beverly Hills to Long Beach. Within these vast areas of this type of ghetto are enormous tracts of vacant land, dereliction and abandoned properties. Ford and Griffin (1979) argued that although this is the dominant image of the black ghetto, the reality is being modified by the emergence of a 'new city' type of ghetto in those parts of the USA which have experienced significant urban growth in the last part of the twentieth century. In cities like San Diego, Denver and Phoenix these ghettos extend from the inner city to rural fringes. The gradient from poverty and poor environments at the inner city end of the sector to affluence and good environments on the fringe is contained within the black community. Ethclasses or social stratifications within the ethnic group find separate spatial expressions within the ethnic sector; there are segregated socio-economic status groups within the black community. Although the emergence of this fifth type of ghetto suggests structural assimilation among

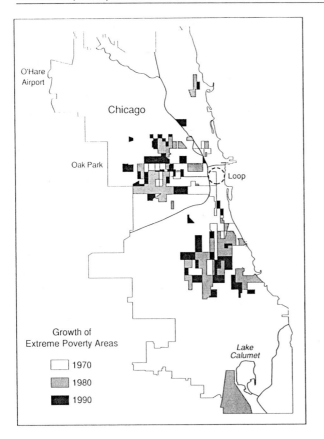

Growth of
Extreme Poverty Areas

☐ 1970

▦ 1980

■ 1990

Figure 10.5 Poverty areas in Chicago, 1970–90

some sections at least of the black population of the USA, there are no signs that the ghetto is dispersing. Fears and prejudices rooted in generations of segregated residential areas will take many years to dissipate. This discussion has focused on black ethnic groups but the rise of Hispanic minorities has been the feature of southern cities. In Los Angeles, Hispanics by 1980 formed a group of 816,076 in the city and 2,144,022 in the county; there have been lesser but still significant growths of Asian communities.

One focus of attention in recent research on ethnic minorities in US cities has been the emergence of these sharp polarities within the groups. Wilson (1987) emphasized these trends in his studies of black communities highlighting the problems experienced by what he termed the 'truly disadvantaged'. This group occupied the older inner city parts of the historic ghetto and had begun to acquire features of residualization, marginalization and exclusion **within** the black residential areas. Marks (1991) emphasized the extreme problems which beset traditional ghettos with high unemployment, few job prospects, the collapse of family life and the rising incidence of crime and drugs. A reliance on welfare and a dramatic rise in numbers of black and Hispanic female-headed, lone-parent families was an indicator of change. Anderson (1978) portrayed such areas as dangerous places where people had to find new rules of conduct, localized codes of street etiquette and mental notations – all components of a strategy for survival in the mean streets of the inner city. Wilson saw the loss of community as a key factor. Whereas the inner city ghetto before the 1960s showed 'the features of social organization, including a sense of community, positive neighbourhood identification and explicit norms and sanctions against aberrant behaviour' (Wilson 1987: 3).

The underclass ghettos of the 1990s had lost these features. Many changes could be related to the outward movement of upward socially mobile and traditionally constituted black families. These were the groups which gave stability, social cohesion and social control and their removal took away this social structure and also removed potential leaders and organizers. The outcomes are strong social gradients within the black residential sector and substantial inner-city minorities 'hopelessly mired in poverty' (Aponte 1991). Figure 10.5 shows the changing geography of poverty areas in Chicago between 1970 and 1990. These mainly black areas have increased in territorial extent but have decreased in population.

Immigrants and ethnic areas in British cities

There were ethnic minorities in the UK before the 1950s. An estimated 727,000 Irish migrants lived in England in 1851; there were 300,000 Jews by 1920 and black populations in British ports, such as Bristol, Liverpool and Cardiff, could be dated back several centuries. It was however the influx of immigrants from countries of the New Commonwealth during the 1950s and 1960s that gave substantial ethnic minorities. The main immigrant groups, from the West Indies, India, Pakistan and Bangladesh, have followed classical patterns of immigration. They arrived with many disadvantages associated with the ideological 'baggage' from their colonial history, with a lack of relevant employment skills and education, and found these exacerbated by the discriminatory practices of the host society. As a generalization, replacement theory is most relevant to the task of understanding the niche which they occupy in both social and geographical space. They found employment in the least desirable jobs; they obtained housing in substandard parts of the inner city and their segregation, although it allowed avoidance and preservation, was the product of their marginalization within the host society.

Early ethnic minorities were numerically small and shared poor environments with the low-income indigenous population and, often, the established Irish communities. With continuing immigration and numerical growth, levels of segregation increased and there were ethnic 'majorities': Peach (1996) noted that the Northcote ward in Ealing (London) had a non-white presence of 90.2 per cent (total population 11,177) and Spinney Hill ward in Leicester of 82.5 per cent (10,035). Scale is important and the highest proportion of non-white population in a municipality was 44.8 per cent in the London Borough of Brent (243,080). There was marked segregation between ethnic minorities with the more recently arrived Bangladeshis showing highest and most persistent levels of separation. Whereas part of the segregation, of an order 10 to 15 per cent, can be explained by socio-economic characteristics (Peach *et al.* 1975), it is clearly an ethnic basis of separation which is occurring.

Detailed case studies have been conducted in the city of Birmingham (Jones 1970; 1979) where, in 1971, the 'coloured' minority of 92,632 comprised 9.3 per cent of the total population but by 1991 had reached a total of 206,800 (Mason 1995). In the early 1960s, the location of the ethnic minority groups could be summarized as being inner city and conforming to both a 'fabric effect' – they fitted into available low-cost accommodation – and to a replacement model – they moved into spaces vacated by the indigenous population. By the 1970s, continuing demographic change – out-migration of whites, in-migration and natural increase of immigrants – had consolidated these concentrations at higher densities. Clusters were 38 to 51 per cent non-white composition and different ethnic groups occupied separate parts of the inner city, with Pakistanis, for example, in parts of south Birmingham, such as Saltley and Small Heath. Since 1971 the picture of changing levels of segregation have become more complex and generalizations are elusive. Peach (1996) showed that whereas Black Caribbean levels of segregation were declining, this was not true of the south Asian groups. Part of the explanation lay in attitudes towards public sector housing as while Black Caribbean households had taken up that housing option and had achieved some dispersal, south Asians remained rooted to owner-occupancy in the low-cost sector of the housing market.

The role of public sector housing has been significant in British cities. Although this sector has traditionally fulfilled a strong welfare role, there was evidence in the 1960s (Burney 1967) that municipalities were exercising discrimination against immigrant households. Recency of arrival in a city counted heavily against the immigrant group and where rehousing could not be avoided, a series of expedients, such as placement in deferred renewal areas, improved terraces, or old inner city estates, was used. By the 1970s, however, aided by national legislation, the situation had improved and 19 per cent of black households (mainly West Indian) were in public sector housing. Municipalities targeted black populations occupying the most substandard accommodation for rehousing, though these policies sometimes produced conflict. Public sector housing could produce new 'ghettos' but there is some limited evidence that levels of Black Caribbean segregation are decreasing.

South Asians have progressed through a number of housing stages which Robinson (1979) summarized as early pioneer, lodging-house era and family-reunion, suburbanization and municipalization. Early pioneers were single men seeking temporary work; the lodging-house era saw the expansion of this group and a more permanent stay; family reunion witnessed the main movement of women and children to consolidate the settlement of the group. The Asian 'community' comprises a considerable number of ethnically different groups with strong differences between them but there is some evidence for a myth of return or the idea that their housing decisions are based on a belief that overseas residence is temporary. This argument has been used to explain the unwillingness of south Asians to assimilate into British society and to suggest that choice forms a strong factor in their segregation. Even south Asians have moved to private suburbs (suburbanization) or to public sector estates (municipalization), they have tended to locate near the 'enclave' which houses the majority of the ethnic group and in which its cultural traditions and institutions are maintained (Figure 10.6). Suburbanization of elements of the south Asian population who achieve social mobility has become a feature of cities such as Leicester, Manchester and Glasgow.

The overall balance of evidence remains such as to suggest that in British cities ethnic areas have emerged and are consolidating, though Peach's (1996) conclusion that conditions do not resemble a ghetto are timely. Whereas severe constraints are instrumental in this process, the relevance of choice cannot be disregarded. Public policies have traditionally followed integrationist goals but have often been modified to encompass a much stronger regard for the choices and preferences of the minority groups. Such policies have qualifications. First, as a longer-term goal, the disadvantages which ethnic minorities suffer

Myth of return (strong)	early pioneer :	single men, transient	Difference strong
	lodging house :	single men, longer-stay	
	family reunion :	women and children join men more permanence	
	inner city settlement :	cheap housing Asian landlords cultural institutions	
	suburbanization :	wealthier minority in businesses and professions	
Myth of return (weak)	municipalization :	some move to social housing close to established areas	Difference still strong but more diversity

Figure 10.6 Stages in Asian migration to the UK

through the inequalities present in society and its mechanisms, including the persistence of racism, must be eliminated. The central aim should be to achieve diversity rather than difference. Second, in the short term, positive discrimination and area-enrichment policies must be developed to reduce existing disadvantage. Diversity and a plural society will have little meaning unless the disparities between various distinguishable groups are eliminated.

Other minorities

The focus has been on ethnic minorities and this properly reflects the real nature of minority group segregation in cities. There are other minorities, however, some of which have no ethnic connotation, which deserve mention. Sibley (1992) considered the social construction of the 'outsiders', groups designated as different and stereo typed with a negative image of some kind. The Gypsies, in his case study, fell easily into that category, lacking both acceptability by the dominant society and a territory to which they belong. Gypsies who retain their traditional itinerant lifestyle are classed as outsiders, treated with suspicion and often denied places to live. In the UK, municipalities have found it very difficult to conform with the law and provide designated sites for travelling people. The opposition comes from local residents who associate Gypsies with unacceptable lifestyles, a lack of cleanliness and activities on the margins of legality. The Nimby (not in my backyard) syndrome has been enacted many times as local residents oppose proposals for Gypsy sites.

Other minorities, distinguished by their sexuality, are becoming more visible in western cities and again, for the 'dominant' groups, these are outsiders. Cities have always had districts associated with the 'sex trade' that carry euphemisms such as vice areas and red-light districts. Generally, the attitude of society is that if such activities are to be tolerated, they should be confined to specific areas where they can be controlled and monitored; districts such as London's Soho and the red-light district of Amsterdam are outcomes of this process. The professionals of the sex industry are confined to such districts for the practice of their trade though not necessarily for their residences. In the moral geographies of the city, vice areas are at the lowest point of the scale. A different kind of moral geography has emerged with the clearer emergence of sections of society with different sexual proclivities to those which are generally regarded as normal. Gays and lesbians form minority groups within the modern city and their geographies are being studied.

Forest (1995) studied the West Hollywood district of Los Angeles as an example of a place with a gay identity. His focus was on portrayals of the gay community in the press and, in particular, the attempt by the gay press to link sexual meanings to particular places and thus represent gay minorities in ways similar to ethnic minorities. This concept of diversity and the rights of minorities to occupy specific spaces combats the older image of exclusion or the need to confine 'perverts' and moral failures to excluded places. This perspective suggests that place has a key role in allowing minorities to resist domination, there is some shift from constraint and exclusion to choice and recognition. Places where gays and lesbians are accepted become places where they are empowered and the whole process of 'coming out' is enabled in environments of this kind. Gay territories play significant parts in the evolution of gay identities and subcultures. In West Hollywood, there are symbols of gay identity that conform with the characteristics of many of its inhabitants; place plays a fundamental role in the creation of a 'normative ideal'. Valentine (1993a; 1993b) studied the space behaviour of lesbians in British cities and revealed the difficulties faced by this minority group in a society dominated by a different form of sexuality. Lesbians feel threatened by the ways in which space is organized and expropriated by heterosexuals. Concealment is one way of coping with heterosexual space but relationships develop through networks which may centre on specific areas. Gay places, more likely to be bars or houses rather than districts, are vital and Valentine found that 85 per cent of her sample of lesbians made contact with others through such places. Lesbians feel they are ghetto-ized because their places are often in marginal and run-down urban areas. Yet they offer safety and security from harassment on the basis of a perception of sexuality and in this sense have some of the qualities of defence and preservation discussed elsewhere. Major cities sometimes have visible gay areas and their understanding lies in the social construction of place and the tensions between majority and minority values and forms of behaviour.

Conclusions

The focus of attention in this section has been upon ethnic minority groups in western societies and their residential segregation. Throughout many Third World countries where plural societies are much more common, the issues are more diverse and complex. Residential segregation on ethnic grounds have strong religious and language connotations and are often reinforced by extensive kinship networks and internally organized social systems. Ethnic divisions and ethnic areas, in their diversity of forms, typify cities and maintain their distinctive imprint on urban life. An understanding of their emergence, persistence, and present features lies at least as much in the attitudes and behaviour of the dominant white society as it does in any characteristics of the minorities. As other forms of segregation and difference appear, they reveal familiar traits in both their geographies and their forms of behaviour.

CHAPTER 11

The city as a social world

As the industrial city developed in the nineteenth century, its *raison d'être* was economic activity and manufacturing industries were its driving force, dominating its essential functional features and land-use. Large industries often occupied large tracts of central city space, housing was closely linked to places of employment, power structures were aligned to industrial interests, and the city as the locus of industry and commerce was sharply differentiated from rural areas. As the post-industrial city emerged, the character of the economic institutions changed from manufacturing to services but the urban economy, still the foundation of the city, became more complex with activities that were both more dispersed spatially and variegated by type. At the same time, the social dimension to urban life became more complex and assumed greater significance. Soja (1989), in his *Postmodern Geographies*, tried to express this when he spoke of society becoming contextualised and regionalised around a multi-layered nesting of supra-individual modal localities. Older ideas of urbanism and urban/rural differences had less relevance. Large cities now encapsulate modern trends which have profound effects upon lifestyles and quality of living. Innovation and change are integral to the growth of cities but by no means always in positive ways. In Chapters 11 and 12 some of these changes and the related issues will be explored. Here, the emphasis will be upon the social dimension to urban life, and Chapter 12 looks more generally at social problems in the city.

Terms such as social, economic and political are not discrete, but overlap substantially. Within the social dimension are key features such as the institutions of family and kinship, social networks, friends, neighbours and a sense of place and community. Social behaviour includes visiting friends and the act of neighbourliness as well as more formal and regulated forms of behaviour such as voting in political elections. Interest in behaviour is reflected in a research emphasis on consumption rather than production, and with the ways that people use space in the city. Many forms of behaviour are voluntary and reflect the personalities and preferences of those involved and able to exercise choice, yet much behaviour is involuntary and people are either forced to do things, such as move home in a slum clearance project, or are so constrained by resources or lack of mobility, that real choice is not available.

As a starting point, concepts of environment and behaviour are introduced. One of the city's distinguishing features is that it creates an environment on a scale unprecedented in other forms of settlement. Built environments are the dominant environments for city dwellers. Certainly, cities are placed in natural environments and are shaped by their climate and topography, but it is the built environment that becomes a key influence on everyday behaviour, attitudes and activities. Architects, planners and others concerned with the design of cities have key roles.

Urban environments

The built environment comprises the morphology of the city, the streets, buildings, and open spaces which form the setting for urban behaviour. Built environments are socially constructed and the 'new' cultural geography has focused on this theme and the values with which buildings and spaces are endowed. The meanings attached to space and place, encapsulated in the term 'spatiality', were recognized in earlier writings (Firey 1947), but cultural geography has afforded them new prominence: 'places, landscapes and buildings are 'fields' in which in-group identifications (inclusive identities) are constructed and communicated . . . our urban environments have been adapted in the image of people's belief systems' (Anderson and Gale 1992: 5).

> Urban landscapes are vast monuments to the prevailing social order. They can be read for clues to the ways people have lived and thought through time. Any modern city can provide a point of entry for understanding the workings of the space-economy, of urbanization as a process, and of national material cultures.
>
> (Walker 1995: 33)

A focus upon built environments does not remove some well-known conceptual problems. There are questions on the independence of the environmental variable, its precise definition, the nature of the people-environment relationship, and intervening variables. Built environments may be socially constructed, but they are also physically constructed and have forms which can be modified, a necessary quality as buildings are often not used for the purposes for which they were originally intended. Of the two architectural approaches to urban design, one emphasizes visible form and is aesthetic and abstract in its language; the other is concerned with social usage and studies the behavioural experience of people in different types of designed environment. Both approaches are relevant to an understanding of the interaction between people and environment, as architecture makes a physical representation of social relations in the way it organizes people in space (Boys 1984) The built environment with its buildings, structures, design features and plan, spaces and alignments of streets and paths poses many questions. For example, do high-rise apartment blocks engender particular types of attitude and behaviour? Are population densities or building densities critical variables in understanding social pathology? There are other considerations. Urban environment is a broader concept than built environment; it has economic, social and political significance which affects people in varying ways. The social environment of the city can be divided into the impersonal and the personal. Impersonal social environments are objective and can be measured by indicators of demographic structure or social class, personal social environments are subjective and rest on values, attitudes and forms of behaviour. The concept of spatiality, with its concerns with the production of space and the ways in which it reflects social values offers a link between

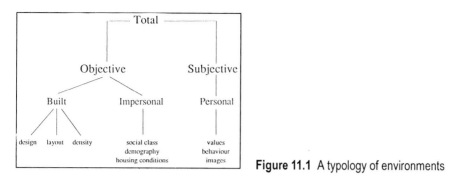

Figure 11.1 A typology of environments

the built and social environments of the city. Urban environment, then, forms a backcloth against which people live their lives. It is not a simple concept. It includes built form, it is imbued with values and meanings, it is multilayered and is a 'palimpsest' in which the past is partially overwritten by the present.

How people relate to the urban environment will reflect their individual differences and the diversities of their past experiences. Michelson (1970) made the useful distinction between mental and experiential congruence with environment. Mental congruence exists if an individual thinks that a particular environment will successfully accommodate his or her personal characteristics, values, and lifestyle; experiential congruence exists if the environment actually accommodates them. The extent to which people adapt to new environments and achieve satisfaction is therefore related to the extent to which mental equates with experiential congruence. Again, Stokols (1978) saw the need to distinguish between primary environments, or those in which the individual spends most time and for which congruence is important, and secondary, which are only used in a transitory way. Figure 11.1 offers a simple typology of environments. The total environment is composed of elements which relate in different ways to different people and contains a variety of scales as well as of types. The built environment has to be seen in context with the social environments formed by the people and activities which occupy space. Whatever the objective qualities these two facets of environment possess, they have to be seen through the filters of people's subjective awareness, understanding and experience. Objective conditions such as overcrowding or substandardness have meaning only in terms of the cognition of the population involved. A planner's definition of overcrowding, for example, may differ substantially from that of a tenement dweller.

Built environment and behaviour

There is a mythology on the relationship between built environment and behaviour. Many of the problems of inner city slums in the early part of the twentieth century, for example, were attributed to the physical conditions under which people lived; overcrowding and substandardness were judged as more significant than poverty and disadvantage. Some of these myths have been exposed, but others persist and there is still insufficient evidence to pronounce on causes and effects. Among the propositions relevant to any examination of environment and social behaviour are the suggested effects of design, distance, and density.

The best known starting point for an analysis of the link between the built environment and behaviour is the study by Festinger *et al.* (1950) of two housing projects at the Massachusetts Institute of Technology, called Westgate and Westgate West. The former consisted of small, prefabricated single-family and detached homes, grouped around courtyards and facing away from access roads, and the latter of two-storey apartment blocks with five apartments in each storey. Festinger *et al.* examined the extent to which design differences affected the formation of friendship patterns and attitudes. In Westgate, the strongest influence was the physical distance between the front doors of the housing units, with most friendships being formed within courts and among near-neighbours. The localized friendship networks also seemed to foster shared attitudinal stances and commonly held views. Isolates from the Westgate friendship networks were typically the occupants of end-houses facing access roads rather than interior courts, or were households where working wives did not participate in the social interaction patterns. For Westgate West, the critical factors were the lines of movement from dwelling-unit to exits and entrances, or functional rather than physical distances. From this study it was argued that the physical matrix within which the occupants of the project lived, formed by both residential proximity and channels of contact, exerted heavy influences on the way in which friendships were formed. Two assertions arose from this classic study. First, that friendships can be determined by physical proximity, and second and more significantly, that groups, however established, exert influence over members through social interaction.

Festinger *et al.*'s study group was composed of students with similar background and age. Kuper (1953) studied residential districts in Coventry in which the dominant house-type was a semi-detached dwelling unit with paths between each set of houses. The placement of doors was found to bring people together and enabled neighbourly contact to turn into more meaningful relationships. Kuper did, however, stress that although proximity and functional distance could bring about contact and interaction, this could have both positive and negative outcomes. Whyte (1957) studied the Park Forest housing area at two points in time with an intervening period of three years. Proximity affected interaction markedly and despite residential change over the three-year period, the same 'homes' were grouped in activity sets. Whyte made a number of observations.

- Children had key roles in establishing contacts.
- People in corner plots were most likely to be isolated.
- People in central locations had the highest levels of involvement.

Whyte's sample population was still uniform. A new housing development attracts people of similar social status, aspirations, and life-cycle characteristics and the significance of this was recognized:

> We emphasize that where the community is heterogeneous one would expect the ecological factors to have considerably less weight than they do in communities where there is a high degree of homogeneity and common interests among the residents.
>
> (Festinger *et al.* 1950: 163)

The significance of this qualification, often ignored by critics, is an essential footnote to the statement of architectural determinism:

The architect who builds a house or who designs a site plan, who decides where roads will and will not go, and who decides, which directions the houses will face and how close together they will be, also is, to a large extent deciding the pattern of social life among the people who live in these houses.

(Festinger *et al.* 1950: 160)

Factors such as age, stage in life cycle and shared interests tend to be neglected. Gans (1972) thought that planners overstated the influence of design as buildings were of secondary importance in comparison with economic, cultural and social factors. Design may hinder or aid relationships but does not per se shape human behaviour significantly. Similarly:

spatial proximity often based on the position and outlook of doors may determine interaction patterns, but this normally only occurs under conditions of real or perceived homogeneity in the population and where there is need for mutual aid.

(Michelson 1970: 190)

Clearly, there is a middle ground between the extremes of architectural determinism and design irrelevance and the polarities may indeed be convenient figments of the critics' imaginations rather than the intentions of the practitioners:

while buildings do not control our lives, architecture does work (albeit in a partial way) together with other aspects of social and economic relations to put people in their 'place' and to describe symbolically and spatially what that place is.

(Boys 1984: 26)

Design factors have often been used as part of a strategy of social engineering. The neighbourhood unit, first introduced as a planning device in Radburn, New Jersey, in 1929, was an explicit attempt to create 'communities' through physical design. Guideline criteria of population size, boundaries, open space provision, services, and traffic layout were used to create both a physical identity and a sense of belonging. At the centre of the neighbourhood unit were the elementary school and community centre; the neighbourhood population size of 7,500 to 10,000, was based on the catchment of an elementary school (Figure 11.2). The 1944 Dudley Report for England and Wales supported the neighbourhood unit principle and planners viewed it as a means of recovering the sense of intimacy and locality which had been disrupted by the scale of urban growth. The evidence for the value of neighbourhood planning is mixed but the principle has proved remarkably resilient. Residential areas have anyway to be arranged in compact forms with local facilities, and this setting is conducive to the development of a local community. Greater flexibility was evident in the plan for Columbia, Maryland. Here housing cluster, neighbourhood and village are components of the city plan, designed to provide basic needs and enable local interaction, in an overall structure which allows choice of movement and accessibility (see Figure 11.2).

A further example of social engineering was the attempt to develop 'socially integrated' housing. Early schemes in British new towns proved unsuccessful as mixtures of social classes led to local fragmentation and polarization of groups rather than integration. Similarly in the USA, progress towards racially integrated housing has met continued

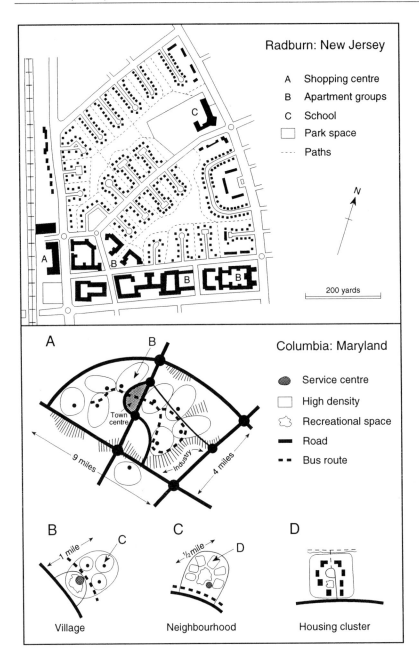

Figure 11.2 Planned neighbourhoods in New Jersey and Maryland

resistance and has achieved limited success. At least two out of every three white Americans live in essentially white neighbourhoods; public housing has become home to the extremely poor and usually non-white population (Dreier and Atlas 1995). The ideal of integrated neighbourhoods remains elusive.

Much research into design influences has been stimulated by the apparent vulnerability of some types of built environment to crime. Newman (1972) studied high-rise public housing

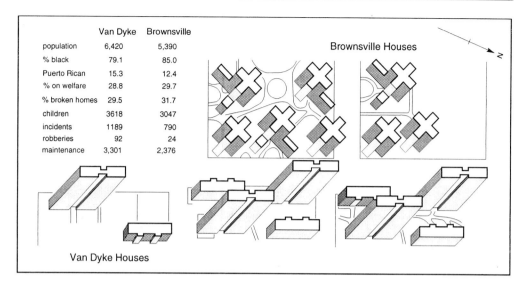

	Van Dyke	Brownsville
population	6,420	5,390
% black	79.1	85.0
Puerto Rican	15.3	12.4
% on welfare	28.8	29.7
% broken homes	29.5	31.7
children	3618	3047
incidents	1189	790
robberies	92	24
maintenance	3,301	2,376

Figure 11.3 Newman's New York case study of defensible space

projects in New York and developed the idea of 'defensible space', a set of primarily design principles aimed at the reduction this vulnerability. Newman compared housing projects with contrasted crime rates and found key differences in design features (Figure 11.3). The upper storeys of high-rise buildings seemed more vulnerable to crime, as did corridors and stairways, which were not well observed, and open spaces which served only to separate buildings. Newman argued that the design principles of defensible space could be introduced to make such environments more liveable. The main principles were:

- Territories must be clearly defined and delineated. Barriers should be used to identify open spaces as extensions of the living block; amenities for a project should be located within the defined territory (territoriality).
- Windows and doors in particular should allow surveillance by residents, who could overlook public spaces and detect strangers. In 1961, Jane Jacobs argued in The Death and Life of Great American Cities that modern design had reduced people's ability to observe and had diminished local social control: Newman echoed these sentiments (natural surveillance).
- The quality of built environment should be improved by avoiding featureless walkways and tiled walls: projects should face out onto safe areas (location).

The defensible space concept provoked criticism, principally on the grounds that it understated social factors, but its broad aims were to create a local sense of identity, to increase safety and improve the quality of life. It sought to place 'greater control within the hands of the community and coincidentally, but just as importantly, allowed the underlying cohesiveness of the community to be articulated' (Mercer 1975: 55). Coleman (1985) followed similar design principles in her studies of public housing projects in London. Her recommendations, such as the removal of overhead walkways and other design improvements, were adopted by several municipalities. Such design schemes will have a positive effect by improving the quality of urban environments and increasing feelings of safety; whether they actually have a longer-term impact on crime rates is more contestable.

Defensible space in practice has laudable aims but design improvements need to be integrated with social and economic policies.

High-rise buildings of flats or apartments continue to attract analyses with findings that demonstrate higher morbidity rates and more neuroses, but these can rarely be isolated as an independent effect of high-rise buildings. There are some people for whom high-rise apartments may pose problems – mothers wishing to supervise young children, old people finding difficulty with stairs or lifts, neighbours seeking opportunities for casual interaction – but it is still difficult to assert any direct causal link between high rise living and social problems. Expensive and well-supervised high-rise blocks appear to be problem-free.

Another hypothesis links levels of crowding and high residential density with anti-social behaviour (Boots 1979). The general supposition that overcrowding creates stress is not conclusively proven and 'those who draw firm conclusions about density and behaviour are either speculating or making astounding inferences from flimsy evidence' (Fischer *et al.* 1975: 415). Whereas population density is a measurable, objective state, overcrowding is experiential and subjective. These relationships are complex, privacy may appear a 'good' and isolation a 'bad' goal but individuals react to these circumstances in a variety of ways. Crowding is best regarded as the complex product of physical, social, and personal characteristics; the main reactions, where they occur, are likely to be psychological rather than physiological.

Urban design and women

The built environment that we have inherited has largely been designed by men and contains assumptions and statements on women's roles in society. Architects construct reality in the sense that their designs contain their ideas:

> about the proper place of women; about what is private and what is public activity and for whom; about which things should be kept separate and which put together; and about what are appropriate behaviours for women in particular locations.
>
> (Boys 1984: 26)

In residential areas, this has meant placing middle-class women, at least, firmly in the home. A typical zoning of home and neighbourhood in time and space, with specific social routines and notions of domesticity, privacy and consumption, sets out 'controls' for women's use of space. Women's means of access were circumscribed and their normal patterns of movement were dictated by their roles as child-carers, home-makers, and shoppers. Wagner (1984) noted that in the US 'greenbelt towns', design reflected this ideal of the suburban nuclear family and woman's role as home-maker. Planners seemed somehow unable to imagine women outside the social context of home and community. For Gregson and Lowe (1995), this ideology is inscribed in space rather than acted out on it and 'home' inscribed with specific visions of women is 'critical to the gender constitution of society'.

Spaces outside the home and local community had similar connotations. Recreational and leisure-time places were designed largely for men with individual public buildings that displayed male priorities and symbolisms. This physical arrangement of the built environment reinforced women's differential access to resources and legitimized the inherent inequalities. Research into women's feelings of safety and fear of crime has shown that urban design influences their willingness to use particular places. Valentine (1990) argued that women's images are the products not only of their perceptions of certain kinds of environments but also of 'the way space is controlled by different groups at different times'. Those groups, whether they be in metro systems, dark areas, or places of entertainment, are almost certainly male and there is little in the design of such places to give women the confidence to move freely around the city.

Summary

There is no simple contention that built environment, through its content, quality or design, affects human behaviour in predictable ways. Yet, the built environment cannot be dismissed as irrelevant. It fulfils the basic functions of shelter and safety and meets the needs of urban dwellers. Built environments can be engineered to improve the probabilities of social interaction, safety or access, but yet design is no guarantee of such outcomes or of the form they might take. Whereas local physical arrangements are not irrelevant to ways in which individuals or groups behave, they are rarely the main determinants. As Boys argued:

> while buildings do not control our lives, architecture does work (albeit in a partial way) together with other aspects of social and economic relations to put people in their 'place' and to describe symbolically and spatially what that place is.
>
> (Boys 1984: 26)

Statements on the ways urban environments affect people need to be partial and prudent if they are to have any lasting value and credibility.

Local social interaction

Whereas geographers have established research into some types of interaction such as shopping trips and journey to work, social relations or patterns of friendship have been less well explored. One hindrance relates to definitions and classifications. The notion of 'friendship' poses significant measurement problems, issues of kin and non-kin relationships remain unresolved, and there are several caveats concerning the 'quality' of relations and the use of ideas such as social networks. Some of the central assumptions of spatial interaction studies do not apply. Unless social interaction focuses on a key institution, such as community centre or church hall, there is no point of conflux to which people are drawn. Studies of social interaction often need to consider large numbers of origins and destinations and flows which are not necessarily reciprocal, the outcome of which is a complex web of relationships.

Allan (1979) defined a 'sociable relationship' as one which an individual enters into purposefully and voluntarily for primarily non-instrumental reasons. This type of relationship excludes business or contractual arrangements and focuses upon systems of

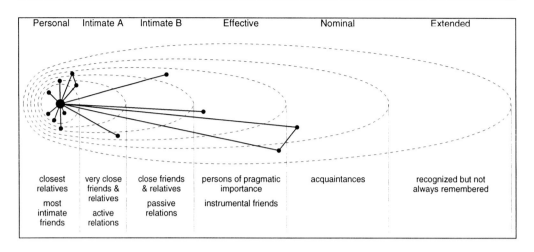

| Personal | Intimate A | Intimate B | Effective | Nominal | Extended |

closest relatives | very close friends & relatives | close friends & relatives | persons of pragmatic importance | acquaintances | recognized but not always remembered

most intimate friends | active relations | passive relations | instrumental friends

Figure 11.4 Boissevain's typology of friendships

exchange, on emotional and affectional ties and the social environments within which they are placed. Boissevain (1974) used social network analysis to study patterns of friendship and though his empirical studies were of atypical groups, he did offer some general concepts. First, his research methodology warranted replication; second, he defined the roles involved in social interaction. Some of these roles were discrete, others were interdependent but all contributed to the web of social relationships. Third, within the key roles of kinship and friendship, he formed a useful typology of relationships (see Figure 11.4). It is in the personal and intimate cells of this typology that Allan's non-instrumental relationships are most clearly contained.

Although kin and non-kin have similar roles in some forms of social interaction, they are more generally different in kind. Allan (1979) argued for a distinction between those human bonds which can be made and unmade at will (friends) and those which cannot (family). The extent to which people use opportunities for social interaction varies enormously; some people are highly active and are involved with numerous contacts in a diversity of settings; others, through choice or circumstance, are far more isolated. Irving (1978) used the terms 'social lions' to describe the former and 'social recluses' to describe the latter.

How is the quality of a relationship defined? Allan (1979) allowed the participants themselves, guided only by some broad 'rules of revelance', to form their own definitions. Clearly, this can be justified as friendship is personal and subjective, but other studies have used objective indices. Irving (1977; 1978) developed a set of indices relating to the intensity, frequency and duration of social contacts and added an index of dispersion to indicate the extent to which relationships were centred upon a small number of key interactors. Figure 11.5 records this classification along with typologies devised by Raine (1976; Herbert and Raine 1976) and Abrams (see Bulmer 1986). Irving also devised three indices labelled kin-orientation, localization, and social network; the social network index generalized on the form of friendship patterns among a set of individuals, ranging from close to loose-knit.

Central to the social network approach is the notion that it is possible to view the social relations of individuals as a scattering of points connected by lines, giving a graphical and

Irving (1978)

Interaction types	Duration features	Frequency features
1. Low intensity	Half-day or less	Less often than once a week
2. Long frequent	Whole day or more	Less often than once a week
3. Middle range	One hour or more	Once or twice a week
4. Short frequent	Half-day or less	More often than twice a week

Raine (see Herbert and Raine 1976)

Type of relationship	Form of social interaction
1. Acquaintance	Pass time of day if we meet, but never in the house
2. Quite friendly	Chat in street if we meet, but rarely, if ever, go in house
3. Friendly	Always chat when we meet, only occasionally go in house (1/month)
4. Very friendly	Chat regularly in street, frequently visit home (1 or 2/week)
5. Very close friend	Chat daily, regularly visit home(4/week)

Abrams (see Bulmer 1986)

Type of relationship	Form of social interaction
1. Acquaintance	Awareness of neighbours, casual greeting
2. Sociable	Chatting, visiting, shopping together
3. Communication	Exchange of information, gossip
4. Participation	Invite to family occasions
5. Collective involvement	Local neighbourhood events

Figure 11.5 Classifications of social interaction

geometrical quality. The points are persons and the lines are social relationships, so that each person can be viewed as a star from which lines radiate to other points, some of which are interconnected. In this personal network, persons in direct contact are in the primary (personal) zone, but may also be in contact with others whom the initial 'star' individual may not know, but could meet via others. Within the secondary (intimate or effective) zone are the 'friends of friends' and the network can be developed sequentially in this way. Applying social network analysis poses problems. There is the issue of boundedness or setting the limits of a 'manageable' network; a fixed number of people can be determined by giving each individual a set number of contacts or by restricting links to within the primary zone. Another issue concerns the relative strength of the links or the content of a relationship. Wellman (1987) identified four types of links or ties which he labelled as active, interactive, intimate and confident; in his study of a Toronto neighbourhood (East York), he estimated that 2,700 adults would be known to an average resident but only 400 of these would be actual ties, links or acquaintances of some kind.

Social network analysis has valuable research roles. It offers an organizational framework to study social interaction, ensuring that individual relationships are seen within a broader context: 'Coalitions, groups, classes and institutions are formed of people who, in different ways are bound to each other. Together they form the constantly shifting networks of social relations that we call society' (Boissevain 1974: 232).

Social interaction varies among different groups of people. Social class differences are significant and generally low-income people show a greater reliance on kin and local social interaction. Professionals tend to have less localized friendship networks and the duration of their contacts is longer. Raine (1976) suggested that middle-class relationships were sustained by regular, if not very frequent, exchange visits. Comparisons of middle- and low-income groups are blurred by differing definitions of sociability and the varying roles of kin and non-kin. Although low-income sociability is often kin-oriented, non-kin relationships are typically tied to specific situations such as workplace or club and may lapse if those points of contact end. Middle-income friendships have greater flexibility and are less tied to specific 'contexts'. Among low-income groups, kin often remains an integral part of everyday lives but geographical dispersion of middle-income families means less physical contact with kin and modified relationships. Visiting friends at their homes is more typical of middle-income people, but visiting is a middle-class form of sociability and different, but equally meaningful, forms of social exchange typify low-income households.

Age and stage in life cycle influence social interaction. Stages, such as child-rearing, contain constraints as young children tie parents to the home. Children can also facilitate social interaction by drawing parents together and cementing the bonds of kinship through their involvement in family sociability. Children act as catalysts in the generation of friendship among groups of mothers whose dependence on neighbourhood as a source of friends tends to increase at this stage. Friendships, even among the middle-class, rarely survive residential change and here the contrast with kin is clear. Class, age and family type all affect social interaction but there are personality differences and special circumstances which confound neat generalizations.

The concept of place

Attachment to place is an important quality of urban life. Attempts to theorize place vary. Is it best regarded in material (structural) terms as an outcome of the competition for, or designation of, space, or in interpretive terms as the locus of embedded values and meanings? Researchers have rehearsed these different views on place and the extent to which it can be regarded as a social construction. Massey (1993) made several key points in her progressive concept of place:

- It is absolutely not static.
- It does not need to have boundaries in any formal sense.
- It does not need to have a single, unique identity but can be full of internal differences.
- Its specificity arises from the wider relations in which it is set, the interactions of the wider and the more local, and the 'layers' of linkages over time.

There are many expressions of place attachment that range in scale from nationalism and regional identity, to civic pride and boosterism, and to a neighbourhood sense of place. Hall (1966) developed this idea of scale by using the five senses of touch, thermal, smell, sight and sound and relating them to the zones of human relations. These zones, illustrated in Figure 11.6, range from body territory or the personal space of an individual to public territory in which the individual moves and interacts but can be relatively anonymous. Similarly, Lyman and Scott (1967) suggested a four-part typology of human activity spaces

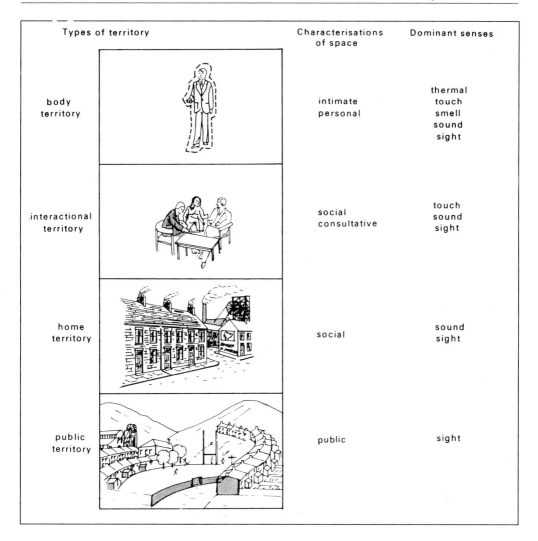

Types of territory		Characterisations of space	Dominant senses
body territory		intimate personal	thermal touch smell sound sight
interactional territory		social consultative	touch sound sight
home territory		social	sound sight
public territory		public	sight

Figure 11.6 Zones of human relationships

which they labelled body territory or an individual's personal space; interactive territory or small group transactional space; home territory or the local setting for social ties outside the home; and public territory or the wider setting with which a person has only general familiarity. N. Smith (1993) in his 'scaling places' used a typology composed of body, home, community, urban, region, nation and global.

Traditionally, geographers have begun their studies at the scale of community and have had little to say about body or home. This has changed with the rise of studies of women in geography and the idea that the body can be a 'cultural locus of gender meanings'; Shurmer-Smith (1994: 351) noted an interest in 'Kleinian notions of inner space which take geography right down into the stomach and bowels in contemplating the anorexic/bulimic desire for self-control'. Home has also assumed more significance with feminist geography. As Gregson and Lowe (1995: 225) stated: 'for the most part, the home – like the body – remains a significance silence in geography'. They go on to argue that studies of middle-class households, at least, and of their reproduction, necessitates an engagement with the ideology of the home. Home is at the same time a place upon which women may impose their identity and value as haven and, also, a place within which they are constrained by a male dominated world. The notion that women's place belongs in the privacy of the home is one that feminists contest with varying success; the 'liberated' women of western democracies are far removed from women in more fundamentalist Muslim societies.

Local community

It is at the point at which social interaction is linked with places within the city that the issue of local community or neighbourhood becomes relevant. The concept of 'community' is elusive and Hillery (1955), for example, identified 94 different definitions in relatively common usage. Community can be applied to many forms of human association but of the 94 definitions, 70 included the criteria of place or territory, common ties and social interaction. Home area is a term close to the idea of local community and British Community Attitudes Survey did in fact use it in its examination of public views on community. The term territory has an ecological meaning as an area dominated by a single animal or group as an exclusive preserve. This has been translated into human terms as people's sense of territoriality. Suttles (1968), in his study of the Addams area of Chicago, showed how a segment of urban space of less than a square kilometre in area, had been subdivided into easily recognized ethnic territories. Each territory had a distinctive social order with a localized frame of reference and behaviour. Youth groups often possess strong territorial associations and their 'turfs' are resolutely defended from outsiders. Ley and Cybriwsky (1974a) demonstrated how youth gangs in inner Philadelphia occupied territories which were sharply demarcated by graffiti – the 'imprints' of specific groups. With greater proximity to the edges of a group's territory, the graffiti became more strident and abrasive in its assertions, it was both a territorial marker and a statement of local empowerment. Boal (1969) used the concept of territoriality in Belfast to demonstrate the sharp divisions between Protestant and Catholic communities. Clonard and Shankill, respectively 99 per cent Catholic and Protestant, had separate patterns of socio-spatial interaction to accompany the residential segregation. Constraints and the heightened need for group cohesiveness or security often exaggerate the need for territoriality; the greater these constraints, the more completely contained within territories group activities will be.

The term neighbourhood suggests not only an identifiable territory to which individuals feel some attachment but also some sense of group cohesion. Early definitions of neighbourhood referred to an area in which there was the habit of exchanging visits, articles and services, and generally doing things together: 'a territorial group the members of which meet on common ground within their own area for primary school activities and for spontaneous and organized social contacts' (Glass 1948: 124).

Definitions such as this require both clear identity of a place and also internal social cohesion. Does this combination of circumstances commonly exist? There are various ways of tackling this question. One approach is to recognize that the urban area does fall into physical units, such as a housing estate built at a particular time, and these often correspond with residential groups, with some measure of social and demographic homogeneity. These

Neighbourhood type	Qualities	How defined
Recognized area	spatial identity legibility	images of city mental maps
Morphological unit	physical definition common design features recognizable limits	observation morphological mapping
Social area	social homogeneity demographic unity	social area analysis census indicators
Local activity system	local social interaction local nodes or points of conflux	activity studies trip patterns
True community	sense of belonging social cohesion identify with place	cognitive maps social interaction common bonds 'communion'

Figure 11.7 Types of neighbourhoods

are not necessarily neighbourhoods, however, until qualities such as shared values and regular social interaction can be identified. There have been attempts to form typologies of neighbourhoods to reflect these differences (Figure 11.7). A recognized area is a loosely defined place which can be named; a morphological unit has physical uniformity; social areas have social-demographic unity; local activity systems contain movements around nodal services such as stores or schools; true communities incorporate other features but add the vital ingredients of local social interaction, common ties and shared values. Using these key indicators of social interaction, common ties, and place identity, a distinction can be made between loose and close-knit neighbourhoods, with gradations in between. This raises other questions. Why should some neighbourhoods possess less social cohesion than others? How do neighbourhoods change over time? Bell and Newby's (1978) distinction between community and communion offered a useful perspective. Community, it was argued, involved an implicit sense of belonging in a taken-for-granted situation; any social area with recognizable boundaries could constitute a community. Communion rested upon a form of human association which involved affective bonds, it implied an active and involved group rather than one which was passive and apathetic. Community could at any time be transformed into communion by an event which affected the neighbourhood as a whole, or by an individual or group who acted as a catalyst. The issue could be the threat of a local school closure or a road-widening scheme; its appearance could transform a latent group into an active association.

Boundaries are of interest. Morphological units have physical and visible boundaries such as the physical barriers presented by main roads or open spaces. Social areas have boundaries, probably less visible, set by the building blocks of census small areas. Boundaries of local activity systems are defined by the catchments of local schools or the 'market' areas of neighbourhood shopping centres. True community may include these features but adds the dimension of a subjective sense of place and affective ties. How can the boundaries of true community be estimated?

Behavioural sciences invoked the concept of 'cognitive mapping'. Lee (1968), a social psychologist, studied the perceptions of Cambridge housewives by asking them to sketch

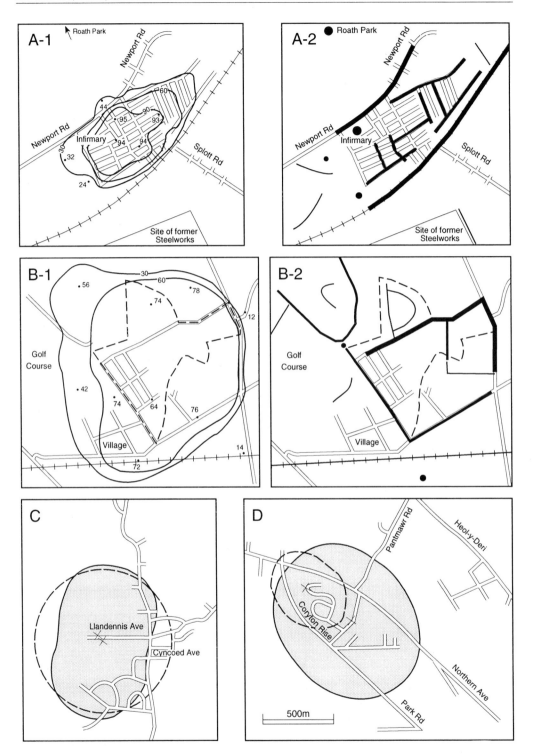

Figure 11.8 Images of neighbourhoods in Cardiff

neighbourhood boundaries on maps. They produced a wide range of boundaries but 80 per cent were able to delineate their neighbourhood. The outcome dubbed as a 'spaghetti map' showed little consensus in detail but there was what Lee termed evidence of 'consentaneity' or a general, shared agreement of what neighbourhood comprised. Herbert and Raine (1976) developed techniques to identify images or mental maps of neighbourhood in Cardiff. Respondents in six different parts of the city were asked, first, to state which sites from a given list were inside their neighbourhood; and second, to identify the edges of their neighbourhood. Marked differences were apparent among types of residential districts (Figure 11.8). The high-status area was defined in an extensive way, with little more than 60 per cent consensus at any one point, a low-status area was highly localized with a 90 per cent level of consensus. The boundaries that people identified were often real barriers such as railway lines or main roads but key landmarks, such as parks and hospitals, were also frequently nominated. Large public sector estates, sometimes designed as neighbourhood units, were segmented, in the images of their inhabitants, into smaller, more manageable units . A more quantitative device to define neighbourhood is the standard deviational ellipse. This tends to produce idealized shapes but they are indicative of the compactness and directional biases of residents' images of neighbourhoods.

The concept of neighbourhood has a chequered history in the social science literature and Wellman (1978) suggested a triad of schools of thought which he labelled as community lost, community saved and community transformed. Community lost related to ideas such as *gesellschaft* and urbanism that involved the break-down of face-to-face primary relationships and the loss of any local sense of belonging. The idea of 'community without propinquity' in a society which was becoming increasingly mobile and less locality-based, also belongs to this school. As it was originally expounded by Webber (1963), the concept seemed appropriate to specific places of high mobility and much less so for others. With new interests in globalization in the 1990s, the task of reconciling the local with the global is once again on the agenda:

> So where is community here? It may be nowhere . . . people can reside in one place and have meaningful social relations almost entirely outside it and across the globe people use the locality as site and resource for social activities in widely differing ways according to the extension of their sociosphere.
>
> (Albrow 1997: 52–3)

The argument has new contexts but is in danger of repeating the mistakes of emphasizing the potentials at the expense of the realities of urban life.

'Community saved' was the counter-argument that neighbourhood remained a vital part of urban life. Evidence was found in the 'urban villages' of places like Boston's North End, New York's Greenwich Village and London's East End, where social interaction and community flourished. Within such neighbourhoods, primary face-to-face relationships, characterized by emotional cohesion, depth and continuity, persisted. The roots of the community-saved school are found in the early twentieth century as was the advocacy of the 'neighbourhood unit principle'. Such planned neighbourhoods, it was believed, could recapture the natural qualities of the old neighbourhoods or quarters of Paris, Venice and Florence, with their focal points of churches or squares and local sense of place. The planned neighbourhood unit principle followed schemes such as the Garden City movement, social settlements, and garden suburbs and found its clearest expression with Perry's (1939) design for Radburn, New Jersey.

The design details for neighbourhood units are important, but what are the purposes and underlying assumptions of neighbourhood planning? There was clearly an early idealism that viewed neighbourhood as a device to improve the quality of life and a mechanism for 'social engineering'. The aim was to produce physical order, to encourage face-to-face relationships, to promote local togetherness, feelings of identity, security and stability, and to counteract the perceived downside of city life. The success of neighbourhood planning is difficult to assess. Whereas 'true communities' are hard to find, planners have often succeeded in creating acceptable urban environments with the opportunities for local social interaction. Neighbourhood planning has its critics: 'The problem with the neighbourhood unit idea is not, therefore, that it cannot be shown to coincide with the existence of a local system, but that it misinterprets the nature of this system' (Bell and Newby 1978: 288).

In this type of judgement, the stress on a local basis for human relationships confuses a 'sufficient' with a 'necessary' condition; proximity in space often leads to close human bonds but is not essential for community to develop as some of the strongest groups, religious or specialist interest, do not share a territorial base. Yet planners have retained faith in neighbourhood units: 'The pervasiveness of its influence and use, despite professional reservations and intellectual repudiations, suggest the power of the neighbourhood unit as a construct' (Banerjee and Baer 1984: 27)

Community transformed (Wellman 1978) was a compromise position. Urban communities, it was argued, were moving throughout a phase of adjustment but not decline, local place retained its importance as the base for activities, community action and identity. Over time, this importance had probably been reduced but not eliminated. Whereas 'true communities' are usually exemplified by exceptional neighbourhoods, such as Boston's North End and London's Bethnal Green, it is reasonable to observe that even in very large cities, people are not 'placeless'. They certainly have more choices of where to go and for what activity, many will display aspatial behaviour at times but locality remains a significant context for social interaction. Choice and flexibility can be incorporated into urban design without losing the roles of locality.

As neighbourhood units remain significant elements of planning strategy, so neighbourhoods or local communities remain important in urban life. There has been a rebirth of localism with the emergence of groups seeking some level of political de-centralization. Neighbourhood associations and community councils have expanded in the 1980s and 1990s and locality-based action groups have responded vigorously to urban environmental issues. Again, awareness of local community groups to externalities and issues that affect the status of their neighbourhood has increased. Community action has developed on several fronts and neighbourhood has assumed new roles, sometimes linked with a new interest in the forms which citizenship can take and the ways in which it is expressed. In addition to serving as a base for local services and activities, the concept of neighbourhood as place involves a sense of belonging to a home area. Neighbourhood can act as a refuge or haven within a large city and is a social world with which its residents identify closely. The growth of niche communities, intended to house people of a particular age-group or set of preferences, represents a reinforcement of these ideals. People identify with place and attribute to it a set of values and meanings which they may seek to preserve. Many examples of campaigns to save or protect communities show how this can occur and support is often forthcoming from people living outside a neighbourhood as well as from those within it (see Anderson and Gale 1992).

Can the roles of neighbourhood be used in constructive and positive ways? Planners have clearly used neighbourhoods in attempts to achieve a better quality of urban life and, more recently, the 'community question' has been linked with concepts such as the delivery of welfare services and community care. De-institutionalization policies in the area of mental health were prompted both by a rising demand for hospital beds and doubts on the value of prolonged institutional care. They had the effect of returning many mentally ill people to residential areas, but could neighbourhoods cope and was community care a viable option? Community-based services require resources, organization, a set of positive, informal attitudes. Vulnerable individuals need a protective envelope against the stresses of urban life, but all the evidence suggests that the 'caring neighbourhood' in this sense is a rarity. The 'carers' are family and close friends rather than neighbours; for those in need – mentally ill, disabled, and the elderly people – kin remains the safest answer. Community responses have often been to oppose the siting of clinics and shelters and to leave the caring role in the hands of a small minority. This argument must be balanced by the need to protect local residents if they are at risk from disturbed individuals. The passing of Megan's Law in some states of the USA, that requires disclosure of the names and addresses of known child sex offenders who are released into communities, has made this issue a central debate.

People and space: activity patterns in urban settings

Activities in the city are many and varied: 'Each individual has a moving pattern of his [*sic*] own, with the turning points at his home, his place of work and his shopping centre during the week and his recreation grounds on a holiday or a Sunday' (Hagerstrand 1971: 144).

Some activities, such as work and school, are fixed in place and time with regular patterns of movement at constant frequencies; others, such as shopping and recreation, are more variable. There are different nodes for the activities of different groups, men and women, children and adults, elderly and young people. Movements in space are responses to locations of activities, the form of the urban system, and the quality of physical channels of movement.

Well-defined 'rhythms' of movement or regular flows along particular channels at particular times are complemented by a wide variety of 'voluntary' movements and activities. Movements within the city are affected by realities and also by ways in which urban space is perceived. Awareness space is that part of the city of which an individual is aware and which forms his or her image of the city. Action space is that known part of the city for which an individual holds some direct experience and evaluation. Activity space contains the locations with which the individual has direct contact as a result of regular day-to-day activities. Activity space will vary with roles such as those of family member, neighbour, worker, student, club member and holiday-maker, all involving different movements. The roles of family member and neighbour involve small spatial orbits and frequent contact; these activity spaces are circumscribed but intensively used. Common movements are:

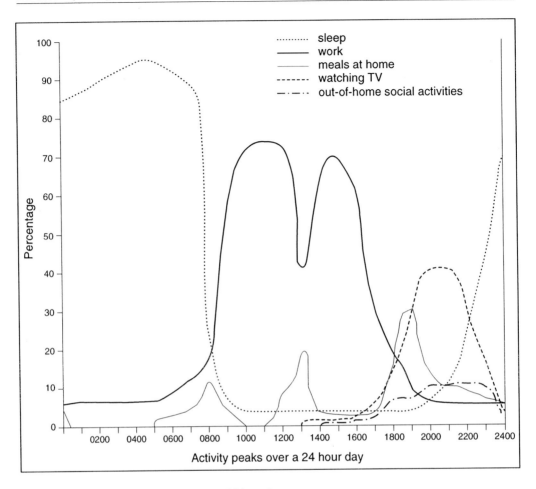

Figure 11.9 Time rhythms of activity over a 24 hour day

- Within and near the home.
- Within and near the sites of activities such as work, school and shops.
- Between these places and home.
- To use specialized services on an irregular basis such as holiday sites and conference centres.

Housewives with young children, elderly people and those who are immobile are all likely to have highly localized activity spaces displaying the constraints on their access to urban space. The more roles an individual adopts, the more diverse are the activity spaces used.

Adding time to geographical space has given a new dimension to the study of activity and movement. Time has always been an implicit component of activities research and the time-budget qualities of urban living patterns are well understood. Once routines and regularities in individual behaviour are identified, generalizations on patterns of movement over a specific period of time can be formed. Figure 11.9 shows typical daily rhythms of sleep, work-trips and recreational activities. Figure 11.10 identifies key locations, and relates these to blocks of time and the constraints of availability. Work and school demand fixed hours,

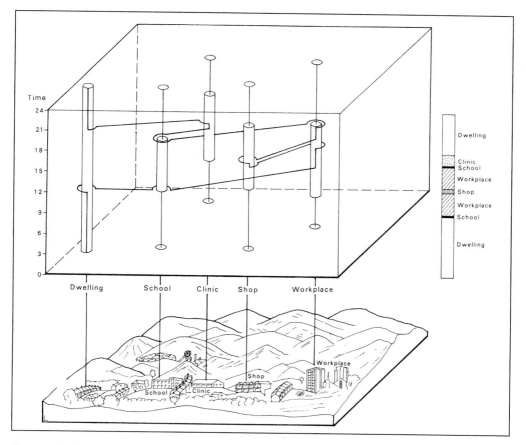

Figure 11.10 Time and space in a working woman's day

shops have greater flexibility for consumers, and social interaction has flexibility within the convention of 'reasonable' hours of visiting. This rhythmic pattern forms part of a highly integrated and coordinated structure within which individual life-patterns must be contained. There is a simultaneous timing of many people's hours of work – imposed by the needs of industry, commerce and administration – which has strong effects on those not directly involved such as retired people and housewives. Different nodes will have different weights for different kinds of people. The housewife with children will be heavily committed to crèche, school, and shops while the working professional has wider orbits revolving around work and the associated social round. Despite flexi-time, most work movements continue to be placed within narrow time bands. Generalizations emerging from studies are, first, there is a 'structure' of traditional routines and practices which imposes constraints; second, there is a physical framework of facilities which needs to be synchronized in both time and space; third, the basic building blocks are individual households and the daily and weekly routinized rhythms around which their activities are patterned. Notions of the dominance of physical movements in activity patterns are contested by the emergence of new forms of cyberspace and the uses of the World Wide Web and Internet to access services and allow interaction. The concept of the Information City is closer to reality as the new communications revolution makes greater use of advanced forms of information technology and in some places a form of 'electronic city', with homes, offices, and businesses all linked to an area network, is already in existence.

Consumer behaviour

Of necessity, there is an interactive relationship between systems of consumer services and the spatial patterns of behaviour of the urban population. A close and predictable relationship, however, does not exist between the location of services and ways in which they are used. As the development of systems of services responds to a wide range of formative influences, so too are patterns of behaviour similarly complex. To develop a better understanding of the characteristics of the systems of services in the city, this section focuses upon studies of consumer behaviour.

The normative models: central place theory and spatial interaction theory

There have been attempts to derive norms from a priori reasoning to model spatial behaviour. Central place theory offered an early deductive theoretical basis for the development of hierarchical systems of service centres. A consumer was expected to use the nearest centre offering the good or service required. From this expectation, the 'nearest centre assumption' or the 'movement minimization hypothesis' is suggested as a basic behavioural tenet. However, this axiom is regarded as a serious overstatement of behavioural realities. Shoppers respond to a range of factors reflecting their social characteristics, the availability of transport, the types and combinations of goods and services required, and knowledge of alternative shopping opportunities. Similar findings have been reported for the use of medical services and it is clear that as urban consumers become more mobile and the range of service facilities more complex, the behavioural assumption of central place theory explains between only a half and a third of trips. Nevertheless, it still provides a useful introduction to consumer behaviour and confirms the continuing significance of the 'friction of distance' for spatial behaviour in the city. A household survey of 2,130 respondents drawn randomly from the census wards of Swansea (Thomas and Bromley 1993) showed a strong proximity effect despite the wide range of grocery shopping opportunities and high levels of car ownership (Figure 11.12).

Spatial interaction theory provides a more precise prediction of consumer behaviour using deductively derived norms. Based upon the earlier 'law of retail gravitation', Lakshmanan and Hansen (1965) postulated a probabilistic reformulation of the gravity model more appropriate for the intra-urban situation. Alternative service facilities for residents were allocated varying degrees of probability in direct proportion to the relative attraction of the centre; to the distance between the centre and the residential area; and in inverse proportion to the competition exerted by other centres. More simply, the choice of visiting a particular shopping centre was determined by a trade-off between the attraction of a centre, the constraints of distance, and the competition of other centres in the vicinity. A model was designed to estimate the shopping expenditure flows between any residential area (i) and shopping centre (j) in a system, to predict the turnover of any shopping centre (Figure 11.11).

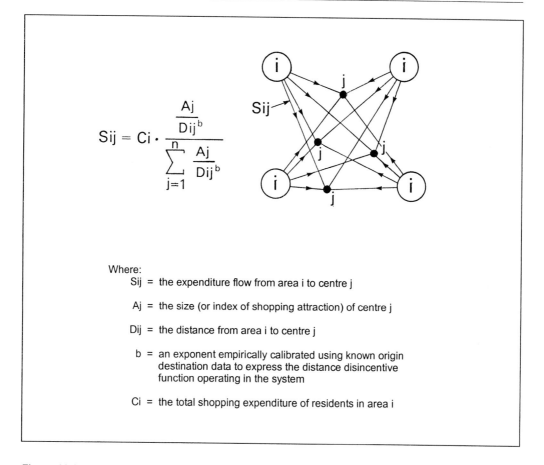

Figure 11.11 The intra-urban version of the gravity model

The three assumed determinants – the attraction of centres, the disincentive of distance, and the competition of alternative centres – all appear to exert a strong influence on shopping behaviour and no significant additional factor has yet been consistently identified. Thus, it is not surprising that increasingly sophisticated variants of this model have been used widely to predict shopping and other service utilization behaviour.

These models are not without difficulties that centre on the issue of obtaining suitable data. Measurements of shopping centre attractiveness require expensive data collection exercises, as do the derivation of distance matrices and shopping interaction data with which to calibrate the model for a base date. Similarly, the extrapolation of the parameters of the model forward to predict consumer responses is problematic. For these reasons, developments of such models have focused on technical rather than practical issues, although approximations of the complex behavioural interactions between residential areas and service facilities are available (Rogers 1992). Such findings have been widely used by retailers in the USA to make optimal store location decisions, while in the UK both Tesco and Marks & Spencer have used similar methods. Refinements and re-evaluations of early models have allowed the development of alternative methodologies for the analysis and prediction of consumer behaviour that offer greater precision to our understanding of consumer behaviour in cities.

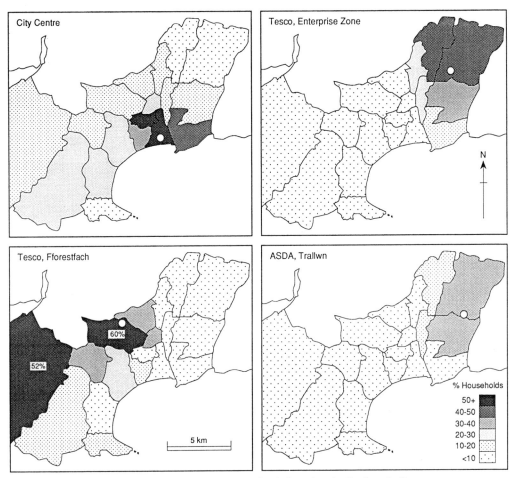

Figure 11.12 Origins of customers at selected main food-shopping destinations in Swansea

The behavioural approaches

With behavioural approaches, the emphasis is on inductive methods and the analysis of questionnaire survey data obtained from individual respondents. Such information enables theories of consumer behaviour to be evaluated and improved and also has shorter-term practical value for planning. Trade area studies of specific stores or centres use information from shopper surveys, while aggregate surveys investigate random samples of consumers drawn from city-wide residential areas. Both yield consistent and similar results for western cities. For all types of shopping centres there is a strong tendency for them, at all hierarchical levels, to draw most of their customers from nearby areas, and the higher the hierarchical level of the centre the wider this area will be. Trade areas also tend to overlap both within and between hierarchical levels, suggesting behaviour consistent with the intra-urban version of the gravity model. Such behaviour is replicated for the use of medical facilities in the USA.

The trade areas of shopping centres in Greater Swansea demonstrate these effects (Table 11.1). The CBD has a primary trade area of 10 miles radius from which 85 per cent of its customers are drawn. This contrasts with the more locality-based Aberafan shopping centre.

Table 11.1 Retailing in Swansea

A Trade areas in Greater Swansea (% respondents)

MIles travelled	Swansea CBD 1988 (139,000 m)	Aberafan District Centre 1978 (22,000 m)	Enterprise Zone Retail Park 1985 (35,000 m)
0–1	15.1	44.4	15.2
1–2	18.6	28.4	13.8
2–3	13.0	8.2	13.5
3–4	13.8	3.1	12.9
4–7	17.3	8.8	19.8
7–9	6.3	0.8	9.9
10–20	6.0	5.6	8.1
20+	9.8	0.0	6.2
No. of respondents	905	258	676

B Location of shopping trips by car ownership in Swansea, 1986

Type of shopping/location	Car-owning households (%)	Carless households (%)
Food		
City centre	15.4	37.6
District centre	9.8	20.3
Local/other	5.7	11.4
Superstore/retail warehouse	69.1	30.7
DIY/decorating		
City centre	19.4	51.9
District centre	7.2	9.9
Local/other	4.8	6.0
Superstore/retail warehouse	68.6	32.3
Carpets		
City centre	39.1	54.9
District centre	6.3	5.6
Local/other	13.1	18.1
Superstore/retail warehouse	41.5	21.4
Furniture		
City centre	43.2	60.0
District centre	6.9	8.9
Local/other	11.1	13.4
Superstore/retail warehouse	38.8	17.7
Clothing/footwear		
City centre	78.1	79.3
District centre	9.7	8.9
Local/other	3.3	5.9
Superstore/retail warehouse	8.9	5.9

However, the car-oriented Enterprise Zone Retail Park has a trade area similar to the CBD despite being only one-quarter its size. In fact, superstores draw customers from distances of up to 10 miles, and characteristically, upwards of 10 per cent of their customers travel from even further afield. The greater attractions of the planned, car-oriented, regional shopping centres in the UK are reflected by their extensive primary trade areas, drawing around 80 per cent of customers from a 20 mile radius (Thomas and Bromley 1993a). Clearly, the modern out-of-town shopping centres are different and this highlights the difficulties involved in the calibration of the models mentioned in the previous section.

The factors associated with variations in consumer behaviour include the combined influence of personal mobility, social status and income. In the UK there is a polarization of shopping behaviour patterns between the more affluent car-owning households and the usually less affluent car-less. For major grocery shopping and DIY purchases, the Swansea survey demonstrated the dominance of the superstores and retail warehouses for these purchases by the car-owning households (69 per cent) (Bromley and Thomas 1993a). By contrast, the car-less shoppers continued primarily to visit the traditional shopping centres for these goods (Table 11.1) and also, to a lesser extent, for purchases of carpets and furniture. The differential did not extend to clothing and footwear, largely because this type of store had not decentralized at the time of the survey. A study of the impact of the Merry Hill regional shopping centre in the West Midlands demonstrated this social polarization effect over the full range of goods and services (Perkins 1996). A social exclusion effect seemed to influence the nearby less-mobile lower-status communities who remained dependent upon the declining facilities of Dudley.

The polarization effect creates a gradual transference of the expenditure of the more affluent out from the traditional neighbourhood, district and CBD shopping centres to the new superstores, retail warehouses and regional shopping centres. Inevitably, the economic vitality and viability of the traditional centres, with their less affluent consumers, are undermined. A spiral of decline can be recognized, particularly where new facilities have been developed near to the old (Thomas and Bromley 1993a).

Age-structure of the consumer group also has an effect. Families with pre-school children and those over 60 years old are constrained in their shopping behaviour, although the differentials are less than those noted for mobility (Bromley and Thomas 1993a). These groups have high allegiances to local facilities for convenience goods, reflecting the constraining influence of young children in the case of younger families and a combination of the inertia of established shopping patterns and infirmity for elderly people.

For use of medical services, proximity is an important determinant of visits to family doctors in the UK, but the nearest centre assumption has to be significantly qualified. Alternative influences include proximity to workplace or shopping centres, and hours of opening. There may be social barriers, such as perceived 'hostile territories' en route to the surgery, or perceptual barriers, such as a limited knowledge of the transport network or of alternatives. Patients may be affected by the personal attributes of the doctor or patterns developed at former residence.

Evidence for patterns of surgery attendance in the UK (Joseph and Phillips 1984), suggests that behaviour is as complex as that for convenience shopping trips, despite the supposedly invariant quality of service offered. Where several practices were accessible, the high status groups used local surgeries, but not necessarily the nearest. This inconsistency seemed related to personal choice and car availability. By contrast, the low status respondents conformed to a 'dual attachment' pattern, either attending the nearest surgery, or, if there was convenient public transport, a city centre practice usually near a former residence. This latter 'relict pattern' effect accounted for between one- and two-thirds of the attendance patterns of the low-status groups. The centralization of general practitioner services into larger but fewer practices has begun to assert a 'spatial monopoly effect' (see also Chapter 8). This causes patients to attend their nearest practice, which can be at some distance in suburban and rural areas. This is socially regressive and is likely to affect the least mobile sections of the community.

Evidence from New Zealand, even in the context of a fee-for-service system supplemented by Government subsidy, indicates similar findings. In the small town of Gisborne, patterns of surgery attendance were highly localised, although not necessarily confined to the nearest surgery (Hays *et al.,* 1990). Again, the significance of proximity was paramount. However, the least mobile groups similarly displayed the most constrained patterns of behaviour; while, paradoxically, Maori patients were those least spatially constrained due to the preference of the ethnic community for a particular practitioner. A more recent study, also undertaken in New Zealand, offers additional insights into the relatively localised patterns of behaviour for primary health care in Western societies (Barnett and Kearns, 1996). In the context of the development of market-driven health care reforms initiated in 1987, they examine the degree to which patients displayed 'consumerist' 'shopping around' patterns of behaviour in their choice of two private accident and medical clinics in Auckland. In fact, only 3 per cent of patients were swayed by price considertions despite the service discounting policies operated by the clinics. Again, ease of access was the major determinant (59 per cent) of the localised patterns of behaviour combined with the convenience of long opening hours (43 per cent). However, for the poorest respondents, physical access was an even more important influence, again suggesting the likely socially regressive results contingent upon the progressive centralisation of primary care. The localised patterns of behaviour and low 'consumerist' traits were considered to reflect the specifics of health care utilisation behaviour which departs significantly from the kinds of market-orientated behaviour typical of the shopping situation. These were neatly articulated earlier by Leavey *et al.* (1989). The need for health care is spasmodic or minimal, so alternative opportunities are only intermittently considered; the urgency of many medical consultations tends to preclude 'shopping around'; while the asymmetry of information held by doctor and patient tends to develop a passive patient role and the accentuation of faith and trust in the medic. By contrast, relatively few will travel outside their local areas, with the exceptions of relic patterns associated with former residences, and those associated with culture specific requirements, or imposed by financial or other social constraints.

The disadvantaged consumer

Increasing social polarization suggests that for some sections of the community 'constraints' are more important than 'choice'. Low income and low levels of personal mobility restrict the lowest social classes and ethnic minorities. Policies have largely ignored the needs of these groups and a class of 'disadvantaged consumers' can now be identified in relation to both shopping and use of medical services.

In the UK, independent convenience stores, smaller supermarkets in inner cities and the peripheral council estates have all experienced decline as outcomes of corporate restructuring of the largest multiple grocery retailers in favour of the development of superstores, and their subsequent competitive impact on the smaller local stores (Guy 1996). More affluent and mobile grocery shoppers benefit from accessible bulk purchasing in modern premises, which includes a price advantage (Bromley and Thomas 1993a). By contrast, disadvantaged consumers suffer the 'double deprivation' of limited access to the newer forms of retailing, and continuing dependence on the limited choice, higher prices and poorer quality premises of the remaining local facilities (DoE 1992). Larger, centralized group practices and health centres have produced similar effects, although the remaining inner city facilities have retained a reasonable measure of accessibility for nearby residents and users of public transport.

Variations in levels of personal mobility indicate the scale of the problem. Currently in Britain approximately 65 per cent of households have access to a car, but there is a range from over 85 per cent in middle- and upper-status neighbourhoods to around 40 per cent in low-status housing areas. Low levels of personal mobility typify mothers with young children and elderly people who have most need for easily accessible shopping and medical facilities (Westlake 1993). Public transport is not always the answer since both mothers with young children and the aged widely report difficulties coping with the services (DoE 1992) and the alternative of walking with bulky goods for any distance is not really acceptable.

Research findings are equivocal. New convenience store chains have emerged to fill the 'market niche' vacated by the large multiples and provide a more versatile range of accessible 'neighbourhood' services. They have partially redressed the decline in accessibility for the less mobile, and offer a supplementary 'top-up' function for the remainder. The 7–Eleven chain and the group purchasing partnerships between independent retailers and wholesalers such as Spar are notable cases. At a larger scale, KwikSave has developed discount supermarkets aimed at the same market niche, while the entry of 'deep discounter' European competition from Aldi, Lidl (Germany), Netto (Denmark) and Ed (France) is indicative of the perceived retailer opportunities at this end of the grocery market (Guy 1996).

However, this revitalization has mostly affected traditional shopping centres in suburbs, usually at some distance from a superstore. Many peripheral former industrial communities, small town, district and neighbourhood shopping facilities have continued to decline (Thomas and Bromley 1995). Less-mobile residents of one such settlement in South Wales had a level of dependence upon the local facilities consistent with the concept of the disadvantaged consumer with consumer behaviour that reflected constraint rather than choice (Bromley and Thomas 1995). Comparable situations exist in other former industrial communities and in rural areas where the high personal mobility of the majority and competition from newer facilities still leave the residual disadvantaged. Again, some inner city communities and residents of peripheral local authority estates, may be in the same position, though: 'a comprehensive up to date description of low income consumers' food shopping behaviour does not exist across a broad range of locations' (DoE 1992: 72).

Disabled people are also disadvantaged consumers. It has been estimated that 9 per cent of the British population experience permanent or temporary mobility handicaps due to physical, sensory or mental impairment (Imrie 1996). There are policies designed to improve the physical access of buildings, through the improvement of access to car parks, buses and lifts, provision of wheelchair access via ramps and the removal of obstacles such as

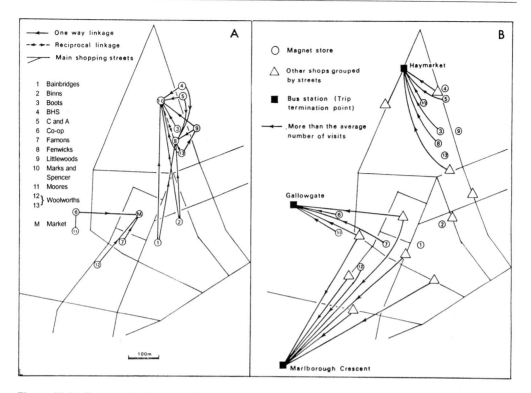

Figure 11.13 Factors affecting shopping behaviour patterns within a central area: Newcastle upon Tyne. Shopping linkages between 'magnet' stores (greater than 25%). Shopper linkages with selected trip termination points

kerbs. Also, local authorities are developing 'Shopmobility Schemes' to enhance their access to central shopping areas by providing appropriate wheelchairs and scooters (DoE 1992). The problems of the vision-impaired and blind in particular, have also generated applied research (Golledge 1993). In the UK the Disability Discrimination Act 1995 sought to develop proactive policies to redress the obstacles to access to public facilities encountered by disabled people, although progress in this direction has a long way to go.

New technology can improve the shopping opportunities of those with mobility constraints. The experimental Gateshead Shopping and Information Service by Tesco, the Borough Council and Newcastle University in 1980 focused on infirm and elderly people and mothers with young children; it established a computer-based ordering system at branch libraries and via a telephone link to the Social Services Department. The orders were then delivered to the homes of consumers. For convenience goods, Electronic Home Shopping will be viable only on a subsidized service for the housebound due to its labour-intensive characteristics (Westlake 1993).

Ethnic minority groups typically have not only low income and mobility but also some culture-specific consumer demands and preferences, particularly for convenience goods and financial and personal services. Shopping facilities in ethnic areas reflect local consumer demand and a particular subsystem of shopping facilities can be identified with small inefficient shops, high prices, low quality goods, fewer services, upwards of 25 per cent of outlets catering for culture-specific products and a general air of dilapidation. In the UK, there are exceptions to this. In some of the largest ethnic areas, economic and social progress is reflected in environmental improvement and a rich variety of quality goods and services. Southall shopping area, central to the Asian community in Middlesex, is a notable example.

Given the variations of the socio-economic characteristics of neighbourhoods and the decentralization of services into fewer but larger car-oriented locations, spatially disadvantaged consumers were an inevitable outcome. Without further research, it is not yet possible to judge whether they are merely inconvenienced by restrictions on choice or form a significant minority.

Shopping behaviour within centres

The detailed manner in which shoppers use a centre can have a considerable influence upon the commercial viability of particular sites. The lack of integration of pedestrian flows, transport termini and shop locations can result in 'dead space' and unlettable shop units, with detrimental effects on commercial or public investment, and adverse environmental problems. The determinants of recurrent patterns of behaviour, the attitudes of shoppers to varying spatial arrangements of facilities, and the attainment of the most efficient and satisfying spatial organization of functions, are all research themes.

Bennison and Davies (1980) studied pedestrian flows in Newcastle upon Tyne (Figure 11.13) and interviewed shoppers in a variety of locations. They suggested the primary importance of large 'magnet' or 'anchor' stores on recurrent behaviour patterns and also the importance of trip termination points at bus stops and car parks. These findings offer general principles for the improvement of circulation patterns in city centres.

Bromley and Thomas (1989) studied two unplanned retail parks and found recurrent patterns of behaviour despite the predominance of car-borne linkages between stores. Store functions and their relative spatial proximity were relevant and there was a clear influence of 'comparison' and 'complementary' linkages between alternative furniture, furnishings, clothing and footwear outlets. 'Spinoff' shopping linkages originated from the superstores and DIY stores, while differences in the social profiles of 'discount' stores and the 'upmarket' outlets suggested the importance of 'market segmentation' considerations for shopping linkages. Spatial proximity was a positive generative force, irrespective of the functional characteristics of stores, and peripheral location had adverse trading implications. A spatially compact form was an advantage offering proximity, centrality, less car-borne traffic, and more pedestrian linkages.

Brown (1992) reviewed methods for investigating patterns of shopping behaviour within centres including pedestrian counts, questionnaire surveys and pedestrian 'tracking', as well as tracking by video-camera technology. Problems include consumers' 'recall', and the ethical issues associated with the use of some of the 'covert surveillance' methods have become major issues (Beck and Willis 1995). Study of shopping behaviour within cities is providing information relevant to the planning and design of shopping centres and is likely to influence decisions on pedestrianization, layout of malls, balance of selling space, and the optimal locations of public transport and car-parking facilities.

Consumer behaviour and the geography of consumption

There is a renewed engagement with theories of consumption and consumer behaviour. Following Gardner and Sheppard (1989), this perspective argues the need for a sound base in economic analysis and its relationship to the broader cultural and social context within which it operates. With more flexible modes of post-Fordist production and the proliferation of consumer demands in an increasingly affluent society, the 'retailer' has been able to assert increasing control over both manufacturers and consumers. This has created a new 'retail culture' in which multiple retailers are prime movers in economic enterprises and in the development of a contemporary culture in which patterns of consumption are a major feature of social relations and personal identity. Ideas such as 'You are what you buy' suggest the need to place the relationships between the capital and the consumer into higher relief in retail geographical analyses. Wrigley and Lowe (1996) called for a 'reconstructed' retail geography with both a stronger emphasis on 'retail capital and its transformation' and a more definitive 'cultural perspective'.

Affluence and personal mobility have presented opportunities for retailers and shopping centre developers to provide new sites of consumption alongside the old, catering for a highly differentiated market (see also Chapter 8). The more prosaic forms of superstores and retail warehouse parks have reached an apotheosis with the emergence of extravagant mega-malls characterized as 'cathedrals of consumption'. Regeneration of city centres with indoor shopping complexes and refurbished buildings and new 'festival shopping' complexes on derelict sites have become common features of major cities. Places where large numbers of people congregate offer markets to be 'colonized' by retail development. Large international airports, railway stations, hotel lobbies, concourses of office buildings and even large hospitals have all to varying degrees accumulated shopping activities. The addition of pharmacies, dry cleaners, petrol stations and banking services to superstores reflects similar forces, along with the addition of convenience retail functions to petrol filling stations. Car boot sales have become the 'quintessential postmodern consumption sites' (Gregson and Crewe 1994: 266). Leisure or tourism faciles are often added to retailing, heralding a conflation of formerly separate functions often accompanied by a carnivalesque atmosphere (Newby 1993). In effect, postmodern society has witnessed a proliferation of consumption sites for an increasingly discerning clientele.

These studies of consumer behaviour focus on micro-spatial facets of behaviour in relation to the subjective meanings attached to the built environment and the conceptualization of shopping as a social activity or cultural pursuit. This contrasts with more traditional studies concerned with regularities in the broader spatial patterns of consumer behaviour, location of shopping attractions and trip destinations in shopping centres.

Ducatel and Blomley (1990: 223) developed the view that retailers and shopping centre developers were involved in the 'premeditated configuration of retail space in an attempt to induce consumption'. Goss (1993) suggested that the 'new places of consumption' were idyllic contexts, products of a combination of the devices of show business (Las Vegas), advertising (Madison Avenue) and theme parks (Disney). Their promoters were characterized as the 'captains of consciousness' and the 'high priests of capitalism'. Developers saw shoppers as objects to be mechanistically manipulated by the strategic placing of shopping attractions in relation to 'plotted paths, set lures and planted decoys', while the semiotics (Gottdiener 1995) of signs and symbols, and noises and smells experienced in the centres create feelings of well-being, nostalgia or exotica, and a permanent carnival or festival atmosphere. The shopping centre becomes the ultimate 'hedonopolis' with place names, such as Europa Boulevard and Bourbon Street at the West Edmonton Mall, used as semantic metonyms to invoke a sense of 'elsewhereness', while iconic metonyms, such as atria, clocks, fountains and piazzas, equally create positive manipulative emotions. At the same time, the use of public art and occasional classical musical performances provide a 'high culture' legitimation for consumption. However, the presence of security guards and electronic forms of surveillance places significant restrictions on the forms of informal activity associated with more traditional shopping centres. In effect, 'If you are not patronizing the mall, you are loitering and can be removed', while the informal congregation of 'nuisance' groups such as youths ('malingering') and derelicts is actively discouraged (Hopkins 1991). The developer-retailer is represented as a conspirator aiming to 'dupe' the consumer into expenditure rather than a businessperson attempting to obtain a return on investment by providing a pleasurable shopping, social and recreational experience. Part of Goss's message, therefore, subverts the aims of the developer by informing a gullible public and reclaiming the shopping centre as public space.

The commercial aim is consumer manipulation for commercial ends, but the degree to which consumer behaviour is deterministically related to environmental design is debatable as Goss's analysis is largely based on personal observation and intuition. Many consumers may ignore or miss the subtlety of the design mechanisms and respond pragmatically to the convenience and attractions on offer. A survey of three regional shopping malls in the USA (Bloch et al. 1994) used the analogy of the shopping mall as a consumer 'habitat', and classified shoppers according to their patterns of behaviour and derived benefits. Four major groups were defined as 'enthusiasts' (24 per cent), 'traditionalists' (28 per cent), 'grazers' (20 per cent), and 'minimalists' (28 per cent); and only the enthusiasts responded to the full array of design features in the modern shopping centres. The traditionalists had predetermined shopping requirements, the gazers indulged in impulse buying, while the minimalists were largely oblivious of the design devices. It is unlikely that there is a simple deterministic relationship between shopping centre design and consumer behaviour. To a substantial degree, the shopping centre developer has to be mindful of the need for a broad appeal. Nevertheless, the Goss approach provides important insights into the possible relationships between shopping centre environmental design and consumer response.

Geographies of consumption have not sought primarily to understand the determinants of spatial patterns of consumer behaviour in shopping centres per se. Instead, the cultural studies approach, with its emphasis on understanding the social and cultural meanings of consumption behaviour, is far more significant. From this perspective, consumption in the post-modern world has replaced production as the central focus of social life, while commodity purchasing patterns define a person's social identity in terms of gender, age, ethnicity or sexual orientation (Shields 1992). The consumer has a high degree of 'sovereignty' in the way in which consumption is undertaken in accordance with individual lifestyles and personal identities. Shields believes that consumer behaviour in the new 'places of consumption' reflects a complex 'dialectic structuration' between the individual and the environment rather than reflecting a simple deterministic or manipulative relationship.

The principal aim of this approach is to understand the meaning of the consumption process for the individual and for social groups and to inform the retail providers of the types of goods and services, shopping environments, and social situations which appeal most to the various sections of the increasingly segmented retail market. Much of this work focuses on theory formulation and introspection but Holbrook and Jackson's (1996) empirical analyses of the Brent Cross regional mall and Wood Green shopping centre in north London is an exception. They used a combination of questionnaire surveys, focus group discussions and ethnographic research to provide a 'more grounded analysis' of contemporary consumption. This new perspective has not yet provided substantial insights additional to those offered by existing approaches. Shopping, for example, is portrayed as 'a skilled social accomplishment, providing both pleasure and anxiety, its meaning varying according to the social context . . . [in which the] reference point remains the family' (Holbrook and Jackson 1996: 194).

Many of the findings, such as the fact that the social characteristics of the shoppers in the two centres reflect the characteristics of the local catchment areas, could be anticipated from existing studies. Yet a combination of quantitative and qualitative methods together with this explicit theoretical perspective is ultimately likely to yield more socially sensitive insights into the nature of consumer behaviour and contemporary consumption.

The main principles developed in this section have general application to consumer behaviour in the city. The growth of leisure facilities has prompted similar patterns of movements. Some leisure facilities are neighbourhood-based and act as local points of conflux and schools often have general community use out of teaching hours. Other leisure facilities need more central locations and the growth of multipurpose leisure centres has been a feature of British cities. Again there are specialist facilities such as playing fields and athletics tracks which generate their own patterns of movement. All can be investigated from the approaches developed in the context of studies of consumer behaviour.

Voting behaviour

With some forms of behaviour, concern is less with the idea of movements over space than with a behavioural process and its spatial outcomes. Voting is a form of behaviour, sometimes obligatory, which occurs at long but not always predictable intervals, and that has tended to increase in frequency with new tiers of government, the use of referenda and the resort to opinion polls. The principle of one person/one vote is now virtually universal but there are several types of electoral system. In the widely used plurality system, the candidate or candidates who poll most votes in a given constituency, regardless of the form of the majority, is elected. Proportional representation, in which voters rank-order the candidates, has the general aim of allowing the overall distribution of votes for each party to have some effect. Dáil Éireann, for example, the Irish parliament, has 144 deputies drawn from multi-member constituencies by a proportional representation system of single transferable votes. Whereas the plurality system often produces a majority government with a minority of the overall vote, proportional representation often leads to fragmentation and the lack of a clear winner.

The most explicit geographical input to voting behaviour is the spatial framework of areas for which representatives are elected. All facets of these areas, including their size, shape, composition and stability, are clearly critical determinants of the outcomes of voting behaviour. The possibilities of using these criteria as determinants have been understood since at least 1812 when Governor Gerry of Massachusetts earned himself a place in history by authorizing a rearrangement of constituency boundaries designed to produce a particular electoral result. The process of 'gerrymandering' has since been widely used and can take several forms. One strategy is to seek out districts of strength, and, for example, place all white middle-class voters in one constituency and guarantee a result; another is the excess vote strategy which concentrates as much of the opposition vote as possible in a small number of areas to give massive majorities but only a small number of successful candidates; a wasted vote strategy disperses opposition votes over a large number of constituencies so that they always remain insufficient to achieve a majority; and the silent gerrymander involves not changing electoral districts to coincide with population change and thus allowing imbalances to emerge. The silent gerrymander in particular has led to an over-representation of rural and an under-representation of urban areas but local government reform has tackled this problem with reapportionment and the redrawing of boundaries. For British parliamentary constituencies, reports of a Boundary Commission recommended substantial changes in the early 1980s; one outcome was a decline in inner city and an increase in suburban representation as boundaries were adjusted to match population change. Despite this, further adjustments were needed before the 1997 General Election and reflected the pace of change. Main guidelines in the British case are equality of electoral size (set at around 63,000 for England), compactness and avoidance of irregular shape, conformity with major local government units, and awareness of the issues concerned with uniformity or heterogeneity within areas.

The constituency spatial framework is a highly influential factor in determining the outcomes of the electoral process. Although re-districting by an overall body, such as the British Boundaries Commission, strives to be impartial and objective, this is very difficult to achieve in practice and there are inevitably trade-offs which have some partiality as any set of objective criteria are over ridden by expediencies. Political parties and individual candidates are faced with an imperfect set of constituencies at any one point in time, the exact form of which is critical especially in plurality electoral systems. In terms of party competition, votes in 'marginal' constituencies are often more important than in others. Parties may concentrate 'vote-buying' in some constituencies whereby large funds are spent on promoting a particular candidate or issue. Johnston (1979: 137) suggested that the allocation of political money 'is spatially biased by the electoral geography of the relevant territory'. The vote-buying model – the more spent on a campaign, the more votes a party receives – has some provenance. Very large sums of money can be involved, as shown in US Presidential campaigns, and forms of vote-buying are various with funds being targeted at specific areas or causes.

There are other influences on voting behaviour. There is an assumption that politics, in the form of beliefs, values and actual voting behaviour, is strongly related to class. As classes tend to be residentially segregated, there is a geography of elections which reflects these biases. In the UK, working-class districts like the Rhondda consistently elect Labour representatives, whereas professional and rural 'county' areas traditionally elect Conservatives. In the USA, the most likely sources of Republican support are in rural conservative districts and suburban municipalities, whereas Democratic allegiance is traditionally higher in industrial regions and inner cities. In addition to traditional allegiances, there is evidence that high socio-economic status areas produce higher turnouts on election days and therefore greater support for favoured parties. In the UK, where voting is not compulsory, the major objective of parties is to convert marginal voters and, where local circumstances dictate, to encourage 'tactical voting' in order to defeat an established candidate. Canvassing is normally concentrated in areas in which known support exists. The 'party-effect' or class allegiance is general but other factors may become influential.

Ways in which information, or the party-line, on a particular issue, reaches individual voters influence voting responses. Pieces of information which are partisan to the extent that they advocate a particular issue or person are sometimes termed cues. Cues originate from the parties, from trade unions, pressure groups, media and the whole network of acquaintances which an individual may possess. Voting behaviour is much affected by the reception of cues from politically relevant sources. The extent to which a cue is accepted is in part a function of the standing of its source, the force of the argument, and the predisposition of the recipient. Cues are affected by biases such as distance from source, credibility, and relevance within local social networks.

Several 'effects' influence the acceptance of cues. A relocation effect occurs where an elector moves into an area dominated by people of a particular political persuasion and may convert to the majority point of view. A neighbourhood effect occurs when the consensus view in a particular area influences the voting behaviour of all its residents, even though some may have been initially inclined, from class or race origins, to use their votes differently. Individuals, perhaps the less committed, may be affected by a contagion effect, or the product of accumulated informal debate and 'bits' of information. A friends and neighbours effect occurs when the candidate receives extra support in a district in which he or she is very well known, such as birthplace, school, home or place of work, but generally this effect is not thought to be high with estimates of less than 5 per cent. A territorial protection effect occurs when residents of an area perceive an imminent threat to their interests and vote for the party most likely to protect them. In the late 1960s, an uncharacteristic swing towards the 'right' and to the Conservative Party in selected West Midlands constituencies, at a time when the national swing was 3 per cent in the opposite direction, reflected fears of the growth of immigration and 'coloured' communities. Special interest effects, such as anti-gun or anti-abortion lobbies, are becoming more common and often target particular constituencies or sitting representatives. In local elections, issues relating to externalities, such as which party will build a new school, protect a hospital casualty department, or oppose a new highway development, are common.

The right to vote has often been achieved after many decades of struggle; it is only in the 1990s for example, that Black South Africans have been given that right, but once it is attained, elections are frequently typified by apathy and low turnouts. Political awareness, however, has grown in relation to many issues which are outside normal politics. The Green movements, anti-nuclear protests, and animal rights campaigns are examples of political consciousness finding strong expression and sometimes, as with the Green parties, finding a foothold on the political stage. At a local community level, pressure groups and residents' associations have performed similar roles. Local community action is increasingly evident and greater accountability has become a key factor in the government of cities.

Women in the city

Statements on human behaviour are often too general. With residential mobility, for example, households are used as collective units and the variation within them is not examined. Some group differences are well understood – elderly people, ethnic minorities, and social classes – but there has been a less sustained focus on gender as a variable. It is true that some of the mainstream research areas, notably the study of shopping behaviour, were in fact studies of women's behaviour, but this was rarely made explicit and it failed to point up some of the key issues on the place of women in male dominated societies. This imbalance is rapidly being redressed and results have added an important dimension to our understanding of behaviour in the city. A first essential is that the study of women should not assume a uniform group. Kay (1996) noted that feminist researchers have long argued that viewing women as a single group is almost as great a crime as ignoring them completely. There is extreme diversity along the familiar lines of class, race, tastes, preferences and proclivities.

The place of women in society still varies dramatically from one part of the world to another. There is a so-called 'liberalization' of women in many western societies but this contrasts sharply to the place women occupy in other societies. As the Taleban assumed control over Kabul, Afghanistan, in 1996, there was a dramatic change in the lifestyles and liberties of women in the new and fundamentalist, Islamic regime. Even within countries such as the UK, there are differences between groups such as recent Asian immigrants and native British population. It can be argued that we are still looking at 'degrees' of male dominance but change is evident in most societies. Changes in attitudes are important but other changes include the growth of women in the labour force and the changing nature of both family life and household composition. In 1950 in Britain, 38 per cent of women in the workforce were married; by 1970 this had risen to 63 per cent. In terms of the total labour force there was a process of 'feminization' (Lewis and Bowlby 1989) with women forming 45 per cent by 1985. The labour market still posed some major problems for women – unequal wages, limited access to higher level jobs, dominance of 'service' types of employment – and they were also more liable to comprise the 'flexible workforce' of those on part-time or short-term contracts. About 60 per cent of women aged 18 to 60 are now in paid work and their place in the labour force has changed dramatically. Yet, Kay (1996) noted that women's work involvement continued to be shaped by their family roles and was different from that of men. There have also been changes in family composition. Taking the narrow definition of a traditional family in which the husband works, the wife stays at home, they have two children and for whom this is the first marriage, less than 5 per cent of households now fall into this category. There are more single-parent families. Defining the traditional family more broadly as married couples with one or more dependent children captures 29 per cent of households. These are indicators of change but the outcome is that 'most women's lives no longer conform to the pattern of unpaid married women living at home, caring for children, and doing the housework while the man goes out to earn the money' (Lewis and Bowlby 1989; 220).

Despite these salient facts, the average women still spends 75 per cent of her adult life in marriage and carries the main burden of domestic and child-care roles. Even women in paid work undertake 300 per cent more hours of housework than men; the traditional roles of wife and mother are little changed. As Harriet Harman (1989) argued, long hours of paid work discriminate against women by creating norms of employment they find difficulty in meeting. (In May 1997, Harriet Harman became Minister for Women and Secretary of State for Social Security in the newly elected Labour government.)

Women's activities in the city are inhibited by difficulties of arranging work schedules to conform with domestic duties and with their need to find access to public service facilities. Studies of housewives' time-budgets showed that the variety of constraints upon their time, such as cooking and food preparation, controlled and dominated a large part of the day and that care of young children consumed large amounts of time. Households with young children typically allocate three to four hours each day to basic child-care and the demands of older children, such as the need to convey them to and from activities, are not inconsiderable. There is a gender role constraint that disadvantages women in both work and social circumstances. The term gender relations signifies the social relations between men and women which underpin male dominance; the differences are largely of social construction rather than of biological determination.

> Much of the substance of feminist geography has focused on the ideas about the social construction of space, the way in which women's spatial freedoms are curtailed family obligations, ideas about morality, vulnerability and access to transport.
>
> (Shurmer-Smith 1994: 350)

A range of leisure pursuits is more readily available to males, many settings for sociability are male preserves, and female sociability tends therefore to be more constrained. Jackson and Henderson (1995) showed that women often felt more constrained by conditions such as family commitments, lack of partners, access, and ability to play certain sports, but stressed the significance of variations between women. Home and neighbourhood offer arenas of action for women, who, because of their limited personal mobility and the demands of a child-centred family existence, may in reality have a spatial range that is no greater than that of a small child. As women spend more time at home, it is they who have to cope with household emergencies and with local issues, such as lack of play space in the neighbourhood or inadequate services. Any contraction of public services, such as the closure of crèches and nursery schools, reduction in public transport provision and supply of local facilities, tends to impact on the quality of women's lives.

Women have problems of access: about one-third own cars and only half the women in car-owning households have regular access to the family car. There is a reliance on public transport and yet the multiple roles of worker, mother and housewife may make more demands on daily travel. In the Reading flexi-hours scheme, all of the men, but only 50 per cent of the women, had access to a car. An early San Francisco survey found that 42.5 per cent of all females aged 19 years or over lacked personal access to a car compared to 18.7 per cent of males. Social and economic time-rhythms continue to reflect a traditional view of male and female roles yet many of the difficulties of the working wife arise from the dissonance between the demands of the job, family commitments and this kind of macro-structure. Societal rhythms of the times allocated for sleep, work and school have changed more slowly than female availability for paid work, though there are societal differences with, for example, greater female involvement over a wider range of occupations in the USA. Working wives have to use early evenings and weekends, what might 'normally' be regarded as leisure times, for household chores.

The different geographies of women are now well understood as part of the study of urban behaviour. Traditional forms of work organization and family roles are only slowly changing and their impact remains considerable. As many have argued, there is great variation among women in their travel needs, role aspirations, and preferred activities; cities need to provide the circumstances under which this diversity can be accommodated.

The child in the city

Many children grow up in cities, their world is an urban world which enlarges from home, to locality, to city as they move from childhood to adulthood. Studies of the spatial learning experiences of children often take as a starting point the four-phase developmental framework of Piaget and Inhelder (1956):

> The sensorimotor stage (up to 2 years of age) is that during which the child defines his/her place in the world through tactile senses and the manipulation of objects.

> In the pre-operational stage (between the ages of 2 and 7 years) children acquire awareness of a few topological properties of space such as proximity, separation, enclosure, surrounding and order; recognize home as a special place with strong emotional attachment and develop elementary notions of territoriality. This phase represents the transition between the stage of intuitive thought and behaviour and later stages which contain clearer evidence of organization.

> The concrete operational stage (between ages of 7 and 11 years) is marked by increasing ability to represent environment and to recognize connections between topological properties in an integrated system.

> The formal operations stage (from 11 years of age) reveals an increasing ability to use abstract spatial hypotheses which use symbols and transformations. Topological transformations involve rules of proximity, separation and sequence, whereas geometrical transformations involve metric relationships coordinating space with outside reference points.

This constructivist approach argues that spatial learning is based on experience. Piché (1977), broadly in accord with Piaget's theory, found that children progressed from an egocentric confusion of self and environment, with space defined entirely in terms of personal actions, to a practical apprehension of Euclidian space in which objects, including self, had positions. Children began to analyse routes into segments and imagine directions at the intuitive stage; they also referred to landmarks and displacements within their own intuitive representations and could not yet construct overall cognitive schemes with flexibility or reversibility. Older children in Piché's sample often failed to close the network but were able to represent it and to predict shorter routes. Other evidence has shown that children could draw routes from home to school but whereas the youngest children drew straight lines, older children could show changes in direction (Downs and Stea 1977). Other studies have focused on the contraints placed by parents on children's behaviour and here the general statement is that constraints are only gradually removed with increasing age and that girls are more constrained than boys. Fears for safety are dominant themes in terms of constraints with availability of adequate play-space and leisure activities as important themes. There have been several major studies, notably the Toronto *Child in the City* project and the work summarized by Matthews (1992), that have illuminated the urban worlds of children.

Disabled people in the city

Western cities still make few concessions to the special needs of disabled people and both Gleeson (1996) and Imrie (1996) argued that disability was a critical but neglected issue and one of the 'forgotten arenas' for research. Disabled people may suffer from impairment, disability or handicap: 'conserving the notion of **impairment** as abnormality in function; **disability** as not being able to perform an activity considered normal for a human being; and **handicap** as the inability to perform a normal social role' (Oliver 1990: 4).

These definitions are contested and one argument is that whereas impairment can be located in physical or mental illness, disability is the product of society's inability or unwillingness to create the conditions under which disabled people can achieve normal behavioural expectations. The scale of the problem is difficult to measure but McConkey and McCormack (1983) estimated that out of every 100,000 people in a European city, 1,870 would have some form of physical or mental impairment and a further 1,100 who suffer impairment in some other form. In the UK, the office of Population Censuses and Surveys (OPCS 1988) estimated that 4.3 million had mobility problems, 2.6 million had hearing problems and 1.7 million had severe sight problems.

Many of the problems of disabled people could be ameliorated by sensible provision in mobility and transport. Pavements and sidewalks are often poorly maintained, dropped kerbs for wheelchairs and Braille surfaces for blind people are infrequent, traffic signals and crossings make few concessions to disabled people, toilets and other facilities are often unsuitable, and lighting is rarely of a high standard. Much of the responsibility for these kinds of facilities and other aspects of the urban environment lies with the municipal authorities and they are constrained by cost; private transport companies are slow in providing easy-access buses for similar reasons and legislation may be the only way to achieve some of the goals. The welfare services accept responsibilities but often lack the resources to carry them out with the result that disabled people, like mentally ill and elderly people, have to rely upon family and friends.

There are competing theories of disability which may be capable of reconciliation. The theory of personal tragedy locates the problem with the individual and his/her physical or mental impairment; fate has decreed that there is a set of disabled people. The theory of social oppression takes the view that disability is the social product of a society which has not made proper provision for the needs of the impaired. Language such as 'cripple' or 'spastic' stigmatizes and excludes the disabled person whereas a caring society would seek to integrate and to include. This debate often overlaps with that on the competence of academics who are not disabled to research disability: can the condition be understood only by those who experience it? Hall (1995) has tried to close the gap between these two views of disabled people and argued that both rest on assumptions of dualism such as mind-body, able-disabled, normal-abnormal. Far better to regard the body as an unfinished creative entity, we are what we are, and regard disability as the product of neither the body's medical condition nor of societal attitudes, but as a complex interaction between the two.

Cognitive mapping

Spatial learning processes help in understanding spatial behaviour but behavioural geography has focused on imagery and cognitive mapping drawing on Boulding (1956) who argued that human behaviour depends upon the images or the pictures of the world which we carry around in our heads. There is another view that humans have an innate sense of spatial orientation, comparable to their senses of smell and taste. Terms such as 'imaginary maps' and subjective 'life space' suggest a connection between the internal order of attitudes, traditions, and aspirations and the spatial order external to the individual. Kulhavy and Stock (1996) argued that someone learning a map relied on two cognitive processes. Control processes match the map with information already in memory; the memorial system adds modes of representation and the resources needed to store and maintain the map in memory.

A cognitive map depicting an individual's subjective view of environment is a difficult and ambiguous concept. Hart and Moore (1973) used the term to imply a visual image with some of the properties of a conventional map – 'the internalized reconstruction of space in thought'. This narrow view of the 'mental map' or cognitive cartography had support: 'It is an internalized, predominantly visual structure, and it is dissociated conceptually from affective connotations' (Boyle and Robinson 1979: 63).

Downs (1970) used a threefold typology with 'evaluative', 'preference' and 'structural' components. The last category, structural, was concerned with the identity of space perceptions and the mental adjustments of space users, but again its significance is queried: 'We accept that cognitive maps play only a minor and intermittent role in effective thinking and that it is misleading to impute to them any great significance in the co-ordination of our spatial activities' (Boyle and Robinson 1979: 64).

This argument allows mental maps little place in those routine activities which dominate normal patterns of urban living. When special activities, such as a visit to a new shopping centre or search for a new home, arise, they prompt particular responses which may include consulting maps or formal information-seeking. Subjective images of the city which are generally held may be influential but are not likely to be relied upon in a detailed way. Given this line of argument, mental maps have some intrinsic interest but are of limited use in explaining behaviour; people learn about spatial environments by direct experience, by studying maps, or both.

The task of identifying the cognitive maps which people hold, especially in some conventional graphical form, has raised a number of measurement problems. Measurement can be based upon verbal responses but, more generally, researchers have examined 'graphic' responses and people's ability to draw images of the city. Lynch (1960) demonstrated the potential of sketch maps in Boston. Other ways of identifying cognitive maps have involved completion tests in which respondents are presented with an incomplete cartographic stimulus and are requested to add detail. Cloze procedure involves the superimposition of a grid upon a map from which some cells are subsequently deleted. Respondents are then asked to add detail to the blank cells. There are critical intervening factors in these procedures. Size of grid and density of detail on the original map will influence outcomes and any procedures that require people to use or draw maps introduce new sources of error. Sketches require the ability to draw, cloze procedures involve the ability to 'read' maps and to use the information which they contain. Individuals have these abilities to varying degrees and it is noticeable that many experiments have used groups, particularly students, with 'controlled' levels of ability. Boyle and Robinson (1979) compared maps of Sunderland that had been constructed by correspondents with sharply contrasted cartographic skills and experiences. Whereas those with skill and experience drew a conventional map with places and routes in relative positions, those without could construct only a long transect route from home to city centre. Kulhavy and Stock (1996) concluded that map representation is a function of an individual's experience of maps and perception of the map-learning task in hand.

Other procedures avoid the necessity for drawing skills, though it is argued that cognitive maps derived from sources such as verbal descriptions lack the memorial qualities of those obtained from visual depictions of space. None the less, respondents can be presented with a list of sites and asked if they are, or are not, parts of their neighbourhood. The sites are pre-selected but the procedure allows generalized cognitive maps to be derived. Photographs can be substituted for named sites but here the quality and content of the photography become critical variables. Ranking or scoring places in terms of desirability has been a common approach. Such exercises can be conducted within cities – preferences among residential neighbourhoods or shopping centres – or nationally – preferences among regions of a country. Such exercises have some interest but are of limited value. There are typically local preferences, which affirm the preference for present place of residence, and a general tendency to opt for aesthetically more attractive places with amenable climates or unspoiled environments. Preferences or choices made in an unfettered way without necessity to account for costs or other practical constraints are unlikely to reveal realistic results. Lynch's (1960) seminal work on Boston provided systematic ways of measuring urban images and his typology of paths, landmarks, nodes, edges and districts has been widely adopted. Map images contain both features and structural information. Lynch's classification is of features or specific locations; structural information forms the spatial referent of the relative locations of features. Other studies have been concerned with the legibility of cities or the ability of visitors and residents to recall its salient features; places like Amsterdam with its canals and Paris with its boulevards and monuments, tend to be among the more legible.

Conclusions

The themes discussed in this chapter relate to the 'social dynamic' in urban life. The social world of the city is profoundly affected by economic and political forces, but the social dynamic does add its own dimension. Behaviouralism, with its focus on agency, is explicit in studies of spatial learning processes and cognitive mapping; more complex are the concepts of space, spatiality and place, which involve both structure and agency and intertwine the objective and the subjective, location and meaning. Topics such as urban neighbourhood have practical relevance and are established planning tools and the continuing need for applied qualities and an ability to relate research to public policy can be exemplified by a review of social problems of the city.

CHAPTER 12
Social problems and the city

The emergence and subsequent increase of social problems has often been associated with the growth of cities. To some extent this association is an inevitable consequence of the scale and intensity of urbanization, society's problems become starkly evident within an urban environment as problems **in** the city mirror conditions in the society of which it is part. There is also an argument that some problems are products **of** the city and the set of conditions which urbanization creates; they are **place-problems**. Societies contain inequalities that find sharp expression in urban areas, conflicts arise as material and social aspirations are not matched by opportunities. This chapter focuses upon problems manifested in cities that include inequality, poverty, disadvantage and the many hazards of urban life. Some of these problems are as old as cities themselves, others are of recent origin. Although the emphasis here is on 'social' problems, economic structures and processes are always relevant, and underlying indicators, such as unemployment rates and investment trends, are critical.

A focus on problems runs the danger of being a focus on surface manifestations rather than causes, on agencies rather than structures. It will be important therefore to probe the roots of problems and not merely to describe their observable characteristics. Again, the implications of globalization for notions of locality are important. For Giddens (1990: 64) local transformations are as much a part of globalization as are the lateral extensions of social connections across time and space. Local problems need to be reconciled both with the specifics of their cultural milieu and with their place in the outwash of global effects. Questions of definition also arise. The 'problems' most commonly studied are those defined as such by official agencies and presented in their statistical returns on topics such as housing substandardness and crime rates. Social scientists have questioned the assumptions underlying such indicators and have exposed their biases and inaccuracies. Such data are neither neutral nor absolute; they have been defined by the data compilers and involve subjective judgements which often lack theoretical bases. More pragmatically, databases may be incomplete or unrepresentative; national censuses, for example, invariably fail to account for the whole population.

A further criticism of a problems-approach is that its concern with 'visible effects' may lead to reformist and ameliorative stances and a focus on 'welfare policies', and it has been less adept at addressing the deeper sources of inequality. The approach followed in this chapter is to demonstrate the existence of social problems in cities and also to place these within structures and to ask questions of data and definitions. Despite the conceptual difficulties, these are real problems which affect the lives of many people in significant and persistent ways. We do need to portray the quality of urban conditions as well as to identify its origins. Similarly, although welfare policies may ameliorate inequality rather than tackle its causes, in the short term at least, they provide help for those in need. Some problems, such as the living conditions of old people, are more susceptible to short-term measures, while others, such as the deterioration of the inner city, require more radical policies. A focus on problems has value as the means of providing a basic inventory, a portrayal of the extent of human misery, and an essential stage in a broader, longer-term strategy for change.

This chapter begins with a discussion of those current crises of the inner city which have a clear structural origin. The associated issue of urban government is related to inherited patterns of fragmentation of authority in large metropolitan areas, and the varying success of city authorities in regenerating urban economies. Most urban problems are economic, social and political but environmental hazards have assumed greater significance as the thrust towards the sustainable city gathers momentum. The continued development of social indicators and analyses of the quality of life are discussed and, finally, some specific problems such as ill-health and crime in cities will be used to demonstrate ways in which geographical research has been applied to contemporary urban issues.

The inner city and its problems

Through the many centuries of the pre-industrial city and even during the earlier stages of the compact industrial city, there was little sense of a division between 'inner' and 'outer' cities. The inner city problem is the product of the modern western metropolis and often has a legalistic definition as city and suburbs form separate local legislations. The municipalities in cities of the USA, metropolitan boroughs in London and *départements* in Paris, all have some measure of autonomy. Definitions of the inner city usually begin by grouping the relevant administrative units and revealing areas with a number of shared characteristics. These are the oldest parts of the city, they contain most of substandard housing and dereliction, they have residual areas of older industries and transport nodes, but they also have many historic buildings and conservation projects. They share central city space with the main institutions of government, culture and commerce located in the central business district. They are areas starved of investment on a sufficient scale and in which refurbishment is partial and fragmented (Figure 12.1).

The problems that typify inner city areas have been features of the industrial city over several stages of its evolution. A consistent problem is that of the congestion and overcrowding of people and activities into a limited amount of space. As radial transportation routes focused on a central nodal point, so the conditions for convergence were set; as industries demanded easy access to cheap labour, the need for high-density housing, rows and tenements near the factories, was created. A technology which permitted only a basic and localized infrastructure of services and facilities in the nineteenth century promoted the compact city. This kind of central overcrowding is now evident in the large cities of the Third World as they struggle to cope with the sheer weight of urban populations. Industrial cities of the western world have adapted to this basic problem of

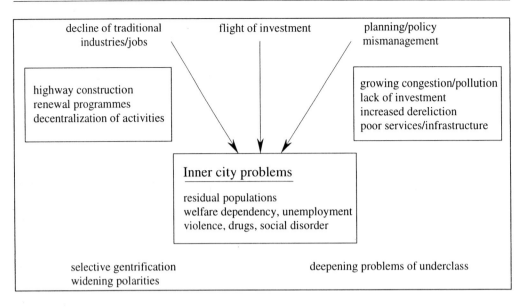

Figure 12.1 Problems of the inner city: some features

inner city congestion by a long process of dispersal of people, housing and activities. Efficient and varied forms of transport allowed the metropolis to emerge. Transport was both the maker and the breaker of cities: it was the maker in the sense that it created a central point of conflux around which the city grew, it was the breaker as its expanding network allowed urban populations and activities to disperse. This ongoing dispersal process, filtering downwards through society, has been a dominant trend during the twentieth century and has alleviated residential congestion in inner city. Many cities continue to experience considerable traffic problems such as shortage of car-parking space and pressures on public transit systems; the 'new' twentieth-century cities of the USA are conspicuous for their alternative urban forms with less reliance on radial transport systems and dominant cores. Dispersal has affected retailing, manufacturing and office functions as well as population; in some places, the congestion of the old inner industrial city has been replaced by a vacuum, with many derelict properties and abandoned land.

For western cities, central densities have remained relatively high but gradients have become shallower, for non-western cities densities have risen in both central and peripheral locations.

A second problem of the inner city is the concentration of poverty and deprivation. In the pre-industrial city, this central area was typified by the symbols of wealth and power but now only the vestiges of that system have survived as heritage buildings or conservation areas. As the wealthy used their prerogative to distance residence from workplace, the inner city began to acquire different characteristics. The new industrial proletariat lived close to their workplaces in what became crowded and often polluted environments. The Victorian slum was established and poverty and substandardness in the inner cities of western Europe were evident by the mid-nineteenth century. Added to this were social problems such as ill-health, crime and segregated districts of immigrant workers creating new tensions. There are many graphic accounts of these urban conditions ranging from the contemporary observations of Mayhew (1862) and Booth (1891) to later analyses attempting to measure conditions such as congestion, overcrowding, poverty and deprivation. In many ways the 'two worlds' of the western city were already present in European cities in the mid-nineteenth century but whereas the social distances between the 'haves' and the 'have-nots' were great, the spatial distances were less marked.

Recent trends in the inner city

The inner city has been no stranger to problems and the processes of social separation towards the suburbs, creating the inner city-outer city dichotomy, have been ongoing for long periods of time. From the early 1970s to the 1990s, awareness of inner-city problems in western cities increased dramatically. It produced the Inner-City Decline thesis, which though now in need of qualification, remains a credible interpretation of urban change throughout these years. If it now needs modification, it is because some of the trends for decline have slowed down and because there have been public and private investments in some inner cities. A number of changes and precipitating conditions can be related to the decline of the inner city. First, there was continuing population loss from inner city areas. By the later 1960s the 'cores' of European cities were decentralizing in absolute as well as in relative terms and over the period 1951 to 1981 the six largest cities in the UK lost over one-third of the populations of their inner areas. The inner city of Paris experienced a population loss of 300,000 between 1968 and 1975 and in Rome the loss was almost 200,000 between 1963 and 1971. These losses largely involved the outward movement of people in a selective way; one outcome was an inner city population which was *residual* and which had distinctive features. Champion *et al.*, (1987) argued that the inner city areas had increasingly become the repository of people with the least economic 'clout' in our society, thereby undermining the quality of life there by creating a situation of multiple deprivation. Studies of some European cities would qualify that generalization and White (1984) noted that west European inner city populations had become polarized with representations of both the very rich and the very poor.

North American urban areas experienced unprecedented population losses from central cities since the early 1970s with the most affected cities being those in the old manufacturing belt such as Cleveland, Buffalo and Pittsburgh, but elsewhere cities such as St Louis and Atlanta also recorded significant losses. The image of the US city changed from one of a high-density, congested but vital centre in which face-to-face relationships could still exist, to that of an ageing, polluted, crime-ridden vacuum typified by declining services, a weak employment base and escalating taxes. There are differences, real and perceived, between cities and some writers' views are of interest: 'LA is the loneliest and most brutal of American cities; New York gets god-awful cold in the winter but there's a feeling of wacky comradeship somewhere in some streets' (Kerouac 1955: 85).

In 1960, the per capita income of the cities was 5 per cent greater than that of their surrounding suburbs; by 1989 it was 11 per cent less. The proportion of poor people living in US cities grew from 32 per cent in 1960 to 42 per cent in 1995 (Dreier and Atlas 1995). In both European and North American cities there have been compensating population flows that have added to the changing character of the inner city. Foreign immigrants from former colonies have moved into inner cities in the UK and the rest of Europe; these movements started as seasonal labour migrations but have tended to acquire permanence. In the USA, the black and Hispanic populations in particular have moved to numerical dominance over large areas of the central city. Mayor Koch of New York estimated that the large majority of the 1 million people who left his city in the 1960s and 1970s were middle class and white, while the large majority of those who moved in were black, Hispanic and poor (*Firing Line* 1979); Mayor Koch was replaced by the first black incumbent of the post in 1989. Racial disadvantage has been at the root of civil disorder since the later 1960s and the Los Angeles riots of 1992 were among the worse in US history, heightening awareness of inner city problems.

Another compensating flow was that related to gentrification, or the return of higher-income households to selected inner city neighbourhoods. Gentrification is selective both in terms of the conditions under which it can occur and of the households it can attract; there is no evidence that it has had a major effect on the higher-income preference for suburbs. As a process, gentrification is in part the product of changing tastes and preferences among middle-income groups, and in part it reflects the willingness of investors to favour specific areas and types of property within the inner city.

Population change is one recognized inner city problem, job loss, particularly in manufacturing, is another. Gordon (1989) reported unemployment rates of twice the national (and London) average in inner London boroughs such as Hackney and Tower Hamlets. Again, this kind of job loss is not new as industries and businesses have been migrating to peripheral highway-based locations for some decades, but closure rather than transfer and the attendant total losses of jobs has become a feature since the later 1960s. A series of studies of the British inner city pinpointed the nature and dimensions of these job losses. Lomas (1975) showed that between 1966 and 1973 there was an overall loss of 200,000 jobs from inner London, 140,000 of these in manufacturing and the rest in services. Gripaios (1977) in a more detailed study of south-east London suggested that 69 per cent of closures resulted from 'deaths' of firms rather than transfer; a Manchester study (Lloyd and Mason 1978) discovered that 85 per cent of the total employment decline from 1966 to 1972 was due to deaths and transfers and most of these were actual closures. Hausner (1987) showed that between 1951 and 1981 the inner cities of the six large UK conurbations lost over 1 million manufacturing jobs, one-half of those which they held in 1951. From these British studies, several generalizations can be made:

- The inner city manufacturing sector has experienced a major downturn.
- Traditional inner city firms have proved particularly vulnerable because of their small size and high costs.
- Some transfers from inner city to outer city (and within the inner city) have occurred, but most losses are associated with total closures.
- Urban redevelopment schemes have had adverse effects on small firms through displacement and higher costs.

These economic downturns and their adverse effects on inner city employment were also evident in US metropolitan areas (Berry 1980). Growth industries increasingly dispersed with older slow-growth industries remaining in the core. From 1969 to 1977, the manufacturing belt in the USA as a whole lost 1.7 million industrial jobs; New York City is estimated to have lost 600,000 jobs between 1968 and 1978. Although there were compensating flows in other sectors, of the 500 large industrial corporations surveyed by *Fortune Magazine* in 1965, 128 had New York headquarters; by 1975 this had decreased to 90. This decline has continued. Fainstein and Fainstein (1995) noted that the old central cities of the manufacturing belt had done exceptionally poorly in economic terms in the later 1980s, and that rising social problems had accompanied this economic decline. These cities show the impact of successive waves of de-industrialization and dis-investment.

The third dimension to the inner city problem is a declining quality of life. Physical environments in the inner city are substandard with low-quality buildings, inadequate services, high densities, and an increasing amount of derelict land. Investment on the edges of US cities added 27 million new dwelling units between 1963 and 1976 and left an inner city starved of capital. Although filtering of older housing stock occurred, abandonment began to typify much of the inner city and the wastelands of dereliction spread. People were trapped in these kinds of environments and it was the disadvantaged, vulnerable and victimized who became concentrated in inner city areas. There they formed an urban underclass of

> persons who lacked training and skills; who either experienced long-term unemployment or had dropped out of the labour force altogether; who were long-term public assistance recipients; and who were engaged in street criminal activity and other forms of aberrant behaviour.
>
> (Wilson 1985: 133)

Knox (1989) showed that for the 100 largest US inner cities, poverty was disproportionately the lot of the black and Hispanic population. In Washington DC 25 per cent of the white population lived in inner city poverty areas compared with 72 per cent of blacks and 46 per cent of Hispanics. Urban underclass is one relevant concept, social exclusion is another. These groups become marginalized and are excluded from the main spheres of employment, good housing and educational opportunities (Figure 12.2).

The poverty areas in many European cities are often occupied by recent immigrants and others on the margins of society; Merlin (1986) identified 400,000 immigrants and 400,000 elderly persons in inner districts of Paris. Sectors of this kind are common in west European cities and are occupied by a transitory population of students, young single adults, immigrant labourers and the very poor. White (1984) described the overall inner city in western Europe as an area of steady population decline with sharp social polarization and some indicators of rising social status. The suburbanization of blue-collar workers in Paris has allowed them to escape the worse consequences of the decline of the inner city employment market.

Poverty areas are typified by multiple deprivation and almost total social exclusion but it would be a mistake though to regard the whole of the inner city as a deprived area; it is a mosaic with some districts of advantage and status close to those of real poverty (Figure 12.3). Inner city problems are most acute in the larger, old industrial cities where the inherited urban fabric has deteriorated and 'residual' populations are trapped in 'residual' environments.

There is ample evidence to demonstrate the variety and intensity of inner city problems. The loss of manufacturing jobs in inner London has deskilled the 'traditional' labour force,

progressive 'flight' from inner city produces suburbs and the outer city	suburbanization
inner city left to later immigrants, some ethnic and other residual groups	filtering
gentrification createsd middle-class enclaves in the inner city	gentrification
low-income suburbs as filtering continues and 'stable' working class move out	filtering
underclass of 'truly disadvantaged' left in abandoned and derelict parts of inner city	abandonment
middleclass move beyond urban fringe	counter-urbanization

Figure 12.2 Urban trends and inner city problems

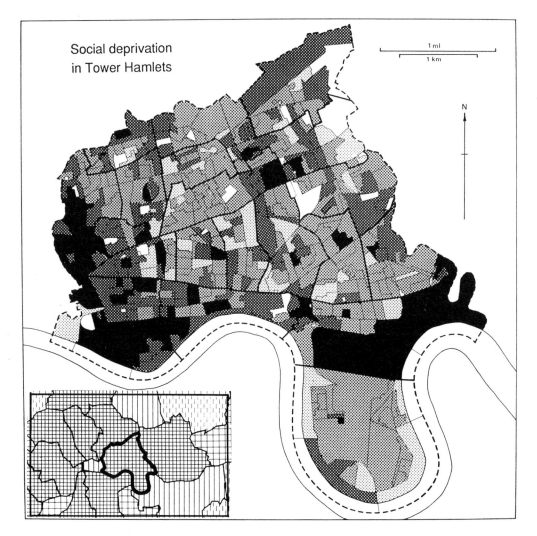

Figure 12.3 Social deprivation in Tower Hamlets, London. Most intense shading shows highest rate of deprivation on a composite index

while pressures for more office space, often speculative, reduced the amount of land available for low-cost housing. Offices generated a demand for labour but this was met by suburban commuters who possessed the relevant skills. Birmingham's traditional role as a base for small-scale traditional industries was sharply affected by the economic decline of the 1970s. The vulnerability of Liverpool's industrial structure was exposed and much of the inner city became a 'waste-land' as a consequence of overzealous clearance schemes. Hausner (1987) showed that between 1971 and 1981, Glasgow, Tyneside and West Midlands were among the twenty British cities which experienced most rapid decline. Whereas London had some success in attracting business services to counteract industrial job losses, Glasgow, Tyneside and West Midlands were still dominated by traditional activities.

Problem estates

Problem areas are by no means restricted to the inner city. Public sector housing programmes have led to the phenomena of problem estates located on urban peripheries yet still typified by deprivation and disadvantage. The Liverpool Inner Area Study stated that concentrations of people at risk were to be found in peripheral estates such as Speke and Cantril Farm (Sims 1984) and elsewhere it has been noted that the scale and concentration of deprivation was increasing in Glasgow's peripheral estates. The inner city then has no monopoly of poverty and deprivation and the 'problem estate' is a feature of many British cities. Such estates acquire unenviable reputations in terms of social behaviour and become 'difficult-to-let' in housing tenancy terms. Some estates in the UK local authority housing sector have been described as disgraceful and degrading; the category of undesirable council property used by Cater and Jones (1989) identified places where overcrowding, lack of amenities, high levels of disrepair, poor services provision and above-average levels of unemployment were prevalent. At Meadowell on Tyneside, Barke and Turnbull (1992) documented an estate with high unemployment, a sense of hopelessness, a thriving drug culture and a high incidence of crime. The question of why such problem estates emerge and persist will be discussed below but these pockets of deprivation can occur throughout the urban area and are most commonly linked with larger-scale public housing projects. Experience in the USA is not dissimilar to that of the UK. McClain (1995) pointed out that many US 'suburbs' were small towns with considerable poverty, unemployment and crime; in 1990 8.7 per cent of the suburban population was below the poverty line and 30.5 per cent of the USA's poor lived in suburbs, 42.4 per cent in cities and 27 per cent in non-metropolitan areas. In European cities, there are many such disadvantaged areas where social problems become acute and social exclusion is evident.

Urban ecological crises

There has been a strong surge towards greater environmental awareness and the need to monitor and protect the ecological habitat. Although many of these habitats are in non-urban locations, they primarily serve urban populations and many country parks and nature reserves have been 'developed' with urban needs in mind. The city itself is an 'ecological

	Type of problem	Pollutants/ sources	Nature of damage	Treatment
People-made	*Air pollution*	sulphur oxides nitrogen oxides carbon oxides hydrocarbons	health hazard loss of amenity	ban on fuels emission control
	Water pollution	industrial commercial waste : sewage	health hazard polluted waterways aesthetic problems	emission control water processing
	Solid waste	industrial domestic building rubble packaging	fire risk health hazard aesthetic deterioration disrupted ecosystem	collection disposal recycling
	Noise and heat	highways industries airports	physical and mental property value	noise shield land-use planning
Natural	*Fogs*	particulates urban climates	traffic hazard safety, stress health	
	Floods	drainage condition flood plain	threat to life and property	channels flood control
	Special events earthquake hurricane drought	geological or climatic conditions	life, property urban system	basic precautions warning systems

Figure 12.4 Types of ecological hazards

habitat' and its condition in these terms has become a matter of increased public concern. Concepts such as the green city and the sustainable city are powerful influences on planning policies and urban strategies. Historically, concerns focused on the squalid conditions of streets, services and housing at particular stages of urban development, such as the industrial cities of nineteenth-century Europe. Contemporaneously in modern cities of Europe and North America, this concern focuses more on control of urban activities and the ways they threaten the natural environment.

There are three main headings under which the ecological issues posed by and within cities can be grouped. First, there is the role of the city as a generator of waste. Urban populations are typified by concentrations of the by-products of human activity from the throw-away garbage of households to the smoke emissions of industrial plants. Second, there are the roles of cities in modifying the local environments in which they are placed, and both climatic and hydrological conditions can be affected in highly significant ways. The growth of urban-industrial societies has been coincident with the types of hazard termed 'quasi-natural' in which the 'urban effect' added to the natural phenomenon produces a malevolent output such as 'smog'. The third group contains the roles of cities in relation to natural hazards or elements in the physical environment harmful to people and caused by extraneous forces. Here it is the built form of the city and the intensity with which it occupies space which places its population at high risk to natural phenomena such as floods, hurricanes, tornadoes and earthquakes. Figure 12.4 lists some of the main ecological hazards in cities. Some hazards are entirely people-made, such as traffic noise, others are purely natural, such as tornadoes, but many are affected by both sets of conditions. The emissions which constitute air pollution are people-made but a set of natural conditions – presence of temperature inversions, lack of ventilation – are necessary before they constitute a major hazard. Similarly, periods of torrential rainfall may produce flood conditions but the high run-off rates of urbanized surfaces and interventions into natural drainage help to produce large-scale flood hazards. The list is by no means complete, but it does provide a set of major categories with which to assess the reality of urban ecological crises.

Comparisons in terms of environmental quality can be made at an inter-urban scale and here the generalizations are largely predictable. First, hazards increase with size of urban area; larger cities entail greater interventions into nature, generate more waste and place more people at risk. Second, some types of cities are more likely to have lower-quality environments than others. Older industrial cities are likely to generate contaminants on a greater scale; many older industrial areas contain the scars on landscape and vegetation that reflect years of industrial urban contamination. More specifically, cities in particular regions – such as Nevada with its high level of radioactive elements in the atmosphere – or which contain particular industrial activities, such as coal-mining or petrochemicals, may be especially vulnerable. Los Angeles, with its combination of local climatic conditions and intense motor vehicle usage, falls into this category. Third, cities in particular geographical locations are at high risk from natural hazards. Cities on floodplains, or near coasts with subsidence or inundation problems (such as Venice), on regular hurricane or tornado tracks, or in earthquake zones (such as San Francisco), all provide examples of this group. How much risk such urban areas face must be a function of probabilities of hazard occurrence, its likely severity, and the measures which have been taken to mitigate the effects.

Classifications of cities according to their overall environmental quality are based upon indicators. Liu (1975) used indicators such as air and water pollution, solid waste output, climatic factors, automobile registrations, and availability of recreational space, to classify US cities. This composite index extended beyond the strict measures of ecological hazard but gave some general indication of inter-city variations. As a generalization, the most favourable US urban environments are found in newer cities, and in the west; the worst are in the older industrial-commercial regions of the north-east and mid-west. Highest concentrations of both air and water pollutants correspond with older centres of heavy industry such as Pittsburgh, Cleveland and Baltimore.

At the intra-urban scale, other generalizations are possible. There is a basic distance-decay effect with pollution levels higher in the central city, with its concentrations of buildings, people, traffic and activities, and lower towards urban peripheries. This effect has been shown in cities such as Manchester and, in US cities, low-income neighbourhoods close to the centre are at most risk. A variety of hazards, such as winter smoke and the 'heat island' effect, adversely influence the health of central-city occupants, especially elderly and under-nourished people, causing chest infections and other respiratory ailments. Local wind conditions may modify the urban 'dust dome' into a 'dust plume' spreading over adjacent rural areas and Terjung (1974) suggested that megalopolitan areas already function as vast pollution 'sheds' on a regional scale.

Air pollution

Air pollution is a closely monitored urban hazard, partly through the notoriety attached to events such as the 1952 London smog and also because of its close links with local climatic conditions. Athens is now thought to have the worst traffic pollution in Europe as a consequence of rising levels of car-ownership, many old vehicles, and local climate; the *nefos*, an ochre-coloured cloud, contains dangerous levels of nitrogen oxide and ozone. Figures are imprecise but Northam (1979) suggested that in the USA, 173 million tonnes of contaminants are released into the atmosphere annually and Kirby (1995) suggested that fossil-fuel burning had released 5 billion tonnes of carbon annually since 1945. Photo-chemical air pollution has been observed in over half the US states, having strong effects on the quality of the air. Of the populated areas of California, 97 per cent had recorded incidence of impaired visibility, 80 per cent suffered plant damage and 70 per cent eye irritation. The automobile constituted the greatest source of emissions by contributing 60 per cent of the state's nitrogen oxides and 80 per cent of its reactive hydrocarbons. In California, all new vehicles must emit 70 per cent less volatile organic compounds and nitrous oxides by the year 2003 (from a 1993 base) and a 1993 European Union directive requires all new cars to be fitted with catalytic converters.

Heat island effect

A city's compact mass of buildings constitutes a strong intervention into local climate affecting exchange of energy, levels of conductivity and contributing to the heat island effect. This effect is produced by the artificial heat generated by traffic, industry and domestic buildings and shows marked temporal variations. Precipitation tends to be higher in urban areas: Bremen has a rainfall 16 per cent higher than its port 1.5 kilometres away, central Moscow records 11 per cent more rainfall than its peripheries. Emitted particulates in the air serve as nuclei in fogs which occur with a frequency twice to five times that typical of rural areas. Urban haze can reduce visibility by 80 to 90 per cent and some of the major ecological 'disasters' in cities have resulted from smog formation. These occur in weather conditions which promote multiple elevated temperature inversions, trap ground air, and prohibit natural ventilation processes in the atmosphere. At Donora, Pennsylvania, in October 1948, the weather situation was such that contaminated air accumulated in the valley in which the city is located, twenty people died and several thousand became ill; some estimates put the deaths related to London smogs in 1952 at 3,000 to 4,000; in New York in 1963, 405 deaths may have resulted from similar conditions. Overall disadvantages of urban over rural areas in percentage terms have been put at 1,000 for contaminants, 26 for visibility and 60 for fogs.

Water pollution

Water pollution has critical roles in urban life as polluted streams cause loss of amenity and can be life-threatening. Cities need clean drinking water and water for industrial purposes, for the maintenance of recreational and biotic waterways, and to service channels for the disposal of waste. Unfortunately, these roles are often in conflict; discharge of heated power station water, for example, may have bad effects on the biotic life of a stream. Supply of drinking water in western cities is now carefully monitored but accidental contamination does occur and poor resource management renders cities vulnerable to shortages during periods of moderate to severe drought conditions. There are policy issues, such as the addition of fluoride to drinking water to counter caries (tooth decay) among children. Despite the fact that clean drinking water is a basic necessity, provision of an adequate supply has often been a slow and piecemeal process and, in the nineteenth century, was often a response to calls for control of disease and fire rather than to meet a basic need. Lakshmanan and Chatterjee (1977) estimated that between 40 and 70 per cent of the urban population of less developed countries lived in districts without safe water or sanitation. Main sources of water pollutants in urban areas are sewered municipal waste and industrial discharges; the problems are well known but, largely because of the prohibitive costs, methods of dealing with them remain primitive. Waste water and raw sewage 'lagoons' are still found in modern US cities; devastating effects of industrial pollution on lakes and rivers have sometimes reached disaster proportions prompting legislative measures and stricter controls.

Solid waste

The amount of solid waste generated by cities is a function of urban population size, affluence and the material conditions of urban life. In Washington DC between 1914 and 1956, paper as a proportion of total waste increased from 45 to 64 per cent; in São Paulo between 1927 and 1969, paper waste increased from 13 to 25 per cent, while organic material declined from 83 to 52 per cent. The increased trade in glass, metals and plastic waste in advanced societies is associated with increases in pre-packaging and decreases in recycling. Western societies were slow to respond to the problem of solid-waste disposal and still in the 1850s, New Yorkers permitted vast quantities of refuse and excrement to accumulate in streets, with severe repercussions on public health. Methods of solid-waste disposal include incineration, recycling and placement in a repository to degrade. Although the advantages of recycling and alternative technologies are well known, land-fill remains an effective and popular method. Land-fill site location is often contested by the Nimby (not in my back-yard) syndrome and the number of municipal land-fill sites in the USA has declined from 5,499 in 1988 to 2,720 in 1998. Many cities have reached a 'solid-waste crisis' and New York, for example, must dispose of 4.3 million tonnes of waste each year. Although many Third World cities are in desperate straits, more of their waste is organic, and Haynes and Hakim (1979) described the situation in Cairo where a programme of maximum recovery was operated. Some types of solid waste are dumped but much is used for fertilizer and is used within the city, with a set of waste entrepreneurs. Itinerant dealers, the *rubabikya*, collect bulk waste for resale, the *zabaline* collect and sort domestic waste and have an allied pig-raising activity, and the *wahiya* are the brokers of the waste enterprise. This is a massive, labour-intensive, recycling operation providing livelihoods for several ethnic groups. There is a cost, however. Rates of infant deaths before the age of 1 year run at 60 per cent among the *zabaline*.

Noise

Noise is an urban environmental hazard. To those who have infrequent contact with high noise levels, it is a minimal problem, to those living or working in close proximity to highways, airports or industrial machinery it is a major urban hazard. People may become accustomed to such high noise levels but this fact does not render them harmless or acceptable. Most urban noise comes from transportation systems, with two-thirds of the outdoor noise that people hear in their homes coming from traffic. Decibels, which measure the intensity of sound on a logarithmic scale, are most commonly used in noise comparisons. It is estimated that 32 million people in the UK are exposed to noise levels above 55 decibels, which the World Health Organization regards as harmful. Readings between 85 and 145 decibels, commonly found in busy streets or near construction work, are more often rated as within the discomfort range with 145 as a level at which physical pain is experienced. Ameliorative measures are possible and it has been estimated that resurfacing roads with porous asphalt would reduce 'road boom' by 85 per cent.

There are increasing controls over pollution levels, often as responses to specific hazard events. Realization of the accumulating effect of motor vehicle emissions, for example, led to new specifications on the design of exhaust systems, to lead-free petrol and other improved car components. Similarly, policies towards domestic smokeless fuels and industrial smoke emission have allowed significant progress towards clean air; greater awareness of problems of the ozone layer has stimulated controls over emissions from household appliances as well as from vehicles and industry. Publicity surrounding the idea of the sustainable city has prompted closer controls of traffic and of pollution; one outcome of the Rio de Janeiro summit was the setting of Agenda 21 inviting cities to form strategies to achieve the qualities of sustainability and an improved quality of life. Many cities have responded with action plans and new forms of environmental control and protection.

Natural hazards

In terms of natural hazards, cities place large numbers of people at risk in constrained spaces and the impact of the city on natural environment is also relevant. Built-up areas interrupt natural drainage and increase flood liability; buildings may accentuate wind effects; cities built on floodplains face risk of water inundation. The epitome of a 'bad' location is perhaps the appropriately named town of Hazard, Kentucky, located on a narrow floodplain of the Kentucky river in a situation which renders it vulnerable to periodic flooding. Houses continue to be constructed on floodplains, even when developers and buyers are aware of the dangers. Runoff rates in urban areas (60 per cent) are much higher than in rural areas (15 per cent).

Coastal cities are vulnerable to a range of hazards and seaboards are often highly urbanized. London has a high level of vulnerability to exceptional tidal conditions on the River Thames, yet it is only in the last quarter of the twentieth century that effective control measures have been taken with the Thames barrier. Most coastal cities have protection strategies – centuries-old in the Netherlands – and can cope with all but extreme events. Abnormal weather conditions can produce disaster, as in the hurricane-prone areas of the US Gulf coast and the tornado-track cities of Texas and Oklahoma. Earthquakes pose a significant threat to urban areas in many part of the world. Generally the regions at risk are well known, but there is a limited amount which technology can achieve and monitoring rather than controlling is the realistic objective. Japanese cities have specialized forms of construction to minimize earthquake effects and emergency procedures yet these served little purpose in the Kobe disaster of 1994. San Francisco's position on the San Andreas fault makes it a well-known city at risk, but legislation to warn against building and occupance in most vulnerable areas has had little effect despite the experiences of 1906 and 1989, (though methods of construction of buildings did ameliorate effects in 1989). There is some evidence that human activity can exacerbate problems; the disposal of liquid waste into deep strata at 3,600 m (12,000 feet) near Denver in the 1960s coincided with a striking increase in earthquake activity.

Better management and strategic planning can reduce the risk and impacts of natural hazards, but there is little control over the hazard itself. Flood control systems can be constructed but there is no control over the movement of hurricanes and tornadoes. A consistent research finding has been that people do not respond to awareness of hazards and there are examples of objections to flood control schemes because of their impact on aesthetic features. The pace and nature of urban growth contain their own priorities for those involved and environmental stress may be relegated in relation to other perceived goals and difficulties. Responsibilities lie with those professionals charged to administer cities and to make decisions in the allocation of funds and resources. They should respond not merely to disaster but also to the more general, ongoing task of ensuring the safety of urban environments.

Social problems

There are problems *in* the city, found throughout society but most evident in urban areas with their concentrations of both people and activities, and problems *of* the city, that are products of the urban environment *per se*. One significant role of urban geography has been that of portraying the extent of these problems and with demonstrating the intensity with which they occur. Unemployment, substandard housing, ill-health, deviance and many other problems are highly clustered in specific parts of the city which suffer from multiple deprivation. Of course, large cities have no monopoly of such problems; unemployment and poverty are just as likely to occur in rural areas or small towns, it is the size and density of the city which sets it apart. It must also be remembered that economic and social problems are both culturally and historically specific; that they are socially constructed; and that deprivation is a relative rather than an absolute concept. Geographers have developed a range of ways in which to study urban problems.

Territorial social indicators

A growing interest in social indicators was paralleled by closer attention to *relevance* or the need to apply research to problems of the real world. This call for relevance was one reaction to the preoccupation with abstract models of the city. Geographers turned to territorial social indicators as quantitative measures of the incidence of social problems in geographical space; they were designed to show where problems occurred. Technical advances included the provision of better spatial recording units, a greater range of statistical indices, and more consistent spatial units over time and place to allow comparability. An outcome was a surge of investigations, based on spatial statistics, into the social conditions in cities, using terms such as level of living, social well-being and quality of life. In principle this was not new. Studies of nineteenth-century British cities and Chicago in the 1920s, for example, had followed similar approaches but now methodology was more precise and concepts were better defined. Figure 12.5 shows the criteria used by the United Nations to measure level of

UN components of level of living	*Criteria of social well-being in the USA*
Health, including demographic conditions	Income, wealth and employment
Food and nutrition	The living environment
Education, including literacy and skills	Health
Conditions of work	Education
Employment situation	Social order
Aggregate consumption and savings	Social belonging
Transportation	Recreation and leisure
Housing, including household facilities	
Clothing	
Recreation and entertainment	
Social security	
Human freedom	

Figure 12.5 Alternative measure of human well-being

living and by David Smith (1973) to measure social well-being.

The use of territorial social indicators was fraught with difficulties. It often proved difficult to find appropriate data of sufficient rigour at the required spatial scale. Again, terms such as quality of life were subjective and held different meanings for different people. There were questions of the measurability of qualities such as love, caring and affection, that were central to people's ideas of quality of life.

Comparisons among cities

At an inter-urban scale, there have been attempts to classify US cities according to the quality of urban life that they offer. Liu (1975) used five broad classes of social indicator – economic, political, environmental, health/education, and social – and Figure 12.6 shows his classification of US cities on the economic and social components. Larger metropolitan areas generally tend to score highly on the economic component with Dallas, Houston and Portland in the south and west, a cluster of manufacturing metros in the mid-west, and emerging cluster of smaller cities in 'sunbelt' states such as Texas shared that status. On the social component, the high-scoring metropolitan areas are found in the Rocky Mountain states and on the west coast, together with the 'newer' urban areas of the plains and broad west. By contrast, the low-scoring metropolitan areas are found east of the Mississippi and in older urban US. Similar studies in different parts of the world have been used to rank or classify cities according to their 'liveability', though the outcomes are very much the products of indices used.

Patterns within cities and the theories of poverty

Territorial social indicators can be used to identify problem areas within cities, to monitor change, and to compare the spatial incidence of various types of problems. Indicators can be used in combination to locate areas of multiple deprivation. Territorial social indicators focus upon the spatial manifestation of problems rather than their causation. As conceptual approaches to deprivation and poverty, the so-called 'theories of poverty' offer some insights into causation.

Deprivation and poverty are difficult to define as a poverty level, for example, is placed at an amount of income, below which households are classed as poor or deprived. This 'level', however, will vary from one society to another according to some internal standard of

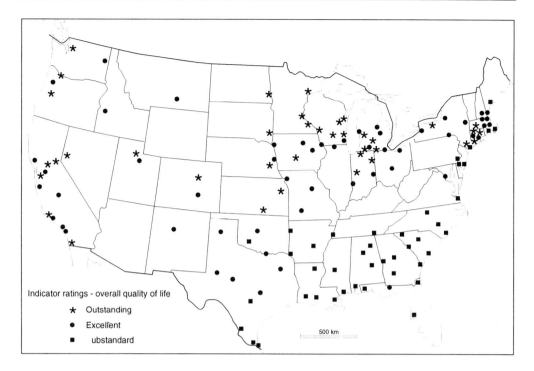

Figure 12.6 Overall quality of life in US cities

assessment. Definitions of poverty are therefore internalized and relative. A poor US citizen will appear affluent in comparison to the Bangladeshi peasant, but has points of reference in middle-income USA rather than in the Third World. Figure 12.7 summarizes some of these theories of poverty:

- **Structural class conflict** theories suggest that poverty and deprivation are the products of particular social formations and the inequalities which they promote and perpetuate. Capitalism, it is argued, invariably produces inequality as it allocates differential rewards in a competitive society; the fact of inequality need not lead to absolute poverty but the critical relative conditions are established. According to this theory, therefore, the causes of poverty lie in the roots of society: any change must be structural.

- **Institutional theory** proposes that poverty develops from the inability of the allocative systems of government and of private institutions to channel goods and services in ways effective enough to reduce or eliminate disadvantage. The failure of bureaucracies to promote awareness of welfare, for example, can lead to unnecessary incidence of deprivation; administrative or investment policy failure may divert resources to other purposes and reduce the ability of the system to eliminate poverty. Kirschenman and Neckerman (1991) focused on the role of employer discrimination which could vary racially and along gender lines.

- The theory of the **cycle of deprivation** suggested that children born into deprived households and (typically) into deprived areas may consistently be faced with fewer opportunities to progress because of their limited access to alternative paths and

Theory	Source of problem	Characteristics of problem	Perpetuating features	Main outcome
structural class-conflict	social formation	unequal distribution of power maintenance of disparities	organization of labour class distinctions	inequality
institutional management	allocative system	uneven distribution of resources inefficient bureaucracies weak communications/ awareness	maintenance of elitism low welfare inputs non-sharing of opportunities	disadvantage underprivilege
cycle of deprivation	social group residential area	few opportunities limited access to social mobility transmission of poor attitudes disadvantaged environment	subcultural norms lack of positive interventions	deprivations low aspirations low achievement
cycle of poverty	individual inadequacies family background	group apathy inherited deficiencies	fatalism failure of welfare services	retardation poverty

Figure 12.7 Theories of poverty

possibilities. A 'cycle' is perpetuated as children go from deprived homes to schools which they share with similarly deprived children, acquire few qualifications or usable skills and, in adulthood, find themselves as uncompetitive in employment or housing markets as their parents were. This theory is often contested but has led to calls for positive intervention into home, school, and neighbourhood in order to compensate for inadequate aspirations, attitudes, and place disadvantage.

• The theory of the **culture of poverty** focused on individual deficiencies. Mead (1992) summarized these as the character deficiencies and deviant values of many inner city residents and the statement has echoes of the older genetic approach. The original theory also, however, suggested a more general lack of aspirations and prevalent fatalism. This theory draws attention to individual disadvantage and the need for positive intervention through educational and social work systems.

Figure 12.8 shows four competing hypotheses developed by Johnson *et al.* (1994) to explain the incidence of high rates of unemployment and resulting poverty in cities.

Earlier studies using territorial social indicators were empirical and showed little awareness of conceptual bases. Typically, these studies analysed large sets of data and selected indicators in intuitive ways. Edwards (1975), however, developed an early link with theory and argued that indicators could be related to a set of key competitive markets (Figure 12.9). This conceptual framework allows the systematic choice of key indicators, and an application of the procedure to the definition of deprived areas in Cardiff showed clusters of deprived areas in part of the inner city and also in older public sector estates such as Ely; these were places where people were conspicuously failing to compete in key markets. In Cardiff it appeared that whereas public policy had succeeded in improving housing conditions, it had been less successful in reducing other forms of social deprivation, such as those affecting educational attainment and employment chances

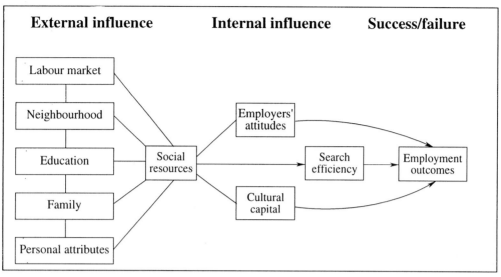

External influence   **Internal influence**   **Success/failure**

Source: Based on Johnson *et al.* 1994
Note: Not all links are shown

Figure 12.8 Factors affecting employment opportunities

	Employment	Housing	Education
Problem	failure to find work failure to find job with good rewards or high satisfaction	inability to obtain mortgage or to own house inability to qualify for good local authority house	failure to obtain good educational qualifications inability to obtain access to educational opportunities
Outcome	unemployment low-skill job low-paid job	substandard housing overcrowding lack of privacy	no educational qualifications few usable skills poor attitudes to schooling
Indicators	per cent unemployed per cent low-skill workers	per cent without household facilities per cent overcrowding or sharing per cent private rented furnished	per cent leaving school without GCSE per cent leaving school at minimum school leaving age

Figure 12.9 Competitive markets and social indicators

Territorial social indicators can be used as instruments to implement area policies or some forms of positive discrimination. Area policies are aggregate policies and are vulnerable to distortions such as ecological fallacy, or the tendency to miss individual differences, and the modifiable area effect, or the dependency of results on the spatial units used. Area policies are none the less effective. It was estimated that by allocating extra resources to 15 per cent of census small areas in Britain, 61 per cent of deprived households would be reached. Boal *et al.* (1978) showed that in Belfast the ten worst-off areas contained 10 per cent of the households, 19 per cent of the unemployed, 27 per cent of the children in care, 19 per cent of delinquents, and 19 per cent of the incidence of bronchitis. This showed not only that some areas have a disproportionate share of disadvantage, but also that they have no monopoly of such disadvantage. Knox (1989) showed how the 'poverty areas' of the hundred largest US cities contained over 60 per cent of the poor population and over 80 per cent of the poor black population. Given these concentrations, policies focused on 'poverty areas', as identified by territorial social indicators, would clearly reach a very large number of those in need. Deprived areas, however defined, do not contain *all* of those in need, neither do they consist wholly of a disadvantaged population. It is this partiality which hinders an effective area policy and is the ecological fallacy effect. Place policies need to be complemented with people policies directed at individuals or households in need regardless of where they live. There are major differences, along racial, gender and age lines, between types of poor people living inside and outside poverty areas. Whereas in US cities the poverty areas contain disproportionate shares of blacks, Hispanics and female-headed families, while elderly people are less well represented. There are sharp, recent trends such as the 'feminization' of poverty with a striking increase in the proportion of poor people accounted for by women. Greene (1994) showed that whereas the areas designated as poor in Chicago in 1970 had a population of 155,000, in 1990 those same areas had a population of only 84,000. Poverty areas in Chicago were increasing in geographical extent but there were fewer people there. Stegman (1995) noted a net out-migration of 3.7 million people from US central cities; left behind was an underclass: 'people, mostly minorities, who are trapped in increasingly isolated, high poverty areas of the inner cities ... woefully unprepared for decent jobs. ... [young people] lose their way into crime and drugs, or slip into habitual dependency on welfare' (Stegman 1995: 1,601–2).

Social indicators derived from official statistics, usually national censuses, often fail to include subjective measures such as feelings, attitudes and values. Other studies, such as that of Fresno, California (see D.M. Smith 1979) have attempted to fill that gap. Results showed some consensus among residents on the significance of health-care costs and drug-addiction levels to personal well-being, but there were class differences. Whereas flood hazards and the growing number of people on welfare were issues for affluent residents, people from low-income areas attached less importance to these and more to access to health-care and availability of jobs: 'what constitutes a social problem in a city depends, then, on who you are and where you live, at least to some extent' (D. M. Smith 1979: 18).

Some specific social problems

Deprivation and poverty are general terms that cover a range of conditions, each of which may constitute a problem in its own right; a number of these are now selected for analysis.

Ill-health

The association of ill-health with particular types of urban environment and with specific districts within cities has been recognized over long periods of time. Compared with global and regional variations of disease, work at the urban scale is sparse. One early example of the spatial ecology of disease in a city was Snow's study of cholera in mid-nineteenth-century London. By identifying a link between a contaminated water supply and the residences of cholera victims, Snow set a precedent for the study of urban diseases. In this example, there was a clear causal link between environment and illness and when the source of contamination was removed, the incidence of cholera declined. Other studies at this time were able to demonstrate that districts of substandard housing, water and sanitation services were breeding places for disease. Rowntree's (1901) survey of the relationship between poor physique, poverty and malnutrition among inner city populations was of similar genre, though the key was poverty and the general social condition rather than some specific feature. As improvements in medical science, sanitation and housing impacted upon western cities, so absolute standards were raised and worst conditions ameliorated.

Concentrations of ill-health remain however. Coates and Silburn (1970) described children in the St Ann's district of Nottingham in the early 1960s as generally being in a poor state of physical development, noticeably smaller and less well developed than children from suburbia; in Belfast, there was a high concentration of infant mortality in the most deprived areas of the city. Outside western societies, many of the historically close correlations between ill-health and living conditions, especially in areas which are badly served in terms of water supply and sanitation, remain part of modern urban life. Lakshmanan and Chatterjee (1977) estimated that nearly 250 million urban dwellers occupied districts without safe water or sanitation in unserviced 'settlements' and these were growing by 12 million persons each year. This type of problem appears to be reaching crisis proportions in less developed countries; in Calcutta, 79 per cent of households occupied a single room, 1.8 million people lived in slums in which latrines are shared among 30 to 50 people, and 63 per cent of households had no regular water supply. Cholera is endemic in the *bustees* or squatter settlements where life is often brief and brutal, and the many refugee settlements produced by conflicts in many parts of the world have created similar conditions.

Other studies of western cities confirm the distinctive spatial concentrations of ill-health. Shannon and Spurlock (1976) recognized 'environmental risk cells' within cities, the inhabitants of which were exposed to above average health hazards. They argued that both health hazards and communicable diseases were distributed differentially across urban landscapes, and individuals in contact with such environmental risk cells, either through residence or activities, were particularly vulnerable. Some of the bases of environmental risk cells are 'physical' such as exposure to atmospheric pollution and therefore to illnesses like gastro-intestinal and respiratory complaints. Others are 'social' and include exposure to localized drug-cultures, to high levels of alcohol consumption and smoking.

Epidemiological studies show clear links between vulnerability to disease and demography. Vulnerability generally increases with age but for particular diseases specific age-groups, household types or persons are most at risk. When demographic variables are controlled, socio-economic status consistently appears to have a strong inverse relationship with ill-health, it is poor people who suffer most from many kinds of ill-health. A major exception has been HIV and AIDS which has affected a range of people and is, according to Dutt *et al.* (1987), the 'bubonic plague' of the twentieth century. North American AIDS was first noted in the three metropolitan areas of New York, San Francisco and Los Angeles which between them contained 67 per cent of all cases in 1983 though it has since diffused to other urban areas. The spatial clustering of AIDS was originally in districts with large numbers of homosexual men but is now far more widespread and affects heterosexuals. One serious concern is large numbers of children being born HIV positive, another is the shift of the disease to the Third World where it is the poor who are at greatest risk. Many contagious diseases have links with poverty and cluster in 'poor' environments within the city. Early studies of Chicago showed correlations of contagious diseases with low income, overcrowding, and adjacency to open water surfaces with a poverty syndrome proving the strongest underlying condition. Haynes (1988) showed that highest lung cancer rates in the UK occurred in inner urban areas – Hammersmith and Fulham in London and Knowsley in Liverpool.

Contagious diseases spread over time and diffusion techniques have proved useful exploratory tools. Pyle (1973) examined measles epidemics in Akron, Ohio, for four periods of outbreak between 1965 and 1970. The clusters of high rates were consistently in central and south-eastern parts of the city despite the fact that numbers of children at risk were greater elsewhere. A diffusion process could be traced from the poverty area in the south-east to the inner city transitional districts, to some suburbs and eventually back to an area near its point of origin. There was some evidence that in the low-income areas, where most of the outbreak was contained, preventive measures were not fully adopted but that in suburban districts the rapid adoption of safeguards halted the spread of the disease. Despite the general improvements in living conditions, vulnerability to disease remains high in specific parts of the city and a feature of the 1990s has been the reappearance in such areas of diseases, like tuberculosis, thought to be controlled. The reasons lie in lax attitudes to vaccination and prevention and the return of high-risk living conditions as disparities between the 'haves' and 'have-nots' grow wider.

Mental illness

Mental illness bridges a gap between physical disabilities and forms of behaviour which might be categorized as deviant. Interest in the analysis of mental illness has broadened from earlier emphases on epidemiology and spatial ecology. Faris and Dunham (1939) provided one of the best known early studies of this kind with data collected for the city of Chicago. They calculated incidence rates of new cases of mental illness, occurring within given groups, over a specified period for 120 community areas within the city and plotted their spatial distributions. The schizophrenic sample of 7,253 cases revealed a regular gradient from 1,195 per 100,000 near the city centre to 111 at the urban periphery. Some disorders such as senile and alcoholic psychoses showed similar patterns but others did not. Manic depression, for example, revealed clusters of cases in peripheral as well as in inner city areas. Most forms of mental disorder, however, clustered in parts of the inner city notably rooming house areas, transient quarters, and skid-rows.

This spatial 'model' with central clusters of mental illness is replicated elsewhere. In Liverpool, there were clear centre-periphery gradients in 1931 and 1954 but a more diffuse pattern in 1973 (see Giggs 1979). Several types of neuroses seemed to cluster in peripherally located public sector housing projects and there is evidence of stress-related illness in high-rise tower blocks. The step from observing patterns to understanding processes has proved difficult. Earlier studies of Chicago proposed a 'breeder hypothesis', linking mental illness with conditions in the local environment and an alternative 'drift hypothesis', which suggested that mentally-ill people moved into particular areas after they became afflicted (Figure 12.10). Both of these hypotheses have something to offer but following discharge of patients from institutions, the increasing numbers of homeless, mentally-ill people supports

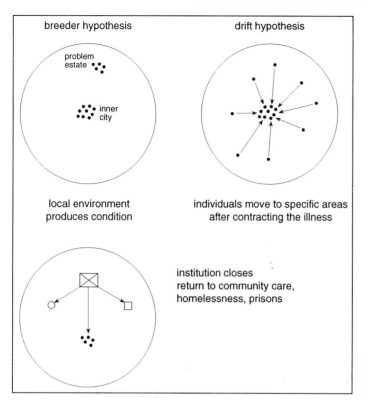

breeder hypothesis

problem
estate

inner
city

local environment
produces condition

drift hypothesis

individuals move to specific areas
after contracting the illness

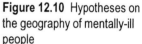

institution closes
return to community care,
homelessness, prisons

Figure 12.10 Hypotheses on
the geography of mentally-ill
people

the drift hypothesis. A link with density or overcrowding has also been argued, though whereas the statistical connection often appears to be clear, its interpretation is controversial. Statistical associations offer guidelines on the ecology of mental disorder, but do not offer causal explanations. Causality in this field is clearly a complex feature and needs to account for individual and genetic differences as well as environmental precipitating conditions. Some forms of mental illness are clearly inherited and 'environment', in the form of home, community and neighbourhood, can also have positive roles in caring for the individual at risk. Spatial ecologies tend to identify those environments which are least successful in these caring roles. Other forms of mental disorder emanate directly from environmental 'stresses', such as overcrowding, lack of support, or fear of crime; some areas of the city contain more sources of stress than others. Importantly, mental illness is a collective term which covers many very different conditions; some of these conditions cluster in space and correlate with particular kinds of environmental conditions, others do not.

Facilities for mentally-ill people require locations and the prospect of a nearby facility is typically regarded as undesirable by local residents; the Nimby syndrome applies. As with so many aspects of human behaviour, mental illness has a social construction and those afflicted are labelled in negative ways by the 'normal' population. Studies show an increase in tolerance towards facilities with distance removed from them residentially in a classical distance-decay effect. De-institutionalization, or policies for the involuntary return of many mentally-ill patients to the community, has had an unprecedented impact on cities and has caused considerable conflict in mental health-care. This conflict (Dear and Wittman 1980) derived from two sources: the assignment problem or matching client to treatment setting,

stages	relevant factors/outcomes
contract illness	age, sex, race class, competences type of neighbourhood
committed to institution	severity of condition treatment mode length of stay counselling
returned to community	ability to cope adequate facilities family support community care
rejects or is rejected by community	homeless turns to drugs/alcohol prison

Figure 12.11 Career paths of mentally-ill people

and the siting problem, or fitting type of facility to community context. Communities resist both facilities and the mentally ill, and new forms of spatial segregation arise from three factors: neighbourhood resistance to facilities; planners' tendency to locate after-care facilities in downtown or central city locations of least resistance; and informal filtering (or drift) towards transient rented areas of mentally-ill people. All of this points to the fact that the cycle has come full circle and 'unwanted' mentally-ill people may once again be clustering in specific inner city areas. Substitution of community for institutional care is proving illusory and close family provide the only real haven for mentally-ill people unless the state reassumes its responsibility for mental health care in a more catholic way. There seems little prospect of this happening at a time when economic considerations continue to outweigh factors of need in government policy (Figure 12.11).

Substance abuse

Substance abuse is an urban problem, though it is a problem **in** the city. As a category, substance abuse covers the many forms of illegal drug-taking and alcohol abuse. Drug abuse, increasingly, is a major urban problem, both in itself and in terms of the behaviour it stimulates: it poses an enormous burden upon those concerned with social control in the city. Heroin is a major drug which though illegal and controlled has become widely available in western cities. Prior to the 1940s, heroin was virtually unknown in the UK and was limited in North America to groups who generally lived outside the law. Pearson (1989) argued that the use of heroin can be likened to a contagion model, spreading by contact and having a strong impact in particular areas because of its reliance on local, largely hidden, networks of suppliers, pushers and users. By the 1980s, heroin was a national problem in the USA, often linked with crime, and was known to be prevalent in specific parts of cities such as east and central Harlem in New York. In the UK there was a three-fold increase in known addicts between 1979 and 1983 and heroin was cheap and plentiful in major cities such as London, Manchester and Glasgow where its use had begun to show correlations with social deprivation and with the so-called sink-estates of public sector housing. Many other drugs such as marijuana, 'crack-cocaine' and their derivatives had become readily available and attracted the young in particular. The drug trade was a major industry with global connections and local networks. Increasingly, much crime is drug related both through the behaviour of affected individuals and as a means of financing the habit.

Although drug abuse, of which heroin is but one example, is a major problem, C. J. Smith (1989) pointed out that ten times as many die as a result of alcohol abuse as from all drugs combined. Data constrain most analysis to a regional scale but Smith and Hanham (1982) showed that the highest US rates for alcoholism were in south-western and north-eastern states along with 'high-spots' in the mid-west, Greater Lakes and Florida. C. J. Smith (1989) showed that in 1983 there were over 12,000 alcohol-related car accidents in New York and over 2,000 deaths from other forms of alcoholism. Alcohol-related admissions accounted for over 1 million patient days in New York hospitals. Alcohol abuse is most widespread in cities and is focused on places of entertainment; in both the USA and the UK there are strong regulatory powers on the location of outlets, times of sales, and constraints on groups such as juveniles. Although alcohol abuse is widespread, the poor tend to fall victim and views on the escapism provided by alcohol and the 'macho' image of the drinker, especially among the youth, remain relevant. C. J. Smith (1989) identified a 'disease model', which sees drinkers as 'different'; a 'social integration model', which views drinking as an acceptable form of behaviour but recognizes problems linked with excesses; and a 'public health model', which aims to reduce consumption. Against this last objective is the fact that alcohol, like tobacco, is a multi-million pound industry and pressures to boost consumption are inevitable.

Homelessness

The phenomenon of homelessness again is not new but its dimensions and changing character are such that it is once more an urgent problem in the city. Venness (1992) showed the changes over time in the status of homeless people and argued that the premises embedded in the 'home ideal', which is both socially constructed and exclusive, should be contested. Figure 12.12 places the homeless in a range of housing classes in the USA at the beginning and end of the twentieth century. Estimates of the number of homeless people in the USA vary from 350,000 to 600,000 and these numbers are thought to be increasing as they are in many European cities. Homeless people form an extreme category of those sections of population suffering from social exclusion; they are

> excluded from many of the markets and services vital to their human development and pursuit of a decent life-style. The European Commision lay the developing problem of social exclusion directly at the doors of rising unemployment and the fragmentation of the job structures.
>
> (McGregor and McConnachie 1995: 1,587–8)

Social exclusion is the product of changes in economic structures and also of the withdrawal of the state from many of its roles in the provision of welfare. Homeless people are the worst victims of these kinds of changes as they become not merely disadvantaged economically but also outcast socially.

> Evicted from the private spaces of the real estate market, homeless people occupy public spaces, but their consequent presence in the urban landscape is fiercely contested. Their visibility is consistently erased by institutional efforts to move them elsewhere.
>
> (N. Smith 1993: 89)

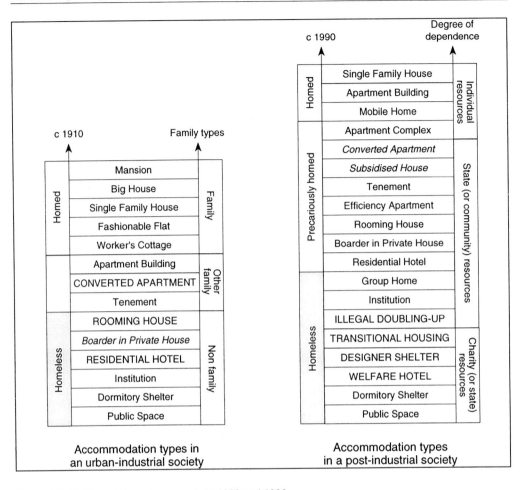

Figure 12.12 Place of homeless people in 1920 and 1990

A significant change is that homeless people now comprise more variety than the stereotype of single men, either following casual work or occupying the skid-rows of US cities. Stegman (1995) thought that one-fifth of US homeless people were families with children; many young people, men and women, are homeless on the streets of major cities such as London, Paris and New York. For many, the basic problem is economic and the lack of employment but this is exacerbated by the lack of housing and in some European cities by the refugee problem. Abandoned children have become a major feature of former socialist societies like Romania, in war-ravaged areas of Europe and Africa and in major cities of Latin America.

Some of the main reasons for increasing homelessness lie with unemployment and the deficiencies of the housing market but there are other factors. The process of *deinstitutionalization* has thrown many mentally-disturbed people onto the streets. Family, community care and state welfare may pick them up for a while but they tend to drift into this type of lifestyle. Stegman (1995) suggested that, in US cities, at least one-third of homeless people were mentally ill and half suffered from alcohol or substance abuse. The advent of crack cocaine has in itself been put forward as a reason for the growth of the young homeless as it is on the streets that their desired lifestyle can be found. Another set of reasons may be found in changing household formations, the decline of the traditional family, of marriage rates and related social norms. All of these add up to less stability and fewer havens to which marginalized individuals can retreat. Some homelessness may emanate from the slum clearance schemes that removed cheap lodging houses and similar shelter on the old skid-rows, but the impact of these schemes varies from one city to another. Public policy must address the problem of homelessness in structural and ameliorative ways. In the USA, $1.7 billion was used to fund local strategies to reduce homelessness in 1995 and Housing and Urban Development, a federal agency, issues 15,000 rental certificates annually to non-profit home providers (Stegman 1995). In the UK, there are many housing providers for welfare dependants in the private sector but financial constraints give the municipalities a limited ability to provide shelter.

Urban crime and delinquency

A consistent finding of analyses of official crime statistics has been the association of high crime rates with urbanization and the growth of cities. Crime rates increase with urbanization and although some societies are well known for 'rural crime', rates are characteristically higher for urban areas. Evidence to support this contention has been available from the early nineteenth century with the statistical mapping exercises in France and the work of social reformers such as Mayhew (1862); it continues to receive confirmation from a variety of contemporary sources. In addition to this link with cities, there are striking regional variations in crime rates and this fact has frequently been demonstrated in the USA. Perhaps the best known North American regional image is that of the 'violent south'; in 1975, for example, the southern states had 42 per cent of the nation's homicides and 75 per cent of its prisoners under sentence of death. Harries and Brunn (1978) recognized a 'traditionalistic political culture' in these southern states which in some way nurtured violence. It was also reflected in the geography of sentencing as the numbers on death row and the actual executions portrayed. These images and those of 'crime cities', like Chicago, endure but many major US cities show high rates of violence. In 1995, New Orleans, with 73 murders per 100,000 population, headed the list, followed by Washington DC (62) and Detroit (46). Gary, Indiana, with a 1995 murder rate of 118 per 100,000, epitomized the problems of the older, smaller, industrial cities with a devastated economic base. Unemployment there was three times the national average, 40 per cent of the children lived in poverty, the town had changed through economic decline and white flight from a racially mixed community to a poor, crime-ridden, black ghetto.

Although these associations of crime with cities and particular regions are real enough, criminologists stress the need for caution in the use of official crime statistics. There are problems of the completeness of data, of the extent to which they may contain biases, and of the ways in which definitions of offences are derived and interpreted. Crime and delinquency are defined by the rule-makers, they reflect particular traditions and value-systems, especially of those empowered to make the rules, they are social constructs proscribed by the criminal law.

Most western societies have experienced increasing rates of crime and this has aroused both political concern and a closer scrutiny of the effectiveness of the criminal justice system. Maguire (1994) estimated that the British *Criminal Statistics* showed a total of notifiable and recorded offences of 5,594,000 in 1992, an eleven-fold increase since 1950. There are marked differences between societies. From 1957 to 1976, the UK crime rate quadrupled and, between 1981 and 1995, the number of crimes recorded by the police increased by 91 per cent. These are high rates but they pall in comparison with the incidence of crime in the USA. In 1975 there were 493 recorded homicides in the UK but 18,780 in the USA. The UK has about one-fifth of the total population of the USA. An interesting press observation is that prompter and more effective emergency medical services in the UK may be a factor in keeping death-rates from assaults low. New York alone had 1,622 homicides, followed by Chicago with 814, Detroit with 663 and Los Angeles with 501. As Oklahoma City's homicide rate passed 100 in 1979 it was described in the local press as 'entering the big league'. As national crime surveys, involving detailed questioning of households on their experience of crime, are carried out, they offer a much clearer picture of the reality. The 1996 British National Crime Survey estimated that there were 19.1 million crimes in 1995 against individuals and their property; these surveys, which have been frequent since the 1980s, suggest a much more stable pattern of crime than that indicated in official statistics. The latter reflect variations in the efficiency of reporting and recording rather than in crime *per se*. Local surveys, such as the Islington Crime Survey, London (T. Jones *et al.* 1986) showed that over a twelve-month period one in two households could expect to fall victim to some form of crime. This was in many ways an exceptional area but it did reveal the extent of unreported crime: nationally, the 1984 British National Crime Survey estimated that only 48 per cent of burglaries, 8 per cent of robberies, and 11 per cent of sexual offences were recorded in official statistics

The facts of the spatial concentration of crime and delinquency in specific parts of the city are well known. In the nineteenth century, observers noted 'crime areas' within cities which acted as breeding grounds for criminals. These 'rookeries' were located in parts of inner London, Manchester and other large cities, places occupied by 'the lowest grade of thieves and dissolute people' (Tobias 1976: 131). Later, much of this type of work was formalized in the studies of Shaw and McKay (1942) in Chicago. Analysing patterns of juvenile crime by community areas, they identified both 'delinquency areas' and regular 'crime gradients' from city centre to periphery (see Figure 12.13).

This model for the spatial ecology of crime within cities has had generality and persistence, though some qualifications are necessary:

- The model was most applicable to North American cities and mirrored a social geography at that time in which the least advantaged occupied inner city areas. Even in the USA there has been evidence that inner city/suburban crime rate differentials are narrowing selectively as low-status suburbs show rising crime rates and the inner cities continue to lose population.
- Where state housing policies transfer low-income people to peripheral estates, high crime rates tend to accompany them and in many parts of Europe the sink-estates have become the most problematic areas. Social condition rather than quality of housing underpins much crime.
- There are different geographies for offenders and offences; the former will correlate with those social environments associated with deprivation and disadvantage, the latter with environments which offer targets and opportunities.

- The many types of offences have different geographies; most robberies, for example, tend to occur in central city commercial areas, most burglaries in residential districts, violence is common in domestic settings but also at places of entertainment and points of conflux.

- Known crime is not all crime and white-collar crime in particular is under-represented in official statistics; Levi (1992) demonstrated that the normal mode of policing and prosecution reproduces local patterns of crime. The regulation of financial crime has been largely ignored by criminologists who are preoccupied by the policing of the working class, yet in 1988, some $1,200 billion was involved in cross-border securities transactions and much more in foreign exchange and commodities futures transactions (Levi 1992). It is in these areas, requiring international policing, that much white-collar crime is located. These and other areas are difficult for the police and success rates in prosecution are not high.

Analyses of spatial patterns of crime have been accompanied by attempts at explanation. Shaw and McKay (1942) measured the statistical associations between delinquency, crime, recidivist and truancy rates against a set of territorial social indicators. They found strong associations between the measures of deviance and indicators, such as substandard housing, poverty, foreign-born population and mobility. Shaw and McKay argued that these correlates had no specific causal significance in themselves but were symptoms, along with delinquency and crime, of some underlying social condition. Their theory of 'social disorganization' expressed this condition and suggested that in the absence of a stable form of society, with legalistically based codes of behaviour and established norms and values, precipitating conditions for deviance would exist. Alternatively, 'subcultural theory' suggested that crime or delinquency areas corresponded with groups of people who shared sets of values, beliefs and behavioural norms which condoned some forms of illegal activities. Alongside many values which were unexceptional, there were some which amounted to a subculture of criminality. These attempts to explain crime are contested. Social disorganization, for example, cannot account for the fact that some crime areas do have an internal social order and cannot be classed as socially unstable. Other theories include a structural approach which locates the roots of criminal behaviour in the inequalities that have been created in a capitalist society, criminality becomes an expected form of behaviour to counter disadvantage and the rules of the empowered minority, genetic theories which regard some forms of criminality as inherited and part of the physical or mental make-up of the individual, and environmental theories which believe that there are particular social conditions which help, form, or precipitate deviant behaviour. Both social disorganization and subcultural theory belong to this last group.

Geographers have argued that there is a valid 'poor environment hypothesis' suggesting that most known offenders are drawn from disadvantaged localities, easily identified by social indicators such as housing substandardness, unemployment, low socio-economic status and weak family life. Poor living conditions spring from the prevalence of inequalities and, therefore, structural and environmental arguments need not be contradictory. All aggregate theories of this kind are vulnerable in the sense that whatever the level of inequality, deprivation or adverse conditions, some disadvantaged individuals turn to crime, but many do not. This raises once again the structure-agency debate and the need to reconcile macro-explanations with individual and local circumstances.

Within the poor environment hypothesis there are specific ideas:

- The **housing class hypothesis** suggests that offender rates are lower in owner-occupied than they are in rented housing areas.
- **Social disorganization,** or the idea that more offenders are found where stabilizing conditions are absent, was supported in the Sheffield study (Baldwin and Bottoms 1976).
- The **poor social environment** hypothesis (Herbert 1976) suggested that higher rates of delinquency would occur in districts where sets of values, norms of behaviour, and in particular low social control of children by their parents, were such that deviant behaviour was tolerated. The evidence here pointed towards a subcultural effect in which residents of delinquency areas appear to hold some sets of values which condone deviant behaviour. The wide issue of the sufficiency of parental supervision has had increased attention with the evidence for the demise of the traditional family.

The idea of 'delinquency areas' was explicit in the early studies of Chicago by Shaw and McKay (1942) and has been replicated in many other studies. Ley and Cybriwsky (1974a, 1974b) examined the distribution of teenage gangs and their 'turfs' or local territories in Philadelphia where graffiti were used as boundary markers to assert territorial claims. Rowley (1978) described the skid-rows of North American cities as 'any dilapidated section of town where petty criminals, degenerates and derelicts hang out'.

The facts of delinquent or crime areas can be established; they are districts within the city containing disproportionate numbers of offenders and in that sense are defined in relative terms. There are questions, however, on the emergence and persistence of such areas. The first of these questions – Why do delinquency areas emerge? – is often difficult to resolve in the absence of detailed historical evidence. Difficult-to-let estates in the British public sector of housing have been studied in these terms as they are both recent and the municipality maintains good records of tenancy and occupance. More general characterizations of these problem estates have been recognized as high rates of tenant turnover, a paucity of recreational facilities and other services, a self-selection process that leads particular kinds of households into these estates, and evidence that local authority housing managers had followed a practice of 'dumping' problem families in particular estates. The last of these factors may have particular relevance as households from slum-clearance areas were often moved *en bloc* to a new estate. Gill (1977) scrutinized housing officials' records of tenants of Luke Street, Liverpool, and found them liberally sprinkled with phrases such as 'not suitable for new property', 'suitable for the Dock area only', and 'not suitable for the Corporation to rehouse'. He concluded that 'it was local planning and housing department policy that produced Luke Street' (Gill 1977: 187).

The suggestion of a strong self-selection process operative among residents of problem estates argues that prospective tenants match estate life to their own aspirations, they may be attracted by low levels of rent and by proximity to family and friends. Barke and Turnbull (1992), in their detailed study of the Meadowell estate on Tyneside, concluded that it was not really until the late 1960s and the 1970s that Meadowell's problems began to match its reputation, and during the 1980s these real problems were accentuated. They suspected that the municipality played a significant part in the development of this downward spiral, especially through inattention to maintenance needs, but factors external to the areas and especially those affecting employment had major impact.

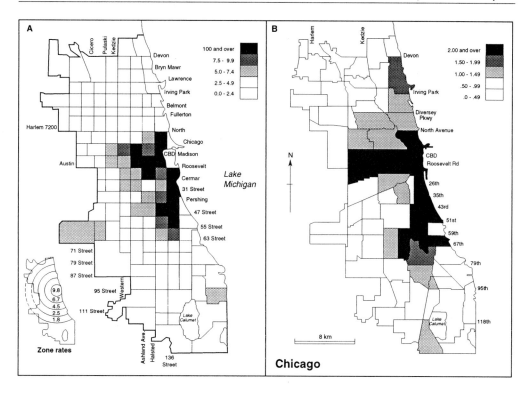

Figure 12.13 Delinquency areas in Chicago

On problem estates, tenants with any kind of social aspiration attempted to leave, those who stayed were either indifferent to the estate's reputation or were desperate for housing. Labels given to problem estates are influenced by the initial occupants and, in Sheffield, one estate was used to rehouse a number of notorious gang-leaders and their associates, while in Cardiff another was made distinctive by the fact that its occupants were largely Roman Catholic and Irish from the old docklands. Once labelled, estates have reputations which are difficult to change even if actual behaviour does not match the label. Damer (1974) demonstrated this for an estate called Wine Alley in Glasgow, a place with a reputation for rent arrears, vandalism and crime, yet this image was based far more upon past rather than present events; Barke and Turnbull (1992) showed a similar situation in Meadowell. Figure 12.14 summarizes factors which may 'produce' a problem estate.

Environmental criminology

Environmental criminology is an approach to the geography of crime which focuses on criminal events and the places at which they occur, the thrust is the offence rather than the offender. As Maguire (1994) argued, greater interest in the victims of crime emerged in the 1980s and this had the effect of focusing attention on the offence and its impact and the questions of where, when and against whom the crimes were committed. Many crimes are reactions to opportunities in the local environment; it is the assemblage of targets, easy access, low surveillance, weak control and poor security which make some places more vulnerable than others. Jacobs (1961) articulated these ideas and they were developed by

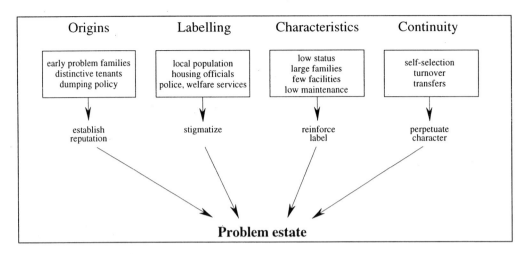

Figure 12.14 Factors contributing to the emergence and persistence of a problem estate

Newman (1972) with his idea of 'defensible space'. From surveys in New York, he suggested that housing projects would be well defended if they were visible, if they had a strong sense of community, and if divisions between private and public space were clearly identified. As a policy, defensible space involved the development of good design principles and effective management of space to reduce vulnerability. Coleman (1985) applied these ideas to public sector housing in London and her Index of Disadvantage measured the extent to which different parts of the city suffered from defects in the design and quality of the built environment. At a more basic level, research has shown that improved street lighting can reduce fear of crime and may, in some circumstances, reduce actual crime levels. Experiments with security cameras in shopping districts have had similar effects though displacement of car thieves in particular to less well guarded areas may be a consequence.

The concept of 'incivilities' can be firmly wedded in environmental criminology. Incivilities occur in the urban environment in forms such as graffiti, litter and vandalism and these serve as early signs or indicators of increasing disorder in a neighbourhood. Figure 12.15 places these in a continuum of forms of disorder and the hypothesis is that they can act as precursors of more serious events. This concept of change over time is shown schematically in Figure 12.16 and the argument is that incivilities arise when there are decreasing levels of local social control, a reducing level of maintenance, and a tendency for 'respectable' residents to begin to leave the area. Unless the process is arrested, a social change beginning with the appearance of incivilities, can become a downward spiral into crime and serious disorder. Another concept which can be discussed in similar terms is that of community crime careers. Here the argument is that residential areas can progress over time in a cyclical manner such that there are stages at which they are much more likely to experience rising levels of criminal activity. The clearest connections are demographic. Estates, for example, suffer most crime and vandalism, at the stages when they have the highest numbers of youths in residence. As these numbers decline through natural demographic change, the incidence of disorder also tends to decline. Other conditions, both external and internal to the estate, affect their crime careers. Local employment opportunities, policing attitudes, social services labelling and the emergence and persistence of problem families and drug cultures, are all relevant.

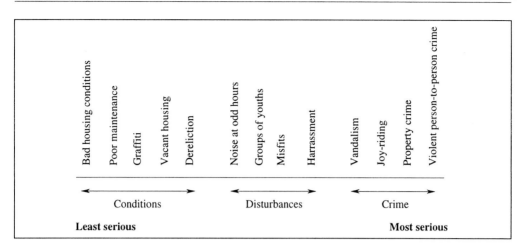

Figure 12.15 Incivilities and forms of social disorder

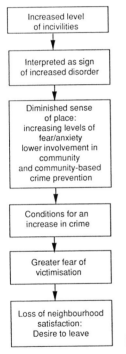

Figure 12.16 Incivilities and neighbourhood change: a model

Environmental criminology offers a number of hypotheses to explain why some residential districts are more vulnerable to offences against property:

- The **offender-residence hypothesis** suggested that areas become vulnerable if they contain many offenders or are close to where offenders live. This idea is based on the fact that most offenders travel only short distances to commit crime.
- The **border-zone hypothesis** suggested that the edges of well-defined neighbourhoods are more vulnerable than their cores, as the latter benefit from clearer neighbourhood identity and social cohesion.
- The **local social control hypothesis** suggested that well-integrated, socially cohesive

neighbourhoods, where residents share a sense of community and share the task of social control, are the least vulnerable.

- The **area variability hypothesis** suggested that 'mixed' areas are more vulnerable, though the kind of mixture is contentious. Mixture is often taken to apply to household types, ethnic composition, and juxtaposition of relative wealth and poverty.

National crime surveys have highlighted the prevalence of fear of crime and London's Islington Survey, for example, revealed that over half the women interviewed avoided going out after dark. Fear of crime is often translated into fear of places and many areas within cities are perceived as unsafe and are carefully avoided. S. J. Smith (1986) argued that fear of crime is heightened among those who are on the 'margins' of society, either in economic or social terms. Real and perceived levels of vulnerability are often in tandem and those who live in vulnerable areas respond by adopting a stronger security consciousness. The ways in which they do this will vary. Wealthier people invest more in security because they have the means to do so and thus feel more protected. Several sections of society feel particularly vulnerable and they may respond with avoidance strategies of various kinds. Women will avoid dark areas and spaces thought to carry risk, elderly people may become virtual prisoners in their own homes, gay men and lesbians seek security in specific areas or social settings where they feel accepted. Valentine (1997) has shown that parents felt their children to be most at risk from abduction (45 per cent) and that they perceive a 'geography of danger' with public parks (60 per cent), shopping centres (34 per cent) and playgrounds (33 per cent) designated as more dangerous places. Virtually all parents in this survey (95 per cent) imposed some kind of constraint upon their children's play and many increasingly encouraged them to spend time at home or to join organized activities; all of these moves were motivated by a felt need for safety.

Geographers have focused on offenders, offences and the local environments in which they occur. There is however a growing interest in the criminal justice system and with the 'rule-makers' rather than the rule-breakers.

- There are issues relating to the policing strategies adopted to cope with crime, from intensive policing of difficult areas to the whole concept of **community policing**. How should these strategies be organized territorially and what effects do they have on crime? The evidence on the effectiveness of differential policing and similar strategies in reducing crime rates is varied and inconclusive, but these are important aspects of police work.

- Are there **crime prevention policies** which can be applied effectively? A major crime prevention policy is that of **neighbourhood watch** which involves residents in surveillance and reporting and is often claimed to reduce local crime rates. The police are involved in these schemes in advisory and 'responsive' capacities but they are mainly citizen initiatives and have been adopted in a variety of forms. Whereas neighbourhood watch undoubtedly can have positive effects by reducing fear of crime and leading to more social-bonding within communities, it is less clear that it actually reduces crime. Again, neighbourhood watch schemes are least prevalent in the localities that most need them and, where effective, they may merely displace crime to less well-protected neighbourhoods.

- Most communities in the UK have **crime prevention strategies** and there has been a range of special initiatives such as the **Safer Cities Programme** in response to an

- *Design security measures*
  - target hardening, locks, doors, windows
  - better lighting, security cameras
- *Social control measures*
  - neighbourhood watch
  - community policing
  - youth involvement schemes
- *Liveable environments*
  - remove graffiti, incivilities
  - improve maintainance
  - create defensible space, sense of space
- *Legalistic control*
  - more intensive policing
  - remove real problem individuals
- *Overall strategies*
  - priority estates, safe cities
  - inter-agency schemes
  - job creation schemes

Figure 12.17 Crime prevention policies

awareness of public concern about crime (Figure 12.17). Measures range from target-hardening approaches, such as the fitting of window-locks and alarms, to social measures in which police work collaboratively with social services to find ways of channelling the energies of youths, in particular, into more positive channels. These measures often have good effects but they are often short term.

- A different type of police strategy involves closer involvement with communities and their problems. Community policing is one expression of this strategy but others include the establishment of **police consultative committees** and forums designed to maintain a dialogue between police and public. Again, these collaborations seem to work best in middle-class communities but the policy needs to be persisted with. Accusations of racism are the most common aimed at the police and evidence does indicate that black youths are more likely to attract police attention. Policies here need to be imaginative and to be both longer term, more recruitment of black police officers, and short term, police counselling on ways to deal with minorities, dimension.

- As a historical example of the impact of the **rule-makers** on the geography of crime, Shumsky and Springer's (1981) study of San Francisco's red light district between 1880 and 1934 is of value. Noting that the locations of both brothels and prostitutes in the city changed over time, they argued that these were the product of changing attitudes and practices within the criminal justice system. As the laws themselves, or local enforcement of those laws changed, so prostitutes relocated their activities in order to avoid being arrested and thus created new 'zones of prostitution'. This changing geography was the outcome of the actions of the rule-makers rather than the rule-breakers and a later study of Vancouver has shown similar characteristics as phases of policing activity result in shifts of 'vice' areas in the city. There is some debate on whether this type of victimless crime should be designated as illegal at all and different interpretations of the law underlie the varying patterns of enforcement.

- In societies where the jury system is used, there is increasing evidence that the make-up

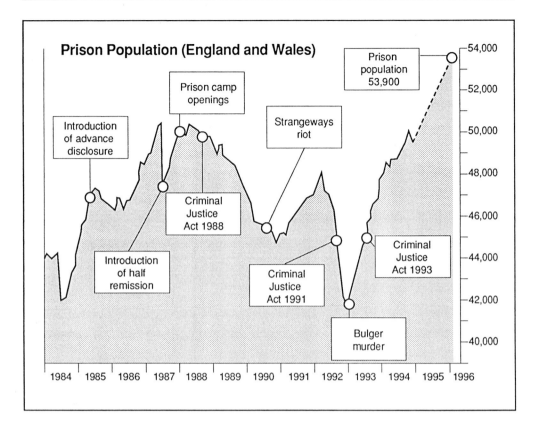

Figure 12.18 Changes in prison population in England and Wales, 18984–96

of the jury is a critical factor in determining outcomes of the criminal justice system. Herbert (1994) argued the need to select jurors from the locality of the offence and/or offender, with the relevant values and background, in order to legitimize the jury system.

The final stage of the criminal justice system involves the courts and their range of punishments. The variations in sentencing patterns have already been referred and it is clear that there are local effects which can be summarized as regional or inter-court differences. Custodial sentences are among the most severe sentences and there is pressure on governments to remove persistent offenders from society. Although contested by the more liberal lobby of penal reformers, the custodial line has been dominant in the 1990s with California's 'three-strikes' rule and the introduction of private prisons to cope with the burden of incarceration. Figure 12.18 shows the fluctuations in prison population in England and Wales since 1984 and the events which may bear some relation to these highs and lows. In 1996 in England andWales, there were 135 state and private jails holding 53,941 prisoners (in France in the same year, there were 183 jails and 52,658 prisoners). In England and Wales 18 new prisons were planned for the 1990s, each holding around 800 prisoners; some of these may replace substandard or out-of-date existing prisons. There are many types of prison from open prisons to high-security establishments but they all face the Nimby problem when it comes to location and the trend is to place them outside urban areas.

Educational disadvantage

'Children from affluent areas (schools) know more, stay in school longer, and end up with better jobs than children from schools that enrol mostly poor children' (Jencks and Mayer 1990: 111).

This generalization raises the key issues of the debate on educational disadvantage. It is clear that children's attainment at school will vary considerably but the questions are whether this variation simply reflects 'natural' ability or whether conditions of class, race, home environment and school intervene. The strongest and most persistent evidence is for a social class effect and this underpins the quotation from Jencks and Mayer. Some of the earliest scientific evidence comes from the study by Jackson and Marsden (1962) *Education and the Working Class* based on an industrial city in northern England. This study was completed at the time of the 11+ selective examination which all children had to sit as entry to state secondary schools: those who passed went to the grammar schools, those who failed to the secondary modern or technical schools. The 11+ produced a major divide among children between those who might go to higher education and the professions and those apparently destined for lower skilled jobs. The Jackson and Marsden study showed that whereas the overall composition of the city was 78 per cent blue-collar/low-income and 22 per cent white-collar/high-income, the corresponding composition of the grammar school population was 36 per cent and 64 per cent. In other words, the white-collar/high-income section of the community won a disproportionate number of places in the grammar schools. Now did this imbalance reflect differences in natural ability, or was the advantage of social background intervening in a major way?

A further dimension to this study threw some light on school and neighbourhood effects. For most elementary schools, the success rates in the 11+ reflected the social class of the residential area in which they were located. However, in some elementary schools with catchments which drew upon a variety of residential areas, the success rates among blue-collar/low-income children were higher. This led to the proposition that these children benefited from contact with strongly motivated children from 'better', more supportive home backgrounds and the overall school effect counteracted a negative social class effect. Some evidence on similar lines was provided by Robson's (1969) study of the 11+ in Sunderland. Here he saw some evidence for a neighbourhood effect, where children in residential areas with some prevalence of positive attitudes to education benefited, and concluded that attitudes of neighbouring families could be more significant than those of the objective social class. Finally, a number of major projects by Douglas (1964; Douglas *et al.* 1986) used a cohort of children born in a particular week in 1946 and monitored their progress through the educational system. With rigorous testing that included controls for intelligence by IQ tests, he still established that differences by social class were evident at primary or elementary school level and increased as pupils moved through secondary or high school. In the USA, Wilson (1959) found some evidence for both a social class and a school effect, though his methodology has been contested. In the Jencks and Mayer (1990) analysis, they concluded that growing up in a higher social class neighbourhood did raise educational attainment but that the evidence for an independent school effect was ambiguous.

The publication of school league tables in the UK in the 1990s has served to put the questions of social class and school effects into sharp focus. These league tables have state

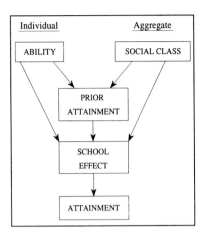

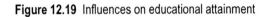

Figure 12.19 Influences on educational attainment

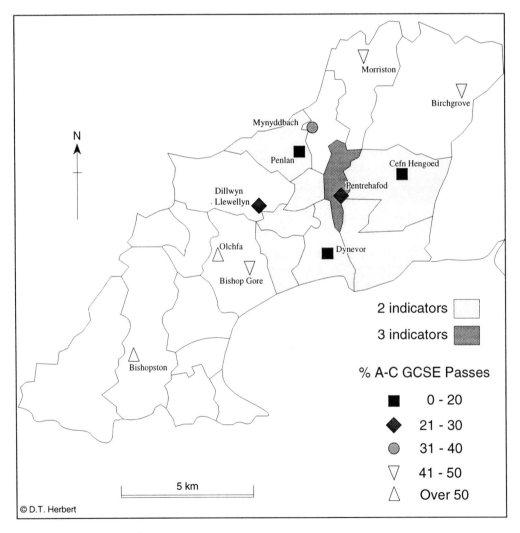

Figure 12.20 Social deprivation and school performance in Swansea, 1994

provenance and are taken as performance indicators for schools which are ranked according to the success rates of pupils entered for national examinations at the age of 16 years. Invariably, schools in the private sector with the advantage of smaller class sizes and pupil support systems record higher rates of attainment and they are closely followed by schools in the public sector which draw upon higher social class catchments. A current debate concerns the relative significance of pupil ability, school, neighbourhood and social class; Figure 12.19 summarizes this set of factors. Although the question is contested, the weight of empirical evidence points firmly towards a social class effect, as the case study contained in Figure 12.20 indicates. In Swansea, there is a close correspondence between attainment and the social class of the school catchment. The rationale is that these successful pupils have better access to home support, a more favourable set of values and aspirations, and better understood objectives. A school effect may exist but it has to be seen as secondary to the impact of social background.

In the USA, these conditions remain relevant but the main issues in high school education have been as much linked with race as with social class. From the 1950s through to at least the 1970s, the issue of school desegregation dominated the politics of education. Lowry (1973) documented the progress of events in Mississippi as devices such as 'separate but equal' and 'freedom of choice' were used by local school boards to hinder the federally driven desegregation process. As key court decisions, such as Brown versus Topeka School Board in 1954 and 1955, Alexander versus Holmes County 1969, and Swann versus Mecklenburg 1971, destroyed the bases of segregation, 'white flight' occurred with white children being taken out of the state education system to create a new kind of separation; it was reported (Evans-Pritchard 1997: 27) that 700,000 US children had been removed from the school system to be educated at home. Despite achievements of legislation, the actual success of measures to desegregate, even in state schools, is questionable. Opposition to 'busing', the main way of achieving school desegregation without residential desegregation, has had considerable success; changes in the thrust of Supreme Court decisions have had the effect of protecting white suburbs from the desegregation process. De Vise (1994) noted that forty years after the Brown versus Topeka decision, *de facto* residential and schools segregation in Chicago remained very high; the lack of school desegregation in Denver's suburbs acted as a major pull factor for white families moving into the metropolitan area (Dwyer and Sutton 1994). Basically, any ideals relating to schools and equality of opportunity cannot make substantive progress without change in the structures upon which they rest. The inequalities inherent in the structure of society will continue to be reflected in varying levels of educational attainment.

Old people in the city

There is growing evidence that elderly people are emerging as a group with distinctive social and spatial characteristics. This is a group, usually defined as people over the age of 65 years, which is growing significantly in western societies as a direct consequence of better health-care and rising standards of living. In the USA in 1900, 4.1 per cent of the population was over the age of 65 years, by 1990 this figure had risen to 12 per cent. In some ways the actual numbers are the most significant and one survey estimated 28.4 million US citizens aged 63 or over in 1976 and 36.1 million in 1991. Warnes (1994) suggested that 18.7 per cent of the British population was of pensionable age in 1991. Similar trends are evident in other

European countries but it is in less developed countries that change is likely to be dramatic. One projection indicates that by the year 2025, 14 per cent of people (1.135 million) will be aged over 60 years and 71 per cent of these will be in less developed countries.

For many older people, increased deprivation is an inevitable consequence of the ageing process and to that extent they begin to constitute a social problem. Many older people are dependants who rely on the state welfare system or a network of family to support them. Retirement from employment is the main loss of income though by no means all elderly people live at subsistence levels; the 'elderly' is not one group with uniform features, but contains as much diversity as the rest of the population. Undeniably, however, there are problems. Many old people, especially women, live alone and become marginalized in economic and social terms. There are stages within the retirement years. In the first of these there is a continuity from normal life with active lifestyles, travel and much self-fulfilment, later stages are marked by catastrophic events which increase dependency and limit this life-style. There is no simple, general chronology to these stages. Some may enter the later stages very quickly, others much later in their lives and the strongest influential factors appear to be health and morale. For simplicity, some researchers refer the stage of the 'old-old' as the over 75s or over 80s, but these are approximations.

The theories of ageing accommodate this idea of stages. Disengagement theory contends that in response to key events, such as retirement from work or loss of a partner, people may turn inwards psychologically and match this with social disengagement with normal routines. Part of the marginalization will be self-imposed and might *in extremis* lead to an excluded elderly group. Activity theory is more positive and suggests that older people will maintain former roles as long as possible despite chronological ageing. If some roles are lost, others will be substituted, and this can help compensate for changed circumstances. There is evidence that 'successful ageing' is achieved by matching the precepts of activity theory and becoming involved in a variety of roles. Continuity theory is a variant of activity theory and proposes a continuous and seamless process of substitution and adaptation, perhaps to successively less demanding activities. A less general concept is the environmental docility theory which refers to the declining ability of old people to cope with 'obstacles' in the environment. Older people are discouraged by obstacles such as busy roads, high curbs, high steps on buses, steep slopes and inadequate labels on buildings. They may forgo access to services and places if access is judged to be too difficult. A great deal can be done to ameliorate problems of this kind and a network of welfare services, with home-helps, meals-on-wheels and home delivery of medicines and other goods, does exist but is patchy in terms of provision.

Western societies have their retirement areas or places that act as retirement migration destinations. Such places are typified by environmental advantages of climate and scenery. Parts of the southern US states, such as Florida, Arizona and California, attract large numbers of retired people; western Canada, and especially Vancouver Island, has a similar function; coastal areas in the UK and parts of southern Europe such as Spain and Portugal can also be classified in this way. The idea of communal homes for elderly people dates from the medieval hospices and almshouses, but in the 1980s and 1990s developers have been active in adding to the range of residential care encouraged by the state's underwriting of fees in both the UK and the USA. Types of homes include sheltered homes, local authority homes, private residential homes, nursing homes and voluntary homes and there were about

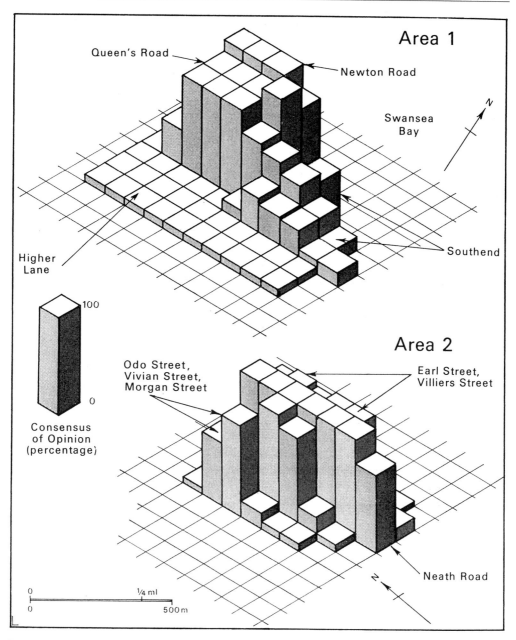

Figure 12.21 Mental maps of elderly people in Swansea

250,000 in such homes in the UK in the late 1980s, with most increase in the private sector. There are also clusters of housing provision in retirement communities, of which Sun City in Arizona is the best known example, retirement suburbs, trailer parks and some sections of 'affordable housing'. More housing, in both the private and public sector, is being dedicated to elderly people and this is creating a trend towards demographic segregation.

For many older people, retirement years are spent in the same urban environments that they have occupied in the later years of their working lives. Ageing *in situ* helps continuity and adaptation and an urban environment, rich in services and amenities, has much to offer elderly people. These will be familiar places with established networks of family, friends and recreational activities Urban environments are not uniformly hospitable. Of the near 7 million elderly people living in US inner cities, many occupy single rooms in cheap rented accommodation and here, as elsewhere, elderly people figure strongly among the residual populations of these central city areas. The poor elderly, with no means to adapt to change, are trapped in deteriorating environments, with a quality of life that is unenviable. In some of the 'problem estates' of British cities, conditions are no better and old people constantly refer to better times and the downward spiral affecting the places they live. Too often elderly people have become targets for harassment, vandalism and petty crime and have good reason to feel vulnerable.

The quality of life enjoyed by elderly people is a function of their financial soundness, their mobility, health and morale. Both quality and quantity of social relationships are important and the burden of care increasingly rests on the state and the family. By and large the popular concept of the caring community is tenuous but elderly people increasingly rely on others to provide basic needs and protection against adverse circumstances. Old people have a strong sense of local place and there are many studies that show the way in which place becomes an important but increasingly local concept. Figure 12.21 shows the mental maps of two groups of elderly people in Swansea and the overriding feature is the constraint of space. Rowles (1978) took this analysis further and showed that old people held a sort of hierarchy of places which he termed home, surveillance area, neighbourhood, and 'other city'. With increasing immobility, actual behaviour, such as trips to other places, diminished, but were substituted by drawing upon the memories or remembrances of past experiences. His idea of fantasy replaced activities with imperfectly remembered episodes from the past:

> The elderly gradually become prisoners of space. Certainly some individuals remain active and mobile into advanced old age . . . for many, physiological decline, economic deprivation and traumatising effects of rapid societal change, herald physical, social and psychological withdrawal. This . . . is accompanied by progressive reconstruction of the individual's geographical life-span and associated intensification of attachment to the proximate environmental context.
>
> (Rowles 1978: 22)

Western cities need to address the ways in which they cope with ageing populations. Are built environments designed for different generations suitable for older people? Do priorities in health-care and social welfare provision need to be readdressed? Do combinations of retirement communities and residential care provide the answers and what of the elderly poor who may fall outside these sectors? Finally, it should be remembered that elderly people should be treated on the basis of need, in the same way as the rest of the population, rather than simply on the criterion of age. But undoubtedly, the needs of older people tend to be greater as they become more dependent and their demands on health-care and welfare are much higher than the rest of the population.

CHAPTER 13

Urban trends and urban policies

The challenge of large cities

The global trend towards greater urbanization continues to dominate processes of human settlement and although not even over time and space, they have produced the large city as a worldwide phenomenon. Nearly half of the world's population, and three-quarters of those in western societies, now live in cities; between 1960 and 1992, another 1.4 billion urban dwellers were added; between 1992 and 2007, another 1 billion will follow (Parker 1995). Major metropolitan complexes of over 10 million people, such as Mexico City (15.1 million), Tokyo/Yokohama (25.0 million), New York/New Jersey (16.1 million) and Shanghai (13.5 million) are found in both developed and developing countries. There is a dynamism in urbanization that is affecting urban systems and their constituent cities in a variety of ways. Whereas advanced societies have been transformed into closely interconnected urban systems with little distinction between town and country, many Third World societies have slower rates of urbanization, more rapid urban growth and strong rural-urban differences. The challenge of large cities is being met in completely different circumstances. Countries such as India, where many of the major cities will be located, lack the capital, the technology and the organization necessary to cope with the enormous pressures of urban population growth and there are already catastrophic problems of over-concentration, poor housing and a lack of basic facilities. The former socialist 'planned' economies in eastern Europe and China occupy a broad intermediate position in which pressures of urbanization exist but have been partially controlled by the absence of free movement between rural districts and the cities. Urbanization pressures in China resemble those in the Third World societies with comparatively low levels of urbanization, 26 per cent, but with strong population controls. Central planning in China aims to harmonize urbanization with industrial and agricultural development and to spread the economic transformation across the city-size spectrum and throughout all regions, but with an estimated reservoir of over 800 million potential rural migrants and evidence of loosening control, contemporary pressures may well confound the realization of these aims. Zhao and Zhang (1995) argued that the Chinese policy of controlling city-size is at odds with the natural forces of industrialization and urbanization. At the same time, in societies where there is less control the problems still exist though they may be different in kind.

The variability of urban form

There are many differences between societies in terms of the types of cities produced by modern urbanization. Governmental roles have been different with, for example, tighter planning controls and more interventionist housing policies in UK than in the USA. In the UK, through to the late 1970s, there was a stronger welfare dimension to housing policy than was evident in a US housing market dominated by market principles. Cities are shaped by the social, economic, governmental, religious and cultural institutions of the wider society of which they are part, but there are more basic considerations such as the availability of space, the amount of inherited urban fabric, and even the 'conservatism' of the British population.

Post-industrial society is becoming increasingly characterized by very large organizations, in both private and public sectors, with people's day-to-day lives being conducted by, or for, large and impersonal bureaucratic institutions. Institutional values and decisions permeate downward through society and corporate decision-making is concentrated in a small number of 'quaternary places' (Friedmann 1995). The growth of such places may well herald a move back towards urban primacy even in the developed world, with 'world cities' acting as control centres in the international capitalist system. Knox and Taylor (1995) rehearsed the 'world city hypothesis' as a model of this evolving world-system of urban places with both global and local roles.

The interplay between 'structural' and local effects, between structure and agency, and the need to relate spatial outcomes to the macro-societal levels at which they originate, has been a theme throughout this text. This 'macro' level can be interpreted in various ways. For Walker (1978) and Harvey (1985) it was the political economy, for Dicken and Lloyd (1981) and Clegg (1996) the organization of big business and the multinational company, and for Vance (1978) the 'institution' in more diverse forms. All of these integrating themes have virtue. Whereas there is an inescapable logic in tracing inequalities in urban environments back to the political economy, there is also merit in tracing the impacts on localities of decisions made in the boardrooms of multinational companies or agencies of the state. This interplay between the global and the local has become a central feature of the globalization debate. Giddens (1990) spoke of globalization and its effects on the transformation of the texture of everyday life and Held (1995) recognized a dualism in which the local was affected by events in other parts of the world but the decisions of local groups could still have wide reverberations (see also Eade 1996).

Cross-cultural comparisons

A further outcome of attempts to integrate structural and local effects has been the addition of new dimensions to the long-established tradition of comparative studies. Such comparative studies, involving contrasted political economies, relate basic structural differences to outputs at the consumption level. They might, for example, focus on specific institutions such as housing finance and related national policies and their relevance to outcomes in local housing markets, or the ways in which different social formations lead to different health-care systems. Much of the thrust towards a better understanding of the urbanization process is emerging from analyses of various parts of the Third World with re-evaluations of theories of urbanization and uneven development.

Modernization theory

Modernization theory recognized major primate colonial cities as the centres of political and administrative power, as well as the focal points of economic control, managing the export of raw materials and the import of manufactured products. It was assumed that the pressures for development would be accommodated by a 'spread effect' from these centres.

Dependency theory

Dependency theory was based on the proposition that the colonial heritage left much of the undeveloped world in state of dependence upon the international capitalist economy with the 'siphoning' of surplus from the colonies to the external control centres rather than its use to stimulate indigenous development. With the increased internationalization of capital and globalization effects, foreign investment has focused on the labour cost advantages of Third World cities and the dependency paradigm has continuing relevance for their space economies (Gwynne 1996).

Globalization

The globalization debate now encompasses many of the divergent strands of urban economic development theory. Few parts of the world are now free from the imperatives of the global economy and the sophisticated networks of trade and business interactions, with ever more efficient information flows, support the concept of interdependence and integration. Are cities reduced to being convenient points in the global economy? Or, more likely, do they retain some autonomy as commercial centres, as economic motors and as centres of creativity and culture. Not only cities of the Third World are at risk from globalization. Dreier and Atlas (1995) stated that economic globalization had transformed the US economy from one based on high-wage industries to one reliant on low-wage services.

Dispersed urbanization

There is support for forms of 'dispersed urbanization' to promote more equitable development and an integrated space economy (McGee 1986) with urban and rural activities contained in small and intermediate urban centres. This model focuses on the commercialization of agriculture by investing in infrastructure, population control, education, health, advice and administration to promote the process of transformation (Rostam 1989). Of prime significance for individual societies are the resource base, the physical environment, the existing urban and transport infrastructure, the demographic characteristics, and ethnic and cultural considerations, along with a more refined knowledge of the manner in which growth impulses diffuse through the system of settlement (Hardoy and Satterthwaite 1986). To date the relative success of the Chinese experience of urbanization (Goldstein 1988) is at least indicative of the need for rather more Draconian policies than currently characterizes much of the Third World, though Zhao and Zhang (1995) argued that to achieve economic growth China should reverse its policies and allow cities to grow. Nagpaul (1988), in an analysis of India, called for a significant 'de-westernization' of thinking and the development of a policy for economic and social development in closer accord with indigenous conditions.

Urban outcomes

In addition to trends, processes and the effects of structural conditions, the physical and functional forms of cities and urban systems are of central importance. City region, metropolis, conurbation, megalopolis and urban region are all attempts to describe the physical expressions of the urbanization process. There is a regional component to British urbanization that reflects post-industrial economic restructuring, and it is expressed in the dynamism of southern Britain and the stagnation or decline of the old industrial regions of the north and west (Martin 1993). The urban outcome is 'megalopolitan Britain' extending throughout south-east England and characterized by 'counter-urbanization' and the integration of urban and rural areas. There are strong local trends within the larger metropolitan areas leading to the decentralization of the new employment opportunities, the decline of the traditional industries, and a heritage of inner city dereliction. Jakle and Wilson (1992) traced the causes of rising levels of dereliction in US cities to the shift of investment to suburbs, the major highway construction programmes that pulled people out of the cities, to the subsidies on home-ownership, and the 'bulldozer' urban renewal schemes. The 'inner city problem' still represents a major challenge for contemporary society and the disparities continue to grow.

There was a regional shift in the USA associated with the decline of the north-east seaboard (the original megalopolis) and the mid-west, and the rise of the 'Sunbelt' with its new metropolitan areas. Urban decentralization became a marked feature accentuating economic, social and political divisions between the inner city and outer suburbs. These trends have at times typified much of western Europe, though always with regional variations (Cheshire and Hay 1989), but during the 1990s many larger European cities have shown a remarkable turn-around (Robson 1994) with the return of population growth to their cores. This urban renaissance has much to do with the rise of the 'competitive city', by no means confined to continental Europe, where cities develop an entrepreneurial style and forms of 'boosterism' or place promotion to great effect. This may involve joint ventures between public and private sectors, local economic strategies, marketing of cities as places of heritage, culture or entertainment, and the forging of networks. Cities compete for grand projects from Millennium funds in the UK, for prestigious events such as the Olympics, for designations such as City of Culture. For Robson (1994) all of this pointed to the role of the 'city as forum' – meeting place, exhibition place and base for information and high-level services.

The characteristic features of urbanization in advanced industrial societies in the late twentieth century are their increasingly dispersed regional forms and socio-economic disparities. Future trends will reflect emerging 'green issues' such as the conservation of energy and land, and pollution controls, and the thrust towards sustainable cities, along with the needs of social and spatial equity. Policies for urban containment allied with social integration are likely to remain for urban systems at all levels. The details of the process of change, however, will reflect the nature and strength of control exerted by central governments. By contrast, Third World urbanization appears posed to create more and larger cities and the attendant urban environmental problem of over-concentration is likely to become marked (Dogan and Kasarda 1988), with economic and social problems reaching a critical level.

Planning and policies in the western city

As urbanization has progressed in the western world, so the interventionist roles of the state, at various levels, became more evident. In some respects the two trends may be only loosely connected but the growth of cities both exaggerates existing problems and creates new ones. There are associated increases in crime rates, pollution levels and traffic congestion, and conflicts arise between alternative users of scarce land resources. Urban policies are needed to cope with inequalities and their local environmental expressions, to manage land and the uses to which it is put, to organize flows of traffic and to impose standards and controls on urban development. In a more fiscal and administrative sense, large cities have problems of government which often require centralized direction. The experience of western societies suggests that planning is a necessary activity and particularly so if any kind of welfare criteria are accepted. These ideals were compromised in the UK in the 1980s and 1990s with reduction of public expenditure, diminution in the powers of local government, and the diminished effectiveness of the welfare state (Blackman 1995).

Geography and urban policy

Urban geography has a long association with the practice of planning and a formulation of urban policies that has generally assumed descriptive and positive roles – providing factual surveys and manipulating models under specified ideal conditions – rather than a normative role which advocates the kind of action needed to produce the best results. There has been a close involvement in physical planning programmes concerned with issues such as urban reconstruction, development control, and land-use arrangements within cities. This type of physical planning, aimed at creating a better environment which, it was believed, would in turn create a better society was especially marked in the UK following the Town and Country Planning Act 1947. There are parallels elsewhere and the concept of the geographer/planner as a career path has become established in several parts of the world. There are other forms of physical planning and design in which geographers have both a strong academic interest and some involvement. Peter Hall (1988) traced the great movements in architecture, planning and design which have progressively changed the face of cities. The City Beautiful movement had expression in nineteenth-century Europe with the boulevards of Paris and Vienna and the great monuments of the capital cities. In the USA, the 1892 Chicago Exhibition stimulated a classical revival in the design of cities and strengthened the cultural dimension of museums, galleries and theatres. Architects such as Le Corbusier and Frank Lloyd Wright had major impacts on the form of cities and planners like Howard, Geddes and Perry brought about new towns and neighbourhood planning. In modern times, highways have transformed cities and the new malls and 'palaces of consumption' become the icons of a post-modern world.

Concerns with natural resources and environmental quality provided another bridge with planning. Cities had clear ecological consequences and issues such as air pollution and flood hazard became of central significance and in need of control. In his review of issues of sustainability in Third World cities, Drakakis-Smith (1995) examined the links between macro- and micro-levels of policy. At the macro-level there are considerations of equity, social justice, basic human needs, self-determination and environmental awareness; at the micro-level, there are specific areas of concern such as the economy, the 'brown agenda' of the physical environment, pollution, waste disposal and recycling, human rights and population change. In western cities, as discussed, Agenda 21 has already begun to influence urban policies albeit in fragmented ways.

Urban planning has established concerns with movement patterns, emphasizing flows and their relationships with land-use arrangements and urban structure, and resulting in the development of models of urban systems which linked movement and land-use (Batty 1978). These efforts exemplify urban geographers in their positive roles and involved mathematical modelling. Work on such models continues but with a diminishing influence on policy-making as the need to match decisions to realities gains precedence. Two related types of models stimulated a great deal of research and application. The first of these was 'optimal location models', or the identification of 'ideal' sites for new urban facilities, and the second was 'optimal regionalization', or the identification of territories or sub-regions within the city which best serve a specific administrative or social welfare purpose.

Spatial analysis and urban policy

Problems of urban education exemplify policy-oriented research using spatial models. Programming models could be used to determine optimal locations for high schools in the USA. The terms of reference for the model were to provide locations for new schools and to allocate students in such a way that the cost of transporting all students to schools was minimized. As constraints on the model, each school was allocated a maximum capacity, an upper and lower limit of black and white students, and the number of new schools to be constructed was specified. Locational algorithms of this kind can be programmed to satisfy various criteria and they are heavily conditioned by these initial assumptions or priorities. Centrographic models seek the 'minimum' point or centre of gravity in a distribution; other types of models seek locations which involve the smallest number of links between nodes on a network, or are designed to ensure that no individual is more than a specified distance from a school. Most models of this kind are strongly based on accessibility criteria and have been widely applied to identify optimal locations for a range of public utility and health services (Massam 1993; Bullen et al. 1996). Other models incorporated a service utilization behavioural dimension (Wrigley 1988) and Multi-Criteria Decision Making (MCDM) techniques in operational research influenced the evaluation of alternative planning policies. Planning aims are converted to a range of data-based evaluative criteria which are then incorporated into a decision-making framework which includes the opinions of alternative interest groups (Massam 1993). Problems tackled in this way include the site selection of public utilities, route alignments of motorways, and the priority rating of competing expenditure. With the advent of Geographical Information Systems (GIS), a major new dimension has been added to the quantitative analysis of urban problems and basic record-keeping within planning departments. This is of major significance and will bring geographical method central to another part of the planning process. In more statistical terms, multilevel modelling allows the interrelationship between various scales of data to be investigated and again has considerable application to planning issues.

Urban education issues can also be used to exemplify the application of systematic regionalization techniques. The need to consider alternative strategies for decentralizing high school administration has led to exercises specifying the required number of areas, a target number of school boards, and a desired size-range of between 25,000 and 50,000 students. The algorithm produced a large number of possible amalgamations which could be reduced by applying further constraints of contiguity, shape and level of ethnic mix. Eventual outcomes of exercises of this kind are often guided as much by political considerations as by the options presented by the model. For example, regionalization procedures which employ basically spatial criteria to minimize distance travelled will typically produce compact 'neighbourhood' catchment areas. As the school population will then mirror residential segregation, this outcome is at odds with policies designed to 'integrate' children along either ethnic or social class lines.

Urban planning and local governance

The progress of urban development has generated the need for state intervention at a variety of spatial scales. The relationship between the scale of urban growth and the nature of state intervention is, however, not necessarily close and is as much a reflection of a particular form of political economy as a response to urban growth (see Chapter 6). Historically, the impact of planning and state intervention on urban development has been much greater in the UK than the USA, but urban concentration both exaggerates existing problems and creates new ones. Conflicts arise over scarce land resources, traffic congestion increases and housing obsolescence, pollution and social problems result from the combined effects of time and economic and social change. As large cities portray society's inequalities in stark relief, there are problems of organization and control that require formal institutions to manage in an efficient way.

In advanced capitalist societies a number of recurrent trends have been identified which have been of central concern for urban planning (see Chapter 5):

- Uneven regional economic development in the post-industrial era has been a pervasive theme with major negative impacts on the older manufacturing areas in peripheral locations.
- Pressures for decentralization and counter-urbanization have been strong within the growing urban regions which have benefited from new service economies and modern high-tech industrial development. Here, urban growth has generated pressures for city-regional forms of planning control.
- Deindustrialization in the older inner cities has created pockets of economic decline, a heritage of environmental dereliction and housing obsolescence, and the social problems associated with the emergence of a disaffected, and often ethnically distinct, underclass.

- The problems of the inner city find parallels in the worst of the social housing estates. The so-called sink-estates suffer from a whole range of malaise including high unemployment, vandalism, crime, drugs and a much weakened family life.
- Parts of central cities in growing urban regions have undergone regeneration. This has involved the development of high status producer service employment and the expansion of tourism, leisure entertainment and specialist shopping activities, along with pockets of gentrification and high status residential development. This has accentuated social polarization in the inner city.
- For McLain (1995), the urban crisis of the city was violence. Cities in the USA were being overwhelmed by waves of assault and homicides, often drug-related. Homicide was the main cause of death for black males aged 15–24 and black females aged 25–44; an 'entire generation of black youth was being wiped out'.

Since the mid-1960s, the urban geographical literature has often contained policy implications aimed at 'improvement' and usually incorporating economic and social equity considerations. Planning is implicit at all spatial scales, often in the 'liberal democratic' or 'welfarist' tradition of economic control. Ideally, the principal role of central government is to identify clear national policy directives for economic change. In the UK and the rest of western Europe, there is a lobby for a strong regional apparatus, principally designed to redress regional economic imbalances. These are complemented by forms of local government control, responsible for the efficient organization of the economic, social, environmental and functional characteristics of the city. A degree of consensus exists on the operational advantages of a 'city-regional' form of local government articulated in relation to 'labour-market' areas, with a localized 'community' level to allow more effective public participation.

In reality, economic imperatives have progressively reduced the significance of 'public' control over the urban development process. In a context of increasing global economic competition, national economies in advanced capitalist countries have tended towards anti-inflationary and monetarist policies of the sort initiated by the 'Thatcherite' governments in the UK and by President Reagan in the USA during the 1980s. This has resulted in a reduction in public sector investment in social welfare policies and planning, and the replacement of the Keynesian mode of economic control by a 'neo-liberal' regulatory environment dominated by private enterprise. Such policies have tended to dismantle the 'local state' and to replace it with a broader conception of 'local governance'. The power of local government has been reduced relative to complex combination of public, private and voluntary agencies responsible for service provision, while the importance of market forces and 'quangos' have also grown progressively in importance (see Chapter 6). At the same time, there has been a tendency towards the relaxation of planning controls to stimulate the market economy.

The UK was a particularly strong advocate of such policies under a Conservative government. Economic growth was the priority and social welfare expenditure was curtailed, paralleled by a loss of confidence in the effectiveness of regional economic development policies. There is now a greater reliance on free-market forces to redress the regional economic imbalances. Disparities associated with the north-south divide have continued into the 1990s, despite a significant degree of inward investment in new forms of manufacturing in the peripheral regions (Martin 1993) and academic opinion continues to support the reinstatement of strong 'local agencies' to reduce the imbalances (see Chapter 5). The disadvantageous economic situation of peripheral region throughout western Europe is a reflection of non-interventionist neo-liberal economic policies (Dunford and Perrons 1994) and the need for planned programmes of public expenditure to initiate economic restructuring is being advocated.

A similar situation exists at the urban scale. There is widespread support in planning circles for a strong 'city or metropolitan regional' scale of local government. Arguably, however, the functional logic of strong city regional government for the delivery of efficient urban planning is being confounded by the pressures exerted by global economic competition and the political responses of national governments. Most advanced capitalist countries have moved some way towards a reduction of the power of local government.

In the context of the British inner city problem, for example, Robson (1988) indicated that the impressive array of policy initiatives has been more than offset by sweeping cutbacks in public expenditure. Similarly, the intermittent relaxation of restrictions on retail decentralization has undermined investment confidence in the traditional city centres (Chapter 8). Transport planners stress that the 'suppressed demand' for car-borne trips in cities will obstruct solutions, based upon a combination of road improvements and commercially based public transport systems, to the problem of transport congestion. Strategies restraining the use of private vehicles and supporting 'subsidized' public transport and 'urban containment' are advocated but are difficult to implement without sufficient public funds (Chapter 7).

Insights into the relationship between urban planning and local governance in Toronto (Filion 1996) have some generality. Urban planning in the Greater Toronto Area has maintained a compact urban region with relatively high levels of public transport use, a healthy inner city, and a strong central business district. The reduction of public sector expenditure over recent years has lessened the likelihood that planning will be able to deliver the bolder post-modern ideals of more public participation and a heightened environmental sensitivity. Using regulation theory to examine the institutional influences, Filion identified a consensus of post-modern planning ideals among the planning institutions in the urban region. There was widespread support for sustaining the quality of the urban environment. Ideally, this would involve maintaining a compact urban form by reurbanizing vacant inner city sites and promoting nodal development at the periphery, both of which would maximize the potential for public transport and reduce car use. However, insufficient public sector finance to initiate developments and to create a stronger metropolitan-wide institutional framework has produced a divergence between these ideals and emerging patterns of urban development.

Regional economic planning is needed to perform a coordinating function by promoting access to central government and a responsiveness to local conditions. The value of metropolitan area planning for coherent policies which avoid the problems of fiscal dislocation between inner cities and suburbs has been widely demonstrated (Chapter 6). However, in a post-industrial economic environment the involvement of private capital in public-private development partnerships has become vital to successful developments and effective planning at both the regional and urban scales. The ideal, therefore, might be a planning system strongly organized via public agencies offering firm 'control' and 'direction', but at the same time able to work cooperatively and effectively with the private sector. This implies the reinstatement of the 'local state', which, arguably, flies in the face of the contemporary economic circumstances, but the 'dismantling' of the local state is neither universal nor immutable. The European Union, for example, is committed to the development of regional institutions to redress regional disparities and there are examples of effective city regional forms of urban government in Metro Toronto and the Tokyo Metropolitan Region. The essence is an effective balance between public and private control over urban and regional development for the overall economic and social good of contemporary societies.

Area policies and urban renewal

Studies of residential differentiation generated a policy interest in local concentrations of urban deprivation. A parallel literature on social indicators and levels of living has developed territorial social indicators which have been used to identify areas which have been considered to warrant special policies and resource allocation. Area policies and the related concept of positive discrimination are closely related research themes. The content of area policies varies considerably from improvements to the physical environment to economic regeneration and social infrastructure development, and they are now used widely where the emergence of a disadvantaged 'underclass' in inner cities and some suburbs, usually exhibiting a potent mix of economic, social, ethnic and racial problems, is a characteristic feature. The decline of the older manufacturing industries had major negative impacts on the economic and social conditions of the inner cities and lower status communities throughout most advanced western economies. The shift from an industrial to a post-industrial society resulted in concentrations of industrial dereliction, deterioration of the residential environment, and economic and social dislocation in inner cities and industrial suburbs, particularly in economically peripheral regions. In the absence of short-term solutions to the problems posed by structural change, area based initiatives were initially used to enhance the physical and housing conditions of the most deprived communities. Subsequently, with the development of a deeper recognition of the complexities of the problem, policies have been broadened to combine physical, social and economic dimensions which aim to develop conditions designed to assist the process of economic and social regeneration in the future.

The interest of the Ford Foundation in the USA in the 1950s with the problems of metropolitan government and inner city research was an early response. The 'grey areas' programme funded research in parts of selected cities such as Oakland and Boston; federal programmes as part of the subsequent 'War on Poverty' legislation similarly focused on inner city districts; while the Housing and Urban Development Office (HUD) sponsored Urban Initiatives in the 1970s.

Similar area-based policies in the UK focused initially on the physical dimension of housing deprivation and involved both clearance and improvement. This focus was perpetuated with the Housing Acts of 1969 and 1974 which introduced the policies of General Improvement Areas (GIAs) and Housing Action Areas (HAAs). GIAs were intended to concentrate assistance through grants to householders, and to local authorities for general environmental enhancement. However, the HAA concept initiated an important policy shift in a social direction. Funding was targeted more definitively towards the alleviation of social stress in highly localized areas defined by indices such as overcrowding, with the aim of upgrading both the physical environment and the related social conditions. Comparable area based policies were being developed contemporaneously for education in deprived communities. The 1967 Plowden Report was initially concerned with primary schools, but its examination of the relationship between urban deprivation and educational disadvantage had far-reaching effects (Central Advisory Council for Education 1967). Deprived areas were identified in which inadequate schooling facilities combined with poor home backgrounds to produce disadvantage. Territorial social indicators, of which the Inner London Education Authority (ILEA) ten-point index was the most widely cited, were used to define Education Priority Areas (EPAs) for the targeting of positive financial discrimination. A similar situation was reflected in the health-care delivery system (Chapter 8). From the mid-1970s the Resource Allocation Working Party of the National Health Service redirected funding to those regions with the highest levels of adverse health indices, while additional financial inducements have also been available to general practitioners working in deprived areas.

These early initiatives culminated in the development of a more broadly based 'Urban Aid' programme to assist areas exhibiting multiple deprivation. The Inner Areas Act 1978, for example, established partnerships between local authority and central government departments for the regeneration of the inner cities of the major conurbations. The early investment of £40 million in 1977–78 was rapidly increased to £300 million in 1986–7, while during the same period a plethora of additional spatial targeting initiatives increasingly involving both the public and private sectors were instituted. These included Derelict Land Grants, Urban Development Grants, Urban Renewal Grants, Commercial and Industrial Improvement Areas, Enterprise Zones, Simplified Planning Zones, Urban Development Corporations, Partnership and Programme Authorities, Task Forces, and City Action Teams, together extending the overall budget to over £2 billion per annum (Robson 1988).

However, the degree of central government financial commitment necessary for urban regeneration had, by the mid-1980s, come increasingly into conflict with pressures exerted by international economic competition and an associated political commitment to reduce levels of public expenditure. In the inner London boroughs, for example, the reduction in the Rate Support Grant was equivalent to five times the investment in the Urban Programme in the period 1979–84. In the context of the 'Urban Aid' programme the problem was exacerbated by an increasingly damaging political divergence between the Conservative Government and Labour controlled local government in the inner cities which resulted in the abolition of the metropolitan counties in 1986, and with it the attendant loss of their potential coordinating function. Consequently, from the early 1980s Robson (1988) suggested that coordination of the various policy initiatives had not been achieved, while the level of investment has not been consistent with the need created by the required scale of industrial restructuring and the problems associated with the inheritance of outmoded infrastructure.

This assessment is consistent with subsequent events. Urban policy in the 1990s has continued to suffer from declining public expenditure, while the 1991 Census indicated that the inner cities had continued to lose population leaving concentrations of the 'urban poor', characterized by unemployed people, lone parents, the ill-housed elderly and ethnic minorities (Robson 1994). These communities continue to suffer from the problems of economic collapse and social dislocation, while high levels of criminality, drug abuse and intermittent disorder were endemic in these areas. A lack of coordination between agencies continues to be evident; the participation of the local communities in the regeneration process has been minimal; and the ethnic minorities have obtained only limited benefits (Robson *et al.* 1993). Nevertheless, urban policy evaluation has not been entirely negative. Modest employment generation has been evident in some of the smaller cities, while the City Challenge schemes initiated in the early 1990s have demonstrated the positive visionary potential of public-private sector coalitions for the economic regeneration of inner cities. European Union resources have also assisted the process, particularly as they are subject to less stringent restrictions, and have, consequently, encouraged strategic thinking in the redevelopment process.

Overall, however, the principal effects of urban policy in the UK has been essentially infrastructural, bringing derelict land back into use and providing shopping centres, leisure facilities, conference centres and transport, while local communities continued to be marginalized by the regeneration process. Thus, Robson (1994) suggested that while the area-based initiatives have now provided some of the economic pre-conditions necessary for urban regeneration, central government has to develop far stronger social policy initiatives if the problems of the inner city are to be redressed. This will require the reinstatement of a politically 'unfashionable' 'welfarist' perspective, the reinvolvement of the 'community' in a process of 'participatory democracy', and a comprehensive policy incorporating 'consistency and compassion'. In the absence of such initiatives, the current area-based policies are likely, at best, to be palliatives rather than solutions to the social problems of the inner city.

A similar situation has developed in the USA. In the 1970s the solution to urban problems was increasingly seen to be based on private sector initiatives, with a shift away from Federal programmes involving assistance to cities and a redistribution of wealth to the poor. However, while success has been achieved in the central business districts of the more fortuitously located cities such as Baltimore and Pittsburgh, the 'market' has not resolved the social problems of the wider areas of the inner cities, particularly in the regions suffering the worst effects of deindustrialization. The urban poor remain largely separated from the regeneration process. In fact, it is now widely considered that Federal programmes such as the Model Cities Programme and the financing of Urban Enterprise Zones in well-defined 'poverty areas' have been insufficient to resolve the problems. Instead, a far stronger Federal involvement in partnership with private enterprise is considered necessary if a significant move towards a greater degree of socio-spatial equity is to result. Stegman (1995) believed that after twenty years of job losses and fiscal stress, US inner cities had lost their capacity to create good jobs and generate robust economic opportunities for those with less than a college education.

Inner city decline also developed in France, Germany, Belgium and the Netherlands in the 1970s. However, the problem has not generally been as great because the environmental dereliction associated with early industrialization was less extensive; a heritage of a greater variety of higher density residential areas combined with a less marked racial dimension of inner city decline have presented fewer obstacles to the regeneration process. Consequently, a range of area-based policies have since the late 1980s achieved a greater measure of success

(Parkinson *et al.* 1993), although it was also considered that the more consistent strategic use of a combination of strategies was an important contributory factor. These included joint ventures between local government and the private sector, often involving higher education institutions; the development of economic strategies based on local advantages; and the marketing of the cities offering high quality environments, entertainment and service facilities. The coordinating activities of the Hamburg Business Development Corporation comprising representatives from the City, major banks and the Chamber of Commerce were considered particularly instructive in this respect.

Area policies now form an important element of urban planning strategies in most parts of the world. Urban geography has contributed much to such policies through its traditional research roles of defining regions, identifying boundaries and describing internal structure. However, irrespective of the criticisms of specific area-based policies, the principle of positive discrimination has been subject to widespread scrutiny. A recurring theme has been that the 'disadvantaged' living outside designated policy areas do not benefit from the targeting of resources. This has prompted an ongoing debate focusing on the distinction between 'people poverty versus place poverty' (Knox 1989).

Strong counter-arguments, however, occur. Johnston (1992b), for example, suggested that concentration *per se* in the inner city of the USA of criminality, poor schooling, or the displacement of these areas from new suburban job opportunities can accentuate the effect of inherently disadvantageous conditions. In effect, the cycle of poverty is characterized as a problem of as well as in the city. Thus, area-based policies can be justified on economic grounds since, for example, the costs of riots resulting from the concentration of the disaffected and alienated might be avoided, while the targeting of scarce resources towards adverse conditions is likely to be most cost-effective. Clearly, area-based policies relating to environmental, economic and social conditions are insufficient in themselves to resolve the problems of the inner city, but need to be supplemented by wider policies which address the root causes of the problems. Nevertheless, many forms of deprivation are locally concentrated and will continue to require spatially based investigation and policies. Robson (1994), in his evaluation of British urban policy saw positive benefits from both public expenditure and the public-private partnerships. Whereas there had been a lack of strategic thinking and financial priorities, area-based schemes had often been the most effective. Fainstein and Fainstein (1995) urged a US urban policy that focused on job creation, job retention, less racial isolation and a coherent mix of economic, physical and social initiatives.

Community action and community care

Despite some revival in the concept of individualism during the 1980s, issues of citizenship, community involvement and public participation have been recognized for some time. The 1969 Skeffington Report in the UK was specifically concerned with public participation in planning and its recommendations affected local procedures. Smith (1980) argued that the re-emergence of neighbourhoods as a basis for the decentralization of problem-solving and service provision represented an implicit belief that localism and smallness are associated with a higher quality of life. There is less evidence for these community movements in the UK but the Community Councils and Community Health Councils established as part of local government and health administrative reform in 1974 have promoted a move in the same direction. There continues to be an impetus for community organization from within communities themselves. In the UK, the Community Organizing movement has appeared in several large cities as a reaction against a 'chaotic privatized future' with extremes of wealth and poverty and a belief that people feel safer in organized networks and communities (Stokes and Knight 1997). Blackman (1995) saw the need for the public sector to adjust to a situation in which empowerment and citizens' charters were becoming the icons of good practice. However, while the need for a local community perspective should be addressed as an ongoing project, economic stringency combined with increasingly centralized controls has often redirected academic attention more strongly towards forms of crisis management (Curtis 1989; Mohan 1989).

The 'caring community' provides another avenue for policy-orienated research, particularly in relation to elderly and mentally-ill people. The 'medical model' of care has been rejected for all but the most difficult of personal situations due to the damaging health effects associated with inappropriate placements and the inflexibility of the kinds of care offered in an institutionalized environment (Warnes 1989). 'Normalization' is the attempt, to accommodate elderly persons in their own homes and to integrate mentally-ill people into communities in which people live normal day-to-day lives. This has involved a variety of innovations and experiments in domiciliary social and nursing support services. Voluntary agencies can help only those at the 'bottom of the pile and turn away far more people than those to whom they can offer some kind of care' (White 1989).

The economic value of such policies, which tackle the 'bottomless pit' of health-care, has received wide acclaim, but the policy is fraught with difficulties. Adequate community care can be as costly as institutional care and the burden shifts from state to family, with no assurance that 'caring community' will work. White (1989) estimated that there were 6 million people in the UK caring for sick, disabled or elderly relatives on a voluntary basis. To the special cases of elderly and mentally-ill people who are vulnerable, and to the provision of social and health-care services can be added the rising tide of the homeless and the failure of housing services. Fainstein and Fainstein (1995) viewed neighbourhood based initiatives as inadequate in the face of the economic effects of globalization and the flight of capital. 'Just as firms are required to pay the clear-up costs of environmental pollution, they should assume the costs of community abandonment'(Fainstein and Fainstein 1995: 631).

Social justice and welfare

Optimal locations and regions, area policies, and community-based action are elements of a broad strategy to achieve a more equitable distribution of resources in space. There have been attempts to mould these strands into a general theory and the concept of territorial social justice (Smith 1994). David Smith traced urban geography's concerns with relevance, inequalities and moral geographies and argued that the time had come for a re-engagement of the discipline with ethics, morality and social justice. The term 'social justice' was taken to embrace both fairness and equity in the distribution of goods and services; it involved treating people rightly or fairly in a variety of ways. Empirically both needs and provisions are measurable, at least through aggregate indices, although conceptually a 'just distribution' is more difficult to articulate. Early studies were concerned with ways in which the allocation of resources to one territory affected conditions in another. The idea of externalities was an important concept with residential locations determining access to both 'goods' and 'bads' and leading, potentially, to conflicts in the urban environment. Harvey (1973) identified need, contribution to the common good and merit as the components of social justice. Areas of special difficulty with an accumulation of social deprivation may justify positive discrimination to achieve these qualities. Territorial social justice, in many ways a derivation of the area policy, emerged as a mechanism for resource-distribution to accommodate externalities and other inter-area effects and respond to areas of special disadvantage.

David Smith's (1977) ideas on a geography of human welfare run parallel with concepts such as social justice and the just distribution of resources. His attempt to redefine human geography as the study of 'who gets what, where, and how' rested on the premise that welfare themes permeate the whole of human geography. For Smith, the scope of human geography can be summarized as:

- description or the empirical identification of territorial levels of well-being
- explanation or the study of cause and effect, the origins of patterns
- evaluation or judgement on the desirability of alternative geographical states, the form of desired distributions
- prescription or the statement of policies needed to achieve change
- implementation or the assuming of roles needed to carry through policies for change.

This remains a useful framework for action and many urban geographers both by their research and by their actual involvement in key areas of urban decision-making have followed its precepts. As David Smith concluded, the main message is that geographers should return to the theme of social justice in both theory and practice:

> Without a better sense of the value of normative theory, without more willingness to enter the politics of prescription, geography is powerless to challenge the subtle ideologies that legitimise enduring social inequalities.
>
> (Smith, 1994: 72)

Summary and conclusions

Urban geography has eclectic qualities as practitioners pursue different methodologies towards diverse ends. In one sense this demonstrates the ability to develop new paradigms, but in another it creates problems that require resolution.

First, there is the central issue of whether an urban geography remains a recognizable and viable field for study. The traditional focus of urban geography as a kind of regional geography at the urban scale with its quest for the elusive synthesis and its overwhelming breadth continues to hold interest, at least at an introductory level. Also the notion of studying the city in a holistic way, with as much emphasis on interrelationships as on separate strands, has considerable modern relevance.

The second issue involves the kind of role which urban geographers can fill in the fields of policy and decision-making in the last part of the twentieth century. The spectrum of possibilities is wide and includes traditional descriptive roles, classifications of land-use, portrayal through indicators of the extent of people's inhumanity, prescription of ameliorative policies which 'positively discriminate' under a general umbrella of socio-spatial justice or welfare; or advocacy of radical reform from a belief that inequality will continue, and this is a proper course. There is room for the descriptive fact-finding and the evaluative model-building. There is also room, and must be, for a range of beliefs among urban geographers which leads them towards analysis of economic and social problems from different assumptions and towards different views of what a better society might be. Some may criticize society from a fundamental belief that the whole order is wrong, others may criticize but will have a far different view of the extent of the malaise or of the scale of necessary change. Evidence so far suggests that if the choice is between evolutionary change within the framework of existing institutions or revolutionary change which overthrows existing orders, most urban geographers by sentiment are very firmly committed to the former of these paths.

A final and cautionary note first sounded by Hare (1974) remains valid today. He argued that in the development of major policy issues there are no real experts, things are too complex and interconnected for 'expert' views to be accepted without question. Academic disciplines and public policy-making were seen as separate and distinctive domains, geography as a discipline is largely irrelevant, and effective individual commitment by a geographer is more important than the general application of geography itself. Urban geography must properly seek to extend its contribution to the study of problems and the formulation of policies, but in the end it is likely to be one contribution among others and rarely a specific solution in itself. As a field of study, however, urban geography remains both definable and dynamic and capable of producing students well grounded in the understanding or urban patterns, processes, problems, prescriptions and policies.

References

Abrams, C. (1964) *Man's Struggle for Shelter in an Urbanizing World.* Cambridge, Mass.: MIT Press.

Abu-Lughod, J. L. (1961) 'Migrant adjustment to city life: the Egyptian case', *American Journal of Sociology*, 67, 22–32.

Adams, C. T. (1990) 'Housing policy', in A. Heidenheimer, H. Heclo and C. T. Adams (eds) *Comparative Public Policy*. New York: St Martin's Press.

Albrow, M. (1997) 'Travelling beyond local cultures: socio-scapes in a global city', in J. Eade (ed.) *Living in the Global City: Globalization as a Local Process*. London: Routledge, 37–55.

Alexander, I. and Dawson, J. A. (1979) 'Suburbanization of retailing sales and employment in Australian cities', *Australian Geographical Studies*, 17, 76–83.

Alihan, M. (1938) Social Ecology. New York: Columbia University Press.

Allan, G. A. (1979) *A Sociology of Friendship and Kinship*, London: Allen and Unwin.

Alonso, W. (1963) *Location and Land-Use*, Cambridge, Mass.: Harvard University Press.

Amin, A. and Thrift, N. (1995) 'Globalisation, institutional "thickness" and the local economy', in P. Healey *et al.* (eds) *Managing Cities: The New Urban Context*. Chichester: Wiley, 91–108.

Ampe, F. (1995) 'Technopole development in Euralille', in D. Banister (ed.) *Transport and Urban Development*, London: E & FN Spon, 128–35.

Anderson, E. (1978) *A Place on the Corner.* Chicago: University of Chicago Press.

Anderson, K. and Gale, F. (1992) *Inventing Places: Studies in Cultural Geography*. Melbourne: Longman Cheshire.

Angotti, T. (1993) *Metropolis 2000. Planning, Poverty and Politics.* London: Routledge.

Aponte, R. (1991) 'Urban Hispanic poverty, disaggregations and explanations', *Social Problems* 38, 516–28.

Badcock, B. (1984) *Unfairly Structured Cities*, Oxford: Basil Blackwell.

Badcock, B. (1995) 'Building upon the foundations of gentrification: inner city housing development in Australia in the 1990s', *Urban Geography* 16, 70–90.

Baldwin, J. and Bottoms, A. E. (1976) *The Urban Criminal.* London: Tavistock.

Banarjee, T. and Baer, W. C. (1984) *Beyond the Neighbourhood Unit: Residential Environments and Public Policy.* New York: Plenum.

Banister, D. (ed.) (1995) *Transport and Urban Development.* London: E & FN Spon.

Barber, J. (1993) 'Why bother subsidizing suburban transit routes?', *Toronto Globe and Mail* 27 July.

Barke, M. and Turnbull, J. (1992) *Meadowell: The Biography of an 'Estate with Problems'.* Aldershot: Avebury.

Barlow, I. M. (1991) *Metropolitan Government.* London: Routledge.

Barnett, J. R. and Kearns, R. A. (1996) 'Shopping around? Consumerism and the use of private accident and medical clinics in Auckland, New Zealand', *Environment and Planning A* 28, 1053–1075.

Bartelt, D., Elesh, D., Goldstein, I., Lean, G. and Yancey, W. (1987) 'Islands in the stream: neighbourhoods and the political economy of the city', in I. Altman and A. Wandersman (eds) *Neighbourhoods and Community Environment*. New York: Plenum, 1163–89.

Batty, M. (1978) 'Urban models in the planning process', in D. T. Herbert and R. J. Johnston (eds) *Geography and the Urban Environment*, vol. 1. London: Wiley, 63–134.

Beck, A. and Willis, A. (1995) *Crime and Security: Managing the Risk to Safe Shopping.* Leicester: Perpetuity Press.

Bell, C. R. and Newby, H. (1978) 'Community, communion, class and community action: the social sources of the new urban politics', in D. T. Herbert and R. J. Johnston (eds) *Social Areas in Cities.* London: Wiley, 283–301.

Bell, D. (1974) *The Coming of Post-Industrial Society.* London: Heinemann.

Bennison, D. J. and Davies, R. L. (1980) 'The impact of town centre shopping schemes in Britain: their impact on traditional retail environments', *Progress in Planning* 14, 1–104.

Berry, B. J. L. (1961) 'City size distributions and economic development', *Economic Development and Cultural Change* 9, 573–87.

Berry, B. J. L. (1973a) *The Human Consequences of Urbanisation.* London: Macmillan.

Berry, B. J. L. (1973b) *Growth Centers in the American Urban System*, 2 volumes. Cambridge, Mass.: Ballinger.

Berry, B. J. L. (1976) 'The counterurbanization process: urban America since 1970', in B. J. L. Berry (ed.) *Urbanization and Counterurbanization.* New York: Sage.

Berry, B. J. L. (1980) 'Inner city futures: an American dilemma revisited', *Transactions, Institute of British Geographers* NS5, 1–28.

Berry, B. J. L. (1991) *Urban Growth in the United States and Kondratieff Cycles: Long-wave Rhythms in Economic Development and Political Behaviour.* Baltimore, Md: Johns Hopkins Press.

Berry, B. J. L., Barnum, H. G. and Tennant, R. J. (1962) 'Retail location and consumer behaviour', *Papers and Proceedings of the Regional Science Association* 9, 65–106.

Berry B. J. L., Simmons, J. W. and Tennant, R. J. (1963) *Commercial Structure and Commercial Blight*, Research Paper no. 85. Department of Geography, University of Chicago, Chicago.

Blackman, T. (1995) *Urban Policy in Practice.* London: Routledge.

Bloch, P. H., Ridgway, N. M. and Dawson, S. A. (1994) 'The shopping mall as consumer habitat,' *Journal of Retailing* 70, 23–42.

Blomquist, W. and Parks, R. B. (1995) 'Unigov: local government in Indianapolis and Marion County, Indiana', in L. J. Sharpe (ed.) *The Government of World Cities: The Future of the Metro Model.* Chichester: Wiley, 77–89.

Boal, F. W. (1969) 'Territoriality on the Shankill/Falls divide', *Irish Geography* 6, 30–50.

Boal, F. W. (1978) 'Ethnic residential segregation', in D. T. Herbert and R. J. Johnston (eds) *Social Areas in Cities.* London: Wiley, 57–95.

Boal, F. W. (1987) 'Segregation', in M. Pacione (ed.) *Social Geography: Progress and Prospect.* London: Croom Helm.

Boal, F. W., Doherty, P. and Pringle, D. G. (1978) *Social Problems in the Belfast Urban Area: An Exploratory Analysis*, Occasional Paper no.12. Department of Geography, Queen Mary College, London.

Boddy, M., Lovering, J. and Bassett, K. (1986) *Sunbelt City? A Study of Economic Change in Britain's M4 Growth Corridor.* Oxford: Clarendon Press.

Bodenheimer, T. S. (1989) 'The fruits of Empire rot on the vine: United States health policy in the austerity era', *Social Science and Medicine* 28, 531–8.

Boissevain, J. (1974) *Friends of Friends: Networks, Manipulators and Coalitions.* London: Blackwell.

Booth, C. (1891) *Life and Labour of the People.* London: Williams and Margate.

Boots, B. N. (1979) 'Population density, crowding and human behaviour', *Progress in Human Geography* 3, 13–63.

Borchert, J. G. (1988) 'Planning for retail change in the Netherlands', *Built Environment* 14, 22–37.

Bose, A. (1971) 'The urbanization process in south and southeast Asia', in L. Jakobson and V. Prakash (eds) *Urbanization and National Development.* Beverly Hills, Calif.: Sage, 81–109.

Boulding, K. (1956) *The Image: Knowledge of Life and Society.* Ann Arbor: University of Michigan.

Bourassa, S. C. (1995) The impacts of borrowing constraints on home ownership in Australia, *Urban Studies*, 32, 1163–73.

Bourne, L. S. (1975) *Urban Systems: Strategies for Regulation.* Oxford: Clarendon Press.

Bourne, L. S. (1976) 'Housing supply and housing market behaviour in residential development', in D. T. Herbert and R. J. Johnston (eds) *Spatial Processes and Form.* London: Wiley, 111–58.

Bourne, L. S. (1982) *Internal Structure of the City*, London: Oxford University Press.

Bourne, L. S. (1993) 'The demise of gentrification: a commentary and prospective view', *Urban Geography* 14, 95–107.

Bovaird, T. (1993) 'Analysing urban economic development', in R. Paddison, J. Money and B. Lever (eds) *International Perspectives in Urban Studies*. London: Jessica Kingsley, 9–40.

Boyle, M. J. and Robinson, M. E. (1979) 'Cognitive mapping and understanding', in D. T. Herbert and R. J. Johnston (eds) *Geography and the Urban Environment*, vol. 2. London: Wiley, 59–82.

Boyle, P. and Halfacree, K. H. (1997) *Migration into Rural Areas: Theories and Issues*. Chichester: Wiley.

Boys, J. (1984) 'Is there a feminist analysis of architecture?' *Built Environment* 10, 25–33.

Braidwood, R. J.,and Willey, G. R. (eds) (1962) *Courses towards Urban Life: Archaeological Considerations of Some Cultural Alternates*. Chicago: Aldine.

Breheny, M. (1994) *Urban Decentralisation and Transport Energy-Efficiency*, Discussion Paper 20. Department of Geography, University of Reading.

Bromley, R. D. F. (1979) 'The function and development of colonial towns: urban change in the Central Highlands of Ecuador, 1698–1940', *Transactions, Institute of British Geographers* 4, 30–43.

Bromley, R. D. F. and Thomas, C. J. (1989) 'The impact of shop types and spatial structure on shopping linkages in retail parks: planning implications', *Town Planning Review* 61, 45–70.

Bromley, R. D. F. and Thomas, C. J. (1993a) 'The retail revolution, the carless shopper and disadvantage', *Transactions Institute of British Geographers* 18, 222–36.

Bromley, R. D. F. and Thomas, C. J. (1993b) *Retail Change. Contemporary Issues*. London: UCL Press.

Bromley, R. D. F. and Thomas, C. J. (1995) 'Small town shopping decline: dependence and inconvenience for the disadvantaged', *International Review of Retail, Distribution and Consumer Research* 5, 433–56.

Bromley, R. J. (1980) 'Trader mobility in systems of periodic and daily markets', in D. T. Herbert and R. J. Johnston (eds) *Geography and the Urban Environment*, vol. 3. Chichester: Wiley, 133–74.

Brooks, J. S. and Young, A. H. (1993) 'Revitalising the central business district in the face of decline: the case of New Orleans', *Town Planning Review* 64, 251–71.

Brown, S. (1992) *Retail Location: A Micro-Scale Perspective*, Aldershot: Avebury.

Brown, S. (1993) 'Retail location theory: evolution and evaluation', *International Review of Retail Distribution and Consumer Research* 3, 185–229.

Bullen, N., Moon, G. and Jones, K. (1996) 'Defining localities for health planning: a GIS approach', *Social Science and Medicine*, 42, 801–16.

Bulmer, M. (1986) *Neighbours: the Work of Philip Abrams*. Cambridge: Cambridge University Press.

Burgess, E. W. (1925) 'The growth of the city', in R. E. Park, E. W. Burgess and R. D. McKenzie (eds) *The City*, Chicago: University of Chicago Press.

Burke, J. (1975) 'Some reflections on the pre-industrial city', *Urban History Yearbook*, 13–21.

Burney, E. (1967) *Housing on Trial: A Study of Housing and Local Government*. London: Oxford University Press.

Buttimer, A. (1976) 'Grasping the dynamism of the life-world', *Annals, Association of American Geographers* 66, 277–92.

Canadian Geographer (1991) Special volume of articles on the West Edmonton Mall, 35(3), 226–305.

Carpenter, J. and Lees, L. (1995) 'Gentrification in New York, London and Paris: an international comparison', *International Journal of Urban and Regional Research* 19, 286–303.

Carter, H. (1977) 'Urban origins: a review', *Progress in Human Geography* 1, 12–32.

Castells, M. and Hall, P. (1994) *Technopoles of the World: The Making of the 21st Century Industrial Complexes*. London: Routledge.

Cater, J. and Jones, T. (1989) *Social Geography: An Introduction to Contemporary Issues*. London: Edward Arnold.

CEC (Commission of the European Communities) (1992) *The Impact of Transport on the Urban Environment*. Brussels: European Commission.

Central Advisory Council for Education (CACE) (1967) *Children and their Primary Schools*, Report of CACE, Chairman Lady Plowden. London: HMSO.

Cervero, B. and Landis, J. (1995) 'Development impacts of urban transport: a US perspective', in D. Banister (ed.) *Transport and Urban Development*, London: E & FN Spon, 136–56.

Champion, A. G. (1992) 'Urban and regional demographic trends in the developed world', *Urban Studies* 29, 461–82.

Champion, A. G. (1995) 'Internal migration, counterurbanisation and changing population distribution', in R. Hall and P. White (eds) *Europe's Population: Towards the Next Century*. London: UCL Press, 99–129.

Champion, A. G. (1997) 'Studying counterurbanization and the rural population turnaround', in P. Boyle and K. H. Halfacree (eds) *Migration into Rural Areas: Theories and Issues*. Chichester: Wiley.

Champion, A. G., Green, A. E., Owen, D. W., Ellin, D.J . and Coombes, M. G. (1987) *Changing Places: Britain's Demographic and Social Complexion*. London: Edward Arnold.

Chance, J. K. (1975) 'The colonial Latin American city: pre-industrial or capitalist?' *Urban Anthropology* 4, 211–28.

Chandler, T. and Fox, G. (1974) *3000 Years of Urban Growth*. New York: Academic Press.

Cheshire, P. (1995) 'A new phase of urban development in Western Europe: the evidence of the 1980s', *Urban Studies* 32, 1,045–63.

Cheshire, P. C. and Hay, D. G. (1989) *Urban Problems in Western Europe: An Economic Analysis*. London: Unwin Hyman.

Childe, V. G. (1950) 'The urban revolution', *Town Planning Review* 21, 3–17.

Chorley, R. J. and Haggett, P. (1967) *Models in Geography*. London: Methuen.

Christaller, W. (1966 [1933]) *Central Places in Southern Germany*, trans. by C. W. Baskin, Englewood Cliffs, NJ: Prentice Hall.

Clapham, D. (1995) 'Privatisation and the East European housing models, *Urban Studies* 32, 679–94.

Clark, P. and Slack, P. (1976) *English Towns in Transition, 1500–1700*. London: Oxford University Press.

Clarke, M. and Stewart, J. (1994) 'The local authority and the new community governance', *Regional Studies* 28, 201–19.

Clegg, J. (1996) 'The development of multinational enterprises', in P. W. Daniels and W. F. Lever (eds) *The Global Economy in Transition*. London: Longman, 103–34.

Cloke, P., Philo, C. and Sadler, D. (1991) *An Introduction to Contemporary Theoretical Debates*. London: Paul Chapman.

Coates, K. and Silburn, R. (1970) *Poverty: the Forgotten Englishman*. Harmondsworth: Penguin.

Coe, N. M. (1996) 'Uneven development in the UK computer services industry since 1981', *Area* 28, 64–77.

Coleman, A. (1985) *Utopia on Trial*. London: Hilary Shipman.

Conzen, M. R. G. (1960) *Alnwick, Northumberland: A Study in Town Plan Analysis*, IBG Monograph no. 27. London: Institute of British Geographers.

Conzen, M. R. G. (1962) 'The plan analysis of an English city centre', in K. Norborg (ed.) *Proceedings of the IGU Symposium in Urban Geography*. Lund: CWK Gleerup.

Cooke, P. (ed.) (1989) *Localities*. London: Unwin Hyman.

Cooke, P. (1996) 'Reinventing the region: firms, clusters and networks in economic development', in P. W. Daniels and W. F. Lever (eds) *The Global Economy in Transition*. London: Longman, 310–27.

Cowgill, D. O. (1978) 'Residential segregation by age in American metropolitan areas', *Journal of Gerontology* 33, 446–53.

Cowlard, K. A. (1979) 'The identification of social (class) areas and their place in nineteenth century urban development', *Transactions, Institute of British Geographers* 4, 239–57.

Cox, K. R. and Johnston, R. J. (1982) *Conflicts, Politics and the Urban Scene*. London: Longman.

Crang, P. and Martin, R. L. (1991) 'Mrs Thatcher's vision of the "new Britain" and the other sides of the "Cambridge phenomenon"', *Environment and Planning D: Society and Space* 9, 91–116.

Crosby, B. C. and Bryson, J. M. (1995) 'The Twin Cities Metropolitan Council', in L. J. Sharpe (ed.) *The Government of World Cities. The Future of the Metro Model*. Chichester: Wiley, 91–109.

Crowe, P. R. (1938) 'On progress in geography', *Scottish Geographical Magazine* 54, 1–19.

Curtis, S. (1989) 'Community welfare services in the inner city', in D. T. Herbert and D. M. Smith (eds) *Social Problems and the City: New Perspectives*. Oxford: Oxford University Press, 176–96.

Curtis, S. and Taket, A. (1996) *Health and Societies. Changing Perspectives*. London: Edward Arnold.

Dahya, B. (1974) 'The nature of Pakistani ethnicity in British cities,' in A. Cohen (ed) *Urban Ethnicity*. London: Tavistock, 77–118.

Damer, S. (1974) 'Wine alley: the sociology of a dreadful enclosure', *Sociological Review* 22, 221–48.

Daniels, P. W. (1996) 'The lead role of developed economies', in P. W. Daniels and W. F. Lever, (eds) *The Global Economy in Transition*. London: Longman, 193–213.

Daniels, P. W. and Lever, W .F. (eds) (1996) *The Global Economy in Transition.* London: Longman.

Daniere, A. G. (1995) 'Transportation planning and implementation in cities of the Third World: the case of Bangkok', *Environment and Planning C* 13, 25–45.

Daunton, M. (1990) *A Property-owning Democracy: Housing in Britain.* London: Faber and Faber.

Davies, R. L. (1984) *Retail and Commercial Planning.* London: Croom Helm.

Davies, R. L. (ed.) (1995) *Retail Planning Policies in Western Europe.* New York: Routledge.

Davies, W. K. D. (1967) 'Centrality and the central place hierarchy', *Urban Studies* 4, 61–79.

Davies, W. K. D. (1972) 'Conurbation and city region in an administrative borderland: a case study of the Greater Swansea area', *Regional Studies* 6, 217–36.

Davis, K. (1974) 'Colonial expansion and urban diffusion in the Americas', in D. J. Dwyer (ed.) *The City in the Third World.* London: Macmillan, 34–48.

Davis, M. (1990) *City of Quartz: Excavating the Future in Los Angeles.* London: Vintage.

Davoudi, S. (1995) 'Dilemmas of urban governance', in P. Healey *et al.* (eds) *Managing Cities: The New Urban Context,* Chichester: Wiley, 225–30.

Dear, M. J. and Wittman, I. (1980) 'Conflict over the location of mental health facilities', in D. T. Herbert and R. J. Johnston (eds) *Geography and the Urban Environment,* vol. 3. London: Wiley, 345–62.

de Pater, B. (1996) 'The Hague has awakened: urban renewal and urban revitalization', *Geografie* 5, 4–11.

De Planhof, X. (1959) *The World of Islam.* Ithaca, NY: Cornell University Press.

Dennis, R. and Clout, H. (1980) *A Social Geography of England and Wales.* Oxford: Pergamon.

Devas, N. and Rakodi, C. (eds) (1993) *Managing Fast Growing Cities. New Approaches to Urban Planning and Management in the Developing World.* Harlow: Longman.

De Vise, P. (1971) 'Cook County Hospital: bulwark of Chicago's apartheid health system and prototype of the nation's public health hospitals', *Antipode* 3, 9–20.

De Vise, P. (1994) 'Integration in Chicago forty years after Brown', *Urban Geography* 15, 454–69.

Dicken, P. and Lloyd, P. E. (1981) *Work, Home and Well-Being.* London: Harper and Row.

Dickinson, R. E. (1948) 'The scope and status of urban geography: an assessment', *Land Economics* 24, 221–38.

DoE (Department of the Environment) (1992) *The Effects of Major Out-of-town Retail Development.* London: HMSO.

DoE (Department of the Environment) (1993) *Merry Hill Impact Study.* London: HMSO.

DoE (Department of the Environment) (1994a) *Transport, Planning Policy Guidance 13.* London: HMSO.

DoE (Department of the Environment) (1994b) *Vital and Viable Town Centres: Meeting the Challenge.* Report of the study undertaken by Urban and Economic Development Group (URBED) in association with Comedia, Hillier Parker, Bartlett School of Planning, University College London, and Environmental and Transport Planning, Department of the Environment, London: HMSO.

DoE (Department of the Environment) (1994c) *Sustainable Development: The UK Strategy.* Cm 2426, London: HMSO.

Dogan, M. and Kasarda, J. D. (eds) *A World of Great Cities: The Metropolis Era,* vol. 1, Newbury Park, Calif.: Sage.

DoH (Department of Health) (1989) *Working for Patients: The Health Service Caring for the 1990s,* Cm 555. London: HMSO.

DoH (Department of Health) (1992) *The Patient's Charter: Raising the Standard.* HMSO: London.

DoH (Department of Health) (1995) *Health and Personal Social Statistics for England.* London: HMSO.

Domosh, M. (1992) 'Controlling urban form: the development of Boston's Back Bay', *Journal of Historical Geography* 18, 288–306.

Dorling, D. and Cornford, J. (1995) 'Who has negative equity? How house price falls in Britain have hit different groups of home-buyers', *Housing Studies* 10, 151–78.

DoT (Department of Transport) (1996) *Transport: The Way Forward,* Cm 3234. London: HMSO.

Douglas, J. W. B. (1964) *The Home and School.* London: MacGibbon and Kee.

Douglas, J. W. B., Ross, J. M. and Simpson, H. R. (1968) *All Our Future,* London: Peter Davies.

Downs, R. M. (1970) 'Geographic space perception: past approaches and future prospects,' in C. Board (ed.) *Progress in Geography,* vol. 2. London: Edward Arnold, 65–108.

Downs, R. M., and Stea, D. (1977) *Maps in Minds,* New York: Harper and Row.

Doxiadis, C. A. (1968) *Ekistics: An Introduction to the Science of Human Settlement.* London: Hutchinson.

Drakakis-Smith, D. (1995) 'Third world cities: sustainable urban development', 15, *Urban Studies* 32, 659–77.

Drakakis-Smith, D. (1996) 'Less developed economies and dependence', in P. W. Daniels and W. F. Lever (eds.) *The Global Economy in Transition.* London: Longman, 215–38.

Dreier, P. and Atlas, J. (1995) 'United States housing problems, policies and politics in the 1990s', *Housing Studies* 10, 245–69.

Drennan, M. P. (1996) 'The dominance of international finance by London, New York and Tokyo', in P. W. Daniels and W. F. Lever (eds) *The Global Economy in Transition.* London: Longman, 352–70.

Ducatel, K. and Blomley, N. (1990) 'Rethinking retail capital', *International Journal of Urban and Regional Research* 14, 207–27.

Duncan, J. S. (1992) *The City as Text: The Politics of Landscape Interpretation in the Kandyan Kingdom.* Cambridge: Cambridge University Press.

Duncan, O. D. and Duncan, B. (1955) 'Residential distribution and occupational stratification', *American Journal of Sociology* 60, 493–503.

Dunford, M. and Perrons, D. (1994) 'Regional inequality, regimes of accumulation and economic development in contemporary Europe', *Transactions, Institute of British Geographers* 19, 163–82

Dutt, A. K., Monroe, C. B., Dutta, H. M. and Prince, B. (1987) 'Geographical patterns of AIDS in the United States', *Geographical Review* 77, 456–71.

Dwyer, C. F. and Sutton, C. J. (1994) 'Brown plus forty: the Denver experience', *Urban Geography* 15, 421–34.

Dwyer, D. (1986) 'Chengdu, Sichuan: the modernisation of a Chinese city', *Geography* 71, 215–27.

Eade, J. (ed.) (1996) *Living in the Global City: Globalisation as Local Process.* London and New York: Routledge.

Edwards, J. (1975) 'Social indicators, urban deprivation and positive discrimination', *Journal of Social Policy* 5, 275–87.

Emmi, P. C. and Magnusson, L. (1995) 'Further evidence on the accuracy of residential vacancy chain models', *Urban Studies* 32, 1,361–7.

Engels, F. (1844) *The Condition of the Working Class in England* (reprinted 1969), London: Panther.

Engels, F. (1872) *The Housing Question* (reprinted 1954). Moscow: Progress Publishing.

Evans, A. (1973) 'The location of headquarters of industrial companies', *Urban Studies* 10, 387–95.

Eyles, J. and Woods, K. J. (1983) *The Social Geography of Medicine and Health.* London: Croom Helm.

Fainstein, S. and Fainstein, N. (1995) 'A proposal for urban policy in the 1990s', *Urban Affairs Quarterly* 30, 630–4.

Faris, R. E. and Dunham, H. W. (1939) *Mental Disorders in Urban Areas.* Chicago: University of Chicago Press.

Feldman, L. D. (1995) 'Metro Toronto: old battles – new challenges', in L. J. Sharpe (ed.) *The Government of World Cities: The Future of the Metro Model.* Chichester: Wiley, 203–25.

Festinger, L., Schachter, S. and Back, K. (1950) *Social Pressures in Informal Groups.* Stanford, Calif.: Stanford University Press.

Fielding, A. J. (1982) 'Counterurbanization in Western Europe', *Progress in Planning* 17, 1–52.

Fielding, A. J. (1994) 'Industrial exchange and regional development in Western Europe', *Urban Studies* 4–5, 679–704.

Filion, P. (1996) 'Metropolitan planning objectives and implementation constraints: planning in a post-Fordist and postmodern age', *Environment and Planning A* 28, 1637–60.

Fine, J., Glenn, N. D. and Monts, J. K. (1971) 'The residential segregation of occupational groups in central cities and suburbs', *Demography* 8, 91–102.

Firey, W. E. (1947) *Land Use in Central Boston.* Cambridge, Mass.: Harvard University Press.

Firing Line (1979) Radio interview with Mayor Koch of New York City.

Fischer, C. S., Baldassare, M. and Oske, R. J. (1975) 'Crowding studies and urban life; a critical review, *Journal, American Institute of Planners* 31, 406–18.

Ford, L. and Griffin, E. (1979) 'The ghettoization of paradise', *Geographical Review* 69, 140–58.

Forest, B. (1995) 'West Hollywood as a symbol: the significance of place in the construction of a gay identity', *Environment and Planning D, Society and Space* 13, 133–57.

Forrest, R., Gordon, D. and Murie, A. (1996) 'The position of former council houses in the housing market', *Urban Studies* 33, 125–36.

Fox, K. (1985) *Metropolitan America: Urban Life and Urban Policy in the United States, 1940–80*. London: Macmillan.

French, R. A. and Hamilton, F. E. I. (eds) (1979), *The Socialist City: Spatial Structure and Urban Policy*. Chichester: Wiley.

Frey, A. (1973) 'The teaching of regional geography', *Geography* 58, 119–28.

Frey, W. H. (1994) 'The new urban renewal in the United States', in R. Paddison, J. Money and B. Lever (eds) *International Perspectives on Urban Studies 2*. London: Jessica Kingsley, 131–67.

Friedmann, J. (1973) *Urbanization, Planning and National Development*. Beverly Hills: Sage.

Friedmann, J. (1978) 'The urban field as a human habitat', in L. S. Bourne and J. W. Simmons (eds) *Systems of Cities. Readings on Structure, Growth and Policy*. New York: Oxford University Press, 42–52.

Friedmann, J. (1995) 'Where we stand: a decade of world city research', in P. L. Knox and P. J. Taylor (eds) *World Cities in a World System*. Cambridge: Cambridge University Press, 21–47.

Friedmann, J. and Wolff, G. (1982) 'World city formation: an agenda for research and action', *International Journal of Urban and Regional Research* 6, 309–44.

Friedmann, J. and Wulff, R. (1976) *The Urban Transition: Comparative Studies of Newly Industrializing Societies*. London: Edward Arnold.

Frost, M. and Spence, N. (1993) 'Global city characteristics and central London's employment', *Urban Studies* 30, 547–58.

Gans, H. J. (1962) *The Urban Villagers*. New York: Free Press.

Gans, H. J. (1972) *People and Plans*. New York: Basic Books.

Gardner, C. and Sheppard, J. (1989) *Consuming Passions: The Rise of Retail Culture*. London: Unwin Hyman.

Garreau, J. (1991) *Edge City: Life on the New Frontier*. New York: Doubleday.

Giddens, A. (1984) *The Constitution of Society: Outline of the Theory of Structuration*. Cambridge: Polity Press.

Geddes, P. (1915) *Cities in Evolution*. London: Williams and Norgate.

Giddens, A. (1990) *The Consequences of Modernity*. Cambridge: Polity Press.

Giggs, J. A. (1979) 'Human health problems in urban areas', in D. T. Herbert and D. M. Smith (eds) *Social Problems and the City: Geographical Perspectives*. Oxford: Oxford University Press, 84–116.

Gilbert, A. (1982) *Urbanization in Contemporary Latin America: Critical Approaches to the Analysis of Urban Issues*. New York: Wiley.

Gilbert, A. (1993) *In Search of a Home: Rental and Shared Housing in Latin America*. London: UCL Press.

Gilbert, A. (1994) *The Latin American City*. London: Latin American Bureau.

Gilbert, A. (1996) 'Urban growth, employment and housing', in D. Preston (ed.) *Latin American Development: Geographical Perspectives*. Harlow: Longman, 246–71.

Gill, O. (1977) *Luke Street*. London: Macmillan.

Ginsburg, N. S. (1986) 'Some reflections on urbanisation in South-east Asia', in M. P. Conzen (ed.) *World Patterns of Modern Economic Change*. Chicago: University of Chicago, 195–216.

Glass, R. (1948) *The Social Background to a Plan: the Study of Middlesbrough*. London: Routledge and Kegan Paul.

Gleeson, B. (1996) 'A geography for disabled people', *Transactions, Institute of British Geographers* 21, 387–96.

Goheen, P. G. (1970) *Victorian Toronto 1850–1900: Patterns and Processes of Growth*, Geography Research Paper 127. University of Chicago.

Golant, S. M. (1980) 'Locational-environmental perspectives on old-age segregated areas in the United States', in D. T. Herbert and R. J. Johnston (eds) *Geography and the Urban Environment*, vol. 3. London: Wiley, 257–94.

Goldstein, S. (1988) 'Levels of urbanisation in China', in M. Dogan and J. D. Kasarda (eds) *A World of Great Cities: The Metropolis Era*, vol. 1. Newbury Park, Calif.: Sage, 187–224.

Golledge, R. G. (1993) 'Geography and the disabled: a survey with special reference to vision impaired and blind populations', *Transactions, Institute of British Geographers* 18, 63–85.

Gordon, I. R (1988) 'Resurrecting counter-urbanisation: housing market influences on migrations from London', Institute of British Geographers Conference, Loughborough.

Gordon, I. R. (1989) 'Urban unemployment', in D. T. Herbert and D. M. Smith (eds) *Social Problems and the City: New Perspectives*. Oxford: Oxford University Press, 232–46.

Goss, J. (1993) 'The "magic of the Mall": an analysis of form, function, and meaning in the contemporary retail built environment', *Annals, Association of American Geographers* **83**, 18–47.

Gottdiener, M. (1995) *Postmodern Semiotics: Material Culture and the Forms of Postmodern Life.* Oxford: Blackwell.

Gottmann, J. (1981) *Megalopolis: The Urbanized North eastern Seaboard of the United States.* Cambridge, Mass.: MIT Press.

Gottmann, J. (1976) 'Megalopolitan systems around the world', *Ekistics* **243**, 109–13.

Gottmann, J. (1983) *The Coming of the Transactional City.* Institute for Urban Studies, University of Maryland, College Park, Maryland, USA.

Graham, S. (1995) 'The city economy', in P. Healey *et al.* (eds) *Managing Cities: The New Urban Context.* Chichester: Wiley, 83–89.

Greeley, A. (1969) *Why Can't They Be Like Us?* New York: Institute of Human Relations Press.

Greene, R. P. (1994) 'Poverty area stability: the case of Chicago', *Urban Geography* **15**, 362–75.

Gregson, N. and Crewe, L. (1994) Beyond the high street and the mall: car boot fairs and the new geographies of consumption in the 1990s, *Area,* 26, 261–7.

Gregson, N. and Lowe, M. (1995) Home-making: on the spatiality of daily social reproduction in contemporary middle-class Britain, *Transactions, Institute of British Geographers,* 20, 224–35.

Grimaldos, A. I. and Ferrer, C. A. (1995) 'The Barcelona Metropolitan Area', in L. J. Sharpe (ed.) *The Government of World Cities. The Future of the Metro Model,* Chichester: Wiley, 33–55.

Gripaios, P. (1977) 'The closure of firms in the inner city: the south-east London case 1970–75', *Regional Studies* **11**, 1–6.

Guy, C. (1994a) *The Retail Development Process: Location, Property and Planning.* London: Routledge.

Guy, C. (1994b) 'Whatever happened to regional shopping centres?', *Geography* **76**, 291–312.

Guy, C. M. (1996) 'Corporate strategies in food retailing and their local impacts: a case study of Cardiff', *Environment and Planning A* **28**, 1575–602.

Guy, C. M. and Lord, J. D. (1993) 'Transformation and the City Centre', in R. D. F. Bromley and C. J. Thomas (eds) *Retail Change: Contemporary Issues.* London: UCL Press, 88–125.

Gwynne, R. N. (1996a) 'Industrialisation and urbanisation', in D. Preston (ed.) *Latin American Development: Geographical Perspectives.* Harlow: Longman, 216–45.

Gwynne, R. N. (1996b) 'Trade and developing countries', in P. W. Daniels and W. F. Lever (eds) *The Global Economy in Transition,* London: Longman, 239–62.

Hagerstrand, T. (ed.) (1971) *Information Systems for Regional Development.* Royal University of Lund, cited in L.S. Bourne (ed.) (1971) *Internal Structure of the City.* New York: Oxford University Press, 244.

Haggett, P. (1965) *Locational Analysis in Human Geography.* London: Edward Arnold.

Hall, P. (1966) *The World Cities.* London: Weidenfeld and Nicolson.

Hall, P. (1985) 'The people: where will they go?' *The Planner* **71**, 3–12.

Hall, P. (1988) *Cities of Tomorrow: An Intellectual History of Urban Planning and Design in the Twentieth Century.* Oxford: Basil Blackwell.

Hall, P. (1995) 'A European perspective on the spatial links between land use, development and transport', in D. Banister (ed.) *Transport and Urban Development* London: E & FN Spon, 65–88.

Hamnett, C. (1991) 'The blind men and the elephant: the explanation of gentrification', *Transactions, Institute of British Geographers* **16**, 173–89.

Hamnett, C. (1992) 'The geography of housing wealth and inheritance in Britain', *Geographical Journal* **158**, 307–21.

Hamnett, C. (1994) 'Social polarisation in global cities: theory and evidence', *Urban Studies* **31**, 401–24.

Hardoy, J. E. and Satterthwaite, D. (eds) (1986) *Small and Intermediate Urban Centres. Their Role in National and Regional Development in the Third World.* London: Hodder and Stoughton.

Hare, F. K. (1974) 'Geography and public policy: a Canadian view', *Transactions, Institute of British Geographers* **63**, 25–8.

Harman, H. (1989) 'A pattern set for men', *The Independent,* 14 November.

Harries, K. D. and Brunn, S. (1978) *The Geography of Laws and Justice.* New York: Praeger.

Harris, C. D. and Ullman, E. L. (1945) 'The nature of cities', *Annals, American Academy of Political and Social Science* **242**, 7–17.

Harris, N. and Tewdwr-Jones, M. (1995) 'The implications for planning of local government reorganisation in Wales: purpose, process, and practices', *Environment and Planning C* 13, 47–66.

Harris, R. (1993) 'Industry and residence: the de-centralisation of New York, 1900–40', *Journal of Historical Geography* 19, 169–90.

Hart, R. A. and Moore, G. T. (1973) 'The development of spatial cognition: a review', in R. M. Downs and D. Stea (eds) *Image and Environment*. Chicago: Aldine, 246–88.

Hartshorn, T. A. (1992) *Interpreting the City*. New York: Wiley.

Hartshorn, T. A., and Muller, P. O. (1989) 'Suburban downtown and the transformation of metropolitan Atlanta's business landscape', *Urban Geography* 10, 375–95.

Harvey, D. (1973) *Social Justice and the City*. London: Arnold.

Harvey, D. (1977) 'Government policies, financial institutions and neighbourhood change in United States cities', in M. Harloe (ed.) *Captive Cities*. London: Wiley, 123–39.

Harvey, D. (1982) *The Limits to Capital*. Oxford: Blackwell.

Harvey, D. (1985) *Consciousness and the Urban Experience*. Oxford: Blackwell.

Harvey, D. (1989) *The Condition of Postmodernity*. Oxford: Blackwell.

Harvey, T. (1996) 'Portland, Oregon: regional city in a global economy', *Urban Geography* 17, 95–114.

Hatt, P. K. (1946) 'The concept of natural area', *American Sociological Review* 11, 423–7.

Hausner, V. A. (ed.) *(1987) Urban Economic Change: Five City Studies*. Oxford: Clarendon Press.

Haynes, K. E. and Hakim, S. M. (1979) 'Technology and public policy: the urban waste management system in Cairo', *Geographical Review* 69, 101–8.

Haynes, R. (1988) 'The urban distribution of lung cancer mortality in England and Wales, 1980–83', *Urban Studies* 25, 497–506.

Hays, S. M., Kearns, R. A. and Moran, W. (1990) 'Spatial patterns of attendance at general practitioner services', *Social Science and Medicine* 31, 773–81.

Healey, P., Cameron, S., Davoudi, S., Graham, S. and Madani-Pour (eds) (1995) *Managing Cities: The New Urban Context*. Chichester: Wiley.

Held, D. (1995) *Democracy and the Global Orders: From the Modern State to Cosmopolitan Governance*. Cambridge: Polity Press.

Hendriks, F. and Toonen, T. A. (1995) 'The rise and fall of the Rijnmond authority: an experiment with metro government in the Netherlands', in L. J. Sharpe (ed.) *The Government of World Cities: The Future of the Metro Model*. Chichester: Wiley, 147–75.

Herbert, D. T. (1976) 'Urban education: problems and policies', in D. T. Herbert and R. J. Johnston (eds) *Social Areas in Cities, vol. 2, Spatial Perspectives on Problems and Policies*. London: Wiley, 123–58.

Herbert, D. T. (1994) 'Venue v. vicinage: the siting of trials and the pursuit of justice', *Urban Geography* 15, 411–14.

Herbert, D. T., and Raine, J. W. (1976) 'Defining communities within urban areas', *Town Planning Review* 47, 325–38.

Herbert, D. T. and Thomas, C. J. (1982) *Urban Geography: A First Approach*. Chichester: Wiley.

Herbert, D. T. and Thomas, C. J. (1990) *Cities in Space: City as Place*. London: David Fulton.

Hicks, D. A. and Nivin, S. R. (1996) 'Global credentials, immigration, and metro-regional economic performance', *Urban Geography* 17, 23–43.

Hiebert, D. (1995) 'The social geography of Toronto: a study of residential differentiation and social structure', *Journal of Historical Geography* 21, 55–74.

Hillery, G. A. (1955) 'Definition of community: areas of agreement', *Rural Sociology* 20, 111–23.

Hillier Parker Research (1996) *Shopping Centres of Great Britain: A National Survey of Retailer Representation by Trading Location*. London: Hillier Parker May & Rowden.

HOC (House of Commons) Environment Committee (1994) *Shopping Centres and their Future: volume 1, Session 1993–94*, London: HMSO.

Holbrook, B. and Jackson, P. J. (1996) 'The social milieux of two north London shopping centres', *Geoforum* 27, 193–204.

Holly, B. P. (1996) 'Restructuring the production system', in P. W. Daniels and W. F. Lever (eds) *The Global Economy in Transition*. London: Longman, 24–39.

Hopkins, J. S. P. (1991) 'West Edmonton Mall as a centre for social interaction', *Canadian Geographer* 35, 268–79.

Horvath, R. J. (1969) 'In search of a theory of urbanisation: notes on the colonial city', *East Lakes Geographer* 5, 69–82.

Hoyle, B. (1995) 'A shared space: contrasted perspectives on urban waterfront redevelopment in Canada', *Town Planning Review* 66, 345–69.

Hoyt, H. (1939) *The Structure and Growth of Residential Neighbourhoods in American Cities*. Washington DC: Federal Housing Administration,

Hurd, R. (1903) *Principles of City Land Values*. New York: Record and Guide, 19–21.

Imrie, R. (1996) *Disableism and the City*. London: Paul Chapman Publishing.

Irving, H. (1977) 'Social networks in the modern city', *Social Forces*, 867–80.

Irving, H. (1978) 'Space and environment in interpersonal relations', in D. T. Herbert and R. J. Johnston (eds) *Geography and the Urban Environment*, vol. 1, Chichester: Wiley, 249–84.

Jackson, B. and Marsden, D. (1962) *Education and the Working Class*. London: Routledge & Kegan Paul.

Jackson, E. and Henderson, K. A. (1995) 'Gender-based analysis of leisure constraints', *Leisure Sciences* 17, 31–51.

Jackson, P. and Penrose, J. (eds) (1993) *Constructions of Race, Place and Nation*. London: UCL Press.

Jackson, P. and Smith, S. J. (1984) *Exploring Social Geography*. London: Allen and Unwin.

Jackson, P. and Thrift, N. J. (1995) 'Geographies of consumption', in D. Miller (ed.) *Acknowledging Consumption: A Review of New Studies*. London: Routledge.

Jacobs, J. (1961) *The Death and Life of Great American Cities*. New York: Vintage Books.

Jacobs, J. (1969) *The Economy of Cities*. New York: Random House.

Jahn, H. A. (1991) *Le Nouveau Paris: l'iconothèque*. Dortmund: Harenberg Kommunikation.

Jakle, J. A. and Wilson, D. (1992) *Derelict Landscapes: The Wasting of America's Built Environment*. Lanham, Md: Rowan and Littlefield.

Jakobson, L. and Prakash, V. (eds) (1971) *Urbanization and National Development*. Beverley Hills, Sage.

Jefferson, M. (1939 'The law of the primate city', *Geographical Review* 29, 226–32.

Jencks, C. and Mayer, S. (1990) 'The social consequences of growing up in a poor neighbourhood', in M. McGreary and L. Lynn (eds) *Concentrated Urban Poverty in America*. Washington DC, National Academy, 111–86.

Jenkins, R. (1986) *Racism and Recruitment: Managers, Organizations and Equal Opportunities in the Labour Market,* Cambridge: Cambridge University Press.

Johnson, J. A., Oliver, M. L. and Bobo, L. D. (1994) 'Understanding the contours of deepening urban inequality: theoretical underpinnings and research design of a multi-city study', *Urban Geography* 15, 77–89.

Johnston, R. J. (1972) 'Towards a general model of intra-urban residential patterns: some cross-cultural comparisons', *Progress in Geography* 4, 83–124.

Johnston, R. J. (1979) *Political, Electoral and Spatial Systems*. Oxford: Oxford University Press.

Johnston, R. J. (1980) *City and Society: An Outline for Urban Geography*. Harmondsworth: Penguin.

Johnston, R. J. (1982a) 'The local state', in Johnston, Geography and the State. London: Macmillan, 187–260.

Johnston, R. J. (1982b) *The American Urban System: A Geographical Perspective*. London: Longman.

Johnston, R. J. and Pattie, C. J. (1996) 'Intra-local conflict, public opinion and local government restructuring in England, 1993–95', *Geoforum* 27, 97–114.

Jones, E. (1960) *The Social Geography of Belfast*. Oxford: Oxford University Press.

Jones, K. and Simmons, J. (1990) *The Retail Environment*, London: Routledge.

Jones, P. N. (1970) 'Some aspects of the changing distribution of coloured immigrants in Birmingham, 1961–66', *Transactions, Institute of British Geographers* 50, 199–219.

Jones, P. N. (1979) 'Ethnic areas in British cities', in D. T. Herbert and D. M. Smith (eds) *Social Problems and the City: Geographical Perspectives*. Oxford: Oxford University Press, 158–85.

Jones, T., McLean, B. and Young, J. (1986) *The Islington Survey*. Aldershot: Gower.

Joseph, A. E. and Phillips, D. R. (1984) *Accessibility and Utilization: Geographical Perspectives on Health Care Delivery*. London: Harper and Row.

Kaplan, D. H. and Schwartz, A. (1996) 'Minneapolis-St. Paul in the global economy', *Urban Geography* 17, 44–59.

Kay, T. (1996) 'Women's work and women's worth: the leisure implications of women's changing employment patterns', *Leisure Studies* 15, 49–64.

Keane, M.C. (1985) 'Ethnic residential change in Belfast, 1969–75', unpublished Ph.D. thesis, Queen's University, Belfast.

Kerouac, J., (1955) *On the Road*. Harmondsworth: Penguin.

King's Fund (1995) *Tackling Health Inequalities: An Agenda for Action*. London: King Edward's Hospital Fund for London.

Kirby, C. (1995) 'Urban air pollution', *Geography* 80, 375–92.

Kirby, D. A. (1983) 'Housing', in M. Pacione (ed.) *Progress in Urban Geography*. London: Croom Helm, 7–44.

Kirschenman, J. and Neckerman, K. (1991) 'We'd love to hire them . . . but: the meaning of race for employers', in C. Jencks and P. Peterson (eds) *The Urban Underclass*, Washington DC: Brookings Institution.

Knox, P. L. (1978) 'The intra-urban ecology of primary medical care: patterns of accessibility and their policy implications', *Environment and Planning A* 10, 413–35.

Knox, P. L. (1989) 'The vulnerable, the disadvantaged, and the victimized: who are they and where do they live', in D. T. Herbert and D. M. Smith (eds) *Social Problems and the City*. Oxford: Oxford University Press, 32–47.

Knox, P. L. (1995) *Urban Social Geography: An Introduction*. Harlow: Longman.

Knox, P. L. and Taylor, P. J. (1995) *World Cities in a World System*. Cambridge: Cambridge University Press.

Kulhavy, R. W. and Stock, W. A. (1996) 'How cognitive maps are learned and remembered', *Annals, Association of American Geographers* 86, 123–45.

Kuper, L. (1953) *Living in Towns*. London: Cresset Press.

Lakshmanan, T. R. and Chatterjee, L. R. (1977) *Urbanization and Environmental Quality*, AAG Resource Paper 77–1. Washington DC: Association of American Geographers.

Lakshmanan, T. R. and Hansen, W. G. (1965) 'A retail market potential model', *Journal of the American Institute of Planners* 31, 134–44.

Lamarche, F. (1976) 'Property development and the economic foundations of the urban question,' in C. Pickvance (ed.) *Urban Sociology: Critical Essays*. London: Tavistock, 85–118.

Lampard, E. E. (1965) 'Historical aspects of urbanisation', in P. M. Hauser and L. P. Schnore (eds) *The Study of Urbanisation*. New York: Wiley, 519–54.

Langton, J. (1975) 'Residential patterns in pre-industrial cities: some case studies of the seventeenth century,' *Transactions Institute of British Geographers* 65, 1–27.

Langton, J. (1978) 'Industry and towns, 1500 to 1730', in R. A. Dodgson and R. A. Butlin (eds) *A Historical Geography of England and Wales*. London: Academic Press, 173–98.

Lawton, R. (1972) 'An age of great cities', *Town Planning Review* 43, 199–224.

Lawton, R. (1979) 'Mobility in nineteenth-century British cities', *Geographical Journal* 145, 206–24.

Lawton, R. and Pooley, C. G. (1975) *The Urban Dimensions of Nineteenth Century Liverpool*, Department of Geography Project Working Paper 4. Liverpool University.

Leach, S. (1994) 'The local government review: from policy drift to policy fiasco', *Regional Studies* 28, 537–49.

Leavey, R., Wilkin, D. and Metcalfe, D. H. (1989) 'Consumerism and general practice', *British Medical Journal*, 298, 737–9.

Lee, T. R. (1968) 'Urban neighbourhood as a socio-spatial schema', *Human Relations* 21, 241–68.

Lever, W. (1996) 'Market enlargement: the Single European Market', in P. W. Daniels and W. F. Lever (eds) *The Global Economy in Transition*. London: Longman, 291–309.

Levi, M. (1992) 'Policing the upper world: towards and global village', in D. J. Evans, N. R. Fyfe and D. T. Herbert (eds) *Crime, Policing and Place: Essays in Environmental Criminology*, London: Routledge, 217–32.

Lewis, J. and Bowlby, S. (1989) 'Women's inequality in urban Britain', in D. T. Herbert and D. M. Smith (eds) *Social Problems and the City: New Perspectives*. Oxford: Oxford University Press, 213–31.

Lewis, O. (1966) 'The culture of poverty', *Scientific American* 215, 19–25.

Ley, D. (1977) 'Social geography and the taken-for-granted world', *Transactions, Institute of British Geographers* NS2, 498–512.

Ley, D. and Cybriwsky, R. (1974a) 'Urban graffiti as territorial markers', *Annals, Association of American Geographers* 64, 491–505.

Ley, D. and Cybriwsky, R. (1974b) 'The spatial ecology of stripped cars', *Environment and Behavior* 6, 53–67.

Liu, B. C. (1975) *Quality of Life Indicators in United States Metropolitan Areas, 1970*. Washington DC: US Environmental Protection Agency.

Lloyd, P. E. and Mason, C. M. (1978) 'Manufacturing industry in the inner city: a case study of Greater Manchester', *Transactions, Institute of British Geographers* **NS3**, 66–90.

Lomas, G. M. (1975) *The Inner City: A Preliminary Investigation*. London: London Council of Social Services.

Lord, J. D. (1988) *Retail Decentralization and C. B. D. Decline in American Cities*, Working Paper 8802. Institute of Retail Studies, University of Stirling.

Lorenz, A. (1996) 'Inward investment booms', *Sunday Times*, 13 October.

Lösch, A. (1954) *The Economics of Location* (translated from 1940 version by W. H. Woglom and W. F. Stolper). Yale New Haven: University Press.

Loukaitou-Sideris, A. (1993) 'Privatisation of public open space', *Town Planning Review* **64**, 139–67.

Lovering, J. (1995) 'Creating discourses rather than jobs: the crisis in the cities and the transitional fantasies of intellectuals and policy makers', in P. Healey *et al.* (eds) *Managing Cities: The New Urban Context*. Chichester: Wiley, 91–108.

Lowry, M. (1973) 'Schools in transition', *Annals, Association of American Geographers* **63**, 167–80.

Lyman, S. M. and Scott, M. B. (1967) 'Territoriality: a neglected sociological dimension', *Social Problems* **15**, 236–49.

Lynch, K. (1960) *The Image of the City*. Cambridge, Mass.: MIT Press.

Mabogunje, A. L. (1974) 'The pre-colonial development of Yoruba towns', in D. J. Dwyer (ed.) *The City in the Third World*. London: Macmillan, 26–33.

Mabogunje, A. L. (1986) 'Backwash urbanisation: the peasantisation of cities in sub-Saharan Africa', in M. P. Conzen (ed.) *World Patterns of Modern Economic Change*. Chicago: University of Chicago, 255–72.

Mackinder, H. J. (1902) *Britain and the British Seas*, London: Heinemann.

Maguire, M. (1994) 'Crime statistics, patterns, and trends: changing perceptions and their implications', in M. Maguire, R. Morgan and R. Reiner (eds) *The Oxford Handbook on Criminology*. Oxford: Clarendon Press, 233–91.

Mallett, W. J. (1994) 'Managing the post-industrial city: business improvement districts in the United States', *Area* **26**, 276–87.

Marks, C. (1991) 'The urban underclass', *Annual Review of Sociology* **17**, 445–66.

Marshall, J. N. and Wood, P. A. (1995) *Services and Space: Key Aspects of Urban and Regional Development*. London: Longman.

Martin, R. (1993) 'Remapping British regional policy: the end of the north-south divide', *Regional Studies* **27**, 797–805.

Mason, D. (1995) *Race and Ethnicity in Modern Britain*. Oxford: Oxford University Press.

Massam, B. (1993) *The Right Place: Shared Responsibility and the Location of Public Facilities*. New York: Longman.

Massey, D. (1984) *Spatial Divisions of Labour*. London: MacMillan.

Massey, D. (1988) 'What's happening to UK manufacturing?" in J. Allen and D. Massey (eds) *The Economy in Question*. London: Sage, ,45–90.

Massey, D. (1993) 'Power geometry and a progressive sense of place', in J. Bird, B. Curtis, T. Putnam, G. Robertson and L. Tickner (eds) *Mapping the Futures: Local Cultures, Global Change*. London: Routledge, 59–69.

Massey, D. and Meegan, R. (1982) *The Anatomy of Job Loss*. London: Methuen.

Massey, D. S. and Denton, N. (1993) *American Apartheid: Segregation and the Making of the Underclass*, Cambridge, Mass.: Harvard University Press.

Matthews, M. H. (1992) *Making Sense of Place: Children's Understanding of Large Scale Environments*. Hemel Hempstead: Harvester Wheatsheaf.

Matthew, M. R. (1993) 'Towards a general theory of suburban office morphology in North America', *Progress in Human Geography* **17**, 471–89.

Mayer, H. (1954) 'Urban geography', in P. E. James and C. F. Jones (eds) *American Geography: Inventory and Prospect*. Syracuse, NY: Syracuse University Press, 142–66.

Mayer, J. D. (1986) 'International perspectives on the health care crisis in the United States', *Social Science and Medicine* **23**, 1056–65.

Mayer, M. (1995) 'Urban governance in the post-Fordist city,' in P. Healey *et al.* (eds) *Managing Cities: The New Urban Context*. Chichester, Wiley, 231–49.

Mayhew, H. (1862) *London Labour and the London Poor*. London: Griffin-Bohn.

Maynard, A. (1994) 'Can competition enhance efficiency in health care?' Lessons from the reform of the U.K. National Health Service', *Social Science and Medicine* 39, 1433–6.

Mazur, A. (1991) *Downtown Development – Chicago: 1989–92*. Chicago: City of Chicago.

McConkey, R. and McCormack, B. (1983) *Breaking Barriers: Educating People about Disability*. London: Souvenir.

McGee, T. G. (1971) *The Urbanization Process in the Third World: Explorations in Search of a Theory*. London: Bell.

McGee, T. (1986) 'Circuits and networks of capital: internationalisation of the world economy and national urbanisation', in D. Drakakis-Smith (ed.) *Urbanisation in the Developing World*. London: Croom Helm, 23–36.

McGee, T. G. (1967) *The South-east Asian City*. London: Bell.

McGregor, A. and McConnachie, M. (1995) 'Social exclusion, urban regeneration, and economic re-integration', *Urban Studies* 32, 1587–600.

McKinnon, A. C. (1989) *Physical Distribution Systems*. London: Routledge.

McLain, P. (1995) 'Thirty years of urban policies', *Urban Affairs Quarterly* 30, 641–4.

Mead, L. (1992) *The New Politics of Poverty*. New York: Basic Books.

Mercer, C. (1975) *Living in Cities*. Harmondsworth: Penguin Books.

Merlin, P. (1986) 'Housing politics in the old centre and the development of ghettos of marginal groups,' in G. Heinritz and E. Lichtenberger (eds) *The Take-Off of Suburbia and the Decline of the Central City*. Stuttgart: Steiner Verlag, 228–34.

Michelson, W. A. (1970) *Man and his Urban Environment*. Reading, Mass.: Addison-Wesley.

Ministry of Transport 91963) *Traffic in Towns, Report of the Steering Group and Working Party appointed by the Minister of Transport under the Chairmanship of Colin Buchanan*. London: HMSO.

Mogridge, M. J. H. (1987) 'The use of rail transport to improve accessibility in large conurbations, using London as an example', *Town Planning Review* 58, 165–82.

Mohan, J. (1989) 'Health-care policy issues', in D. T. Herbert and D. M. Smith (eds) *Social Problems and the City: New Perspectives*. Oxford: Oxford University Press, 126–41.

Moore, E. G. (1972) *Residential Mobility in the City*, AAG Resource Paper 13. Washington DC: Association of American Geographers.

Morrill, R. L. (1987) 'The structure of shopping in a metropolis', *Urban Geography* 8, 97–128.

Mumford, L. (1938) *The Culture of Cities*. London: Harcourt, Brace and Co.

Mumford, L. (1961) *The City in History*. London: Secker and Warburg.

Munro, M. (1987) 'Residential mobility in the private housing sector', in M. Pacione (ed.) *Social Geography: Progress and Prospect*. Londonm: Croom Helm, 31–61.

Munro, M. (1995) 'Homo-economicus in the city: towards an urban socio-economic research agenda', *Urban Studies* 32, 1,609–21.

Murphy, R. E. (1972) *The Central Business District: A Study in Urban Geography*, London: Longman.

Muth, R. F. (1969) *Cities and Housing*. Chicago: University of Chicago Press.

Myrdal, G. M. (1957) *Economic Theory and the Under-Developed Regions*. London: Duckworth.

Nagpaul, H. (1988) 'India's great cities', in M. Dogan and J. D. Kasarda (eds) *A World of Great Cities: The Metropolis Era*, vol. 1. Newbury Park, Calif.: Sage, 252–90.

Nelson, R. L. (1958) *The Selection of Retail Locations*. New York: Dodge.

Newby, P. (1993) 'Shopping as leisure', in R. D. F. Bromley and C. J. Thomas (eds) *Retail Change: Contemporary Issues*. London: UCL Press, 208–28.

Newman, O. (1972) *Defensible Space*. New York: Macmillan.

Nijman, J. (1996) 'Breaking the rules: Miami in the urban hierarchy', *Urban Geography* 17, 5–22.

Nilsson, J., Dicken, P. and Peck, J. (1996) *The Internationalization Process: European Firms in Global Competition*. London: Paul Chapman.

Northam, R. (1979) *Urban Geography*. New York: Wiley.

Oc, T. and Trench, S. (1993) 'Planning and shopper security', in R. D. F. Bromley and C. J. Thomas (eds) *Retail Change: Contemporary Issues*. London: UCL Press, 153–69.

Oliver, M. (1990) *The Politics of Disablement*. London: Macmillan, Basingstoke.

OPCS (1988) *The Prevalence of Disability*. London: HMSO.

Paaswell, R. E. (1995) 'ISTEA: infrastructure investment and economic development', in D. Banister (ed.) *Transport and Urban Development*, London: E & FN Spon, 36–58.

Pahl, R. E. (1979) 'Socio-political factors in resource allocation', in D. T. Herbert and D. M. Smith (eds) *Social Problems and the City: Geographical Approaches*. London: Oxford University Press, 33–46.

Paris, C. (1995) 'Demographic aspects of social change: implications for strategic housing policy', *Urban Studies* 32, 1623–45.

Parker, J. (1995) 'Many splendoured things, a survey of cities', *The Economist* July, 3–4.

Parkinson, M., Dawson, J. P., Evans, S. R. and Harding, A. P., (1993) *Urbanisation and the Functions of Cities in the European Community*. Brussels: European Commission.

Peach, G. C. K. (1979) 'Race and space', *Area* 11, 221–2.

Peach, G. C. K. (1996) 'Does Britain have ghettos?' *Transactions, Institute of British Geographers* 21, 216–35.

Peach, G. C. K., Winchester, S. W. and Woods, R. I. (1975) 'The distribution of coloured immigrants in Britain', in G. Gappert and H. M. Rose (eds) *The Social Economy of Cities*. New York: Sage, 395–414.

Pearman, H. (1994) 'On the road to nowhere land', *Sunday Times* 20 November, section 10, 12.

Pearson, G. (1989) 'Heroin use in its social context', in D. T. Herbert and D. M. Smith (eds) *Social Problems and the City: New Perspectives*. Oxford: Oxford University Press, 307–22.

Perkins, S. (1996) 'The social effects of retail decentralisation: a multi-method impact assessment of the Merry Hill regional shopping centre, West Midlands', Unpublished Ph.D. thesis, University of Wales, Swansea.

Perry, C. (1939) *Housing for the Machine Age*. New York: Russel Sage.

Piaget, J. and Inhelder, B. (1956) *The Child's Conception of Space*. London: Routledge and Kegan Paul.

Piché, D. (1977) 'The geographical understanding of children aged 5 to 8 years', unpublished doctoral thesis, University of London.

Pinch, S. (1985) *Cities and Services: The Geography of Collective Consumption*. London: Routledge and Kegan Paul.

Pirenne, H. (1925) *Medieval Cities*. Princeton: Princeton University Press.

Poole, M. A. and Boal, F. W. (1973) 'Religious residential segregation in Belfast in mid 1969: a multi-level analysis', *Institute of British Geographers Special Publication* 5, 1–40.

Pooley, C. G. (1977) 'The residential segregation of migrant communities in mid-Victorian Liverpool', *Transactions, Institute of British Geographers* NS2 364–82.

Preston, D. (ed.) (1996) *Latin American Development: Geographical Perspectives*. Harlow: Longman.

Prestwich, R. and Taylor, P. (1990) *Regional and Urban Policy in the United Kingdom*. London: Longman.

Pyle, G. F. (1973) 'Measles as an urban health problem: the Akron example, *Economic Geography*, 49, 344–56.

Radcliffe, S. A. (1996) Race, gender and generation: cultural geographies', in D. Preston (ed.) *Latin American Development: Geographical Perspectives*. Harlow: Longman, 146–64.

Radford, J. P. (1976) 'Race, residence and ideology: Charleston, South Carolina in mid-nineteenth century', *Journal of Historical Geography* 2, 329–46.

Radford, J. P. (1979) 'Testing the model of the pre-industrial city: the case of ante-bellum Charleston, South Carolina', *Transactions, Institute of British Geographers* 4, 392–410.

Raine, J. W. (1976) 'Social interaction and urban neighbourhood', unpublished Ph.D., University of Wales, Swansea.

Rakodi, C. (1995) 'Rental tenure in cities of the developing world', *Urban Studies* 32, 791–811.

Ratcliff, R. V. (1949) *Urban Land Economics*. New York: McGraw-Hill.

Rees, P. H. (1979) *Residential Patterns in American Cities: 1960*, Geography Research Paper 189, University of Chicago.

Reissman, L. (1964) *The Urban Process: Cities in Industrial Society*. New York: Free Press.

Relph, E. (1976) *Place and Placelessness*. London: Pion.

Rex, J. A. and Moore, R. (1967) *Race, Community and Conflict*. London: Oxford University Press.

Reynolds, J. (1993) 'The proliferation of the planned shopping centre', in R. D. F. Bromley and C. J. Thomas (eds) *Retail Change: Contemporary Issues*. London: UCL Press, 70–87.

Roberts, B. (1978) *Cities of Peasants*. London: Edward Arnold.

Robertson, K. A. (1995) 'Downtown redevelopment strategies in the United States', *Journal of the American Planning Association* 61, 429–37.

Robinson, V. (1979) *The Segregation of Asians within a British City: Theory and Practice*, Research Paper no. 22. Oxford University School of Geography.

Robson, B. (1969) *Urban Analysis*. Cambridge: Cambridge University Press.

Robson, B. (1988) *Those Inner Cities*. Oxford: Clarendon Press.

Robson, B. (1994) 'No city, no civilization', *Transactions, Institute of British Geographers* 19, 131–41.

Robson, B., Parkinson, M., Bradford, M. G., Deas, I., Garside, P., Hall, E. and Robinson, F. (1993) *Evaluating the Impacts of Government Urban Policy*, Report to the Department of the Environment. London: DoE.

Rogers, A. and Uto, R. (1987) 'Residential segregation re-theorized: a view from southern California', in P. Jackson (ed.) *Race and Racism*. London: Allen and Unwin, 50–69.

Rogers, D. (1992) 'A review of sales forecasting models most commonly applied in retail site location', *International Journal of Retail and Distribution Management* 20, 3–11.

Rossi, P. A. (1955) *Why Families Move*. Glencoe, Ill.: Free Press.

Rostam, K. (1989) 'Rural service centres in Malaysia: a study of the settlement geography of Hilir Perak', unpublished Ph.D. thesis, University of Wales, Swansea.

Rowles, G. (1978) *Prisoners of Space: Exploring the Geographical Experience of Older People*. Boulder, Col.: Westview.

Rowley, G. (1978) 'Plus ça change . . . : a Canadian skid row', *Canadian Geographer* 22, 211–24.

Rowley, G. (1993) 'Prospects for the central business district', in R. D. F. Bromley and C. J. Thomas (eds) *Retail Change: Contemporary Issues*. London: UCL Press, 110–25.

Rowntree, B. S. (1901) *Poverty: A Study of Town Life*. London: Macmillan.

Sancton, A. (1995) 'The Montreal urban community', in L. J. Sharpe (ed.) *The Government of World Cities: The Future of the Metro Model*. Chichester: Wiley 131–46.

Sant, M. and Simons, P. (1993) 'The conceptual basis of counterurbanization: critique and development', *Australian Geographical Studies* 31, 113–26.

Sassen, S. (1991) *The Global City: New York, London, Tokyo*. Princetown, NJ: Princeton University Press.

Sassen, S. (1994) *Cities in a World Economy*. London: Pine Forge Press.

Saunders, P. (1980) *Urban Politics*. Harmondsworth: Penguin.

Saunders, P. (1981) *Social Theory and the Urban Question*. London: Hutchinson.

Schaefer, F. K. (1953) 'Exceptionalism in geography: a methodological examination', *Annals, Association of American Geographers* 43, 226–49.

Schiller, R. K. (1986) 'Retail decentralization – the coming of the third wave', *The Planner* 72, 13–15.

Seamon, D. (1979) *A Geography of the Lifeworld: Movement, Rest and Encounter*. London: Croom Helm.

Shachar, A. (1994) 'Randstad Holland: a "world city"?', *Urban Studies* 31, 381–400.

Shah, S. (1979) 'Aspects of the analysis of Asian immigrants in London', unpublished D.Phil. thesis, University of Oxford.

Shannon, G. W and Cutchin, M. P. (1994) 'General practitioner distribution and population dynamics: Munich, 1950–90', *Social Science and Medicine* 39, 23–38.

Shannon, G. W. and Spurlock, C. W. (1976) 'Urban ecological containers, environmental risk cells and the use of medical services', *Economic Geography*, 52, 171–80.

Sharpe, L. J. (1976) 'The role and functions of local government in modern Britain', in Layfield Report, *The Relationship between Central and Local Government*. London: HMSO, 203–20.

Sharpe, L. J. (ed.) (1995) *The Government of World Cities: The Future of the Metro Model*. Chichester: Wiley.

Shaw, C. R. and McKay, H. D. (1942) *Juvenile Delinquency and Urban Areas* (revised edition, 1969). Chicago: Chicago University Press.

Shaw, M. (1977) 'The ecology of social change, Wolverhampton 1851–71', *Transactions, Institute of British Geographers* NS2, 332–48.

Shaw, M. (1979) 'Reconciling social and physical space, Wolverhampton 1871', *Transactions, Institute of British Geographers* 4, 192–213.

Shevky, E. and Bell, W. (1955) *Social Area Analysis*. Stanford, Calif.: Stanford University Press.

Shevky, E. and Williams, M. (1949) *The Social Areas of Los Angeles*. Los Angeles: University of California Press.

Shields, R. (1992) *Lifestyle Shopping: The Subject of Consumption*. London: Routledge.

Short, J. R. (1984) *An Introduction to Urban Geography*. London: Routledge and Kegan Paul.

Short, J. R. (1989) 'Yuppies, yuffies and the new urban order', *Transactions, Institute of British Geographers* 14, 173–88.

Shumsky, N. L. and Springer, L. M. (1981) 'San Francisco's zone of prostitution', *Journal of Historical Geography* 7, 71–89.

Shurmer-Smith, P. (1994) 'Cixous' spaces: sensuous space in women's writing', *Ecumene* 4, 349–62.

Sibley, D. (1992) 'Outsider in society and space', in K. Anderson and F. Gale (eds) *Inventing Places: Studies in Cultural Geography*. Melbourne: Longman Cheshire, 107–22.

Simon, H. A. (1957) *Models of Man: Social and Rational*. New York: Wiley.

Sims, D. (1984) 'Urban deprivation: not just the inner city', *Area* 16, 299–306.

Singh, R. P. B. and Singh, R. L. (1986) 'Urban changes in India', in M. P. Conzen (ed.) *World Patterns of Modern Economic Change*, Geography Research Paper. University of Chicago, 175–93.

Sjoberg, A. (1960) *The Pre-Industrial City: Past and Present*. New York: Free Press.

Sjoberg, A. (1965) 'Cities in developing and in industrial societies', in P. M. Hauser and L. F. Schnore (eds) *The Study of Urbanization*. New York: Wiley, 213–63.

Sjoberg, A. (1973) *Scientific American, Cities: Their Origins, Growth and Human Impact*. San Franscisco: W. H. Freeman, 25–39.

Skinner, G. W. (1985) 'Rural marketing in China: revival and reappraisal', in S. Plattner (ed.) *Markets and Marketing*. New York: University Press of America, 7–47.

Smailes, A. E. (1953) *The Geography of Towns*. London: Hutchinson.

Smith, C. J. (1980) 'Neighbourhood effects on mental health', in D. T. Herbert and R. J. Johnston (eds) *Geography and the Urban Environment*, vol. 3. London: Wiley, 363–415.

Smith, C. J. (1989) 'Alcoholism and the alcohol control policy in the American city', in D. T. Herbert and D. M. Smith (eds) *Social Problems and the City: Geographical Perspectives*. Oxford: Oxford University Press, 323–41.

Smith, C. J. and Hanham, R. Q. (1982) *Alcohol Abuse: Geographical Perspectives*. Washington DC: Association of American Geographers.

Smith, D. M. (1973) *The Geography of Social Well-Being in the United States*. New York: McGraw-Hill.

Smith, D. M. (1977) *Human Geography: A Welfare Approach*. London: Edward Arnold.

Smith, D. M. (1979) 'The identification of problems in cities: applications of social indicators', in D. T. Herbert and D. M. Smith (eds) *Social Problems and the City: Geographical Perspectives*. Oxford: Oxford University Press, 13–32.

Smith, D. M. (1994) *Geography and Social Justice*. Oxford: Blackwell.

Smith, N. (1987) 'Dangers of the empirical turn', *Antipode* 19, 59–68.

Smith, N. (1993) 'Homeless/global: scaling places', in J. Bird, B. Curtis, T. Putnam, G. Robertson and L. Tickner (eds) *Mapping the Futures: Local Cultures, Global Change*. London: Routledge, 87–119.

Smith, S. (1993) 'Social landscape: continuity and change', in R. J. Johnston (ed.) *A Changing World: A Changing Discipline*. Oxford: Blackwell, 564–75.

Smith, S. J. (1986) *Crime, Space and Society*. Cambridge: Cambridge University Press.

Smith, S. J. (1987) 'Residential segregation: a geography of English racism', in P. Jackson (ed.) *Race and Racism*. London: Allen and Unwin, 25–47.

Soja, E. (1971) *The Political Organization of Space*, Commission on College Geography Resource Paper 8. Washington DC: Association of American Geographers.

Soja, E. (1989) *Postmodern Geographies*. London: Verso.

Stegman, M. A. (1995) 'Recent United States urban change and policy initiatives', *Urban Studies* 32, 1,601–7.

Stokes, P. and Knight, B. (1997) *Organizing a Civil Society*. Birmingham: Foundation for Civil Society.

Stokols, D. (1978) 'Environmental psychology', *Annual Review of Psychology* 29, 253–95.

Stren, R. (1992) 'African urban research since the late 1980s: responses to poverty and urban growth', in R. Paddison, B. Lever and J. Money (eds) *International Perspectives on Urban Studies 1*. London: Jessica Kingsley, 210–33.

Suttles, G. D. (1968) *The Social Order of the Slum*. Chicago: University of Chicago Press.

Swyngedouw, E. (1996) 'Producing futures: global finance as a geographical project', in P. W. Daniels and W. F. Lever (eds) *The Global Economy in Transition*. London: Longman, 135–63.

Taeuber, A. F. (1988) 'A practitioner's perspective on the index of dissimilarity', *American Sociological Review* **41**, 884–9.

Taeuber, K. E. and Taeuber, A. F. (1965) *Negroes in Cities: Residential Segregation and Neighbourhood Change.* Chicago: Aldine.

Taylor, G. (1949) *Urban Geography.* London: Methuen.

Terjung, W. H. (1974) 'Climatic modifications, in I. R. Manners and M. W. Mikesell (eds) *Perspectives on Environment*, Resource Paper 13. Washington DC: American Association of Geographers.

Thomas, C. (1988) 'Moscow's mobile millions', *Geography* **73**, 216–25.

Theodorson, G. A. (1961) *Studies in Human Ecology.* New York: Harper and Row.

Thomas, C. J. and Bromley R. D. F. (1993) 'The impact of out-of-centre retailing', in R. D. F. Bromley and C. J. Thomas (eds) *Retail Change: Contemporary Issues.* London: UCL Press, 126–52.

Thomas, C. J. and Bromley R. D. F. (1995) 'Retail decline and the opportunities for commercial revitalisation of small shopping centres: a case study in South Wales', *Town Planning Review* **66**, 431–52.

Thomson, J. M. (1977) *Great Cities and their Traffic.* London: Gollancz.

Tickell, A. and Peck, J. A. (1995) 'Social regulation after-Fordism: regulation theory, neoliberalism and the global-local nexus', *Economy and Society* **24**, 357–86.

Tobias, J. J. (1976) 'A statistical study of a nineteenth century criminal area', *British Journal of Criminology* **14**, 221–35.

Togo, H. (1995) 'The metropolitan strategies of Tokyo: towards the restoration of balanced growth', in L. J. Sharpe (ed.) *The Government of World Cities: The Future of the Metro Model.* Chichester: Wiley, 177–201.

Townroe, P. (1995) 'The coming of supertram: the impact of urban rail development in Sheffield', in D. Banister (ed.) *Transport and Urban Development.* London: E & FN Spon, 162–86.

Tuan, Y. F. (1968) 'A preface to Chinese cities', in R. P. Beckinsale and J. M. Houston (eds) *Urbanisation and its Problems.* London: Oxford University Press 218–53.

Turner, J. F. C. (1967) 'Barriers and channels and housing development in modernising countries', *Journal of American Institute of Planners* **32**, 167–81.

Urry, J. (1995) *Consuming Places.* London: Routledge.

Valentine, G. (1990) 'Women's fear and the design of public space', *Built Environment* **16**, 288–303.

Valentine, G. (1993a) 'Negotiating and managing multiple sexual identities: lesbian time-space strategies', *Transactions, Institute of British Geographers* **18**, 237–48.

Valentine, G. (1993b) '(Hetero)-sexing space; lesbian perceptions and experiences of everyday spaces', *Environment and Planning D, Society and Space* **11**, 395–413.

Valentine, G. (1997) 'My son's a bit dizzy and my wife's a bit soft: gender, children and the culture of parenting', *Gender, Race and Culture* **4**, 37–62.

Van Weesep, J (1994) 'Gentrification as a research frontier', *Progress in Human Geography* **18**, 74–83.

Vance, J. E. (1966) 'Housing the worker: the employment linkage as a force in urban structure', *Economic Geography* **42**, 294–325.

Vance, J. E. (1971) 'Land assignment in pre-capitalist, capitalist, and post-capitalist cities', *Economic Geography* **47**, 101–20.

Vance, J. E. (1978) 'Institutional forces that shape the city', in D. T Herbert and R. J. Johnston (eds) *Social Areas in Cities.* Chichester: Wiley, 97–125.

Venness, A. R. (1992) 'Home and homelessness in the United States: changing ideals and realities', *Environment and Planning D: Society and Space* **10**, 445–68.

Vise, P. de (1971) 'Cook County Hospital: bulwark of Chicago's apartheid health system and prototype of the nation's public health hospitals', *Antipode* **3**, 9–20.

Wagner, P. L. (1984) 'Suburban landscapes for nuclear families: the case of the green-belt town in the United States', *Built Environment* **10**, 35–41.

Walker, R. (1978) 'The transformation of urban structure in the nineteenth century and the beginnings of suburbanisation', in K. R. Cox (ed.) *Urbanisation and Conflict in Market Societies.* Chicago: Maaroufa Press, 165–212.

Walker, R. (1995) 'Landscape and city life: four ecologies of residences in the San Francisco Bay area', *Ecumene* **2**, 33–64.

Walker, R. (1996) 'Another round of globalization in San Francisco', *Urban Geography* **17**, 60–94.

Wallerstein, I. (1989) *The Modern World-System*, New York: Academic Press.

Walmsley, D. J. (1988) *Urban Living: The Individual in the City*. Harlow: Longman.

Ward, D. (1964) 'A comparative historical geography of street-car suburbs in Boston and Leeds 1850–1920', *Annals, American Association of Geographers* 54, 447–89.

Ward, D. (1971) *Cities and Immigrants*. New York: Oxford University Press.

Ward, D. (1975) 'Victorian cities: how modern?' *Journal of Historical Geography* 1, 135–51.

Warnes, A. M. (1989) 'Social problems of elderly people in cities', in D. T. Herbert and D. M. Smith (eds) *Social Problems and the City: New Perspectives*. Oxford: Oxford University Press, 197–212.

Warnes, A. M. (1994) 'Cities and elderly people: recent population and distributional trends', *Urban Studies* 31, 799–816.

Webber, M. (1963) 'Order in diversity: community without propinquity', in L. Wingo (ed.) *Cities in Space*. Baltimore, MD: Johns Hopkins University Press, 23–54.

Weber, A. F. (1899) *The Growth of Cities in the Nineteenth Century: A Study in Statistics*. New York: Macmillan.

Westlake, T. (1993) 'The disadvantaged consumer: problems and policies', in R. D. F. Bromley and C. J. Thomas (eds) *Retail Change: Contemporary Issues*. London: UCL Press, 172–91.

Wellman, B. (1978) *The Community Question: The Intimate Networks of East Yorkers*. University of Toronto.

Wellman, B. (1987) *The Community Question Re-evaluated*, Research Paper 165. Centre for Urban and Community Studies, University of Toronto.

Wheatley, P. (1963) 'What the greatness of a city is said to be: reflections on Sjoberg's pre-industrial city', *Pacific Viewpoint* 4, 164–88.

Wheatley, P. (1971) *The Pivot of the Four Quarters*. Chicago: University of Chicago Press.

White, P. (1984) *The West European City: A Social Geography*. London: Longman.

White, J. (1989) 'Social cushions and asylum on the street', *The Independent* 14 November, 18.

Whitehand, J. W. R. (1967) 'Fringe belts: a neglected aspect of urban geography', *Transactions, Institute of British Geographers* 41, 223–33.

Whyte, W. H. (1957) *The Organization Man*. New York: Anchor Books.

Williams, C. C. (1992) 'The contribution of regional shopping centres to local economic development: threat or opportunity?' *Area* 24, 283–8.

Wilson, A. B. (1959) 'Residential segregation of social classes and aspirations of high school boys', *American Sociological Review* 24, 836–45.

Wilson, W. J. (1987) *The Truly Disadvantaged: The Inner City, The Underclass and Public Policy*. Chicago: Chicago University Press.

Wirth, L. (1928) *The Ghetto*. Chicago: University of Chicago Press.

Wirth, L. (1938) 'Urbanism as a way of life', *American Journal of Sociology* 44, 1–24.

Wirth, L. (1945) 'Human ecology', *American Journal of Sociology* 50, 483–8.

Wolpert, J. (1965) 'Behavioural aspects of the decision to migrate', *Paper and Proceedings of the Regional Science Association* 15, 159–69.

World Bank (1995) *World Development Report*. Oxford: Oxford University Press.

Wrigley, N. (ed.) (1988) *Store Choice, Store Location and Market Analysis*. London: Routledge and Kegan Paul.

Wrigley, N. and Lowe, M. (eds) (1996) *Retailing, Consumption and Capital. Towards the New Retail Geography*. Harlow: Longman.

Xu, X., Ouyang, N. and Zhou, C. (1995) 'The changing urban system of China: new developments since 1978', *Urban Geography* 16, 493–504.

Young, M. and Willmott, P. (1957) *Family and Kinship in East London*. London: Routledge & Kegan Paul.

Zhao, X. and Zhang, L. (1995) 'Urban performance and the control of urban size in China', *Urban Studies* 32, 813–45.

Zipf, G. K. (1949) *Human Behaviour and the Principle of Least Effort*. Reading, Mass.: Addison-Wesley.

Zorbaugh, H. W. (1929) *The Gold Coast and the Slum*. Chicago: University of Chicago Press.

Zweig, S. (1942) *The World of Yesterday*. Vienna.

Subject index

Page numbers representing figures are in **bold**; those for tables are in *italics*.